When a Flower Is Reborn

ROSA ISOLDE REUQUE PAILLALEF

❧ When a Flower Is Reborn

THE LIFE AND TIMES OF A MAPUCHE FEMINIST

Edited, translated, and with an introduction

by Florencia E. Mallon

Duke University Press Durham and London 2002

© 2002 Duke University Press

All rights reserved

Printed in the United States of America

on acid-free paper ∞

Designed by C. H. Westmoreland

Typeset in Minion by Keystone Typesetting, Inc.

Library of Congress Cataloging-in-Publication

Data appear on the last printed page of

this book.

For the Mapuche, my people,

with the hope that they may see reflected in my words their

own diversity, as part of our struggle for self-determination

in this new century.

 CONTENTS

Where I've most easily been able to find that superior being is in the places where someone says, there's nothing else to be done. There I find something that speaks to me. When a flower is reborn amidst all that filth, it tells you there's still a moment of hope, and that our love for the earth, for nature, for human beings, must open each day toward the world, toward people, toward all of us.

—ISOLDE REUQUE, *April 1997*

✤ ACKNOWLEDGMENTS

ISOLDE: *I thank Günechen, God, for having given me life as part of an aboriginal people rich in customs and wisdom, among whom we breath fresh air and new life every day. I thank my parents for giving me life and for understanding that a woman can step outside the boundaries of her home, her community, her county. Thanks also to all the Mapuche who have been part of the indigenous social movement from September 12, 1978, until today, for teaching me about our past and our present, and for opening up my vision toward future generations.*

FLORENCIA: *I thank María Elena Valenzuela, for first putting me in touch with Isolde. Thanks also to Magaly Ortiz, who transcribed the tapes of our interviews, and to E. Gabrielle Kuenzli and Yesenia Pumarada Cruz, who helped with the translation. Valerie Millholland, Miriam Angress, and several anonymous readers for Duke University Press also labored hard to make this book a reality.*

ISOLDE AND FLORENCIA: *We are grateful that we found each other, and for the way our friendship and collaboration took on a life of its own. The book is no longer a dream! Our collaboration has not been merely a scientific one but has also encompassed our commitment to, and passion for, social justice and for a deeper understanding of society. We thank our two families, who were able to recognize the special importance of our work together, and who gave us their unconditional support, welcoming us into both households with open arms. The best proof of this is the special friendship our children, Lily Reuque and Ramón and Ralph Stern, have developed among themselves. We both lovingly accept and share this challenge for the future: that our friendship will continue long after our project has been completed.*

NOTE ON PRONUNCIATION

Words in *mapunzugun* will adhere to the following unfamiliar rules. When at the beginning of a word or syllable, the "x" denotes a "tr" sound with the soft English "r". At the end of a syllable, the "x" denotes a "sh" sound in English. The "g" denotes a "ng" combination in English.

"I'm going to tell you a little about my life, you see, so that we can get to know each other better," Isolde Reuque Paillalef says at the beginning of her testimony. These were the first words she spoke to me during our first formal interview on November 29, 1996. We had talked on the phone a couple of times, setting up our meeting, and I had earlier heard from my Santiago colleague María Elena Valenzuela a summary of the role Isolde had played as a Mapuche feminist leader, including a description of how María Elena had gotten to know Isolde on the Chilean delegation to the International Women's Conference in Beijing earlier that year. I met Isolde at the Café Raíces, an experiment in the blending of indigenous cultures, musics, jewelry, and cuisine from all over Latin America that had existed in downtown Temuco for about eight months. Though we were not aware of it at the time, the Café Raíces was already on its last legs when the two of us began to get to know each other across one of its tables.

What was perfectly clear to me at that moment were my reasons for wanting to get to know Isolde. Less than a year before I had taught a course on oral history and testimonial literature at the University of Wisconsin in which we had read the most recent experiments in the genre as well as reviewing some of the classics. We had also discussed recent critiques by feminist and postmodern literary critics. In such a context, one of my goals was to explore the possibility of collaborating with a Mapuche woman in the production of a feminist testimonial. I was searching for a horizontal or egalitarian relationship, inasmuch as this was possible. I was not interested in a story that could be "typical" or "representative" of any group, and in any case I doubted that such typicality could be claimed by any one person. I wanted to collaborate on a *testimonio* whose author/subject could dialogue and reflect with me about the political and cultural complexities of her people and her culture.

From what I already knew at the time of our first conversation, Isolde

Reuque could very well be exactly the person I was looking for. I had already interviewed another woman who was a Mapuche intellectual and leader, a woman who held a position of some importance in the *Corporación Nacional de Desarrollo Indígena* (Indigenous Development Corporation—CONADI) and had gotten along very well with her. But for a series of reasons, the most important of which was that she was always too busy at her job, we had not been able to find time for a second conversation. The other Mapuche leader I had interviewed, moreover, was an eminently urban woman. While I was not looking for the "exotic" by focusing on the countryside, and although I was only four months into an incredibly complex research project, still at a loss as to the overall conceptualization, I had already read enough in secondary and primary sources to understand that the relationship between urban and rural, between community and town, was conflictual and complex in Mapuche culture. From early in the twentieth century, organizations of urban Mapuche intellectuals had attempted to erase their cultural differences and integrate into mainstream Chilean culture. Indeed, by the 1930s, only a few Mapuche intellectuals continued to revindicate the religious and family traditions that many acculturated Mapuche urbanites themselves labeled as "barbarian."[1] And even though my earlier interviewee was of a different generation, in which respect for rural Mapuche traditions was now de rigeur among urbanites as well, I began to suspect that her lack of personal rural experience placed finite limits on how far our conversation could progress. Indeed, in my conversation with María Elena in Santiago, I had asked whether Isolde had a connection to a rural community. María Elena had emphasized that she did.

Looking back on these questions now, four years after our first meeting, I can see much more clearly how I, too, was participating in the romanticization of Mapuche rurality as somehow containing the "essence" of Mapuche culture. In 1992, when the first Chilean census encouraged people to self-identify as members of distinct ethnic groups, many Chileans were surprised to learn that nearly a million people fourteen years or older, or 9.6 percent of the country's total population in that age group, self-identified as Mapuche. Equally surprising, perhaps, was that 79 percent of the Mapuche population lived in urban areas, 44 percent in the Santiago metropolitan area alone. Only 15 percent of the country's Mapuche population lived in the IX Region, or La Araucanía, which had historically been considered the group's main territory, though of this population nearly 70 percent continued to live in rural areas. In such a context, my search for a rural connection might seem somewhat nostalgic or out of touch. Yet at the same time there were at least two good reasons underlying my intuitive preference for a rural connection. First, most anthropological research on the Mapuche had focused on rural areas, precisely because it was in the rural land-grant communities that, after their military defeat in the 1880s, the Mapuche people had reconstituted their culture and identity. And second, as Isolde Reuque's testimony makes clear, the revitalized Mapuche ethnic movement that emerged in the late 1970s, even though led mainly by urbanized intellectuals, privileged rural communities as the fountain from which would issue the linguistic, ritual, and political currents of renewal.[2]

The Mapuche indigenous organization that was founded in 1978 was part of a wider trend in Latin America and more broadly. Internationally, indigenous leaders from a variety of groups, such as the American Indian Movement (AIM), had begun, over the previous few years, to formulate an agenda in the context of international human rights policy. Through organizations like the World Council of Indigenous Peoples (of which Melillán Painemal, one of the founders of the Mapuche organization, was vice president), indigenous leaders participated in defining United Nations policies and resolutions for oppressed people within existing nation-states, policies that began to multiply in the 1970s as the UN considered the fate of women, ethnic and national minorities, and aboriginal peoples. As part of an ever more international discourse around human rights, indigenous rights were put squarely on the agenda of progressive church groups, international human rights agencies, and some national governments. In this context, national movements revindicating indigenous peoples' cultural identity and rights to political recognition and autonomy within existing nation-states began to multiply around the globe. By 1992, with the celebration of the Quincentenary of the conquest of the Americas, mobilization had spread dramatically and some governments in the western hemisphere were debating or even ratifying the UN Convention for the Elimination of Racial Discrimination, and ILO Convention 169 on Indigenous and Tribal Peoples.[3]

Isolde and I got along famously at our first meeting. She was honest, intellectually acute, self-confident, and had a sharp sense of humor. A month later, when I read the transcription of our first interview when preparing myself for my next trip to Temuco, I noticed several places where I had attempted to show her how much I already knew, as a reaction to my own insecurities as a *wigka* (non-Mapuche) and semi-*gringa*. But she was very patient with me and did not let my ignorance and posing irritate her, even when I interrupted an important discussion to show her how much I knew. In fact we got along so well during our first conversation that, at one point, I decided to lay my intellectual cards out on the table. I remember telling her (although this did not end up on tape) that I would like to explore the possibility of collaborating on her testimonio or life history. I proposed the following conditions. First, that she would be the principal author, and her name would appear first on the book's title page, with my name further down as editor. Second, that she would receive transcriptions of all our conversations and would have the last word as to the version that would be published. Third, that I would take care of the transciptions and of organiz-ing the text into an initial narrative order, though she would then have final right of revision. Fourth, that she and I would each have the opportunity to write our own introductions and conclusions. And finally, that all of this meant quite a lot of work for us in the next six months. She seemed imme-diately interested and we agreed to meet again the following week, before I traveled back to Santiago.

When I proposed these conditions of collaboration to Isolde, I was influ-enced by the collaboration between North American anthropologist Lynn Stephen and María Teresa Tula, Salvadoran human rights activist and mem-ber of the Committee of Mothers and Relatives of Political Prisoners, Dis-appeared and Assassinated of El Salvador (CO-MADRES). Among all the testimonios I had read, Tula's life history had inspired me most in thinking about the genre as a horizontal collaboration.[4] It would take me longer to understand, from Isolde's point of view, what was attractive about my offer. I remember that at first she mentioned that it was something she had already been thinking about, but that she never found the time, among the folds of her daily life, to sit down at her computer and write. And she invited me to her house in the Pedro de Valdivia neighborhood of Temuco, a two-story structure she and her husband had been building, piece by piece, since their marriage some years before.

I arrived at her house on December 3, 1996, about tea time. I struggled uphill, three blocks of unpaved road from the bus stop, staggering under the weight of a backpack full of notes and photocopies accumulated during a day's research, somehow also hauling my laptop computer. In preparation for our conversation I had passed by the market to buy a bag of *yerba mate*, an herb used to brew a caffeinated tea that, although drunk widely in Argentina, Uruguay, Paraguay, and southern Brazil, in Chile had a more marked association with Mapuche culture. I already knew, from previous experience and conversation, that bringing yerba was a sign of my willingness to sit awhile, drink a mate brew, and let the conversation wander where it might. I had already listened several times to the tape of our previous conversation and had come prepared with a series of questions about the Mapuche movement between 1978 and 1995, wanting to deepen my understanding of Isolde's political role over those years, as well as to hear more of her analysis of the changes that had occurred. We talked for more than three hours and were joined at various points by her husband and one of her sisters. Isolde opened up about her frustrations in the Mapuche movement, and I began to get a clearer picture of the complexities of her role and that of other leaders.

At the end of 1996 Isolde found herself finishing up an extremely intense and important stage of her political and personal life. Since her involvement in the human rights movement at the beginning of the Pinochet dictatorship in 1973, she had been a part of the social and political movements in Chile across a quarter of a century. During the dictatorship she had first participated in the Christian base communities, moving then into the Mapuche ethnic movement. During the transition and democratic consolidation, in addition to continuing her work in Mapuche organizations, she had helped found and unify the indigenous women's movement, representing it as part of the Chilean official delegation to Beijing, and had participated ever more organically in the party politics of the Concertación, the center-left coalition that emerged from the antidictatorship movement to occupy the presidency throughout the 1990s. As became clear in our first conversations, Isolde had an intense desire to look back across this quarter century of leadership and participation, reflecting on the past in order to define more clearly the path she needed to follow into the future.

Isolde shared this desire to reflect, this sense that an important stage had just ended, with many activists in the Chilean antiauthoritarian movement. When in 1990, after a dramatic, nearly decade-long struggle against the

Pinochet dictatorship, the Chilean people had reestablished democratic rule with the election of Patricio Aylwin, there was a period of rejoicing. Victory was at hand! Foreign human rights activists who had accompanied the process, political observers of the electoral transition, and even some of the international NGOs packed up their tents and went home. In a situation in which international observers, foundations, and funding agencies all pronounced Chile transformed and gave the country a clean bill of democratic health, local activists in a broad variety of social movements were left alone to try to make sense of their experiences in the struggle against authoritarianism. After so much suffering, so many struggles and sacrifices, how did one return to normal? This became even more difficult in the new climate that included not only political consolidation and bargaining, modernization and economic growth, but also, and ever more clearly, military impunity. Slowly a post-transition pall fell over many: that much-praised, much yearned-for, much-celebrated democracy was not what people had expected. The international community, much more present during times of struggle and transition, was less able to hear the new attempts at reflection and political innovation with which some activists tried to quiet their hunger for a democracy that could never be the same again. Ironically, in some cases there was even nostalgia for the forms of unity and solidarity that had been possible under dictatorship. This was the situation when I arrived in Chile in 1996 and when Isolde and I began our conversations.

Things have changed quite a bit since then. In December 1997 a new era began in the Mapuche social movement as communities in Lumaco, to the northwest of Temuco, began to challenge the expansion of large lumber companies. Direct action, especially in the form of land invasions, has spread through southern Mapuche communities in both the VIII and IX regions, and protests against other megadevelopment projects have also continued and multiplied. Also, since the arrest of Augusto Pinochet in a London hospital in 1998, the willingness of the Chilean judiciary creatively to confront the question of impunity and human rights abuses has increased dramatically. As a result, a number of military officers, including Pinochet himself (who has, since returning to Chile in 1999, been stripped of his immunity), have been charged with human rights crimes. But none of this seemed possible in 1996 and 1997, when Isolde and I held the bulk of our conversations for this testimonio.

After our interview at her house at the beginning of December 1996, my next visit to Temuco was in January 1997, when I spent the whole month in the region doing archival research and fieldwork. I was extremely busy, in part because my fifteen-year-old son, on summer vacation, had come with me. But Isolde was even busier than I, something that with hindsight I understood was connected to her post-Beijing obligation to lecture on the results and future plans emerging from that conference. During the whole month we managed only one half-hour conversation. When I dropped by her house to give her the transcriptions of our previous interviews, I had to leave them with a neighbor. I began to understand why she had told me, during our first interview, that she never had the time to sit down and write. In fact, I began to wonder whether our planned testimonio would actually materialize. On the positive side, however, an entire month in the Temuco archives, combined with intense fieldwork in a Mapuche community near the coast, helped me reach the top of my first conceptual mountain. For the first time during my research I had a clear view of my project as a whole and could easily discern the research path to follow over the next months.

My work with Isolde was, in fact, a tangent that developed from a broader research project. When I had first arrived in Chile in August 1996, my goal had been to write a general history of the Mapuche people and their relationship to the Chilean state across the twentieth century. I soon realized that the ambition of my project had been based on an overly superficial understanding of Mapuche history. As I came partially to understand the stunning diversity of historical and cultural adaptations lived by distinct subgroups, even individual communities, within the Mapuche, it became clear that I would have to trim the scope of the project to something more manageable. Not wishing to cut my time period, I instead latched onto the idea of limiting the project regionally to a few case studies that, because of their internal diversity, could represent at least a part of the complexity and variety I had begun to see. By the end of January 1997 I had managed to identify four communities or subregions that were satisfactory case studies: the region of Lonquimay, a mountainous area near the Argentine border with a number of Pewenche communities; the community of Juan Catrilaf, immediately south of Temuco city; the community of Nicolás Ailío, west of Temuco and near the Pacific coast, in a region where people considered themselves Lafkenche; and Isolde's community of Chanco, south of Temuco in an area that had previously belonged to the province of Valdivia.[5] While not all these case studies could be developed with equal depth, the breadth provided by comparing cases with this much ecological, cultural, and historical diversity struck me as important. And after a month of focusing on archival research and fieldwork in Nicolás Ailío, I was even more convinced that this new formulation of my project would be viable.

February was a month of vacation and family obligations, so when I returned to Temuco in mid-March I came armed with a new and fresh determination to advance rapidly in the conversations with Isolde. Since the first time we had talked, when she had told me a bit about her community, I had wanted to visit Chanco with her and get to know her family and neighbors, perhaps do some research on the history of the community. When I had suggested this possibility before, Isolde had always seemed interested but we had never been able to confirm a date for our visit. On March 14, having just arrived from Santiago, I called her on the telephone and immediately proposed that we visit Chanco. This time we firmed up a date for that very same weekend. That Sunday, with Isolde's help, I filled several bags with groceries at the local supermarket and presented them as a gift to her mother after having gotten off the bus and climbed the hill to her house. We spent the afternoon talking, eating, and drinking mate, with her parents, her sister, and daughter. I managed a short interview with Isolde's father, don Ernesto Reuque, *logko* (leader) of the community. Isolde's younger sister Elvira introduced me to several of the members of the community's youth group and showed me the library they had founded to help schoolchildren with their homework.

Being in Chanco, part of the district of Pitrufquén, helped me bring together materials I had gathered in the archives with people's memories and lived experience. As Isolde had already explained to me several times, her community had a *título de merced* under the name of Rosario Coñoen viuda de Lefihual, as part of the process of settlement of the Mapuche people after they were militarily defeated in the early 1880s. A título de merced was the original land grant given by the Chilean government to a Mapuche extended-family lineage, of which a total of approximately 3,000, varying tremendously in size and quality of land, were given by the end of the 1920s. Chanco's original title had not been formalized by the Comisión Radicadora—the central state agency in charge of titling Mapuche lands—

until mid-1910, and in the ministerial archives in Santiago I had seen that the formalization of titles in Pitrufquén had been especially delayed, perhaps because the district was south of the city of Temuco and belonged to the province of Valdivia. As a result of this delay the Mapuche communities of the area had faced repeated land problems and boundary disputes with national and foreign colonists who had moved into the district. At the same time, at the moment the title was formalized the community Coñoen de Lefihual was already very small, made up of a total of fourteen persons organized into three family nuclei. Neither the Reuque nor the Paillalef families had formed part of the original community's family tree; it was only after the community was subdivided into individual plots—comparatively early, under the first Land Division Law passed in the late 1920s and enforced through the 1930s—that additional families were able to settle there. Isolde's father don Ernesto Reuque, whose family had formed a part of the original group settled to the east of the railroad tracks, in the community of Antonio Millao, was one of the new arrivals, for he purchased the land where they live today in 1947 from Marcelina Millaleo, a household head listed in the original title.[6]

By the time Isolde's family bought land in Chanco, the process of division, sale, and reconstitution of property had already resulted in a fragmentation of the area's Mapuche communities and an erosion of cultural practice.[7] It is hard to say, as Isolde herself points out, if the division was the cause of fragmentation and cultural loss, or if a certain degree of cultural fragmentation already existed in the region and helped prepare the ground for the subdivision and sale of community lands. Isolde believes that the process occurred in both directions at the same time, with each element reinforcing the other. At the same time this process also facilitated further economic differentiation within the indigenous group, something that was dramatically highlighted in one of the stories told in Chanco about the previous generation of leaders from several of the area's communities.

It seems that in the nineteenth century, the families of several *caciques* from the region had made a contract with the devil. At that time, near the present location of the road to Corte Alto, there still was a patch of virgin forest. Every year the heads of these families held a great banquet in that forest that lasted an entire night, and the food was served on dishes of gold and silver. The families who participated in this devil contract enjoyed wealth and prosperity, but at a high cost. One of the women became a *machi*, or healer-shaman, who was allied with an evil spirit; her daughters and granddaughters were forced to migrate to the city to escape the powers of evil. People also remember that the pact led directly to a major epidemic. The crisis and conflict brought about by these events led to a shakeup in the community's leadership structure, and a *kona* or commoner, someone not belonging to the lineage of the cacique, took over the position of logko (literally, "head") in Chanco. This is something that only happens in Mapuche culture at moments of grave crisis; and this is how the Reuque family took over leadership in their community. People still say that one of the sons of the original pact makers, born in the community of Navarro in 1913, joined the group and pledged to remain single; that is why this person is still so wealthy. Even today, people say, you can tell he has remained faithful to the devil pact, because every time there is a death in the community, this old man rejuvenates.

I first heard this story from Isolde's mother, doña Martina Paillalef, Isolde's sister Elvira, and Isolde's daughter Lily, on May 20, 1997. The conversation began as a joke, when the three women wanted me to stay in Chanco and not return to Temuco that evening. Since they knew I was interested in stories about the community, they offered it to me as a "prize" for postponing the inevitable, almost as a "Thousand and One Nights" to keep me from getting on the bus. The historical veracity of the story and its details is less important than the series of moral and cultural judgments it makes about the problems of fragmentation and materialism, and the consequences of individualism and excessive ambition. It also serves as a dramatic example of how Chanco was and is different from my other case studies, none of which subdivided their lands in the 1930s. While Nicolás Ailío also went through a process of acculturation, in which people began leaving aside Mapuche customs and integrating more into a popular peasant culture, the process was experienced differently, more as generalized poverty and a common need to migrate in search of work. And the community of Juan Catrilaf militantly held onto Mapuche language and customs, in part by maintaining a fairly rigid surveillance over marriage customs, dress, and language use within the boundaries of the community.[8]

My first visit to Isolde's family and community went quite well and I think helped set the tone for our next interview in Temuco the following Wednesday. Together with her sister Elvira, Isolde turned more intimate and reflective. They both shared experiences with me about what it means to be a woman in Mapuche culture, as well as the difficulties they had faced in establishing romantic relationships. Isolde even explained why she felt so comfortable in her relationship with her in-laws. There was something about the dynamic of that conversation, which included as well a description of the ups and downs Isolde had experienced, years earlier, after giving birth to her daughter at a very young age, that convinced me that we had reached a new level in our communication. The three of us also discussed an outline for the book and began trying out possible titles.

It was in this conversation that I began to appreciate how Isolde arranged her story around particular incidents or watersheds in her life, moments that then became nodes of meaning that helped her organize her experience.[9] One of these, I learned, was her pregnancy and the birth of her daughter Lily. Single motherhood marked and ostracized her in deep and painful ways and ultimately, I think, helped shape her sense of being different or separate from the mainstream. The choices she made—carrying the baby to term and refusing to put her up for adoption—helped confirm, for Isolde, her capacity for courage and independence. Her parents' willingness to provide a home for Lily, despite her father's original anger and objections, also cemented a special closeness that remains to this day. Having gone through such a process, moreover, inscribed in Isolde a distinctive form of feminist sensibility and empathy through which she constructed her own view of Mapuche femininity and what she considered the proper relationship between Mapuche women and men. It lent a special ferocity to her criticisms of what she termed *caciquismo*—the claim by some Mapuche men to a particular kind of "warrior masculinity" in which they have a right to multiple partners, something that she associated with a significant portion of today's male leaders in the Mapuche movement. Ultimately, I believe, her experience as a single mother was central to her commitment to feminism.

At the same time, however, her feminism, as a conscious, organized part of her political activity and identity, was relatively late in developing. Isolde became a Catholic and human rights activist first, and this led her into the Mapuche ethnic movement. Once she was there, as she herself points out, the Mapuche movement—and her own Mapuche identity—became paramount in her life. It was only after the transition to democratic rule in Chile, and after the grassroots work that prepared the way for the passage of the Indigenous Law, that Isolde turned her attention to the task of founding a Mapuche feminist organization. As she told me many times, she is Mapuche first, and Mapuche second; only third is she a Catholic, a political party activist, or a feminist. It is because of these priorities, as well as the timing of her feminist political organizing, that the theme of feminism does not appear until the last chapter of this book.

And yet, over and over in recent years, her feminism has productively doubled back into her Mapuche activism. Her feminist sensibility has helped her understand the complexities and contradictions of her role as a Mapuche leader. It has also helped her cement friendships with Mapuche women of many distinct political stripes, precisely because they share the common bond of experiencing discrimination as women in the Mapuche movement and as Mapuche in the feminist movement. After more than twenty years as an activist, it is her feminist sensibility that helps her explain the combination of power and marginality in her status as a "female elder," something male elders in the movement do not face in the same way. It is because her feminism has provided such an important lens as she narrates and reflects back on her life that Isolde's identification as a feminist legitimately belongs in the title of this book.

When I returned to Temuco in April 1997, I found that a small crisis had developed. One of the elders of Isolde's community, with whom we had talked during the previous visit in order to set up an interview for my return, had decided that he could not be interviewed for free. He had discussed the situation with his daughters, who had suggested that Isolde would certainly be making money by helping a gringa with a book, and that he should receive payment as well. Isolde had responded that there were other people in the community and that we did not have to interview him. Isolde's mother had found out first and had been bothered by the situation; Isolde's voice, too, sounded bothered on the phone. Only later, however, did I understand that the incident had revealed a protective feeling toward me on the part of Isolde and her family, since they had chosen to take my side in a conflict with other members of the community about what I was doing in their midst.

Tying this incident to conversations Isolde, Juan, and I had about the

Mapuche movement, especially about the many rumors and debates that in the 1980s swirled around Mapuche leaders and their relationship to NGOs and the funds being disbursed, I have also come to understand that the presence of a foreigner with a camera and tape recorder resuscitated old envies and painful questions. As Isolde makes clear in her discussion of the Mapuche movement, a strong and militant idealism about Mapuche culture was combined, from the very beginning, with an equally strong desire for social and economic advancement, for greater prosperity and progress. When specific Mapuche leaders made connections with international organizations and began to travel, most people believed that these individuals would return from Europe with their suitcases full of money. In reaction to this, an important node of meaning around which Isolde constructed her identity and her story concerned her stubborn independence and incorruptibility, such that she received less money than other leaders because she criticized NGOs and their excessive administrative costs. Particularly in this context, it is easy to see why it would distress Isolde to realize that some of her neighbors might suppose that she was working with me for money. In addition, I think this incident also highlighted another central element of her identity: her sense of strangeness and marginality, even in her own culture and community. While this feeling could very well have originated in her experience with single motherhood, for a variety of reasons, as she explains, her political activism deepened it.

Indeed, Isolde's feelings of strangeness and marginality, her need to find herself in her own culture and society, form another crucial node of meaning that provides order and coherence to her story. When she became one of three founding members of the *Centros Culturales Mapuches* in September 1978, she was the only woman and the youngest of the three; she was also the only one who did not speak *mapunzugun*. Having grown up without speaking the Mapuche language or performing key rituals, in a privatized community undergoing a process of assimilation, she felt a stranger in her own land. Her commitment to Mapuche activism, emerging from her work in the Catholic human rights movement, became her ticket back into her own culture; yet at the same time, working in the movement reproduced her own sense of being different and, somehow, not entirely "authentic."

Part of this difference was cultural. Her descriptions, at various moments of her testimony, of the cultural events the *Centros Culturales* sponsored in

Lumaco symbolize this most directly and poignantly. She herself speaks of being in a different country, of experiencing the sounds, sights, and smells as if she were a foreigner. Yet at the same time, as an outsider looking in she was motivated to learn and to be educated in her own culture by the people in the communities she helped organize. She then took this knowledge back to her own community of Chanco, where she led an effort to resuscitate Mapuche politics and culture and successfully reorganized the local *gillatun*.[10] She also helped a local machi, who had given up her commitment to healing and spirituality when her son had disappeared during the dictatorship, to return to the fold and become the machi for Chanco. A reconstituted community and a newly revitalized machi together struggled to remake local Mapuche identity.

In a sense, this rebuilding and revitalization of Mapuche identity and ritual—and especially the narratives attached to the process among the participants—had much in common with processes in other parts of Latin America. Among peoples and cultures as distinct as the Guatemalan Maya, the Nicaraguan Miskito, the Bolivian Quechua and Aymara, and the numerous indigenous peoples of Colombia, Brazil, and Ecuador, the revitalization of indigenous custom and identity was a conscious part of a new political project of ethnic unity. In many places, previous processes of cultural change and the erosion of traditional practices made necessary a reorganization, at times a relearning, of language and ritual. This became part and parcel of many indigenous revitalization movements.[11]

Isolde also lived her sense of marginality and difference in the Mapuche movement at a political level. As the youngest and only female member of the original three-person leadership, she was the one least marked politically by the previous regime, and the one closest to the Catholic Church. She speaks of this in physical terms, as if it left an imprint on her forehead designating her a Christian Democrat, something that in the earlier years of military dictatorship was an immediate cause for suspicion among people on the left (in part as a reaction to this mark, she did not formally join the Christian Democratic Party until 1994). Especially after the left wing of the Mapuche movement took over the *Centros Culturales* in 1983, this suspicion became a rumor that she had actually been working for the intelligence services.

We traveled to Chanco again on Saturday April 19, planning to return the next day. We had decided to stay overnight with her family, thinking that we would have plenty of time to talk to other people in the community and also to continue our own conversations. When we got to her family's house, however, after the customary greetings, initial conversations, and sharing of the inevitable mate brew, Isolde informed us that she would have to return to Temuco that same night for a political meeting. I should still stay the night, she insisted, and we could continue our conversations the next day when she returned. When I replied, a bit disappointed, that this had not been our original plan and asked why she had not told me of the change before we left Temuco, she chuckled and said something like well, but why did I not take it as a golden opportunity? I could talk to her family, even gossip about her, behind her back!

We did not gossip about her, but with her mother doña Martina Paillalef, sister Elvira, daughter Liliana and older brother Lionel, we did talk a long time that night. For almost two hours, while drinking mate and wine, we filled two cassettes with a discussion of such diverse topics as the origins myth of the Paillalef family (Lionel had read it in a book), doña Martina's childhood, the experience of going to school for Mapuche children, the ups and downs of the 1993 Indigenous Law and of the transition to democracy, and the complexities involved in any attempt at the preservation of minority cultures. We ended up laughing and joking, and Lionel threatened me with stealing a swiss army knife of mine to which he had taken a liking (before leaving Chile I gave it to him as a gift). When Isolde returned the next morning she received positive reports from all concerned, and in the afternoon we found a relatively secluded spot where we could continue our conversation. That day we filled four cassette tapes with a series of discussions about the most important events and moments in the development of the Mapuche movement, using my accumulated research in the newspapers of the time as a starting point. Isolde also suggested I follow up on additional dates of importance in the movement, as well as deepen my research in specific newspapers, when I returned to Santiago. At some point we also decided to include in the book the conversation I had had with her family.

These April interviews marked a watershed in our project. Though it was always difficult for us to know how far we had gone (until one night in May, when we were sitting at the kitchen table in her house in Temuco, the fact we had finished suddenly hit us in the face), in April we were both sure we had advanced more than halfway. On my laptop computer we composed a final draft of the book outline that would become our map through the final interviews. But our watershed was about more than the volume of interviews already recorded; it was also about trust. Returning on the bus to Temuco that Sunday evening, Isolde confided in me that she had never before brought an outside researcher to work in her own community. Though she had collaborated with a number of other scholars and had introduced people to her family in a personal or social sense, earlier research collaborations had usually featured her in-laws rather than her own kin. Opening her family and her community to me had been a sign of trust, as well as a test; luckily I had passed muster and been accepted. In June, at a seminar held in Temuco with representatives from several of the Mapuche communities where I had done research, people were asked what they had gotten from their collaboration with me. Isolde said, with gentle and playful humor, that she had learned things about her community she had never known, not only by going with me to interview some of the elders, but also (she could not resist a chuckle) from the conversations they held after I had already left.

Getting to know and love the Reuque Paillalef family has been for me an exceedingly important experience, both personally and for how it has helped me understand Isolde in new and different ways. But even more, the conversations I had with her family changed the form taken by this testimonio. When Isolde and I decided to include in it the opinions of other family members, I think we began to fashion a different kind of text. Though not the first testimonio to include other family voices—Sidney Mintz's *Worker in the Cane* comes to mind, where in addition to Taso Zayas's voice we hear that of his wife, Elí Villaronga[12]—what has made this book distinct is the repeated mixture of perspectives, and the fact that a variety of additional family members express their opinions along the way. Beyond the participation of individual relatives within Isolde's story, especially her sister Elvira and her husband Juan, the way the "family chorus" interrupts Isolde's narrative in chapters 1 and 3 may seem initially confusing or choppy. But there actually is a rhyme and reason to the placement of these chorus sections, in the sense that they complement or provide a counterpoint to the larger picture being drawn by Isolde—on growing up in Chanco; on the nature of culture, community and ritual; on the implications of government policy and of the Indigenous Law of 1993.

The end result is a text that is inhabited by different perspectives and visions of Mapuche history and culture. Despite the fact that Isolde and her brother Lionel belong to the same political party, for example, their views about the history and culture of their people are quite different. Disagreements between family members; the conversations, joking, and laughing that went on; the lack of resolution on some points or problems where different individuals had diverse points of view—all of this contributes, I believe, to making this a rich and living testimony about a culture in the process of change, fragmentation, and reconstitution.

Attempting to render or transcribe a living oral text, however, has proved easier said than done. The process has deepened my respect for practitioners of the oral history genre who have, for years, debated the problems of transcription, of how to fashion a written text from an oral performance.[13] When one becomes a part of the production process rather than a consumer of already existing texts, debates about "authenticity," about the intrusion of the interviewer into the "purity" of the subaltern text, suddenly seem much less relevant. Simply reproducing the words, as spoken, in written form no longer seems a faithful rendition of the original narrative. Facial expressions and inflections of voice can lend a totally different meaning to the same written words. In fact, I've begun to think of a testimonio more as a play, as a text written to be performed or recorded in a performance, rather than as a strictly textual narrative. Indeed, the reader is encouraged to think of the text as a dramatic performance, with the interactions between the characters being as much a part of the plot as what they actually say.[14]

In a related way, my conversations with Isolde's family also prompted me to rethink my own role in the construction of this narrative. While I never doubted that this testimonio was and had to be, first and foremost, Isolde's, when I saw that other family members were inhabiting small but important pieces of the analysis I felt more comfortable with the role I have played. In general, when reorganizing the transcriptions of our conversations to create a roughly chronological and topical narrative, I have edited minimally in order to give written flow to what is eminently an oral text. I moved from one place to another the materials that, because of topic or narrative line, made more sense somewhere else. I am aware that even this relatively small intervention, by providing chronological and topical coherence to a set of decentered conversations, may increase or decrease the significance of particular themes.[15] In addition, by removing repetition or concentrating most references to one issue or event in one place, I provide greater narrative coherence but may remove clues about the importance of events, or their relationship to one another. I also deleted my questions from the written text when they seemed redundant and Isolde's discussion continued unaffected before and after. When I expressed an opinion, or elaborated at greater length than was necessary, I retained the question so that the reader can better understand the interaction between us that prompted Isolde to expand on a particular topic.[16] Very occasionally, to improve the flow when material had been moved from one place to another, I inserted a question to help link the themes one to the other—but these inserted questions were never more than informational queries. Beyond informing the reader about these changes, the only other thing I can say is that, after five years of working with this story—talking it with Isolde; checking the transcriptions against the original tapes; reading it over and over to glean the key themes and forms of organization it contained; taking it back to Isolde and correcting and clearing the final Spanish manuscript with her—I think we've done the best job we can.

Added to this, however, is the problem of translation, and here Isolde, given her relatively limited English, cannot be a "partner in crime." A rough draft of the translation was produced by two project assistants, E. Gabrielle Kuenzli for chapters 1 and 2 and Yesenia Pumarada Cruz for chapters 3, 4, and the conclusion. I corrected and quite substantially revised that rough draft, working from the original Spanish manuscript, as well as doing the original translation of our combined afterword. I tried, as much as possible, to reproduce the conversational forms and expressions, the jokes and laughter, interruptions and interactions with others that formed a part of what we did. But inevitably, as many have said, translation also involves at least some form of invention or transformation; I have no choice but to take responsibility for that.

A final issue that emerged for me in this context was the extent to which I needed to provide context for a reader unfamiliar with Chilean and Mapuche history. No matter how much or how little background I decided to present, it was by definition intrusive to Isolde's narrative and to our conversations. I have therefore opted to include much of this information in the endnotes, while still attempting to keep these to a minimum. For this reason it is important for the reader to follow along in the endnotes as well as the text, since at various points an important dialogue is established. And while this is, in and of itself, an interruption, it is both necessary and less cumbersome than placing all the additional information in the text.

The result of all this work is an experimental narrative, whose only conscious literary experimentation may be the imitation of theater rather than novel in its structure. In our first attempt at publication in Spanish, we saw that this could be a liability, for nowadays it is hard for a publisher to take a chance with an experimental text that does not follow a traditional narrative line. Nonetheless, after several discussions, Isolde and I decided to keep the present structure, which attempts to represent the way we talked it. We hope it gives the reader an idea of how Isolde struggled, in a dynamic and committed fashion, to make sense of the historical, cultural, and political processes of the past twenty-five years, processes of such central importance to Mapuche and Chilean history. Besides, I think we both agree that one thinks and lives one's life, not with a traditional linear structure, but at multiple levels, and with the interruptions and contradictory participation of different people. As far as possible we have left it that way; and when we recorded what has become the afterword in August 1998 and my son Ramón was present and participated in the conversation, it also seemed important to us that his questions and comments remain in the text. And finally, in its actual form this testimonio represents as faithfully as possible Isolde Reuque's poetic style of thinking and talking. Indeed, she is not only a woman with "a talent for writing poetry"; in eminently Mapuche style, she also has a talent for speaking poetically.

In the first year after I left Chile, I managed to complete the organization of an initial draft of the book-length testimonio that had emerged from our conversations. In August 1998 I traveled again to Temuco and with Isolde and her husband Juan we went over the text, correcting some errors in mapunzugun, taking out some personal references or other comments that, when making the transition from a personal conversation to a written text, no longer seemed appropriate. I also took Isolde a first draft of this introduction, on which she made comments, after which we recorded an introduction and conclusion based on a reading of everything written to that point. This text is thus a reflection of conversations that have not ended, of friendships still deepening and in progress; upon publication it is inevitable that it will freeze in time a whole set of experiences, a life, a network of friendships and social relations that continue to evolve and grow.

Since ending my residence in Chile in August 1997, I have reflected many times on the friendship Isolde and I are still building. On one side, I have thought a great deal about the differences between us—of life experience and cultural background; social position, education, professional connections; economic privilege and country of residence, with all the differential access this entails. I have also considered how the balance of power between us has changed over time. If we started from an initial position in which I depended a great deal more on her, trusting that she would teach me about the Mapuche people and their experiences, that she would take me to her community and help me understand, we have now gotten to a place where, even if she has authorship, right of ownership, and the right to all the royalties that emerge from this text, I have the contacts for publication. My position has been further strengthened, ironically, by our difficulties with publication in Chile, since the first version of the book will come out (not because we wished it) in English. In this sense her desire, her need to share her point of view about the conflicts and successes, pain and happiness that she has seen and experienced in the Mapuche movement over the past quarter century, must necessarily find ultimate realization through my professional and academic connections. All of this makes our friendship a complex relationship that operates at multiple levels; I cannot presume a false and easy equality between us. In fact all the debates, all the criticisms that have emerged from within anthropology in the last twenty years prevent me from pretending an equality of circumstances between the two of us.[17]

At the same time, I do not want to misinterpret nor exaggerate the differences that separate us. On one side they are important and are based on such structural, overdetermined factors as social class, imperialism, even the Spanish conquest and over five hundred years of racism. But on the other side, the two of us have managed to build a friendship that involves two specific people who, for a series of distinct reasons, have been able to communicate with and appreciate each other despite the barriers and differences that separate us. Thus I would also like to reflect a bit on which factors I have come to see as important in the construction of our friendship.

I have come to believe that Isolde Reuque and I became friends because we both felt like outsiders in our own environments. During one of our conversations, when she was explaining to me why she had stayed with her husband despite their many problems, she said it was because they were both "like black sheep." This expression, especially its sense of connection in marginality, also has a great deal of relevance for me. In Isolde's case, as I have already suggested, she has narrated her life around a series of central themes denoting separation, marginality, and difference. More than once, when describing her participation in an aspect of Mapuche culture, she has constructed herself as the outsider, almost the anthropologist (*la curiosa*, as she laughingly, and more than once, referred to herself). When her sister Elvira turned to me one evening in 1999, when we were drinking mate in Isolde's Temuco kitchen, and said: *Tía, eres una bisagra cultural* ("Auntie, you're a cultural hinge"), Isolde was captivated by the concept. Still, even though she allowed that I was a *bisagra* in my own right, she was more interested in how she herself was already the hinge connecting Chilean society to Mapuche culture. Rather than playing the role of the mediator who brings to light an "authentic" voice, therefore, I have become the scribe who facilitates Isolde's mediation between two worlds.

My side of this cultural experience involved learning, when I returned to Chile in 1996 after more than twenty years, that I really did not belong anywhere. Despite my long absence my Chilean family, originally from the traditional landowning elite, accepted me back with deep and uncondi- tional love and welcomed my husband and children warmly and affection- ately. Nonetheless I felt out of place in the post-Pinochet prosperity of upper-class Santiago and sought desperately to find an alternative way of connecting to the land where I was born, preferably along the margins of dominant society. At the same time I did not entirely reject the privilege provided by my family connections, using it strategically in order to sched- ule an interview with a southern landowning family and gaining their confidence by telling them that a great-uncle of mine had been president of the republic. When I expressed my distaste to Isolde about having done this, she laughed at me; but I think the mocking was tinged with affection and with a form of recognition based on her own familiarity with the pain of living on the boundaries of a social and cultural world.

In short, I think we both needed this testimonial, and the friendship that arose alongside it. Ever more isolated within an ethnic movement to which she had given the previous quarter century of her life, forced to witness its ebbing strength at the precise moment when the dynamic unity of its first ten years would have been crucial for self-defense, Isolde needed the platform provided by the book we were aiming to write.[18] She is a person who does her best writing in an oral format (she insisted to me, repeatedly, that this is a general Mapuche trait; few Mapuches, she said, have taken well to the written medium; they are much better at long and florid speeches). Thus she needed me, and the research assistants I contracted for in Santiago, to transform her spoken thoughts into a written narrative. For my part, I needed the vindication, recognition, and simple acceptance I received from Isolde, her daughter, her sister, and the rest of her family. I needed an interlocutor from within Mapuche society who could help me understand and evaluate the many complexities—cultural, political, social— I had encountered; in Isolde, her sister Elvira, and her husband Juan, I found exactly that. And finally, given the closed and insular nature of the "Mapuche Studies" community into which, as an outsider, I found it hard to enter, I also hungered for the approval she gave me as an analyst of her society and culture who cared deeply and looked beyond the surface.

If our connection in marginality has strengthened our friendship, it has also made more difficult the publication of this testimonio in Spanish. Because Isolde is not a "typical" Mapuche leader—she is Christian Democrat, strongly Catholic, with a history of opposing or criticizing the Mapuche left and the NGOs, feminist—what she has to say is not easy to accept in most circles. Because I am neither an anthropologist nor an accepted *Mapuchista* scholar within the Chilean academy, my process of recognition as a legitimate mediator has been rocky and slow and is still a work in progress. From all of this has come this book. We present it, with all its limitations and eccentricities, as the product of an evolving friendship and intellectual conversation based on mutual honesty and trust.

As I write this, I cannot help but think back to Isolde's chuckling remark in June 1997, when she publicly reminded me that much of what she learned in relation to my visits emerged from the conversations that happened after I had already left. Like Rigoberta Menchú's famous concept of "secrets," all narrative is as much about what does not get said as about what does.[19] One layer to this is what Isolde knows and has chosen not to tell me. Another layer involves what she knows, has told me, but has asked me not to tell. A final layer is what I've learned, sometimes without her knowing it, and have chosen not to tell. Her relationship with her family, some aspects of her experience in the Mapuche movement, and perhaps especially her relationship with her husband Juan to some extent cross through all three layers. At various points in our conversations, we revisited each of these key themes in her life and filled them in to the extent that was possible and comfortable. The balance we have achieved between speech and silence reflects the respectful negotiation between two human beings that constitutes our friendship.

Inevitably, however, remaining "secrets" fly in the face of an academic's quest for "objectivity," as the recent controversy surrounding Rigoberta Menchú and David Stoll makes clear. In February 1998, when I sent Isolde the first two complete chapters of her testimonio, I included in the package a copy of Rigoberta Menchú's first memoir. I knew that Isolde and Menchú had been part of the same indigenous tour of Europe in 1992, but I also explained to her on the telephone my other motivation for sending her the book. "When your book is translated into English," I said, "in the United States people will inevitably compare you to Rigoberta Menchú. It's important to begin thinking about what that comparison might mean."

We had that conversation before David Stoll's critique of Menchú became public, but I had already heard rumors that a U.S. anthropologist had been questioning the "truth" of her autobiography. I also knew that Menchú's second memoir was about to appear, and that she had retained principal authorship over that one. Thus a reflection about the similarities and differences between Menchú's first autobiography and Isolde's work, especially the different contexts in which they were written and the distinct political motivations that inspired them, seemed crucial to me. I also thought that such a reflection might help us think comparatively and historically about what constitutes a life history, something that has not been done systematically despite the immense international attention and acclaim Menchú's first testimony received.[20]

As by now is fairly well known, Rigoberta Menchú dictated her first testimony to Elisabeth Burgos Debray, a Venezuelan anthropologist living in Paris, two years after Menchú had first gone into exile. At the peak of the Guatemalan army's scorched earth policy, with the traumatically violent deaths of her father, mother, and brother still painfully fresh, Menchú fervently desired to bear witness about the Guatemalan situation to an international audience. She kept quiet about a number of things, she insists in her second memoir, that under other circumstances she could have discussed.[21] According to U.S. anthropologist David Stoll, however, Menchú not only kept quiet about certain things; she actually lied. Now, at no point does Stoll deny that the things Menchú tells us happened in Guatemala; rather he suggests that the story she tells is actually an amalgam of the experiences of many people and communities rather than her individual experience or that of her village. Stoll further suggests that Menchú told her story "under the influence of revolutionary thinking" and to serve the political interests of the guerrilla forces, specifically the Ejército Guerrillero del Pueblo (EGP). And he concludes that an international public—especially human rights activists and North American academics—enthusiastically and uncritically consumed her story because Menchú offered them an attractive complicity in the construction of an "authentic" and "transparent" image of the suffering and consciousness of Guatemalan Indians.[22]

This complicity—that others might call solidarity or collaboration—between a subaltern voice and an intellectual mediator is the fundamental relationship underlying the genre of testimonio, which, over the past twenty years, has undergone a major boom within Latin American studies. The purpose of this genre, which has become both literary and anthropological, is of course to recover the experiences of ordinary people, subaltern in terms of their access to social or political power. In contrast to those whose wealth—or social, intellectual, or political prestige—would permit and even at times require the writing of a memoir or autobiography, ordinary or subaltern people do not live lives that provide them the space for rest or reflection that such a task demands. Thus the need for a collaboration emerges.

The boom in Latin American testimonio, I believe, had its origins in two interrelated processes that, for the purposes of clarity, are best analyzed separately. The first of these trends was the evolution of a literary category by the name of testimonio that was given formal approval when Havana's Casa de las Américas founded its Premio Testimonio in 1970. In fact this was a recognition of the increasing popularity of this type of work, represented at the time, perhaps most dramatically, by Cuban anthropologist Miguel Barnet's *Biografía de un cimarrón* (1968), translated first into English as "autobiography of a runaway slave." This trend was a partial response to the growing enthusiasm for popular experience and heroism inspired throughout Latin America by the Cuban Revolution of 1959, and in many parts of the world by an increase in radicalism throughout the 1960s. According to literary critic John Beverley, testimonio became popular with the revolutionary moment of the 1960s and culminated as a form of *denuncia* (condemnation) during the repression and authoritarianism of the 1970s and 1980s. "It was the Real, the voice of the body in pain, of the disappeared, of the losers in the rush to marketize."[23] But if we think about the process even more historically, we would have to add yet another layer to Beverley's analysis. The popularity of testimonio also coincided with an intellectual and methodological crisis within anthropology that took shape in the 1980s, a crisis that constitutes the second of the two trends alluded to above.

The crisis in anthropology had two origins. The first was a questioning of the scientific discourse that justified fieldwork, within which the relationship between the anthropologist and the "informant" was simply a way to get access to data about culture that could then be generalized and compared across different societies. In April 1984 in New Mexico, a group of English and U.S. anthropologists held a seminar on the subject of ethnography whose results, when published two years later, helped to criticize anthropology's scientific veneer, revindicating personal experience, literary techniques, and even the poetics of "writing culture." The second origin of the crisis was a more open debate about what Sidney Mintz has called, in the Spanish edition of his classic life history of Puerto Rican caneworker Taso Zayas, a tendency "to trivialize the great differences in wealth, opportunity and power that separate the academic from the informant, and to convert into objects those upon whom anthropologists had to depend in order to get access to information."[24] One of the directions in which this crisis led anthropology was toward an encounter with literature, especially with the literary techniques and debates that were trying to break through the more constricting boundaries of the classic academic canon. In both literature and anthropology there was an increasing attraction toward the transgressions of the scientific method and objectivism made possible by postmodernism and poststructuralism.[25]

In this context, some academics influenced by postmodernism avoided the problems of methodology and power inherent in ethnographic work by dedicating themselves almost exclusively to the analysis of already existing texts. Thus did Menchú's autobiography become almost a bible for politically committed postmodern intellectuals, the example always cited as representative of testimonio, which as a genre was thought to revindicate the presence of the "other" because it was a thread woven into the fabric of guerrilla movements, popular resistance, and struggles against authoritarianism. In such a situation the mediation of a foreign intellectual, who recorded and organized the narrative, became an act of revolutionary solidarity rather than of cultural cannibalism. As conceptualized by Beverley, testimonio as a literary genre gave voice to a "collective popular-democratic subject, the *pueblo* or 'people,' " thus resolving, through relations of solidarity, the "deep and inescapable contradictions" between the subject/narrator and the editor. Beverley defined these relations of solidarity as "a sense of sisterhood and mutuality in the struggle against a common system of oppression."[26] But what happens today, in our postrevolutionary and neoliberal world, when liberation struggles have been defeated or at best marginalized? Beverley concludes that, as a genre, testimonio has become "detached" from its original contexts and has thus lost "its special aesthetic and ideological power." To this must be added, argues Javier Sanjinés, that market forces and globalization have destroyed the material and political conditions that used to facilitate the creation of the social movements and utopian dreams that nurtured testimonio. What is left, then? "What is left today," asks Beverley, "of the desire called testimonio?" And he answers: "Chiapas."[27]

What is lost in all of this, in my opinion—and what Stoll challenges us to put on the table once again—is the specific and "atypical" (if there is such a thing as "typical") nature of Rigoberta Menchú's text within the testimonial genre. Testimonial literature and life history have existed in the Latin American field since before the Casa de las Américas legitimized the genre in 1970. An inclusive list of texts would be too long and complex to reproduce here, but it is interesting to note that, before the texts of revolutionary solidarity so celebrated in the 1980s and 1990s—which would include, in addition to Menchú's book, Margaret Randall's texts on Nicaragua, the testimony of María Teresa Tula mentioned earlier, and the story of Bolivian tin mine activist Domitila Barrios de Chungara—a distinct life history and testimonial tradition had already emerged from anthropology. This would include, among other works, the books by Oscar Lewis, the "testimonial novel" and oral histories produced by Elena Poniatowska (who worked as one of Lewis's research assistants in Mexico City) and by Miguel Barnet, and the classic works by Sidney Mintz on Taso Zayas and June Nash on Bolivian mineworkers.[28]

Within this great variety of texts, what stands out about Menchú's work is that it is the only one that is not based on some kind of encounter with the community and/or culture of the narrator/subject. With all the differences among them, and even in the other cases in which texts were produced with a clear political purpose—such as the testimonies of Tula or Barrios de Chungara, or the books edited by Margaret Randall—we find that the works emerge from some kind of encounter between the editor and the narrator/subject's world. In Menchú's case, on the other hand, the testimonio emerges from a series of interviews done in Burgos Debray's house in Paris, and the original purpose was apparently not to produce a testimonial book but instead a magazine article. According to what Burgos Debray said to Stoll in a subsequent interview, it was only after Menchú had left that the editor discovered she had enough material for a book.[29]

Of course, at no point do I wish to suggest that an encounter with the culture or community of a narrator/subject somehow assures a form of "objectivity" that would otherwise be absent. It is precisely the ethnographer's false objectivity that began to be criticized within anthropology in the 1980s, and I have no desire to attempt its resuscitation. Ironically enough, it may be Stoll's own book that provides the most direct cautionary tale on issues of "objectivity." As Arturo Taracena has argued, Stoll's loud claims to objectivity stop at the very moment when he would need to interrogate or criticize his own "informants" or interviewees, so that the only narratives he subjects to scrutiny are those belonging to people with whom he disagrees. Had he extended the critical dialogue with local communities to everyone who was providing pieces of the story, he would have produced a very different text indeed. And yet, as Kay Warren suggests, perhaps this was not Stoll's purpose in any case, since more than a complex ethnography with multiple levels of information and cultural conversation, the book he produced was in the genre of an exposé.[30]

Despite the many cautionary tales regarding objectivity, I nevertheless believe that a dialogue with the narrator/subject's community or culture makes for a richer and more complex text. For the reasons already described, such a dialogue and the resulting complexity were not a part of Menchú's first testimony. What does it say about our own intellectual world that it is precisely this book, among all possible texts in the genre, that becomes the most read, the most cited, and the most celebrated of all testimonial narratives?

In part, the attractiveness of Rigoberta Menchú's autobiography lies precisely in the clarity and simplicity of the message. A young indigenous woman who has experienced unimaginable suffering bears witness to that suffering and calls for international solidarity. A more complex, perhaps even contradictory, message; a reflection at multiple levels that evokes human imperfections and the lack of unblemished heroisms—such a testimony would not have had the same impact on the international community. Another attractive aspect of Menchú's book is that the narrator/ subject takes control of the narrative and does not allow the inevitable mediator to define the issues to be discussed or the answers given to the questions. Thus the widely cited and discussed comment by Menchú, that no one would know all the secrets of her culture and her people. By maintaining control over what she will say and what she will not, Menchú takes on an important form of agency in the relationship between herself as narrator and Burgos Debray as editor.

At the same time we need to place Menchú's book in context and remember when it was published. Throughout Latin America, military dictatorships were abusing the human rights of the populations under their control and then trying to cover up their actions. Wide and well-organized disinformation campaigns were being challenged only by the individual testimonies of repression's victims, whose truth strove to be heard at the international level. The eloquence of individual testimony, of the victims' truth, was a formidable weapon used by movements against repression in the Latin American countries, by international human rights organizations, and also by the truth or restitution commissions set up in several Latin American countries after the fall of military regimes. At a moment of national and international emergency throughout Latin America, therefore, Menchú's personal testimony was acutely moving and powerful. Perhaps it is not superfluous to mention, in this context, the staggering nature of the genocidal violence experienced in Guatemala during more than three decades of civil war, which according to the recently released report of the Guatemalan Truth Commission resulted in the deaths of around 200,000 Guatemalans, more than 90 percent of whom were killed by the army.[31]

In such a context, it is easy to lose sight of the difference that can exist between truth as a weapon of denuncia or condemnation, and truth as a subject of academic debate.[32] In Menchú's first testimony, truth exists as denuncia in the face of repression, pain, military abuse. When it is seen at this level, even Stoll agrees that Rigoberta Menchú's truth belongs to all poor Guatemalans. But when Menchú's testimonio was transformed into an emblematic academic text, denuncia became ethnography. This transformation impoverished debates on culture and experience, because any difference of opinion was seen as an attack on the legitimacy of the denuncia itself. It also impoverished the role of denuncia as a weapon in the struggle for human rights by conflating the testimony of abuse and pain given by repression's victims with a social or cultural text. Ultimately, this transformation also demonstrated that, at a certain level, we are still searching for the simple and transparent voice of the "other": we still have difficulty accepting multiplicity and contradiction. And this is precisely the point made by both Duncan Earle and Victor Montejo, when in separate essays concerning the Menchú debate they suggest that, because there has been a tendency to "canonize" Menchú's version of events, other perspectives and voices concerning Maya culture or the repression suffered by Maya communities have been marginalized and lost from view.[33]

Perhaps it is only now, when we have passed into a different political era, that it becomes possible to reflect more deeply about the complexities and contradictions of subaltern voices and actions. Can we find new ways to narrate and analyze the problems that remain when the war or dictatorship is over, problems that may appear less dramatic yet are not less painful or intractable, such as poverty, subordination, political exclusion, malnutrition, cultural discrimination? Isolde Reuque's testimony, conceptualized, spoken and written in a postcrisis process of deep reflection, challenges us to begin. It calls on us to take up once again, though now in a new context, earlier forms of testimony or life history that formed a part of long-term ethnographic work and of the deep yet consciously complex relationships fostered by anthropological research. A creative yet always conflictual relationship between testimony and ethnography, between life history and fieldwork, suggests an alternative path that may take us beyond the crisis of testimonial narrative as a form of denuncia. Without rebuilding our old illusions of scientific objectivity, accepting the challenge and responsibility associated with a dialogic and postmodern ethnographic conversation, we can begin to open new and deeper narrative forms in our continuing search for ways to tell the stories of ordinary human beings.

Isolde Reuque and I recorded her testimonio in her own country and region, facing an indigenous movement in retreat. I was witness and scribe as she sorted through twenty-five years of political activism, first in the human rights movement and Christian base communities, then as a found-ing member of the Mapuche indigenous movement of the 1970s and 1980s. She was able, at a different historical moment, to take honest and critical stock of the internal divisions and problems of the movements in which she had participated, of the difficulties of organizing a feminist movement within the Mapuche movement and with the Mapuche people. In this sense her testimonio is reflexive and critical precisely where Menchú's was politi-cally urgent. At the same time, when the two women shared the stage during an indigenous tour of Europe in 1992 it was clear that they also shared a commitment to the preservation of the Native cultures of the Americas, cultures that have survived despite the intense pressures and violent aggres-sion produced by centuries of colonialism. This combination of cultural and ethnic commitment, with a willingness to reflect honestly and critically, make Isolde's testimonio an innovative text that moves us beyond denuncia and beyond simple debates about testimonial "truth." By revealing and analyzing the profound and painful contradictions that exist within popu-lar movements, Isolde presents herself and us with a deep challenge: is it possible to renew and reconstruct a commitment to social justice without also reconstructing an excessively simplistic and heroic vision of popular politics? Without the illusion of an easy answer, Isolde shares with us her reflections and experience.

In so doing, and in highlighting both her participation in Mapuche eth-nic revival efforts and in social movements and political parties more gener-ally, Isolde also constructs a new kind of subjectivity as a Mapuche feminist leader. Until now, existing life histories and memoirs of Mapuche individ-uals have tended to remain divided between those of men who have been political leaders and those of women who have represented a more "authentic" or "ancestral" spiritual or cultural voice. With the exception of the life history of logko Pascual Coña, recorded at the beginning of the twentieth century, who claimed authority based on a combination of his knowledge of the old ways and his education in Santiago and the mission school, more recent memoirs by Martín Painemal Huenchual and José Santos Millao have focused on political struggle and mediation and the role of these male leaders in defining a public agenda for their people.[34] By contrast, with the exception of one small and very schematic article about a Mapuche woman who was a leader before and during Salvador Allende's Popular Unity government, and which was published only in English, the stories of Mapuche women have tended to focus on either the experience of daily life or more "traditional" religious or spiritual aspects. Even Sonia Montecino's recent and highly acclaimed novelized biography of a female machi is organized around a process of mediation in which an outsider and non-Mapuche becomes the designated translator and transmitter of ancestral culture and knowledge.[35]

Isolde, by contrast, refuses mediation of this kind, asserting the right to narrate and interpret her own political agency. The result is definitely a hybrid text, both homage to and passionate critique of the Mapuche movement and Mapuche culture. As a woman and an acculturated Mapuche who was forced to find her way back into her own culture, Isolde provides a complex perspective on the beauty and hierarchy of Mapuche political and cultural practice. She provides an innovative perspective on the issue of autonomy within the women's movement, especially as it related to women from oppressed ethnic or racial communities like the Mapuche. She makes important contributions to emerging comparative discussions of indigenous movements and of evolving state policy toward indigenous peoples in Latin America more broadly, exposing the painful trade-offs indigenous activists face when attempting both to pass legislation and to foment social movements and grassroots activism. She addresses, both passionately and directly, the painful Gordian knot that ties grassroots movements to political party structures in Chile (and potentially also in other parts of the world), criticizing political party practices simultaneously from within and without.[36]

Isolde's adamant commitment to her own perspectives and positions— whether as a feminist, a political moderate, or a staunch Catholic—even as she remained in a minority within the Mapuche movement as well as in Chilean society more generally, has forced her to pay a high price, both in isolation and in criticism. At one point in our conversations, she spoke of a deep depression she entered in the mid-1980s, after the *Centros Culturales Mapuches* were taken over by Mapuche militants from the Chilean Communist Party. The resulting split expelled a significant number of the least radical Mapuche communities, and she, along with several of the other leaders, was forced out. It was only after a trip to New Mexico, where she met a Hopi grandmother who had been an activist all her life, that Isolde began to emerge from her slump. "It was an emotional, powerful, meaningful, and painful moment," she told me. This encounter with another indigenous leader and female elder, symbolized by the gift of a turquoise ring Isolde still wears on her hand, represented for her the need to look beyond present-day defeats, both to the past and the future, and to become part of a chain of struggle that did not begin and would not end with her. The setbacks suffered by the Mapuche movement served, then, as a catalyst, both in her efforts to see beyond the immediate process and in her construction of her own political identity as stubbornly optimistic. To this day Isolde sees in her initial experience organizing the Mapuche movement her greatest lessons. Her sense of longing and nostalgia, of yearning and desire for that original moment of revival, is still palpable today. It is a story of heroism. She sees in the communities and traditions of her people the greatest wisdom, not because of some romantic and ancestral purity, but precisely because of survival despite overwhelming odds. "The memories I hold most dear," she told me one day,

are from my travels through Mapuche communities, through the communities in Chiloé, the communities close to the rivers, the lakes, where I find *Günechen* (God), where I can communicate directly with that superior being. That's when I find, I don't know what, but I can cry, laugh, sing. My poetry springs forth, my verses, and I can dream and surround myself in reality, all at once. I think there's much in the wind that blows in each one of those places. Where I've most easily been able to find that superior being, is in the places where someone says, there's nothing else to be done. There I find something that speaks to me. When a flower is reborn amidst all that filth, it tells you there's still a moment of hope, and that our love for the earth, for nature, for human beings, must open each day toward the world, toward people, toward all of us.[37]

A stubborn optimism, with eyes wide open, a romanticism that does not idealize reality—this more than anything else characterizes Isolde Reuque. Her romanticism, her optimism mix in a complex way with an eminently practical view of the world. Throughout her life history she repeats, again and again, some version of the phrase "we have to do what we can, not what we wish to do." Creatively negotiating the contradiction between the ideal and the possible, between reality and desire, Isolde Reuque narrates a life in which she has reconstructed her optimism again and again, finding in it the strength to keep going. That is why we agreed to title her book "When a Flower Is Reborn," a title that symbolizes not only her stubborn spirit,[38] but our shared hope that, in the twenty-first century, the rebirth of the Mapuche movement and of aspirations for social justice will help heal the wounds inflicted on Chilean society by a recent and excessive love of modernity and the market.

CHAPTER ONE

Chanco: Family, Land, and Culture

I'm going to tell you a little about my life, you see, so we can get to know each other better. I'm a poetic woman, my poems and verses were always about the earth, the world, the birds, and the trees. The priest who taught me religion and philosophy in my high school told me that I had a talent for writing poetry, a poetic calling, he said. He told me I should develop my poetic skills, make them public. It hadn't occurred to me to develop this talent on my own before. The routine of life in the countryside didn't help me develop such literary skills. I had to milk the cows, pen the animals, clean the sheds, and transport and sell the milk. Later I developed a routine of work and study; although we were only children, we were assigned chores at a young age in the countryside. It's very common for young children to have chores like taking care of the pigs, the chickens, and the animals in general, the garden, watering the plants and, well, other things too. In the countryside we share the tasks of craft work—spinning, washing, and carding the wool—these chores are divided among us.

So I had no idea about poetry and things, I was a woman of the countryside. Also, I'm the oldest, I have a brother who's really the oldest, but he had a disease called poliomyelitis, or infantile paralysis. The disease left one of his legs badly crippled. So I took on the role of a man-woman, I wore the pants, and with my younger brother we bore the brunt of the work. I didn't do a lot of housework, I worked more in the fields, making fences, plowing, and breaking paths. As soon as I could reach the handle of the plow, I was out there plowing, the oxen jerking me about. Well, this tells you a little about my childhood.

I'm very sensitive, but I don't let my guard down. I developed a thick skin when I was a young child who out of necessity had to take on the responsibilities of the oldest child, plowing, taking care of the animals, milking the cows. My brother got sick with polio when I was two years old. At that time in Chile we didn't have specialists or medicine in our province to cure polio. So Dago and I became the oldest, and then came Pedro. We all had to assume the responsibilities that belonged to the eldest children in a family. My father worked in construction in the city. He also worked in agriculture on the surrounding estates. My mother and we children had to take care of all the household activities.

Those *hualle* trees we have along the edge of our property, we went to get the seeds for those trees from the railroad track when we were children. Those trees are younger than I am. Several of those hualles have been cut down, they're older than my sister Elvira. We went to the railroad track with a cousin of ours who helped us yoke the oxen so we could do our chores, and at first my father got mad at us, but later he realized that we were not doing bad things at the railroad tracks. Then he helped us dig the holes to plant the hualles we'd found by the tracks. Also, people riding in the train would eat apples and throw the cores out the window. From the seeds of these cores little apple trees grew, and we went to get these little trees which sprang up along the tracks as well. At my grandmother's house there were lots of apple trees, more or less as many as we have now at our house, but we were allowed to pick just a few apples to take home with us. If we picked more we were scolded, so we had to make an orchard for ourselves, and that's how we did it.

My oldest brother Lionel and I complemented each other, as he was very good at working in leather. He made and fixed straps, *cabestros* (halters), and cords; he also made yokes, and everything else in leather. Although it's true he didn't work in the fields, we complemented each other. But did he ever like to give orders! He'd sit there, just sit there and say do that, bring me this, take it over there, bring it to me over here. It was terrible. And to top it off I was always running after the pigs: pigs tied up, pigs running loose, they did mischief everywhere, in everyone's crops. I don't know why people just raise them and raise them, without building pigpens or anything. They cause trouble everywhere, that's one of the big problems we had when I was little. We decided to never raise pigs again, because on the one hand it meant a lot of work, and on the other, the pigs could die overnight if they got a fever. When pigs are in heat they are really bad, too; they can bite you and rip out pieces of your flesh.

Anyway, in my community called Chanco, which is near Pitrufquén, there are lots of people with professional titles, such as accountants, elementary schoolteachers, and agricultural extension workers. There are also a few engineers, and let's see, a doctor too; there are twelve electrical engineers. You can count the people who have distinguished professions on the fingers of one hand, they rarely receive important positions. But our community was very atypical in comparison to the others, in part because we're a community that was divided in the 1940s, when the first division of the communities occurred. With this division, descendants began receiving individual land titles from their ancestors, passing the land along through inheritance from the elder to the younger. The process was different in other communities that were divided under the Pinochet Law or the Indigenous Law that existed before, Law 17729. Because our lands were divided early, neither the Pinochet Law nor the current democratic government's law, Law 19253, applied to us.[1]

However, we've been trying to get the government to recognize us, on the one hand, as indigenous communities, and on the other hand, as legally constituted communities. The community into which I was born, in which I was formed and am part of today, doesn't descend from a single family tree, where everybody's related from the start and linked to each other. It's a mixture of the Navarro, Curihual, and Reuque families, where people have been buying land and have formed a community. First we formed a Christian base community and after that we formed an indigenous community. But it wasn't easy. Near our community there's another one in which a machi's son was disappeared. The machi's husband became sick and died from grief and she was left all alone. We talked with her, lifted her spirits and self-esteem, and helped her go on. We adopted her into our community and now she's the machi in our community.

THE REUQUE PAILLALEF FAMILY

FLORENCIA: *Let's begin with the person who knows most about the family, OK? We'll begin with doña Martina, no?*
DOÑA MARTINA: *Why are we going to begin, and where?*
F: *At the beginning.*
LILIANA: *Hey, what time did you get here?*

F: *Why don't you begin with where you were born.*

DOÑA MARTINA: *I was born in Loica.*

F: *What was your childhood like, what happened to you before you came here?*

DOÑA MARTINA: *I don't remember.*

F: *You don't remember anything?*

ELVIRA: *Come on, mom, just tell her.*

DOÑA MARTINA: *Well, yes; it seems my mother left me when I was around six years old. I hardly have any memories of her before she died. So we were left alone, my father and I, and afterward his stepson came to live with us, he was my half brother.*

F: *Was he younger than you?*

DOÑA MARTINA: *He was older. My father got married again to a widow. And I lived with them until my father died when I was thirteen. I stayed there with them until I came here.*

F: *But there in Loica, did you have land?*

DOÑA MARTINA: *Yes, I have some land there, through my father. My husband didn't want to make his home there because he didn't want to be led around by a woman. I told him, let's go there, let's live on that land, but he didn't want to. It was because my mother-in-law said to him: "Sure, you'd go live there because you're bossed around by your wife." So of course he didn't go, and instead we depended on his family. I arrived here, to where my mother-in-law lives, and I stayed a year.*

F: *What were your parents' names?*

DOÑA MARTINA: *Felipe Paillalef Cuminao.*

F: *And your mother's name?*

DOÑA MARTINA: *Marcelina Antilef.*

F: *What kind of work did you do in your father's house?*

DOÑA MARTINA: *I took care of my nephews, of course. You know, I raised them and they don't even come to visit me.*

F: *I bet you had to do lots of work since your mom died when you were young.*

DOÑA MARTINA: *Oh yes, I washed my clothes and my father's, too, since she didn't help us do it.*

F: *Who? Your father's new wife?*

DOÑA MARTINA: *No, my stepbrother's wife.*

F: *Oh, I see.*

DOÑA MARTINA: *She was sickly, so I did the washing, toasted and prepared the flour, and made the bread. At my young age I had all the responsibilities of a woman, and I also took care of the kids. Two of the children were very young, and the others, well, they took care of themselves.*

F: *So when you were ten years old, you were in charge of an entire household like a full-grown woman?*

DOÑA MARTINA: *Yes, I started washing clothes when I was eight years old. My father taught me to wash, and at first we washed together. Later I washed alone.*

F: *And how old were you when you came here?*

DOÑA MARTINA: *I was seventeen years old when I came here in 1946.*

F: *And before that you lived in your mother-in-law's house?*

DOÑA MARTINA: *Yes, at my mother-in-law's.*

F: *So when you left Loica how old were you?*

DOÑA MARTINA: *Seventeen years old.*

F: *So you lived in Loica until you were seventeen years old. And how did you meet don Ernesto?*

DOÑA MARTINA: *Because his sister lived in our house.*

F: *He came to your house to visit his sister?*

DOÑA MARTINA: *Yes.*

F: *And he also saw you?*

DOÑA MARTINA: *Yes.*

F: *And was he very romantic?*

DOÑA MARTINA: *Sort of.*

F: *Only sort of?*

DOÑA MARTINA: *Yes.*

ELVIRA: *What happened, doña Florencia, is that when my mom was about thirteen years old my grandfather died. So she lived with one of my grand-father's stepchildren who was married to my father's sister, and this is how my father got to love her. The nephews she's talking about are also my father's nephews, because they were his sister's children.*

DOÑA MARTINA: *The father of these nephews, my stepbrother, was a drunk; but my grandfather still left him in charge, he made him my guardian.*

ELVIRA: *They left the stepson of my grandfather in charge because my mother was too young. So he was left in charge of all of my grandfather's land and all the possessions that my grandfather left. My mother was very spoiled in those days, she always went out on horseback with my grandfather and he bought her chocolate.*

DOÑA MARTINA: *We use to go to town to eat cookies and drink refreshments in the summer. And in the winter we went to eat cookies and he'd drink a shot of brandy. In the summer we went to enjoy ourselves, we bought drinks, grapes, we went to buy treats rather than vices.*

ELVIRA: *My mother had her own horse she rode to visit the relatives. When my grandfather died, she lost all the investments they'd made.*

F: *I see. So you really enjoyed traveling on horseback?*

DOÑA MARTINA: *Yes.*

ELVIRA: *Those were very good times. My mother's childhood was a beautiful time in her life; she only tells us good things about it. When she lived with her father it was the best time of her life.*

F: *And it seems that you were very close to your father, you were your father's pet, no?*

DOÑA MARTINA: *Yes, I was very spoiled, whatever I asked for he gave me.*

LILIANA: *She enjoyed herself.*

ELVIRA: *The truth is that her biological mother is alive, you know. The biological mother of my mother is alive.*

DOÑA MARTINA: *My grandmother took me in.*

F: *And so when you got here to Chanco you were seventeen years old. You said you arrived in 1946, and you first lived in a room in your mother-in-law's house.*

DOÑA MARTINA: *Yes.*

F: *And how long did you live in the house?*

DOÑA MARTINA: *Not even one year. She threw us out.*

LIONEL: *It wasn't right that . . .*

DOÑA MARTINA: *Yes, she fought with her son and she threw us out.*

F: *What happened? Where did you go?*

DOÑA MARTINA: *Well, we just came here.*

F: *Did you begin building a house?*

DOÑA MARTINA: *No, first we lived in a crate.*

F: *How did that happen?*

DOÑA MARTINA: *The* boldo *tree is still here.*

F: *The* boldo *tree?*

DOÑA MARTINA: *Yes.*

ELVIRA: *This is how a neighbor told me they arrived here, and it made me laugh and laugh. He said they had a crate, a big box made out of wood where they stored the grain. At night my father would flip the box upside down and they would crawl under it to sleep, there under the boldo tree, in the orchard. My mother never told me this story. It was Sebastián Navarro who told me this.*

F: *And how were those times? Difficult?*

DOÑA MARTINA: *Hard, they were very hard times for me, I wanted to leave.*

ELVIRA: *After having been her father's pet when she was very young, she became a young mother with lots of responsibilities. And on top of that, she tells us that her in-laws rejected her.*

F: *So the in-laws didn't approve of you?*

DOÑA MARTINA: *No, they approved of me but they were difficult. And there was no end of problems with my sister-in-law and with a niece who was also my niece. Suddenly they would begin to make problems, they just stirred everything up. Instead of coming to the breakfast table, they got up just to fight. To eat breakfast or lunch in peace was a constant struggle. That's why it makes me furious when my children fight.*

F: *You have bad memories of those times.*

DOÑA MARTINA: *Yes.*

F: *And how long did you live under the boldo tree?*

ELVIRA: *(What do you need, dad?)*

DOÑA MARTINA: *I can't even remember the past (crying). I suffered so much, I don't want to remember. My father left me animals when he died, but afterward I didn't have a single animal, not even the hoof of an animal. They sold my last colt, I still cry for that colt. And now I am old and I still don't have a single animal.*

ELVIRA: *Maybe my mom forgot to tell you that my grandfather traveled doing business. He traveled to the Mapuche territories near Chubut, near the border with Argentina. There are Paillalef from our same family line living there.*

DOÑA MARTINA: *He actually lived over there, he left to live over there.*

ELVIRA: *My mom didn't tell you this part.*

DOÑA MARTINA: *Well no, I didn't. He was there when his wife died and he came back a widower. He left two children there.*

F: *He left two children where? In Neuquén?*

ELVIRA: *No, in Chubut.*

DOÑA MARTINA: *Yes, in the territory of Chubut.*

ELVIRA: *My mother's brothers live there, they traveled there to trade.*

DOÑA MARTINA: *They went to work.*

ELVIRA: *To work, but before they went to trade.*

DOÑA MARTINA: *I don't know.*

F: *I bet they went to work with cattle.*

DOÑA MARTINA: *Yes, it must have been that.*[2]

F: *I think so, because from what I've read, the Mapuche had big herds of cattle, and they followed a long migration circuit from here to Argentina. It was an important part of the traditional economy.*

ELVIRA: *Until the Pacification (the military defeat of the Mapuche) the Mapuches enjoyed a healthy economy throughout the territories all the way to Pitrufquén. The Mapuches were good businessmen, we didn't lack anything but we also didn't have much of a surplus as we traded grain for the animals and goods brought from Argentina, such as wool, weavings . . .*

LIONEL: *But that was before people got to know tobacco and alcohol; after that they traded all they had for a smoke and a drink.*

ELVIRA: *And for brandy.*

LILIANA: *That was at first, because afterward they all traded it for wine.*

ELVIRA: *No, for brandy.*

DOÑA MARTINA: *I wonder how much they traded for the liquor.*

LIONEL: *Remember the bottle everyone drank; what was it called?*

ELVIRA: *There's a book written by Durand which Lily . . .*

LILIANA: *It was called* La frontera, *by Luis Durand.*

LIONEL: *In this book they exchange a piece of land for a bottle of liquor.*

F: *I know the book, it was published by the Quimantú publishing house before it closed.*

LILIANA: *Exactly.*

ELVIRA: *It's a good book. It's very realistic, like the last part of my mother's story she told you. You see, my mother's guardian sold a lot of the land that was left to her.*

LILIANA: *In the book they talk about everything, the messengers, the runners, the bartering networks . . .*

ELVIRA: *Some German immigrants ran a pawnshop in Gorbea, in the neigh-*

borhood of Potricó. *My mother's guardian pawned her saddle, the best tools, my grandmother's jewels, the gourds for mate that were carved with silver, the silver reins, everything. My mother wasn't so little, she remembers it all. He pawned everything, and then he got drunk on all the profits. He sold my mother's animals at whatever price he was offered.*

DOÑA MARTINA: *He stole them from me.*

ELVIRA: *He sold portions of our land, and we were seven people in the family.*

DOÑA MARTINA: *The reins had little barrels of silver woven into the leather. The reins weren't so good, but they were considered good at that time.*

ELVIRA: *Things like that.*

DOÑA MARTINA: *We had a big, thick saddle, like a gaucho saddle, from Argentina, a really good one. Lionel could have used it if we had it, of course we would have made it a bit smaller as it was one of those big Argentine saddles, those that . . .*

LIONEL: *. . . were kind of square-shaped.*

DOÑA MARTINA: *Yes, they were wide, with padding on the sides.*

F: *I've seen that type of saddle, when I lived in Argentina for a few years I used to see them.*

ELVIRA: *All these things we would've had from my mother, we were so young . . . one time Lionel even altered their marriage certificate . . . (They laugh) . . . he changed the ages they had declared.*

LILIANA: *He made himself younger.*

(They laugh.)

DOÑA MARTINA: *No . . .*

LILIANA: *I didn't even know how to write yet and I wrote myself into the family.*

(They laugh.)

ELVIRA: *So something must have remained of this past. My mother says that my grandfather looked like Lionel, they had the same physique, they're both very Paillalef, because they both look like Uncle Nepo.*

DOÑA MARTINA: *No, my father was Nepo's same height, but he was whiter.*

ELVIRA: *He was white, with ruddy skin, hazel-like eyes and a beard.*

LIONEL: *Grandfather Segundo had those same eyes, grumpy old codger that he was.*

DOÑA MARTINA: *My father was like that too at times, suddenly he would be yelling, he just had to.*

LILIANA: *This is why we're so good-looking.*

ELVIRA: *He was a rich old man for those times . . .*

DOÑA MARTINA: *He wasn't that rich, he still raised his animals and sold them himself.*

LILIANA: *And if he did have money, he would've only given it to my mother.*

ELVIRA: *Before, the wealth the Mapuche had was in animals and things like that.*

DOÑA MARTINA: *He bought things with his profits. And since he lived in Argentina he got used to meat and raised his animals to eat and to sell. But he also said he shouldn't leave me that many animals. "Why," he said, "would I leave them to you, if he's just going to sell them anyway?"*

ELVIRA: *He already knew what was going to happen.*

DOÑA MARTINA: *"In the end you'll have nothing left," he said. "I hope he leaves you something, a few animals." But my guardian left me nothing.*

LILIANA: *It's not like he sold everything. That's why now it's so hard to tell the truth.*

ELVIRA: *When her grandfather was still alive and they came to town to shop, my mother went along and they took her to eat cookies and chocolates and drink lemonade.*

LILIANA: *And to drink water from a tap.*

ELVIRA: *She had such a beautiful childhood with her father . . .*

DOÑA MARTINA: *We used to go to the lowlands, just to visit the relatives.*

ELVIRA: *. . . to see Uncle Nepo and the people there didn't know her, they still don't. We just met Uncle Nepo recently.*

LIONEL: *The only one we did know died.*

ELVIRA: *It was then that we found out that we had these relatives, because before we didn't know them, as my father is one of those people who doesn't like to . . .*

LIONEL: *I met Uncle Juanito and we became friends when . . .*

DOÑA MARTINA: *No, it's just that my husband doesn't . . .*

LIONEL: *. . . During the UP[3], and after the coup he went to Argentina.*

DOÑA MARTINA: *It's that he didn't want us to know the relatives, he didn't want to be associated with them because they might take away my inheritance. I didn't think of these things before. There was even one neighbor who pretended to be a relative so that he could take my land away.*

LIONEL: *Geez. (Laughs.)*

ELVIRA: *Yes, well, that's how the family was. It's very nice that Uncle Nepo now loves us like family, and we love him too. We told him that we would've liked to know him and his children earlier. I don't know, at least I would've liked to have had the chance to talk with the kids when I was young. Now they're all professionals, lawyers, psychologists, doctors, engineers. Now they're all professionals and there's no time, not even to hang out. (She laughs.)*

We didn't have that kind of childhood. Now, for example, kids don't work as we did, things have changed. We used to work selling milk, doing odd jobs here and there . . .

LILIANA: *We took care of the pigs.*

ELVIRA: *When I was twelve I sold milk from a backpack I made. I poured out five liters of milk to sell here, another five liters there. Now these little girls who are twelve, thirteen years old don't do anything, they don't even wash the dishes in their house, nothing. We chopped wood, we did everything. Lily's generation was the last one that worked like this.*

LILIANA: *I just missed avoiding all of that.*

F: *That's why you turned out so well.*

LILIANA: *That must be it.*

ELVIRA: *Now, without having to work, they have everything they want without even lifting a finger. We knew what it was to be hungry, we knew what it was to not have shoes to go to town or to school, or enough money for notebooks, we had to put all our subjects in one notebook.*

LILIANA: *When we didn't have pencils our mother gave us pieces of charcoal from the stove.*

ELVIRA: *We couldn't go to the library to do our homework, we could only learn what we could glean from the teacher or in conversations. We never did homework, not because we were lazy but because we didn't have anywhere to get the information, because the teachers . . .*

LILIANA: *That's why we learned to copy really quickly once we got to school, from other students . . .*

F: *If you don't want to, we won't tape these confessions of guilt [cuts off the machine].*

LILIANA: *. . . Ah, censorship. (Laughs.)*

ELVIRA: *Mrs. Mafalda, as pretty and elegant as she was, didn't teach me anything. I don't remember her ever saying anything to me; she didn't give me demerits, either, but she never even noticed enough to ask: "Why didn't you do the work? Or, why do you only have one notebook? How is it that you don't have more notebooks?" We were seven siblings all studying, the money wasn't enough for supplies for all of us. I don't remember that she ever noticed, and anyway I had the idea that the teacher favored the prettier girls . . .*

LILIANA: *And you always thought you were the ugliest.*

ELVIRA: *Yes, I've always had this problem, that I'm sure I'm ugly. There was Gloria Espinoza and some other girls in my class, they were mean. But according to Western concepts of beauty, they were considered beautiful. I remember that the teacher always gave them the seats in the front of the room, she chatted with them. Now that I'm grown up, I don't speak to my old teacher, I don't talk with her because I have bad memories of her.*

LILIANA: *I had this really fat teacher who gave us bad grades. And I cried! We didn't have a lot of homework but I did it all, and all she gave me were bad grades.*

ELVIRA: *Those things happened, and the teachers never asked us, why the scarcity? All they ever noticed was when we didn't do our homework. Now, with the library we've created in the community with books people gave us, the kids can come and use it even on Sunday.*

LILIANA: *What's more, all the children of the younger generation are pretty, I don't think there is anyone now who is ugly and has to take flack at school. I think you were the last ugly child, Elvira. (She laughs.)*

ELVIRA: *Yes, I think my generation was the last. Maybe this is dumb, but I always had the idea that even if a girl doesn't know a thing, if she's pretty she's favored. It didn't matter if I arrived late. And I even took presents to the teacher, milk or kindling for the fire. I arrived early to see if I could get her to like me, but she never even noticed, she never said, "Oh you arrived early and made the fire," nothing.*

LILIANA: *I never took firewood, I only arrived in time to warm myself by the fire.*

ELVIRA: *I took firewood and the teacher never paid any attention to me, she never noticed nor gave me extra points.*

LILIANA: *I got lots of extra points.*

ELVIRA: *Maybe it was because I was a quiet child, maybe because I never did anything or drew attention to myself she didn't notice me. That's probably what happened, the teacher didn't even realize that I was there. Probably because I was so shy and quiet she didn't even know it was me who made the fire in the morning. I'd take matches to make the fire from the few my mother had at home. And she didn't even notice. When I went to high school I was a little livelier and people noticed my presence more, but in grade school . . . I think this must have happened to lots of kids who were shy. The teachers didn't even know they were there. Once a teacher told me that he didn't even notice the quiet children. This was my experience in school. But afterwards I grew wings and soared, now everyone notices my presence wherever I go.*

F: *I'm glad to hear that things have changed. But why? What caused the change so that one generation had to work at a very young age and the following generation didn't?*

LILIANA: *It was cultural and technological change, things like that.*

LIONEL: *It was money.*

LILIANA: *Money and more money, and the ambition for power.*

LIONEL: *More comfort.*

ELVIRA: *It's because the parents stopped working in the countryside and migrated to the cities. In our community everyone works in the city, no one works in the countryside anymore. We even buy our vegetables in town. Before we produced our own milk, vegetables, and eggs.*

F: *So it was a different kind of economy before. Everyone had to work together to produce what they needed.*

DOÑA MARTINA: *Yes, we sold new potatoes, cabbage, cilantro, and other things.*

ELVIRA: *The milk and eggs helped us, they brought a good price.*

DOÑA MARTINA: *We sold milk every day, and when the kids were late I'd sell it.*

ELVIRA: *Our products brought the highest price. We sold chickens with the feathers still on. There used to be a lot of demand for chicken, we sold so many. But then everything began to go wrong, the chicken and the eggs dropped in price. This happened around the time when Lily began to sell.*

LILIANA: *They began to sell white eggs and chickens, they were artificial . . .*

LIONEL: *They were double-breasted chickens.*

LILIANA: *. . . you turned this light on them and they laid an egg every two minutes.*

ELVIRA: *So I think these changes made the younger generation soft, lazy. Sometimes it makes me jealous to see the little girls just strolling around, having a good time.*

LILIANA: *They're all stuck up, they change their clothes all the time.*

ELVIRA: *Now you don't see kids with ripped shoes or old clothes. You don't see kids walking around in the same clothes every day. When we were young we didn't have a lot of clothing. You washed your clothes, waited until they dried, and then put them right back on. We almost always wore the same pieces of clothing. Now children appear with a new outfit every day. Now you can't tell the difference between country kids and city kids. The country kids are even more stylish than the city kids. They have all the luxuries, the church and the library are close, they have everything they need, absolutely everything. There are buses to take you anywhere you want to go, you don't even have to walk short distances anymore. We all walked to high school. In 1984, when I began to attend, I walked to and from school every day, because the bus only ran once a day in the morning. I walked carrying my milk and everything; even the rich kids walked in those days. But this younger generation doesn't even know how to walk, they get tired too fast. The bus drops people off on the edge of town and they can't even walk that short bit. Life has changed a lot, and the town keeps growing out into the countryside. This is changing everything. Not only we Mapuches will disappear, but so will peasant culture as everything becomes more urban.*

F: *The other day when we were walking along the train tracks, Isolde told me that she remembered when she used to jump from tie to tie on the railroad line to get to school. She jumped barefoot from tie to tie as there were lots of rocks in the middle that hurt her feet. So she jumped along like that to school with her shoes in her hand.*

LIONEL: *Lots of kids went to school like that, because the older children taught us to carry our shoes in our hands so they wouldn't get worn out and dirty. We had to arrive at school with clean shoes. When we arrived at Pitrufquén we washed our feet and put on our shoes. They made me take my shoes off and carry them around my neck too.*

ELVIRA: *You'd always get a ride.*

LIONEL: *When I was late I got a ride. I also walked.*

F: *Isolde also told me that you had to buy shoes that were too big so that they would fit longer. But they weren't very comfortable to walk to school in if they didn't fit right.*

ELVIRA: *I got to wear plastic shoes.*

LIONEL: *But in those days at least you could buy a pair of shoes with the money you made selling a sack of wheat. Now you have to sell several bags of wheat to have enough to buy just one pair of shoes.*

ELVIRA: *With one egg . . .*

LIONEL: *. . . you could buy a kilo of salt.*

DOÑA MARTINA: *. . . and you still had a little money left over.*

ELVIRA: *Yes, you still had a little left over. Now what I get from selling one egg doesn't even cover the price of one kilo of salt. Now in order to get the same amount . . .*

LIONEL: *. . . you'd have to add yeast to the salt! (Laughter.)*

ELVIRA: *. . . we bought a kilo of salt with what one egg cost when Lionel was attending the university in Temuco. And with three eggs . . .*

LILIANA: *Afterward we had salt but we didn't have any eggs to eat. (She laughs.)*

ELVIRA: *Eggs were so rare at our family meals then that we all shared an egg, and even then it was usually a privilege reserved for the older children.*

DOÑA MARTINA: *Yes, because we had to sell the eggs.*

LIONEL: *Eggs were expensive.*

ELVIRA: *And now, you know, my nephews eat an egg each. Before, when we were their age, eggs were so expensive. With a dozen eggs the kids could pay for the bus to and from the university for many days. That was in the seventies. Now the price of wheat and eggs has dropped, if you could sell an animal you could buy . . .*

LILIANA: *And the cost of transportation rose, everything else rose in price. Before, you could make money off what you produced. But not anymore, all the prices of the products have dropped.*

ELVIRA: *Now people live in the countryside, comfortably, but they don't earn their living from farming. Lucho, for example, who lives in the countryside but works elsewhere, can buy everything he wants right down to the last sprig of cilantro, but he doesn't farm at all.*

LILIANA: *It's that the land can't support people the way it used to.*

Among the Mapuche there are workers from the countryside who like the rural life, they get married young. In my family we have pretty typical romantic lives in this regard. My older brother always aspired to find a wife, a girl he could talk to a few times and who would accept marriage without all the courtship, without asking much of him. He wanted a woman who was his economic superior, and my brother had a very specific idea of how the woman should look. She should be blond, with blue or green eyes. Or maybe her skin would be a little darker, but she would be his age or younger.

But economically she should be self-sufficient, and he didn't want all the arrangements to take long, he just wanted it to happen quickly, without telling the girl "I love you," without courting her or anything. It was as if he were watching a movie in black and white, and he thought it was in color; that girl didn't exist. My other brother, Dagoberto, the leader of a Christian community, whom you met on Sunday, wants a woman who is the same height as he is. He wants to go out a few times with her, and maybe say "I love you" on the fourth date or so, and maybe on the sixth date ask her to marry him. And if the girl says yes, they'd get married the next week. But she has to like the rural life and share with him.

F: *And meanwhile, would they have as many children as came along?*

That's something we haven't talked much about, but we've talked about my particular situation, since I haven't had children since my marriage, but I did have my daughter much earlier. I've come to the conclusion that my brother doesn't want too many kids, but he does want to have at least three. Three would be fine, four would be sufficient, but under no circumstances as many as my parents had. If we were eight, he'd like to have four. I know he doesn't want to have lots of children, but I don't know if he agrees with using birth control. This is not a subject we've been able to talk about, generally it's not talked about within the family.

F: *But if he doesn't want to talk with his wife about these things, then what happens, happens, right?*

I have to say that I really don't know. My third brother was looking for a wife, too, he was looking for a wife who could share his ideas and principles. His dream was that his wife would be his other half. He was the brother I talked with most, played with most, we dreamed together about what the future would bring before he got married. He fell in love with a girl and began to court her. But her parents didn't approve of my brother. So he broke up with that girl and began to go out with another girl who was also Mapuche. His big goal was to marry a Mapuche girl who would be faithful and obedient and who shared his dreams and objectives. If he was going to be an engineer, his wife had to be of the same social status as he was, and share the same ideas as our mother. Because for my brother—and this is still true—his mother is the best, the most perfect woman he knows. He wants a woman like his mother, someone who is humble and a hard worker, a woman who can resist all the blows life gives.

He also had observed my mother and he knew that he couldn't hit his wife. My father has indulged pretty heavily in domestic abuse. I remember that my mother always had black eyes, you understand? It was my brother who intervened in the situation. I think, too, that the birth of my daughter was an important moment for the family, as was my marriage to Juan. After we were married we went to stay at my parents' house, our first night as a married couple in their home. We had already lived here together in Temuco for a month or so, it was just a normal visit, it wasn't anything unusual. But that night my dad hit my mother, and he hit her because we were married and sleeping together under his roof. The problem that provoked those blows was our sleeping there in his house. My brother could think of nothing else but to tell my daughter, "Go get Mom and bring her here." From that night on my mother didn't sleep in the same bed with my father again.

When I married Juan, my parents stopped sleeping together; as far as we know my father no longer hits her. Now when we're not there, I think they still exchange words, strong words, that vicious cycle which says, "If I don't scold you, if I don't criticize you, if I don't tell you things like that then I don't care about you," as if that kind of abuse was necessary.

F: *For some people, fighting seems to be an inherent part of love.*

Yes, it's like that, it's like a disease that stayed there within them. My brother Pedro and I told ourselves that we didn't want that kind of violence in our own families, that it couldn't be like that with our partners. I talked a lot with my younger brother about this before getting married. He knew me well and we agreed on a lot of things, we talked, you know? After he got married we fell out of touch because he moved to Calama and Chuquicamata to work. It was really too bad.

Pedro is here now. He practically carried out his courtship over the phone and came back to marry the girl. The courtship was like that, they talked a bit in the countryside, then he gave her his telephone number and they started calling each other. After that he came back to get married. He had lived with a different girl before, he had experience with women, and aside from the bad experiences he'd had here, he'd also had a relationship with a girl in Calama. He had bad luck; the girls were unfaithful to him, he caught two of them, so he left. He married a girl from the countryside who was seventeen years old, who supposedly had never been with anybody else and who would keep to the standard he set. That happened in the blink of an eye.

He got married when he was twenty-five, he was no spring chicken, and he was almost ten years older than his wife. The girl wasn't even out of primary school, and he was already an engineer. It seems to me that the age difference caused problems in their marriage. And he began to think that women are all alike, he began to judge them all. And I'll give you one guess as to who ended up defending women! One time when I was furiously defending women's rights, my brother asked me why I worked so hard defending women, when they were all alike. He said, "The best thing about my wife is that she gave me two kids." He had two kids at that point; neither he nor I knew that his wife was already expecting the third.

So there you have the situation. In other words, we return to the main point: Do Mapuches know how to court women? That's the question. Two of my brothers aren't married, exactly because they don't know how to court, they don't want to invest the time. They treat courtship and women as if women had an obligation to marry them.

Three of the sisters in our family are married, and we've all followed our husbands. But I don't know about my brothers-in-law, not the one who lives in Calama—I have a sister who lives in Calama—nor the one who lives here in Temuco. In my case my husband is Mapuche, the other two aren't Mapuche. My husband and I have talked about the fact that a Mapuche man isn't the type to bring you gifts, he isn't about to invite you out somewhere special. If it turns out that you're both going somewhere at the same time, fine; if not you just don't go out together. A Mapuche man will hardly ever hold your hand or walk with his arm around you. Even if you feel it, even if you want it, it doesn't happen. You go somewhere with him, wanting to have a good time, but once you get there you find you've been left alone, in a corner. You have to socialize with the other women and just let him go off and do his own thing. I'm a leader in the Mapuche movement, I have power and presence, and this happens to me; imagine how it must be for the rest of the women. They get this treatment and much more. They work alone in the kitchen. At least I don't have to do that. So, in my opinion, something is lacking in the way Mapuches go about courtship. Something is missing in the way we choose partners and form families, and I've talked to other women about this. We all agree that, in the past, Mapuche men weren't like this, that they used to know how to say beautiful things in the Mapuche language, and that they said them often, anywhere.

ELVIRA: *But Mapuches didn't court each other before, either; it wasn't part of Mapuche culture. My mother tells the story of this woman from her community, doña Angela . . .*

. . . The large woman, who participates in the gillatun . . .

ELVIRA: *. . . and one day she was fetching water and the man who is now her husband walked by. They always saw each other and one day he said to her, "You're coming home with me." And from that day on they were together. One of my father's cousins had a similar experience. My father and my mother also met in the same way. When my mother was young, all the marriages were arranged the way my brother Dago wishes they still were: you see each other around a few times and go home together. Living in a community like this you know people through their families, but that is not the type of courtship we want to have. We don't just want them to tell us "come home with me" and work the details out later.*

In my mother's case she didn't have any courtship. My father worked in the same place as she did. They both took care of animals and later took the sheep to pasture. One day he walked the twelve kilometers to my mother's house. He didn't even talk with my mother's parents, he just told my mother that he'd be back on a certain day at a certain time to get her. Maybe they talked about what would happen if they were found out, about what her relatives would do if they caught them. But he just said, "Listen, when you hear the whistle of the *pidén* bird, when the moon goes down, that will be me." And my dad came back and began to whistle, and my mother came out with her things, and they left together at midnight. They walked all night, they walked twelve kilometers over the hills, until they reached my father's family house. He had never said to my mother directly, "Look, we're going to get married, we're going to live together, we're going to build a house." Things really weren't talked about, they weren't decided ahead of time; at some point, while they were tending the sheep, she must have accepted. He only said to her, "I'm leaving, but I'll be back for you on this day, at this time."

Well. This is really an aside to tell you about romantic relations and to tell you about my two brothers who have not married. I think they have not married because girls today are not just willing to leave their water jugs by the side of the road, or to get up on the rump of a horse, when a man says "come with me." Now people feel the need to talk more, to plan, to share life. Women have really changed in this respect, maybe because of all the bad experiences they've had. Because some women start out with a man, and they haven't gotten very far down the road when they're already pregnant and the man is saying, "I'll be back for you on a certain date, then I'll speak to your father," but he doesn't come back. People have learned to use and abuse each other. Before, a man didn't go away and leave a woman pregnant. No, he was always responsible for what he did, even when he married two or three women. Sometimes it didn't work out and a woman returned home, that happened over the years in some cases. But before, marriages were meant to link communities together and unite them. This is something that has changed over time.

One day my father-in-law and I were talking about why Juan and I didn't have a party when we got married. We had a number of practical problems. I'm seven years older than Juan, and neither of us had the money for a party. The money we had we spent on this property here in Temuco, which we bought as soon as we were married. We bought this property within a month of getting married, and then we built this house, adding on to it bit by bit. We've been working on this house since 1983. But my father-in-law told me that if we'd been married in traditional Mapuche fashion, Juan would have come to get me in my community, accompanied by other people, and would have spoken with my parents. He would have thrown a party at my parents' house, in my community, and then we would have returned to his parents' house to finish celebrating.

F: *Under traditional Mapuche wedding arrangements, wasn't a bride price paid as well?*

Yes, as part of the party held at my parents' house they would also have brought the presents agreed to in the arrangement made with my father. These could include animals, handicrafts, or seeds. Usually they'd also include wheat, potatoes, beans, shallots, blankets, jewelry, pottery, baskets. All of that was included in those days.

F: *Am I mistaken, or was a horse usually part of the exchange?*

Not just one, often several horses were part of the agreement. It depended on . . . the economic status of the Mapuche you were marrying. If the groom was poor, just the logko's servant, he wouldn't be able to give very much. In previous times the community helped out with the bride price, they gave blankets and other items. But there wasn't a set amount, each case was different and depended on a community's ability to pay. That's why some communities were richer than others, and why weddings were done that way, almost like a marriage between communities.

F: *Do some Mapuche communities still practice these traditional marriage customs?*

Yes, especially around Cholchol, Imperial.

F: *And what you described for your mother's generation, that the guy simply showed up and said, come on, let's go, and that was that; I wonder to what extent that, too, was the result of increasing poverty, maybe also migration, cultural change, a whole series of factors, no?*

I think that cultural change and increasing poverty have occurred together for the Mapuche. These two processes happened together because due to poverty people began to migrate and to mix with non-Mapuche society. Education was a big part of this so-called integration. Parents sent their children to school so they could learn to read and write, and the more educated in that generation took non-Mapuche marriage partners as part of the process of "civilizing" themselves. And with these changes, the culture was transformed as well. I'd say now that about eighty percent of marriages, whether between Mapuches or mixed Mapuche-wigka, consist of standard wedding parties like people do everywhere. You know, a good party that lasts a night. The more jaded couples might throw a party that only lasts an afternoon and then it's over. In previous times the parties lasted two, three days, even a week. It took that long to travel between the two communities and carry out the whole ceremonial process. As part of the ritual they had to kill the animals they would eat, and tradition also dictated who supplied the animal, not the groom or his parents but the groom or bride's uncle. There were specific roles for people in the ritual: who killed the animal; who received the stomach or the hide; who grabbed the head or the animal's horns, it had to be the bride's brother or cousin-in-law who held the steer's horns. It was a beautiful ceremony, really, shared by the whole community and in which the whole community participated. A community received the new wife into their midst and gave away the groom as a member of the wife's community. The Mapuche said, "I didn't lose a son, I gained a daughter," or "I didn't lose a daughter, I gained a son." The parents of the bride or groom gave their child both to the new in-laws and to the logko of the new community.

In all our comings and goings, this is being lost, this cultural richness has been lost. Even if we only did a small party that lasted but an afternoon, what I would like—and this is my dream, you see—I would like to spend an afternoon in my house with my in-laws, with a lot of people, and do a traditional Mapuche marriage ritual in which Juan would formally ask for my hand. In this way we don't only give ourselves to each other, but also to our communities, recognizing our obligation to others and to community service. These days marriage is a very egotistical affair between two people who tell each other, "I married you, but not your family and even less your community." That's what happens now. They say, "What's mine is yours," or "What's yours is mine"; but above all the men say, "What's mine is mine."

F: *From a certain point of view, traditional Mapuche courtship was between communities rather than individuals.*

Yes, that's how it was. The courtship lasted a week, but it was clear that the community was implied in the bride and groom's exchange of vows. There was no marriage license in the Mapuche ceremony, nothing on paper, but there were many people who served as witnesses. There is a saying among the Mapuche, that you get married according to three laws: first the law of the community, then civil and then religious law.

F: *I'd like you to tell me more about your in-laws, because you've said several times that you feel very comfortable with them.*

They're young, there are only ten or fifteen years of age difference between us. My mother-in-law just turned fifty; my father-in-law is about fifty-five or sixty. They're very dedicated, very good people, very socially conscious; they believe that a united community can accomplish more than any one person alone. They're also Catholic, but they're Catholic in their own way. Like many Mapuche, they're baptized Catholics because they had to be, or out of respect for the Church, or for some other reason. They believe very strongly in Günechen, in God. They prefer to communicate directly with a faceless God who doesn't have long blond hair, isn't thin or bony, but is instead a supreme being who can do anything.

They respect nature. From them I learned to recognize holiness in nature, in rocks, trees, and water. They took me to a place near the road that leads to their house, near the main street, where a bay tree grows. They told me that the bay tree had been cut down by a man, but had replanted itself. Even though the man cut it all down and threw part of it in the river, the tree started growing again in the same place. Not all the tree came back, but what had been cut down and left there, on the ground, stood straight again. In the middle of the tree is a spring from which water flows. The hotter you are the harder the water flows, like an open faucet. It's on a mountain, surrounded by native trees, and everyone can see it. It's not hidden away or anything. Before it was hidden on a big mountain, but for the last fifty years, since the road was built, it's been in plain view. While deeply respecting trees in general, they also told me that sometimes there were snakes in the trees. I answered that those stories were parables to help children respect nature. In other words, that we shouldn't touch a particular tree because it could cause an allergic rash, what we call *pixtu*. In this way people don't hurt the trees and destroy nature. My in-laws insisted that the power some trees had was real, that it helped God control the rest of nature. That's why, they said, we have so many different kinds of trees. On the road toward Argentina, you can find hualles, oaks, boldos, and araucaria pines (*pewen*). There's a dwarf araucaria, or pewen, where people leave presents: money, handkerchiefs, tee shirts, whatever they want. Having this kind of respect, even reverence, is almost a self-control mechanism for people, because without it they'd rob nature of everything.

They tell me that the same thing occurs with rocks or stones. Stones are also living entities, they grow and develop, they're part of the environment. Some are holy stones, or saints, because the water that flows from them heals people. Other stones are magnetic, they're talismans that can take away people's pains. Maybe a rock itself is not saintly; who knows, my father-in-law would say, how many people have passed their hands over it! But large rocks, tall stones on the hillside or by the river absorb magnetism from the surrounding environment and thus can soothe people's pain. Because of that power, stones can't be removed or taken somewhere else, and any road we build has to go around them. Whether the powerful like it or not, roads have to be built without damaging the rocks and the trees.

Politically speaking, my in-laws belong to the Christian Democratic Party, so I can influence them a lot, just as I influenced my parents and my brothers and sisters. I got them to formally register as party members. But more importantly, we follow the same line within the party, we agree on the way to act and participate politically. I'm sure they watch the news every day to know what's happening with the president, to see who will be the congressional candidate, what are the good and bad campaign slogans. They can criticize one or another party colleague, or they can praise an ally from the broader coalition. The way in which my in-laws reflect upon the political situation can make you question what you thought originally. Since they're from the countryside and still live in the countryside they have a different perspective. Suddenly someone comes along and wants to bring you to their side without really talking or negotiating political perspectives. My in-laws aren't like that, they look at things from all sides, from all perspectives, and they say, "Look, the political party is only one, but it's like being in church. In church we're many individuals and we're supposed to be a single entity at the same time. But in the end, we're really nothing, because each person is there with his or her own vision."

In this sense I get along quite well with them. Every time I've had serious problems with Juan, they've helped me. Even though they're his parents, they talk with me about him, about his defects, and ask me to have patience with him and to hope that the future brings better things. In a way they're like the family, or maybe the friends, I always wanted to have and didn't. My friends don't talk about such personal things because they don't want to get involved. My parents, too, have removed themselves from discussions of my marriage because they didn't want to get involved in such a problematic topic.

My father told me, "Look, it's better that you don't have children if you're always going to be fighting. Why do you want to have kids if you spend so much time out of the house? You have problems with Juan. Of course you do, you're never home." That's what my father says about the situation. But with my in-laws, it's different. They tell me, "You know, a child would really do Juan good." They tell me that he must be frustrated to have married an older woman and can't bring himself to tell me so. My father-in-law tells me, "But I know that he loves you, because when I talk to him, when we talk about things, he tells me that he loves you, that he'll never leave you. He says he's just like that and can't change," my father-in-law tells me. He doesn't say to me, "Be patient, things will change tomorrow." He never says I'm the one who caused all the problems. He says that we're both guilty and that we both have to give a little. He tells me, "Maybe you have to let some of your things go and change a little, be there for him more often, have dinner waiting for him."

The same thing happens with the gillatun. We talk about it, reflect on it. In my in-laws' community five hundred families participate in the gillatun, whereas in my community only thirty participate. In Huilío all the people participate, the young people, the adults, those who speak mapunzugun and those who don't, they're all involved and do their part. Here in my community people are reluctant to participate because they think they'll lose lots of money. They think killing an animal for the gillatun is a wasted expense. They also don't understand that they don't have to kill big animals, like cows or horses. They can simply take a couple of chickens or a sheep, a pig, so that it's not too much for them. As my in-laws say, it's not an issue of bringing enough to feed everyone, it's a question of performing a ceremony. But it's true that there is social pressure to contribute sizeable quantities. The people watch you and if you don't invite them to eat, they'll say that the gillatun was bad because there wasn't enough food for all the people, even if they only dropped by to look. They say, "Ah, they're having a gillatun in Huilío, or in Chanco, everyone will be there. Let's go, too." And you can't kick people out, you have to give everyone who comes to the gillatun a meal. So the gillatun has a sacred, ritual dimension, but it also has a social aspect and even a folkloric aspect. And I've been able to talk about all these issues with my in-laws.

My parents and I couldn't talk about these multiple dimensions of the gillatun. My father becomes obsessed with the social obligation and he gets desperate. He just sits there and says, "Pass me a plate," or "I don't have a plate for him," or "I have to serve so and so." My father-in-law interprets the gillatun very differently. He tells me, "Look, if I attend a gillatun, when it's my turn to host I have to return the favor. It's a moral and a personal obligation, a reciprocity." And yet my father, who doesn't go to other people's gillatun, still feels he has to serve all these people. As my father-in-law suggests, my father really doesn't owe all those people a meal, maybe he just spends and worries too much. But it's hard to make the people who come understand this. Around the time of the ceremony our cousins start arriving from Santiago, my father's nephews, and if we stuck to the notion of strict reciprocity we couldn't take care of them. They come five, six, seven, eight at a time, they bring their children, boyfriends and girlfriends, nieces and nephews. We have to prepare a plate for each person. Even the smallest child needs to be served. So this is a different dimension to the event than just normal participants, the ones who take part in the ceremony. You have to prepare an additional thirty plates, because even if they're not counted among the regular participants, you know these people will arrive.

I can talk about these things with my father-in-law. I can talk with him about many things, about Mapuche traditional dress, about moral and sexual issues. We also discuss politics, religion, and culture, we talk about the customs of different places. These things are very hard to talk about with other people, I can't even discuss such things with my brothers and sisters because we have different priorities, different points of view. I don't know, these things are hard to talk about with other people, but with my father-in-law it's easy to discuss them. If I talked to anybody about my first sexual experiences, it was with my in-laws. I shared with them my concerns and my fears. I talked only with them about these things, I didn't even talk with my mother about it. I should have asked my mother, "Look, are these things normal when you have sex?" But I didn't dare to ask my parents such things; I asked my in-laws instead. With them I could admit that I had lots of fears and doubts.

But it was my father who told me that I shouldn't have frequent sexual relations with Juan. "Your husband's very thin," my father said, "and a wild vixen could come down from the mountains and take him away." I understood that he was telling me to control myself, and to take my husband to the doctor. My in-laws didn't tell me this, it was my father who told me. With my father it went beyond talking. I told him, "Juan has a terrible fever.

His back hurts, and he has a spot where they took out his hernia when he was a child that's giving him problems." It was then that my father told me he knew that many people got carried off by a wild vixen at times like this. He told me so much with that one phrase that I rushed back from Pitrufquén to Temuco and immediately took Juan to the hospital.

I think the most important part of my relationship with my in-laws is our ability to share views on politics and culture. It's the political support they give within the organizations, but also the individual support they give me. They say, "You're a woman, you can do it. Not just anyone can do it, but you can." They also recognize that people have to be united if they're going to change things. It doesn't matter what kind of organization it is that brings people together, it could be a committee, a workshop, a cooperative. My father-in-law is involved in all kinds of organizations, because he realizes that people have to work collectively to improve things. To illustrate this point, he likes to use the example of the supermarket chains. "How many people run those stores?" he asks. "Is it one person? No, there are one hundred, or there are twenty, or there are thirty people involved, you see? There's one manager, but he can't run the stores alone." Often in the speeches he gives in the community he uses this example of the supermarkets, or of the *Sociedad Nacional de Agricultura.* "Why do the large farmers succeed?" he asks. "Because they unite to get access to credit. How do they protect themselves? The truck drivers also: some own the trucks and some drive them. How are they able to unite? Why do they strike from one day to the next, and we aren't able to organize and mobilize like they do?" His speeches helped me develop my own political consciousness, they answered some of my questions and clarified some of my doubts. And my in-laws also see their beliefs reflected in my speeches.

With my in-laws I can even share my commitment to gender issues, as my mother-in-law is also very involved politically. My father-in-law doesn't criticize me for being a leader or going out to meetings. He doesn't make problems for me or say, "Hey, married women stay home because their husbands expect them to." He doesn't say, "It doesn't matter if the man is unfaithful, so long as the woman's not." I won't tell you that they haven't said these things to me in jest. But they also have told me that I have to keep doing what I'm doing. They know me and they trust that I won't do things that they think are bad.

Now, I won't tell you things have been great in my marriage, because they haven't been. I haven't been able to have children, for example, that's one problem. A second problem is that my husband has had many opportunities to run around with other women. On one occasion he left for a couple of months. It really cost him, I know he suffered a lot that time, when he left the house. I'm very strong, incredibly strong on the outside, but I'm extremely sensitive. I really cried a lot, I thought a lot, I took out my pain in many different ways. All of a sudden I'd sit down and write, and then I'd read it later and I'd think, "I wrote this? When, and in what mental condition was I?" I don't know. I'd pick up the paper, and on an impulse I'd throw it in the trash. More recently, though, I've taken to saving what I write, I'm not sure why.

But it was at that point, with Juan out of the house, that my father-in-law told me, "Why should you stay home? There's no reason to stay at home and pine away for this man. He's just one person, and there are many people waiting to hear you speak at the meetings, waiting for you to motivate them. Why should you live and die for just one man? I know he's my son, but he is just one person, no?" So I tell you, I really appreciated his attitude. "He's my son," he told me, "but if the two of you split up you'll still be my first daughter-in-law, my friend, and my daughter. You have to have more energy each day for your work in the organization, you have to participate with more enthusiasm every day."

Knowing that I had their support was such a relief for me, it gave me energy to continue working. At such a difficult moment, having their support was worth more than ten thousand, more than one hundred thousand pesos, because even if you're short on cash you're even shorter on confidence, on optimism. They were there with me through that difficult time. Obviously they didn't come to visit every week, but after all, Juan is their child, he's their oldest son. It's a difficult position to be in, no? But two or three times my father-in-law came by and invited me to stay at his house, and once my mother-in-law stayed here with me. We talked about my situation with Juan the night she stayed here. Or she'd see me in the office and talk with me, or leave me notes. She didn't come to stay with me again, but they were both always there for me.

During our separation there were also political leaders who noticed, and it almost became an issue in the party. Since it was in the summer, some of the politicians were on vacation in Pucón, among them an important national leader in the Christian Democratic Party. He and others took a day off from their vacation to come and talk with me. Their attitude was obviously different, they considered it a political issue. They told me that I was an outstanding individual, that I had won a space for myself politically. That was what mattered, they said, so why did I still care about this guy? I remember saying to the national leader that it was easy for him to say things like that, but it was another thing to live the experience, especially for me. I told him, "Remember that I'm first Mapuche, second a Catholic, and last a Christian Democrat." He reminded me that he was a man, a Catholic, and a Christian Democrat. "On top of that," he told me, "I could put my profession before my allegiance to the Christian Democrats. But it turns out that we all have to establish priorities." He asked me to put my individual and political needs first. It was like telling me that my husband and my marriage were worthless, you see.

But people appreciate things differently at different moments. There have been many people who have told me that my husband isn't worth anything, this or that. It's upsetting to hear such things, because after all, I chose him for a reason, no? Not because I thought he was good for nothing, right? In this sense, I think people's expectations are different. I talked a lot with Gute[4] about politics and the party, about participation and the gains I'd made. We talked about what it would mean for the party to lose its foothold, and what it might mean for me to lose what I'd gained, but Gute always privileged what those losses would mean for the party. So I said stop, wait. I'm not going to kill myself over this, you know? He answered that it was exactly what he was trying to tell me, that I shouldn't lay down and die over it. But he was always cold, wanting to revive my spirit, but from another perspective, completely cold.

With my parents-in-law, as I've told you, it was different. They're always with me, discussing things with me, they've always been in the organization. I send them a letter by bus and I tell them to get some people together, that so-and-so is coming to meet with people, to discuss the situation, on such and such a day. My father-in-law is always there waiting for me when I arrive. I can be bringing a political leader, a representative from an institution, it doesn't matter; he's never let me down. I asked them to help me organize their district and they took me everywhere, established contact people, and were there with me. I can always expect this from them. What didn't happen, though, and what I wish would have happened, was the celebration between our two communities. It's one of my frustrated dreams, but . . .

F: *You mean for your marriage.*

For my wedding. I think these were dreams I had when I decided to marry a Mapuche, to be married according to Mapuche custom. Although I could have married a non-Mapuche man, I chose to marry a Mapuche, the son of a Mapuche leader, who knew how to talk pretty and taught me so many things. I thought we would have something different. But the political situation was difficult then. We were married in 1983, as we were leaving Ad-Mapu. There was a lot of pressure. I had worked for five years full time as the general secretary of the Mapuche movement. I'd let everything else go. Getting married at that moment—I don't know—it was like letting go of everything, getting married with nothing. Those were difficult times, and I think they were difficult for Juan and me, too. Our relationship was beautiful, but there were just too many political problems then. Juan was finishing high school. He had to attend one more year because he was studying accounting. So . . . (Laughs.) Did you hear that? She called me a cradle robber.

F: *I didn't hear, but I saw your eyes, and that was enough! (Laughs.)*

I'm sure it was enough! But I do think that for us, it was a very bad economic situation. On the other hand, I don't think my father was ready to say, "OK, you're getting married, we'll send these things with you and we'll throw a send-off party so you can live in the other community." Conditions weren't right on either side; they were bad for my in-laws, too. They'd just gone through a marriage crisis; my father-in-law had been with another woman for a while. Like all Mapuche men, I want to say, my father-in-law had his fling, and it lasted a long time. Anyway, they were just coming out of this crisis, as I said. In fact, it was our marriage that got them back together again. They were about to separate more permanently. I think our marriage helped to reunite them again; but on the other hand, our marriage also made my own parents stop sleeping together.

ELVIRA: *When Isolde got married, my father tried to arrange our futures for us.*

Since I had a daughter, all the material possessions I might have—from a set of knives, for example, spoons, whatever—went to Liliana. I had a skinny cow, because I have bad luck with animals; it, too, went to Liliana. Every-thing—beds, plates, animals—everything went to Liliana.

ELVIRA: *She has about two or three hectares of land.*

Two and a half hectares. Liliana is the landowner. Everything that I'm not, Liliana is. My father bought five hectares of land. He gave two and a half to Liliana and two and a half to Dago, since my father used Dago's money to buy the land. Their goal was to ensure a bright future for Liliana.

I said I'd take Liliana to live with me. My father refused, my mother refused, and my siblings nearly made mincemeat of me. They weren't ready for Liliana to leave. I talked with Liliana, I told her I was getting married. It shocked her so much she lost weight. She was just a little girl then.

F: *Tell me a little more about Liliana. Did you have her in Santiago?*

Yes. It was a real drama, the whole experience, but it was also a part of life, no? To travel from Pitrufquén to Santiago, without even having been to Temuco; I moved from a small, quiet town to Santiago, huge Santiago. First I stayed with an aunt who wasn't sure if she was staying in Santiago or moving back to Imperial, to her husband's community; or maybe he'd return and she'd stay working in Santiago. Finally they sold the house; I don't know the details of how they sold it. Then I had to go live with another aunt who was single and politically active. She was part of a group that painted graffiti and did other political work, I don't know what all they did. The truth was that I ended up living in a shack with an uncle who drank and an aunt who always arrived late and brought her boyfriends. Things that I would never have seen in my community, I saw and experienced in Santiago. I lived in Santiago from May until September.

When my father found out I was pregnant, he could think of nothing else to say to me except, "Well, you can't get rid of it now, but you'll have to leave the house. I don't want to be embarrassed by you. People will talk and I'll get mad and I'll hit you, and then I'll end up in jail. So it's better if you leave." So I left; and then, even though I did not have their approval, I came back. Because the truth is that things weren't going too well for me in Santiago. I could have stayed and worked, because I was already working and I was beginning to find my niche. I could also have given my daughter up for adoption, but that wasn't for me. I preferred to bring her home. Liliana was born on September 2nd. I stayed at the Joaquín Aguirre hospital until September 10th, then I traveled south on September 18th and arrived home on the 19th.

At first everyone was shocked, which was normal. Then they hid the baby and wouldn't let me take her outside. That lasted a month. After that month was up, my brother Dagoberto took the baby in his arms, brought her out from the back room, and passed her to my father. My father was drinking his mate and holding the baby, and I was standing by the stove trembling. My brothers and sisters were all there, my mother kept serving mate; the tension was terrible. My father held her a good while. The child cooed and he stroked her head. She was so small, only a month old, but she was so cuddly that my father just held her for a good long time. Then he passed her to my mother, and then she passed her to my brother, the same one who had brought her out. He held her a while and then passed her from one sister to the next, and the relationship began to grow, especially with my sister Elvira.

ELVIRA: *She didn't even have a proper bottle, she just had a little rubber duck, the kind you fill with water, and we had to keep filling it up. She'd drink about four of those little bottles at a time.*

Yes, four bottles. Things got more comfortable after that. Liliana could go out in public and she became part of the family. But I needed to work. So I went to work in the parish, from the parish to a teacher's house. She was a music teacher and her husband owned a liquor store. I learned a lot while I was with them. Working and studying wasn't easy. And I continued to work in the parish. I also worked one summer in a flour mill, but I mainly worked in the house. I wasn't the only servant, there was another woman who also worked there and I was her helper. I learned to cook and clean to the lady's liking. I made many friends, with whom I'm still in contact today. Many were from political parties other than the Christian Democrats, like the *Partido por la Democracia* (Party for Democracy, or PPD) or the National Party. I met them long ago, and some still think of me as that nice little girl, but for others I've become a friend. If before I was the children's nanny, today I'm their friend. Today I'm also friends with my English teacher and with the school inspector.

So all these experiences—working at the mill, in the house, at the church—helped me grow and become strong. Especially the parish, which had a different mission in the world, a different set of expectations, helped toughen me up. Because I am tough. If I see someone hurt and I can help him or her, I do. I don't just stand there and cry. If I see a dead person and I can help in some way, I do. I help sick people, too. I don't have problems with all of that.

Although, two or three years ago, I was shocked when I had to go buy a coffin for a friend. The man was a political organizer who had worked a lot with me. He was plowing his land, and a blood clot must have lodged in his brain and he had a stroke. At first he was paralyzed from the neck down. It was terrible; he was still a young man. I went to the hospital and talked with him, I shaved him. A horrible smell emanated from him; it was hard even to enter his room. What he said broke my heart: "Take care of my wife and my son. Please buy me a coffin, you pick out a nice one for me. Organize my funeral, let everyone know so that they all come." You can't cry when someone tells you things like this. When do you cry? When you get home, when you're alone in your room, hours later, when you can think about everything that happened, that's when you cry. I've seen many hard things in my life.

F: *Let's talk a little about your experience in the* Centros Culturales Mapuches. *How did your work in the* Centros *relate to your work in your community?*

The strategy of the *Centros Culturales Mapuches* was cultural revival, through the recuperation of different ceremonies and rituals that had begun to be lost in some communities, but were still alive in others. Some examples are *palin*, and the different kinds of gillatun, practiced in different places; or the *machitun*, which is a healing ceremony. The CCMS also organized different kinds of Mapuche parlor games, such as the *kamikan* and the *awarkuzen*. We also worked on preserving all kinds of Mapuche music. We set up concerts, competitions, and workshops and featured musical instruments and different crafts in order to share knowledge and experience. These were the *Centros'* strategies for getting a lot of people together. The *Centros* also emphasized and organized communal work parties to clean and repair roads, canals, and fences; to build communal pigpens and chutes for removing the horns from and vaccinating animals; to build washtubs for bathing sheep. Any kind of work that could be organized communally, we organized; and it was much more efficient at the communal level, because with a communal washtub you can bathe a lot of sheep!

This strategy which emphasized communal activity was central to our efforts, because we wanted something that would bring us together and create an identity for the group. We wanted to develop what was specifically Mapuche in our speeches, conversations, political platforms; we wanted to emphasize the lyrical and formal aspects of our language, of mapunzugun. The majority of our leaders spoke beautifully in mapunzugun. Obviously, and as an aside, at first I didn't understand a thing. It was my job to present the part in Spanish; my speeches were all about standing up and taking action, about participating and standing together, about brotherhood and solidarity, about ethnic pride, about engaging in *kelluwun*, which is mutual aid between community members. We tried to instill solidarity and revitalize people's religious faith as Mapuches. We emphasized the profound nature of our belief system that's so different from the religious vision of the wigka world.

All this was our strategy for confronting the reality of the dictatorship in which we were living, to get people in the communities united, mobilized, and integrated into the movement. We couldn't organize as Catholics, because there were many Evangelicals and other religious sects among the Mapuche in the countryside. So our strategy was one of cultural and ethnic unity. We decided to do a chain of ceremonies, of gillatun, palin gillatun, or other cultural events. The activity depended on each community, because not every community could do a gillatun when we asked them to.

In many Mapuche communities the gillatun can only be held every four years. The number four is very symbolic for us, as it symbolizes the four cardinal points; also the four levels of a *rewe*. The number four represents about seven sacred things in our culture, among them the number of years between gillatun. So we decided that the communities should hold whatever kind of ritual they wanted, but that the cycle of ritual would end on Conun Hueno hill overlooking Temuco, which is where the last Mapuche uprising occurred before the final defeat, the so-called Pacification, of the Mapuche people. We gave ourselves one year to organize all this.

That's when we began talking in my family, at my house: when was the last time we did a gillatun in our community? Who is our cacique? Why don't we speak the Mapuche language anymore? Because I'm from Chanco, my community became part of the CCMS, almost by definition. And we kept asking ourselves, when was the last gillatun? Who speaks Mapuche? Why don't the rest of us speak Mapuche? Why don't we know how to play palin? Is there a machi in the community? Who is the logko in the community? We asked ourselves questions like these, and with time, we began to find answers. It took effort; no one is a prophet in one's own land, and change doesn't come easily. My community was among the hardest to organize culturally and ethnically, even as it had been easy to organize the Christian base community. This is because we had not only Catholics, but Evangelicals, who tend to resist Mapuche rituals. There are also many people who've had the opportunity to study. Most have completed high school, but some have university degrees, and they all have colonized mentalities when it comes to their Mapuche origins. These professional people, the secretaries, the teachers, they say they're already civilized, and that this Mapuche business is not for them. It was difficult in these cases, because the children of these families didn't want to have anything to do with the gillatun, and they encouraged their parents not to participate either.

It was hard at first to go and visit everyone, then have to visit them again. It was very hard work. In addition, my parents disapproved of my political organizing, because I gave up everything else when I began to work for the Mapuche movement. My parents were really indignant, because they thought I was going to end up a nobody, and they wanted me to finish college and get a professional title in order to secure my future. Well, in a sense they turned out to be right. But we persisted, because we were serious, and thanks to my uncle Vicente Reuque, who helped with the organizing, we managed to carry out the first big meeting. My uncle Vicente is my father's cousin, and he let us use his name. I did the footwork inviting people, but in my uncle's name and in mine. I went door to door, as we'd done for the Christian base communities, when in the month of the Virgin Mary we carried her image from house to house. We did the same thing for the gillatun. I went door to door with my sister Elvira—the youngest, who has now finished a degree in journalism—in order not to go alone. All the people we invited came to the gillatun. A promise to come to a gillatun is serious. If a person says he or she is coming, then they really do.

They elected my father logko, because they said the position used to belong to my father's great-uncle. From there it is passed first to that man's son, who was Vicente Reuque, the same uncle who had helped me organize the first meeting. But Vicente Reuque didn't want to be the logko so they gave the position to my father, and then Vicente died, so my father, Ernesto Reuque, became the logko of our community. So in 1979, after all these things were resolved, our community really got organized. It was hard for me, because my father kept saying no, that ceremony isn't done here anymore, nobody will want to, nobody will support you. But we did a gillatun in my community, after not having done one for twenty-one years. We performed the gillatun and we've never stopped doing it since then. From then on I was initiated into the spirituality and religiosity of my own people.

To begin to do this, without speaking the Mapuche language well was very hard for me. A lot of things I did through intuition, or from what I had learned through participating in the chain of ceremonies in other communities. And so it worked out, and I felt comfortable. But I dropped out of the Catholic University, where I was studying to become a teacher; I just left all that to work in the Mapuche organization. My father didn't find out that I had quit school for six months. But when he did find out, he was very, very mad. He's still mad at me to this day for having left my studies. We haven't stopped talking to each other or anything, but for the first three months after he found out we didn't talk at all. My father always said that the best things his children could have were a profession, land, and an education. That's the best inheritance for Mapuche children, according to my father. He always thought I'd be married someday, and end up dependent on my husband. He didn't want his children to be dependent on others. He wanted us to develop our talents and help our husbands, and not suffer like he has all his life. We'd seen him suffer as we grew up, and it wasn't easy; after all, there were eight of us to support. So with this mentality that my father instilled in me, and the experience I'd had growing up, I tended to work much harder than most of the other movement leaders.

F: *Did you have a machi present at the gillatun you organized in Chanco?*

The machi who participated, and who helped me organize the first meeting, isn't from my community, but she is from my region. She's a woman who has suffered a great deal; she has a son among the disappeared. Because of this, she was afraid to participate in any activity that might suggest she was against the military government.

She is not from Dalpin, the community where she lives, but she married a man from there. The machi is from the region of Quepe, Quepe-Metrenco. She was with her husband for many years. They had several children, but one of her daughters suffered a mishap and died while working as a domestic servant in Santiago. When this happened the machi didn't renew her vows, one would say in non-Mapuche terms, because she didn't renew her commitment to her special helper spirit, or to her community. Time passed, a time of grief, of personal suffering. And during that time, 1973 rolled around and she also lost her son, who lived with her and worked on nearby estates. He was a peasant leader and union organizer.

The machi's son, Pedro Curihual Paillán, was listed in the report issued by the Rettig Commission.[5] The disappearance of their son led both parents into a serious depression. The father even suffered facial paralysis, which then slowly spread to other parts of his body, and finally he suffered a stroke. It was a mild one, because he could still walk, but not easily. Over time his arms and legs got weaker, and he could only shuffle about. The machi had to face the reality of their situation alone, with her son Luis, who lived next door to her. The rest of the children lived far away, in Argentina and in Santiago. One of her children became a major in the police force. The majority of her daughters are married to Mapuche men, but her children who live in Argentina are married to non-Mapuches.

At first she didn't do what other mothers have done when their children are disappeared. She didn't go asking where he was or attempting to find him. She couldn't do this, because both she and her husband became very sick as a result of her son's disappearance. She lived in permanent suffering, in a state of mourning and desperation. When our church group began to visit her, to work with her in 1975 or 1976, we told her that she had to go and find out where he was or what had happened to him, put him on the lists of missing that were circulating at that time. But it was Pedro's girlfriend who presented the writs of habeas corpus and who tried to find out what happened to him, with the support of a solidarity committee we had formed with the help of the Catholic Church. After that the machi and her younger son got involved in trying to find Pedro as well. They looked and looked for him, a mother looking for her son, a brother looking for his brother, but when they couldn't find him, she stopped looking. She didn't search anymore, because each time they tried, it opened up all her wounds.

Only Luis, the younger son, continued to search. He didn't tell his parents anything about his efforts. It was a silent, painful search. I'm the only one who accompanied him as he looked for his brother, as Pedro's old girlfriend finally left. She went toward Argentina. She married a person from Quitratúe, a community to the south of Pitrufquén. She lost contact with our community.

Don Armando, the machi's husband, died and she was left alone once again. That's how twenty, twenty-two years went by and she didn't change her rewe, her personal totem that marks her as a machi. In this ceremony the whole rewe, or totem, is changed; but the renewal is also of her personal commitment, a deepening of her commitment to her personal helper spirit and to her community. During the time in which she didn't perform the ceremony, she also stopped using the items of traditional Mapuche dress, such as the *chamal*. During those years she also stopped using her ceremonial musical instruments and didn't prepare any medicines. In other words, her vocation as machi and healer had been totally lost. Her spirit and dedication were somewhat revived by our 1979 meeting. She was rejuvenated and began to participate again, but only in the ceremony of the gillatun. Beyond that moment she didn't revive her use of traditional clothing or knowledge. She continued to speak Spanish and, when she was invited to join an Evangelical church, she accepted. It seemed that she wanted to shed her vocation, her knowledge, and her Mapuche identity.

Since 1979–1980, when we did the first gillatun, we've continued the cycle. She has found herself in a space about which she had dreamed, where she can speak the Mapuche language and discuss Mapuche themes. At one point she also went to a conference about mapunzugun, and while there she dreamt all night. She dreamt about all the things she'd done before, especially about rituals, cures, and herbs. A few months after the conference, back in her house, she suffered an attack of paralysis on one side of her face. Strangely enough, she went to the hospital to have it treated rather than to another machi. She went to the doctor, with half her face totally deformed. While they were examining her at the hospital, in a matter of seconds, the affected side of her face cleared up, but the other side became twisted. And it just kept clicking back and forth: first one side was twisted, then it was fixed but the other side twisted up, the muscles totally cramped up. Her eyes were fixed in a rigid stare, then the eyeballs turned around with her eyelids pointing upward. She was unrecognizable; nobody had ever seen anything like it before.

After the episode at the hospital, she consulted with other machis. They began to talk among themselves and to diagnose the problem. They blamed the machi for having participated in the conference on mapunzugun. They said people took her picture, that she shouldn't have gone out. They said the dreams she had at the meeting were a sign, and that she shouldn't have accepted an interview and spoken publicly on the radio, nor allowed her grandson to videotape her. The machis blamed her condition on a series of events, without arriving at the real cause, which was that she had left her traditional clothing, the *kultrun* or traditional drum, her knowledge of herbs and traditional healing; in short, she had stopped being a machi. So it became urgent to perform the *ñeikurewen*, the dance of the machi as it is known in that region, as quickly as possible. They did it all within twenty days, because a superior power told the machi that she had to renew her rewe, and when she asked another machi she was told that she would not improve unless she got in touch with her *newen*, or personal spirit. They did the ñeikurewen there, with the people of the community who most believe in our culture, and with members of her original family who came from Quepe-Metrenco.

Without wanting to, I think I played an important role in that ceremony, a very emotional and stressful time for me and for her family. At many points during the ceremony she would say that she didn't want to live anymore, that she was losing her strength, her newen, and her knowledge; that she didn't want to be a machi anymore. In this ceremony there are certain set steps to be followed, and the younger generation didn't have any idea what they were. Her children supported her financially in the ceremony, but they didn't know how the ritual began or ended. They only knew that they were to bring *muday*, a traditional drink made of wheat, and that there should be food for everyone. But they'd never been to a ceremony like that before, and they wanted to consult with us, with me and my husband Juan.

But I couldn't go, because of all the multiple obligations I sometimes bring on myself, or that sometimes chase me down. I couldn't get there ahead of time, I only got there the day before. I arrived at my parents' house, and they told me, "You have to go there immediately, because they've come asking for you many times already." I said I had to drink my mate first, but the moment I finished my sentence they were already at the door, saying, "Let's go, we've been waiting for you." We left immediately, planning what had to be ready in the morning, how it had to be done, who needed to do what. They said they had everything waiting for me, but they weren't sure what to do with it all.

Unfortunately, Juan couldn't accompany me, so I had to face it all alone. My brothers, sisters, and parents had never been to this kind of ceremony, either. I had once been to a ñeikurewen, but I didn't stay the complete first day, nor all night nor the next day; the ceremony takes two days. So I didn't know that much about it, either. The only things I knew were theoretical, or things I had heard in conversation. I had to tell myself, "Look, Isolde, you know everything. And what you don't know, you just make up." I had to show the way, and ask the machi who was serving as guide, in my bad Mapuche, what came next. I had to do this both days: figure out when to beat the kultrun, when to dance, when to find the medicinal herbs, when to dress the machi, when and where to put the new rewe, which had been prepared ahead of time, how to take down the old one. This process took two days: dressing and undressing her correctly, with the new clothing that included the chamal, sash, ribbons for her headdress, blouse, apron; and through dressing her, giving her new strength. It was very beautiful and I learned a lot, but it was also exhausting. It was tiring rather than bothersome; but I did worry and feel stressed out.

I was carrying a feeling of guilt, because I had encouraged that machi to perform the gillatun again, to attend and participate in meetings, to get involved in preserving mapunzugun. I had encouraged her to give testimony as a machi who felt alone, abandoned, because no one else spoke in Mapuche, because no one visited her, because people in the community looked at her strangely, some loving her and others simply scared of her. So it was hard for her, but also for me. How do you make the rest of the community understand that the machi needs their support? How do you make the surrounding communities understand that as well? And how do you make the Mapuche youth understand that the machi is a cultural treasure, part of our heritage?[6]

Luckily, with her living in the community, it's easier to involve people in a new understanding of what it means to be a community. Even the youth group led by my sister, the *Newen Lelfn*, managed to participate in some way in the machi's ritual. One of the young people danced, and that served to motivate and energize the other youth. At first nobody wanted the young boy to participate, because it was a serious ritual, and that meant playing for keeps. And what the group was already doing was not for keeps, then? I told them and their parents that everything we were doing was serious, that none of it was a joke. They still insisted that the machi's ñeikurewen was different, that you had to do it with faith and respect. "Well," I told them, "any ceremony we perform in the community needs to be done with faith and respect."

All these discussions, these ceremonies, these experiences—they form part of the work we've been trying to do over the long run. Because in the community, the people between fifteen and forty-five years old don't have any idea of the terms or concepts in our culture, or of the words in mapunzugun. They can't initiate a conversation in mapunzugun. Those who are forty-five years and older can initiate a conversation, but they're not fluent. They don't use the language in a creative or assertive way. It's here, in the use of the language, for conversation, for public speaking, that we need the creative leadership of the logko. In 1979, when we reinstated the traditional role of the logko, we chose for the position a man with strong values, determination, and physical strength, but who doesn't have the charisma or leadership capacity to move an entire community. I refer to my father. He does have the grace to let his sons and daughters lead the community in his place. He allows me a certain freedom to do what I think is best. My oldest brother collaborates with him. In the gillatun my brother leads the procession of the horses, carrying our community's flag. He therefore occupies a privileged position within the community, although he doesn't speak Mapuche, he can only understand it. And that's how a series of events in our community have contributed to the recuperation of the highest Mapuche ceremony, the gillatun, which we perform every four years. But in my community, we've been performing the gillatun every two, every three, and every four years to make up for lost time. You can perform the gillatun, and through it pray to God, when faced with floods, drought, epidemics, plagues. So with this justification, we've been performing the gillatun more frequently than every four years.

JUAN: *You perform the gillatun to ask for something specific. In the sixties, when there was a disastrous earthquake, there were lots of gillatun. They took just a day to perform, ah? But the central ceremony, the* kamarikun, *is different. It has a fixed calendar and must be performed every four years. The other ceremonies that are held in between are simply gillatun, or* gillai-mawün. *What you call these will depend on what elements the ceremonies contain.*

F: *Speaking of catastrophic events that can spark a gillatun, Lionel told me that after the earthquake in the sixties, your community staged its last gillatun until the one in 1980.*

I don't remember much, I was very young when we did our last gillatun in the sixties. When we were talking with Aunt Elsa yesterday, and were trying to figure out when the last gillatun had been, we guessed it had been about twenty years, but I think you're right, the last one happened in the sixties, after the earthquake. They did lots of gillatun in that period.

Another custom we had to recuperate was how to prepare muday. A few of the older women still remembered how to make muday and had to teach the younger members of the community. The women who played a leadership role in preparing the muday were my mother and Avelina Catrilaf. Doña Avelina made enough muday for three or four households. In the other families Aunt Elsa, Aunt Carmen, and a few more women who still remembered how to make it were able to prepare enough. In the younger households, on the other hand, like Lucho's, they needed help. In Lucho's case, for example, his wife isn't Mapuche, and his daughter is too young, so the other women had to make it for them.

F: *This is the last question I want to ask you about your community. In a document in the* Archivo de Asuntos Indígenas, *I read that the three communities closest to Chanco were divided early on, during the first Law of Subdivision in 1930. Do you think the subdivision created the problems of cultural loss, or do you think an early process of acculturation contributed to the desire to subdivide the communities?*

That's a good question. I think cause and effect worked in both directions at the same time. On the one hand, petitioning for an early subdivision was seen as a mark of "civilization" by some. At the same time, this early division contributed greatly to the loss of community solidarity, it made it hard to live in community. People became more individualistic, more egotistic and small-minded, and looked down on Mapuche cultural practices and forms of knowledge. Although they still maintained some Mapuche customs, like a hearth in the middle of the house (*fogón*) that served as a gathering place, or certain types of food and clothing, they began leaving these things behind little by little—more quickly, it seems, than in other communities. Traditional clothing disappeared, as did the Mapuche language, which no longer was spoken. The ceremonies were gone, people didn't even know what palin was, the awarkuzen and kamikan became foreign to them. Only the women kept up some Mapuche practices in their daily lives, in how they prepared the wool for knitting and weaving, and in the food and drink they served. And of course, we've kept our Mapuche last names. Luckily we've also kept some of our land, because with the subdivision of the communities the land enters the market, and a good part of it was sold to outsiders. That's how Miguel Lacámara obtained the land next door to my family, not for peanuts, but at the going market price. Suddenly our community includes the Donams, the Lacámaras, the Mattes, on one side; and on the other, a host of nonindigenous smallholders. So we end up intermingled with non-Mapuches and isolated from other Mapuche communities, even if these are physically close by. We end up with many people in the communities whose families weren't originally from here.

THE REUQUE PAILLALEF FAMILY

LILIANA: *When you left your parents-in-law and came to live here, mama, did they celebrate the gillatun in Chanco?*

DOÑA MARTINA: *Yes, they did.*

LILIANA: *How many gillatun did you attend before the community stopped holding them?*

DOÑA MARTINA: *I don't know.*

LILIANA: *And did you all go and participate in the ceremony?*

DOÑA MARTINA: *Oh, yes. Your grandfather Marcelino was the cacique.*

F: *Marcelino Reuque.*

ELVIRA: *My father's father.*

F: *What was his other last name?*

LILIANA: *What was grandfather's other last name?*

LIONEL: *Liguillan.*

LILIANA: *Marcelino Reuque Liguillan.*

F: *He was the cacique of this community, then?*

DOÑA MARTINA: *Yes, he was. It seems that he organized the gillatun twice. When he died, our cousin, Juan Reuque, was left in charge. My husband didn't want the position, he said he was too young and that no one would respect him.*

LILIANA: *How old was papa back then?*

DOÑA MARTINA: *I don't know, he just didn't want the position, so Juan Reuque got it.*

LILIANA: *And then was it papa's turn? Is that how papa became cacique?*

DOÑA MARTINA: *Yes. When Juan Reuque died, Vicente Reuque, Gollin's father, took charge, because he was the oldest. When he died, then my husband took over.*

F: *But there were several years during which no one held the gillatun, right?*

DOÑA MARTINA: *Yes, that's correct, they didn't do the gillatun for a number of years.*

LILIANA: *For how many years? Aunt Elsa says fifteen or twenty years went by without holding the gillatun. Is that right?*

DOÑA MARTINA: *I don't know, I don't think it was that many.*

ELVIRA: *I think the last gillatun I can remember happened when I was in high school, when they began to recuperate the ceremony.*

LILIANA: *They say that they began to hold the gillatun again in 1979.*

ELVIRA: *Yes, in 1979.*

DOÑA MARTINA: *I don't know; because when I was in Loica people were always coming here or going there for the ceremony.*

F: *Did you come here, too?*

DOÑA MARTINA: *No, because my uncle wouldn't participate. So I didn't attend, but the neighbors came, the Ekup family and Domingo's mother, Juan Ekup also, they all came and participated.*

F: *So there were lots of people, then.*

DOÑA MARTINA: *At first there were lots of people, but as more and more became Evangelicals, fewer and fewer participated.*

F: *Because the Evangelicals don't participate in the gillatun, do they?*

DOÑA MARTINA: *No, they don't. Even here, right here, it's gotten smaller. Only a few of us participate now.*

F: *Do you remember how things were in 1979 when they began to recuperate the gillatun?*

LILIANA: *Did a lot of people go? Was it beautiful?*

DOÑA MARTINA: *Yes, lots of people went.*

ELVIRA: *Don't you remember, mama?*

DOÑA MARTINA: *Lots of people went; Julia, Vitoco, and Paine were still alive. Not all the people from back then participate now.*

LIONEL: *In what year did you say that gillatun was?*

LILIANA: *In 1979.*

LIONEL: *Wouldn't it have been in 1969?*

ELVIRA: *It was in 1979, because I was in high school.*

LIONEL: *Because it was after the 1960 earthquake.*

ELVIRA: *It was after 1973.*

LIONEL: *Nooo, noo.*

LILIANA: *They say it happened in 1979.*

ELVIRA: *It was in 1979, Lionel.*

LIONEL: *There was a gillatun before 1979.*

ELVIRA: *I don't remember the last gillatun.*

LILIANA: *Who knows when the last one was before 1979. Maybe it was in 1969.*

ELVIRA: *I would have been seven years old then; but I don't remember any gillatun. I never went to any gillatun.*

F: *The earthquake was in 1960.*

LIONEL: *That's right.*

ELVIRA: *I hadn't been born yet.*

LIONEL: *After the earthquake people felt a renewed respect for God, they went back to Church and there was a revitalization of faith among the Mapuche. They made peace among themselves and with God, and they began the gillatun again.*

F: *I've seen several documents that say that after the earthquake there were gillatun held in many different places.*

LIONEL: *Yes. That's when they began to reorganize.*

F: *But it seems that in response to the earthquake in some areas people turned to evangelical religion as well. So there was a gillatun here after the earth-quake?*

LIONEL: *After the earthquake there was a gillatun here organized by Juan Reuque and Vicente Reuque.*

F: *So that would have been the last gillatun before 1979. The last gillatun must have occurred after the earthquake, around 1962.*

LIONEL: *Yes, around there, 1962 or 1963. Then they didn't do gillatun for a while. But the caciques did call another gillatun while Salazar—what was his first name?—was still in charge.*

ELVIRA: *His name was Hilario.*

LIONEL: *Because the old guy was sick, that's why the cycle was broken.*

LIONEL: *At that point the leaders became Juan Reuque and Vicente Reuque. Juanito Reuque was the flagbearer.*

ELVIRA: *They're all dead now.*

LIONEL: *I'm the flagbearer now; maybe I'll die next.*

F: *I don't think so. But there was a period in which the gillatun was not performed, until 1979. But at that point you all participated, right?*

LIONEL: *In 1979 my father headed the gillatun and I was the flagbearer. And before that there were two gillatun in which Juanito Reuque was the flag-bearer and we attended those ceremonies, too. I became the flagbearer after Juan and Vicente Reuque both died and Juanito decided not to participate. Then I carried the flag. I have it right here. I'll carry it until I die.*

F: *Good for you.*

LIONEL: *That's how it was. But if we compare the gillatun of the 1960s and now, I have to say that fewer and fewer people come now.*

F: *So between the 1960s and now, participation has decreased.*

DOÑA MARTINA: *Oh yes! It's really gone down!*

LIONEL: *Recently we've been trying to encourage more young couples to par-ticipate, even if they don't have children, but they don't make up for the people we've lost. Now attendance is about fifteen families per side, so a total of about thirty families participate. Before, about one hundred families entered the gillatun, about fifty families per side.*

F: *Per side?*

LIONEL: *That's right.*

DOÑA MARTINA: *On one side there's Chanco, and from over there, on the other side, there's Loica and Tiltil.*

LIONEL: *There are six communities that participate: Tiltil, Loica, Inoco, Dalpin, Manzanal and Chanco. On one side you have Tiltil and Chanco, and on the other side you have the other four communities.*

F: *And these same communities participated in the gillatun earlier as well?*

LIONEL: *Yes, but many more people participated.*

F: *More people participated earlier. So now you're saying that in total, from all the communities, about thirty families participate?*

LIONEL: *Yes.*

F: *And before one hundred participated?*

LIONEL: *One hundred families.*

LILIANA: *The last time we counted, only seven families were participating from this side. Only seven entered the circle in the last gillatun.*

F: *Why aren't people participating? One reason is obviously the growing numbers of Evangelicals. But are there other reasons for the numbers to go down so much?*

LIONEL: *Acculturation is a big factor. Mapuche culture has lost a lot of its authenticity with the predominance of Spanish culture. In school children are taught to reject and look down on Mapuche culture, and the Mapuche themselves have believed this. It discourages people from participating. I'll give you another example. Here we have an uncle who, even though he's the son of a* cacique, *doesn't participate in the gillatun. He thinks Mapuche ceremonies are for the lower classes, for the uneducated. He has sons who are teachers, so he thinks he can't be involved in things he considers below him. It's so absurd; he doesn't realize that he's speaking badly about himself. But it's a widespread belief, and his attitude is reflected in others who also think that, by participating in a gillatun, they'll lower themselves or become inferior people.*

F: *I read about Mapuche intellectuals living in Temuco around 1910 and 1915. They said the same thing, that the Mapuche people had to do away with their culture and religion in order to become civilized.*

LIONEL: *Yes, some have spoken out against their own people and culture. Yet there have been other Mapuche intellectuals who have advocated on behalf of our culture while working within the dominant system. One family that has been particularly successful at this is the Paillalef family. The cacique Paillalef founded the district of Pitrufquén, and among his descendants we are honored today to count numerous individuals with professional degrees and advanced levels of education; some even teach at the University of Valparaiso. Others hold public positions of great importance from which they promote Mapuche culture while staying within the system. You have to integrate yourself; I think this is the best way to live one's identity while progressing nationally and internationally, and not despising one's own background. When Mapuche people want to have their own flag, their own national identity, and their own territory, I don't agree with them. I think they're wrong.*

F: *You mean the* Consejo de Todas las Tierras.[7]

LIONEL: *Yes. Their approach is not productive; we have to integrate ourselves and belong to the wider society. Because if we break off and push for an autonomous movement, we end up discriminating against ourselves. This kind of self-deprecation is the worst thing for Mapuche culture; it will kill us. There are Mapuches who are part of the Paillalef lineage, the founding family of this district, both young and established professional people, who agree with my position.*

Anecdotally, I should tell you that the cacique Paillalef, as a leader, was a kind of military commando. I like to tell the story of this leader, although when I tell it, no one believes me; they think I'm making it up. But I'll tell you. The cacique Paillalef was the illegitimate son of a young Mapuche woman and an important Spanish official, one of the conquerors who arrived back then. The girl was sixteen years old when she got pregnant. She suffered the worst humiliation imaginable when her community found out that she was pregnant, and that the father was a Spanish officer. People saw the affair as a mockery of the Mapuche by a wigka, and were most offended because the officer had been able to make fun of the girl at the expense of the whole community.

So the cacique of that region, of Arauco, proclaimed that as soon as the child was born, they had to kill it. "We are not going to raise the son of a Spanish conqueror," he said. The girl didn't want them to kill her child. As her pregnancy advanced, she decided to leave the community and she began walking south, until she got to the Temuco area, where she gave birth to her son. She didn't tell anyone who the father was, but the caciques were in touch among themselves; there was a communications network on horseback in those days. So they communicated back and forth, and she was the only stranger in the whole territory to have given birth. They didn't kill the child, but when he was ten, they sent him on a military expedition against the Spanish.

But the expedition was an ambush to get rid of the youth. They told him, "There are some Spaniards over there who are trying to cross the Toltén River and you need to take care of them." They sent the boy out with ten men; imagine that kid in charge of ten men! They thought the Spaniards would kill him instantly, but they didn't kill him or any of his men. Rather, the boy and his men killed the Spaniards and took some of their heads back to show the cacique. The logkos were stumped. "What should we do?" they said. "We have to send him on another expedition. We can't have the son of a Spaniard living among us."

After having survived several other similar ambushes and military expeditions, he ended up here, in charge of guarding the banks of the Toltén River near Pitrufquén. There were two places to cross the river; one here, in front of the Pitrufquén fort, and another place in Villarrica. Crossing at Villarrica was harder. At Fort Pitrufquén the river narrowed to twenty meters or so of deep water, and people could swim across. In Villarrica the river was wider but the currents were slower. They sent the youth to Fort Pitrufquén and the other soldiers stayed at Villarrica. Paillalef got busy constructing barriers, made of tree trunks, along the riverbank. They knew that if the Spaniards won at Villarrica, they'd continue by land and reach Pitrufquén. They set the barriers on fire and no one was allowed to cross the river.

The Spanish arrived from Villarrica; there had been a massacre there, the Spanish had killed huge numbers of Mapuches. So they arrived here and Paillalef had his people ready, and since everything was on fire the Spanish had to attack at a particular place. And so the attack began. They killed lots of Spaniards, and many surrendered. He left them without clothing and took the heads of the dead to the council of caciques in Temuco. He told them, "Here are the heads of the officers," and right there they named him head cacique of the south, turning over to him all the territory between the Toltén and the Calle-Calle rivers.

After the so-called Pacification of Araucanía, the cacique Paillalef incorporated himself into the peace process by forging an agreement with the national government. After that he had very good relations with the government. He was the first Mapuche who learned to read and write. He traveled throughout his territory, between the Toltén and the Calle-Calle rivers, teaching the Mapuche how to read and write. You have to learn, so that the wigka doesn't come and make a fool of you, he would say. He dedicated his life to teaching and imparting culture to the Mapuche. I don't know, maybe it's just a bad habit, and I know it's certainly misunderstood by many, but some of us Mapuche continue to have the same goals. My people have inherited two important legacies: education and the land.[8]

F: *The idea, then, is that there's no contradiction between maintaining Mapuche culture and identity and participating in the broader society . . .*

LIONEL: *Right.*

F: *. . . you can have an education, a profession, and identify as Mapuche. Even though many Mapuche disagree, you're saying that the Mapuche should integrate themselves into the broader society, even though the "education" you refer to means adopting the norms and values of dominant society, no?*

LIONEL: *Yes, but the idea is that to integrate is still better than isolation from society which, I repeat, will lead to self-destruction. I made this very clear on the radio when a Mapuche leader tried to come here and revolutionize our people. Some of our communities are very densely populated and are therefore extremely poor and with a low cultural level. Because of this, these people are more vulnerable to revolutionary messages. I made this appeal over the radio, urging people to disregard the message of this visiting Mapuche, and received congratulations from political leaders and private individuals from around the area.*[9] *That's the idea. I think that when the Mapuche isolate themselves and concentrate too much on their own identity, it's a bad thing.*

F: *Let's talk a little more, in this context, about the recuperation of the gillatun in your region. Because the gillatun is one of the most important ways of unifying the Mapuche and practicing indigenous culture, no? It's a way of constructing Mapuche identity.*

LIONEL: *Of course it is, since it's based on religious faith and on respect for the dignity and uniqueness of the individual. That's why the Pope and the Catholic Church support the gillatun. The Catholic Church is the only church that supports the gillatun. Here there are many young couples who are beginning to show interest in Mapuche culture, have a certain kind of religious belief, and are planning to participate in the upcoming gillatun, even though we've lost the field where we used to perform them.*

F: *What happened to the space you had?*

LIONEL: *There was a field, but the communities never owned it. They just rented it.*

F: *Did you rent it from another community?*

LIONEL: *No, from an individual. I think the last time the lady rented us the field we'd traditionally used was in 1979 for the gillatun. Then we moved to a new space, where we performed the ceremony up until about two or three years ago.*

LILIANA: *Until one year ago. We performed the ceremony in March of 1996.*

ELVIRA: *Yes, in March of last year.*

LIONEL: *Wasn't it two years ago? But now we can't do it there, because the field has been legally divided between two owners. We'll have to look for a new place for the gillatun. We have a few options, but it's not just a question of picking up and moving. There's a whole ritual involved when changing ceremonial sites. If you don't do it correctly, it's not legitimate, it's just not right.*

F: *If I understand correctly, the place itself has a symbolic and spiritual importance . . .*

ELVIRA: *Yes.*

F: *. . . and in many communities, there is a specific place where the gillatun has always been performed, and thus that place has a sacred history.*

LIONEL: *Yes, it's a sacred, holy place, like a Mapuche shrine.*

F: *And that place is reserved just for ritual, no? You can't plant there or do anything else.*

LIONEL: *Right. You can plant there, but not during the year of the gillatun. That year you have to leave the land especially for the ceremony.*

F: *I see. Doña Martina, when Isolde told me about the huge quantity of sopaipillas you made for the gillatun, I was struck by the enormous amount of cooperation and work that was needed to make the ceremony a success. Can you tell me a little bit about what you did, how much work is involved?*

DOÑA MARTINA: *You just make the muday and make the sopaipillas, and kill an animal for the meat, but it's not just for anyone at the gillatun; you serve the people from the community that hosted you the last time, it's like returning the hospitality.*

F: *So every family prepares . . .*

DOÑA MARTINA: *Yes, they prepare a dish for the person who will serve them when it's the other community's turn.*

F: *So it's like . . .*

DOÑA MARTINA: *Of course, it's like having a house guest, you're the host now but you're returning the favor from when your guests hosted you.*

F: *So it strengthens intercommunity bonds.*

LIONEL: *Yes, it encourages social bonds between communities.*

F: *Yes, it creates bonds, but who does all that work to prepare the food and the ceremony?*

LILIANA: *The family does, the whole family.*

F: *So you prepare the muday . . .*

LIONEL: *With wheat.*

F: *. . . in the home.*

LILIANA: *Yes, two or three days before the ceremony.*

F: *And the women do all this work?*

EVERYONE: *The women.*

F: *And the women prepare the sopaipillas too, I imagine?*

LILIANA: *Yes, the men only take care of killing the animal.*

F: *They only kill the animal?*

ELVIRA: *They knock it down and they kill it.*

DOÑA MARTINA: *They also help to cut the meat.*

F: *So everyone participates in the preparation, but perhaps according to the women . . .*

ELVIRA: *Apparently everyone participates, but the men . . .*

LILIANA: *No, I think men and women work equally. For example, the men cut the tree trunks and branches to make the* ramada, *or shelter, where people will be during the ceremony. They take care of those things, hauling and putting everything in its place. I think it's shared work; there are some things the men do and some things the women do at home, like the muday and the sopaipillas, and they prepare the things they're going to take to the field. But the men do the most physically demanding work, they do the ramada, they drag the logs to sit on.*

F: *So all the families that participate in the ceremony have members who enter the circle and dance.*

ELVIRA: *Motivated by faith more than anything else, and even if we don't go to ceremonies in other places.*

LILIANA: *I think that faith and dedication to the culture are what motivate people, more than a dedication to each other, even if you participate back and forth, between communities, as a form of reciprocity.*

ELVIRA: *We admire the faith and cultural dedication of the lady who lives next door, because when we were young, but not so young, she would enter the gillatun with a handcart where she carried two geese and sopaipillas. Even though she was poor, you could see the effort she put into preparing for the ceremony. This last time she arrived with a pig, a couple of sheep, and some beef. She's been changing the kinds of food she takes to the people she owes in reciprocity. Her tremendous faith and dedication motivate us to continue our efforts and to follow her example, especially Lionel. She calls Lionel "cousin," and encourages him, since he's still young. Also, Lionel is the one who takes charge of the whole ceremony, moving around on horseback and organizing things, since my father spends all his time eating . . .*

LIONEL: *I'm the cacique.*

ELVIRA: *Since my father tends to spend all his time eating, it's Lionel who takes charge of the ceremony. It's Lionel who has the job of sacrificing the lamb, the chicken; he's also the one who works with the machi. My father often just sits there, and we have to go get him and tell him, "Dad, you've got to come over here."*

LIONEL: *I'm the one in charge of the sergeants.*

ELVIRA: *At the gillatun you can tell that people in this community like and respect Lionel, but that doesn't carry over to other places.*

F: *So Lionel is a respected and obeyed authority only during the two days of the ceremony?*

ELVIRA: *For those two days, but outside of the ritual sphere Lionel is a political figure.*

LILIANA: *He's a mere mortal.*

ELVIRA: *Yes, a mere mortal, but a respected and popular one. Our gillatun is different from the ceremonies in other parts, because we don't let non-Mapuche participate, and we don't use wine for the ceremony, only muday.*

F: *So outsiders aren't allowed.*

LILIANA: *Outsiders who are not Mapuche.*

ELVIRA: *Yes, only Mapuche people can participate.*

LIONEL: *When they support the culture.*

ELVIRA: *In Huilío, the community of Juan, Isolde's husband, everyone participates in the gillatun, whether they're Mapuche or not. Here only Mapuche participate, but sometimes it's irritating when non-Mapuches stop along the road in their trucks to see what "the little Indians" are up to. We also prohibit wine, but someone never fails to bring some to the ceremony. Even if you're vigilant, things get by you. Some people even bring wine to the ceremony as a gift. Others just go to look, not to participate, even though they're from our community.*

LIONEL: *But the authentic gillatun is performed in honor of God and is similar to the Catholic mass. Both promote fraternity and devotion to God. Partaking of the sacrificial mutton is similar to receiving the host in mass; only those dedicated to what the gillatun stands for participate in consuming the meat at the rewe, which is like an altar. Not just anyone is given meat.*

LILIANA: *The leaders and the caciques . . .*

LIONEL: *Right. Each family that is committed to the gillatun and what it stands for sends a representative to partake of the meat, it's like when you receive the sacred host during mass. The other thing is that the gillatun brings a time of peace, when the outside world and its problems are forgotten and you can share a quiet time with others. You forget about the world for two days to go and talk directly with God, and He is there, listening to His children. People ask for forgiveness for their sins, they lift up their prayers to God, asking for protection in life, for the health of their families, and for a better future. This is the meaning of the gillatun.*

However, there can also be political manipulation during the ritual, even Mapuches taking advantage of other Mapuches. I must consciously admit that some would sell their own brother to the authorities, just to get ahead themselves. This is a very delicate problem, because it is through these manipulations that Mapuche culture loses its authenticity.

F: *Besides the gillatun, do people from this area play palin?*

LIONEL: *Unfortunately no, because of this recurring problem of acculturation. We only have one machi here. And our machi has turned a little bit wigka, because she neglected her sacred duties for a time. According to our cultural norms, every certain amount of time the machi has to do a special ceremony, but two or three times our machi neglected to do it. She just did the ceremony two months ago . . .*

EVERYONE: *In February.*

LIONEL: *In February she renewed her spiritual commitment, renewed her vows as a machi, and made peace with her helper spirit so that she could continue to practice as a ritual specialist. In truth, it was the first time I got to participate in a machi dance of that kind.*

F: *Is this machi dance and ritual you speak of also what is called the* machitun?

EVERYONE: *No, that's a different ritual.*

LIONEL: *The machitun is a ritual in which a sick person is cured; the* machi *dance, known also as the ñeikurewen, is for the machi herself, almost like her spiritual birthday.*

F: *How often do . . . ?*

LIONEL: *She does her ceremony every two or three years. Machis have an altar, a rewe, at their house where they perform the ritual. They invite their most trusted friends and relatives, and those who are committed to Mapuche religion.*

ELVIRA: *She does this ceremony so that her faith, her spirituality, spreads throughout the community. As the machi maintains an important relationship with the community, if people come and support her as she renews her vows she's energized to renew her commitment, and it's like becoming a machi all over again, like when she was first consecrated or initiated. I've read about machi initiation rites in many different publications.*

F: *When she performed her ceremony this past February, how long had it been since the last time?*

LILIANA: *They say that it had been more than twenty years.*

ELVIRA: *More than twenty years.*

LIONEL: *That long!*

ELVIRA: *Even to change the palm leaves that serve as decoration you need help from other people. Even more so to change the rewe, or altar. There are many communities in our area that participate in our gillatun and she should be able to request help from all of them. The last time she did the ceremony twenty years ago, however, nobody helped her; she had to do it all herself with her children. But we saw that her children weren't familiar with the ritual anymore, they went all over asking everyone what should happen next and how it was done. They asked Isolde, they asked all of us. Since we had read a little, we told them what we knew. They didn't know, for example, which horses to use, or the different steps of the ceremony. This was all information she should have transmitted to them.*

I don't know if it's the children's fault. But we know that other machis teach their children about the rituals and communicate Mapuche traditions to them. There are some Mapuche who are the sons of machis who work at the Bank of Chile or teach at the university, but they haven't forgotten how to help their mothers. Even though they live in the city and are married to non-

Mapuche women, they still know what to do and how to help their mothers. But these kids, no. The oldest daughter could remember some things, but other things she'd forgotten. She had to ask people how the ritual was supposed to go. We realized that the machi, who is supposed to be a cultural authority for us, had lost much of her knowledge, and her children had married non-Mapuches. She had been too embarrassed to do the ceremony, because she thought that her sons and daughters-in-law would laugh at her. Only when her embarrassment lifted could she do her ritual again.

Her neighbors weren't like Isolde and Lionel, people interested in and supportive of Mapuche culture. They would hide, they didn't agree with those of us who keep our faith, no one was willing to talk with her or help her. The machi was losing touch with her own spirit. Each machi has a particular spirit, a helper spirit. It was her spirit that told her she had to do the ritual with the community, and also she needed to do it because she was sick. Along with the machi dance, they also did the machitun ritual to try and cure her.

Maybe when she dies she'll take her spirit with her. It's difficult, because it's usually during puberty or adolescence that a daughter or close relative shows signs of being able to inherit the spirit. But that didn't happen in this case. So perhaps in twenty or thirty years we won't have a machi anymore. I think this is a serious danger in several communities, not just ours. What we've managed to recuperate from our culture is the presence of our machi and the renewal of the gillatun and of our faith. But the urban influence is invading our sacred sites, the field where we've held our gillatun—what do you call it? Urban culture is invading our kamarikun. Our site is being . . .

DOÑA MARTINA: *There are a lot of houses there.*

ELVIRA: *. . . used as a construction site. Our site is losing its essential sacred quality and its contact with nature. We need to find a new site, a new kamarikun, but that's not so easy to do. The Indigenous Law says that all sacred ground must be respected and belongs to the community. But here in the district of Pitrufquén the Indigenous Law isn't very effective, because Mapuche territory is surrounded by and encroached upon by individual farms.*

F: *I have to ask something that keeps going around and around in my head as we talk. When we talked about the machi I was struck by the fact that the machi can't practice without the support of the community, and the community can't reproduce itself ritually or spiritually without a machi. The rela-*

tionship goes both ways, the machi and the community depend on each other.

LILIANA: *It's reciprocal.*

F: *Exactly. It seems to me that one of the machi's central problems was that her family and friends abandoned her; she couldn't be a machi like before without a community. That is, until your community adopted her and supported her, no? If Mapuche culture is going to continue to exist, the entire community has to be conscious of and support Mapuche culture, because the community leaders depend on the support of the people to continue the rituals and other cultural forms and pass this knowledge on to the next generation. Elvira, you just told me how worried everyone is that doña Clorinda, the machi, doesn't have anyone to whom she can leave her spirit. You told me you think that her spirit may be extinguished with her when she dies. What will happen if she does take her spirit with her?*

LIONEL: *But the machi doesn't want to give her spirit to any of her children. They have asked for it, and she says no. She says it's too big of a commitment and a sacrifice, and she doesn't want to see her daughters suffer as she did.*

ELVIRA: *Her whole family discriminated against her.*

DOÑA MARTINA: *Because in the middle of the ceremony the spirit took her over and she . . .*

ELVIRA: *. . . went into a trance.*

DOÑA MARTINA: *She lost her head, and when no one else understood her, then they needed the help of a* zugumachife.

ELVIRA: *The zugumachifes are special translators for rituals. They translate the messages for her, because in a trance she doesn't speak the usual kind of mapunzugun.*

DOÑA MARTINA: *She's a machi because a spirit decided that she should be a machi, not because she decided.*

ELVIRA: *She didn't say, for example, when she was fifteen years old, "I want to be a machi . . ."*

LIONEL: *It's inherited.*

ELVIRA: *Priests, nuns, and politicians all decide to be what they want to be. But it works differently with machis; the spirit of a relative enters her and that decides what she is going to be. It can enter her in many different ways; all machis say that at first the spirit begins as a sickness. They get sick, and until they realize what's going on, they stay sick. They can even die. Some girls try to avoid their calling; we've heard stories of young girls who go to Santiago to try to escape their spirit. You can go wherever you want, but the spirit will find you. There was a story on television last year about a girl who was possessed by a spirit and no one understood her, in Santiago they thought she was crazy.*

DOÑA MARTINA: *We saw her story on the program* Laberinto, *on national television. Her grandmother had been a machi, and the girl had grown up with her grandmother.*

ELVIRA: *The girl had her grandmother's spirit inside of her. Actually a lot of illness, both for men and women, is caused by spirits.*

F: *That example reinforces my point that the community and the cultural leaders need to work together so that these spirits are passed down and used to benefit the community.*

ELVIRA: *Yes, there are good spirits and bad spirits. The good spirits can do harm too; it depends on how the individual manages their power. Machis who use spirits to do good are less interested in wealth or worldly possessions, they're more in tune with nature and are simpler and nicer people.*

F: *It seems like community support and the knowledge of the elders are crucial to cultural reproduction and to the future of the machis.*

ELVIRA: *As well as for the logkos. What do we do if the logkos die and their children don't want to take on the leadership position? Before the so-called Pacification, logkos were chosen based on their skill as horsemen and for their ability to negotiate between Spaniards and Mapuches, or between Mapuche communities. After the military defeat, the logko position was handed down based on inheritance. After the logko dies, one of his sons becomes the leader—it's always a son who receives the title. So the sons are in training while they're young, they watch their father and they learn from him. Learn by doing, that's the Mapuche practice.*

That's how Lionel has learned everything he knows, from conversation, but also through watching and participating, like during our machi's ñeiku-rewen. I realized that on the first day, the machi waited for Lionel, not my father. She was desperate that Lionel was late, and once he arrived she sat him in a privileged place and would talk only to him. So the logko is crucial, but when the father dies a son has to be ready to take his place. What if Lionel wasn't interested in taking over the position? Of the three brothers, he's the most dedicated to our community and our culture. Sure he can be

difficult and bossy, but when push comes to shove, when it's time to go public,
he's Mapuchista from head to toe. At other times he can be difficult and it
drives him crazy that we are so Mapuchista, he mocks us privately some-
times, but in public he's as committed as the rest of us. But if Lionel didn't
want the job . . .

LILIANA: *His son would have to do it.*

(Laughter.)

ELVIRA: *. . . if Lionel didn't want to be logko, it would be hard, for example, for*
Dago to do it, because Dago is more Catholic than Mapuche. Lionel, in
many ways, is more Mapuche than Catholic. Dago doesn't have the dedica-
tion to the culture and community that Lionel does, he isn't as serious as the
rest of us. On the day of the gillatun, when Lionel gets up, he does everything
with great seriousness—the ritual preparations, the entrance on horseback,
the gillatun itself—he does it all with sincere faith. During those days, more
or less a week, he's Mapuche from head to toe. But after that . . .

LILIANA: *. . . comes the aftermath. Lionel disappears.*

(Laughter.)

ELVIRA: *It's like the Catholic who only goes to church during Holy Week.*

(Laughter.)

LIONEL: *Or who only goes on Palm Sunday.*

(Laughter.)

ELVIRA: *Yes, it's like the Palm Sunday Catholic, because you don't see Lionel*
again after that. With my brother Pedro, he puts his work first, traveling for
his job. But he also respects our culture. That's why he moved back here from
Calama, so that his children could see what a gillatun was and learn about
their culture.

DOÑA MARTINA: *Yes, so they could see what a gillatun was.*

ELVIRA: *Also, Pedro has the ponchos that belong to the cacique. Lionel and my*
father are using them, but they belong to Pedro. But if Lionel didn't want to
continue the tradition, it would be lost, and so would a good part of our life
as a community. The same goes for those who are the norporrufe, *the*
sergeants of the ceremony. Next door, for example, Millao's son tells me,
"We'll participate until my father dies, but then no more. We'll become
civilized after that." That's the kind of mentality he has. Our cousin Lucho,
on the other hand, has a lot of faith, and we work at it together. He has faith
because we have faith. His father is old, but Lucho will continue to partici-

pate in Mapuche culture after his father dies, because the rest of us will continue to participate. His daughters are also very serious about Mapuche culture, they're in Newen Lelfn, the youth group. His younger daughter Sofia is the most committed to Mapuche culture, but the older one also stands up for Mapuche culture in school. They both want to learn more about the customs; they have faith and they want to learn. This kind of interest has to come from the next generation, it's so important for us to work with the kids. Because there won't always be Lionel and Isolde there to move things along, and what will happen then? We don't want to lose everything we've worked so hard for; we've seen that happen in other places. We also don't want our children to be ignorant of Mapuche culture, as the machi's children were.

F: *So really, it's crucial that the efforts at cultural renewal get transmitted from one generation to the next.*

ELVIRA: *Yes. Everything must get passed on, not just the machi's knowledge, but also the logko's. In that sense my father doesn't say enough. He's very quiet, he doesn't even tell Lionel things. Lionel's the one who participates in everything. He's been to gillatun in Gorbea, and in Meli Rewe, where we have relatives.*

LILIANA: *Meli Rewe.*

LIONEL: *Alto Mirador.*

ELVIRA: *He's been to Huilío, now and then he goes to Carilafquén . . .*

LIONEL: *I've participated in eight different gillatun ceremonies.*

ELVIRA: *So he knows a lot, he's seen a lot. But when he goes it's not only to visit, he also has to learn so that he can share that new knowledge when it's our turn to have the gillatun. It's the work of an entire generation, and if it's not done, the culture begins to die. When I was in Imperial working on my thesis, I realized the gravity of the situation. It's Mapuche territory, and all the girls wear the traditional black dress, or chamal, but if you ask them if they perform the gillatun there, they'll say no. If you ask them if there's a machi there, they'll say no. And if you ask them: "Where do you go when you get sick? To the hospital or to the machi?" they'll say, "How could we go to the machi? Of course we go to the hospital." Many, many things are being lost. And the same type of crisis our machi experienced, was suffered by the machi in Cullinco, Rosa Trahua, and by doña Rosa Barra of Hurilaf. It's happening to most machis, to an entire generation. If the children don't stay close to their parents, there's no one to teach them. In Mapuche culture things are learned informally, by doing; the Mapuche appear in the formal curriculum only as folkloric tidbits. Now with the development of intercultural education, things are changing a little. But many kids are still embarrassed to be Mapuche, a number of the schoolchildren around here don't want to participate in the gillatun. They look at us like oddities, like we're strange birds. Maybe they think we're moving backward in time instead of progressing. They look at us . . .*

LILIANA: *They look down on us.*

LIONEL: *They don't realize that the policemen salute me as I ride into the gillatun on horseback.*

ELVIRA: *This is the generational problem we have; if there's no one to teach the younger people, Mapuche culture begins to fade away. If they don't take the leadership and become the machis and the logkos, the gillatun sergeants of the next generation, the rest of the people can't carry out Mapuche rituals if no one knows what they are.*

Here Lionel and Isolde, the older siblings, are carrying forward the spiritual tradition of previous logkos, such as my father's father, grandfather Marcelino. Although he's not as well known as the cacique Paillalef, his spirit seems attached to the two of them, who like to get involved in politics and in changing society. Some say that don Marcelino also worked with the Germans . . .

LILIANA: *He did speak four languages.*

ELVIRA: *. . . and with the Italians and Swiss that arrived. He'd be wherever they were, giving them advice and talking with them. Other people think don Marcelino was crazy, a good for nothing drifter, because as a muledriver he'd travel all the way to Osorno. My father grew up helping his father with the mule trains, and when we were little he'd tell us about all the trips he'd made. He even told us about California; Florida and California were huge farms owned by gringos . . .*

LILIANA: *And you thought your father had been to the United States. (Laughter.)*

ELVIRA: *People think a lot of different things about don Marcelino. But he did have a gift for getting involved in the world, and also for understanding Mapuche spirituality. It's that combination that we admire so much in him.*

LILIANA: *He had a magical way about him, a gift with people, so when he spoke, even if he said dumb things, people listened.*

ELVIRA: *We also inherited from our ancestors, especially the cacique Paillalef, our Catholic spirit. Pitrufquén was the last territory to be conquered during the so-called Pacification campaign. People don't know that. Pitrufquén was the frontier at a certain point, an important border town. Cacique Paillalef negotiated with the state and with the church for the Mapuche people. He was also baptized. His negotiations were good for the Catholic Church and for us too. That's why we're all Catholic. It's because of the past and the cacique Paillalef. My mother's great-grandfather educated the future generations. Land and education were very important for him. That's the story of why most Paillalefs are Catholics.*

The other logko, my grandfather Marcelino, is not as well known, but he also did important things for the community. It wasn't easy for him; he wasn't rich. No, those two logkos worked hard for what they earned. Grandfather Marcelino and my father worked and worked; we learned from them how important it was to work for what you want to accomplish. They also taught us to value and take care of the land and the animals, and to educate ourselves. Although she was abandoned at a young age, they also told my mother how important it was to educate herself and to take care of the land. My mother still remembers her parents, although they're actually adopted parents, because her birth mother is still alive. She remembers all the spiritual guidance my grandfather gave her when she was very young, and she's never forgotten it. Although my biological grandmother is alive, I don't think of her that way. Our real family is the Paillalefs.

F: *So then there's no contradiction between the Catholic faith and the Mapuche religion?*

LIONEL: *No, no, not at all; to the contrary they support and strengthen each other.*

ELVIRA: *They complement each other.*

LIONEL: *Problems between the Mapuche religion and other religions . . .*

ELVIRA: *. . . happen with Protestantism.*

LIONEL: *Yes, being Protestant and Mapuche doesn't work, because the Protestants don't let the Mapuche participate in any ceremonies. They think the gillatun is pagan.*

F: *Based on our conversation, though, I think I see a difference between the Catholic and the Mapuche religions. Maybe it's less than it used to be, now that the base community movement exists within the Catholic Church. But it seems to me that, at least in its more traditional form, the Catholic faith is more hierarchical; it comes from above and must be transmitted to the faithful through the priest. It seems that the relationship between Catholic leaders and the people isn't as reciprocal as the relationship between Mapuche leaders and the people. I don't know if I'm making myself clear; what do you think?*[10]

ELVIRA: *It's true that, for the Mapuche people, religion permeates daily life, from the moment you're born until the moment you die. Mapuche religion is everything; it's how you interact with others each day, it's how you live your life, it's how you relate to others within your culture. Mapuche religion is everything, really everything.*

F: *In addition, the machi can't exist without the support of the community. She's powerless without her people. The Catholic priest exists whether the people support him or not. He comes from the outside, not from within the community.*

LILIANA: *He's still a priest, regardless of his vocation.*

LIONEL: *But there is also a hierarchy within Mapuche religion. You have, in descending order, the head lineage chief, then the lυgkυs, the sargentos; and the machi is also there. Within the Mapuche religious ceremony you have four people, the gillatufe, who are in charge of the prayers. They direct the prayer sessions for the other people. There are hierarchical similarities with the Catholic religion.*

F: *I see your point.*

LIONEL: *I realized these things around 1982.*

ELVIRA: *He was a student at the university then, and was influenced by theology and all that, and that's why he saw the similarities.*

LIONEL: *I attended the Catholic University of Temuco . . .*

F: *That must have been an important experience for you.*

ELVIRA: *Sometimes he even gets the cross and the rewe mixed up. (Laughs.)*

LIONEL: *And I became director of the campus ministry. I almost became a deacon, but then I seem to have lost ground somewhere along the way. (Laughs.)*

LILIANA: *Maybe rather than talking about a direct relationship between Catholicism and the Mapuche religion, we should talk about the Church supporting Mapuche ceremonials. It's true that Catholic rituals and the gillatun are very different. The religions don't copy each other; long before the Catholic Church was here, the Mapuche religion existed. Rather, I think that the Church has accepted and accommodated to other cultures in the world.*

That's why other cultures appear to share something with the Catholic tradition. Not because I'm Mapuche, but I think the Church has adapted more to our culture than we've adapted our culture to the Church.

F: *I agree with you.*

ELVIRA: *Just as all indigenous people have things in common. Even the indigenous peoples' instruments and dances from South Africa resemble our dances and our kultrun. There is a certain solidarity and identification between indigenous peoples from all around the world. Unless the other person is just totally different, indigenous peoples seem to identify with each other. There's something in the music . . .*

LILIANA: *I think the Spaniards used Catholicism mixed with indigenous elements, to reach the people. The Church knew how to attract people and draw them in. Or at least that's what I think.*

ELVIRA: *This reminds me of what my nephew said to me the other day. He said: "You know, auntie, we Mapuche are the true children of God." "Why?" I asked him. "Because I'm Mapuche, I'm closer to God," he said. "Where did you learn that?" I asked him. "They taught it to us in school," he replied. (Laughter.)*

In some parts of the world, such as Mexico, they were awaiting the arrival of a white stranger. And the Spaniards arrived with Hernán Cortés, and the indigenous peoples thought they were the people their visions had told them would arrive. Both Mexico and Peru had great indigenous civilizations that were very established when the Spaniards came. They were very advanced in art and science, and people today still borrow ideas from these civilizations. Here, where it was so cold, we were not as developed culturally as the ancient Mexicans or the Peruvians, who lived in places where the sun shone all day. They recorded things in stone, while here, information is transmitted orally. Because of that, much of our knowledge was lost when the ancestors died, the information wasn't passed on to the younger generations. The stories we do know, like Lionel's about the cacique Paillalef, get filtered as they pass from mouth to mouth, like a never-ending game of telephone . . .

F: *A story that's changed and enriched each time it's told.*

ELVIRA: *Yes, the stories do change over time. Everyone who tells them adds their own embellishment.*

LILIANA: *And to think Columbus might have said it first. (Laughter.)*

ELVIRA: *Nothing is static, but the stories are still historically valid, even as they change. One day Lionel just came out with that story about the cacique Paillalef.*

LIONEL: *I read it somewhere in a book.*

LILIANA: *Who wrote the book?*

LIONEL: *It's still a manuscript.*

F: *It doesn't seem possible, but I think I'm out of questions.*
   (Laughter.)

LIONEL: *Ask more questions, if you want.*

LILIANA: *If you're done, let's go to bed.*

LIONEL: *I have one last question. Where are you going to put your pocket knife so that I can steal it from you?*
   (Laughter.)

LILIANA: *Shut up. Mapuches are supposed to be honest.*

✤ CHAPTER TWO

The Mapuche Movement under
Dictatorship, 1973–1989

I cut my social, organizational, and political teeth, you could say, with the military coup we had here in Chile. I was a high school student then, and when I arrived for class one morning, they told us the school was closed. When you come to town every day from the countryside, it's hard to find things out ahead of time. We did have a radio at home but we didn't listen to it, because we were always up early milking the cows or delivering the milk. So the news of the military coup surprised my sister and me the morning of September 11, 1973, when we were bringing the milk into town, and we didn't return until the 16th, I think. I delivered milk in town to some priests, and also to some political leaders who lived near my school. In the morning I'd leave the bottles full, and in the afternoon I'd take the empty bottles home again. So it turns out that two of our milk customers went deep into hiding because of the coup, the priest was arrested, and several teachers simply vanished, we never saw them again. That was when we students got together to form a group. It began almost as a joke. We said we'd defend the disappeared, because one of our classmates, Manríquez, had been arrested. We'd say to each other, "Ladrillo is in jail."

As we were young and didn't understand exactly what was happening, we got involved between jokes and laughter, in the middle of these very serious things. Besides, I've always been good at making jokes. In good times and in bad, my face is always full of laughter. And although many people disappeared in Pitrufquén, our town still seemed fairly peaceful. We thought we weren't really experiencing the full effect of the coup, although we did organize to defend those who were in jail, including our classmate and our teacher the priest, who they said was in jail but we really didn't know where he was. He was our religion and philosophy teacher, the one we cared most about and with whom we'd had many interesting conversations. He'd talked to us about life, about the future, about God. He'd put the Evangelicals in their own group and discussed things relevant to them, the Catholics in another group that had meaning for them, and there'd also been a third group for those who weren't baptized and were neither Evangelical nor Catholic. He'd talked to all of us about our rights and responsibilities as people. But at that time, it really was crazy to organize a defense committee and try to free our classmate, Ladrillo.

F: *You called Manríquez "Ladrillo"?*

Yes, we called him Ladrillo because of a Mexican song we knew, which said "Ladrillo is in jail." And so we organized this committee to free Ladrillo, but the truth is that it turned out to be much more than we'd ever imagined. From it came a committee called Civil Defense (*Defensa Civil*), ultimately headed by a man who'd previously served in the Air Force. We managed to get the priest out of jail, and he joined our group and lent us his pickup truck to help us get around. The priest's name was Francisco Lauschman. Of the twenty of us who initially started working with him, only eight stuck with it.

I continued my studies, and graduated from high school in Pitrufquén. As there were no longer enough teachers, I also took on the responsibility of teaching class. We were like student teachers. We were in charge of discipline, and taught class to those in the lower levels. Since I'd completed my second year at the time of the coup, I taught first- and second-year classes. In a pinch, though, I also taught third-year and fourth-year students, although I hadn't even completed the fourth year myself. It was terrible in 1973 and 1974. Those were really difficult years.

Maybe it's a talent I'd had inside me for a long time, but these experiences really helped me stand up in front of people without being afraid. I had to prepare my classes and consult with the teacher. "Prof," I'd say, "what are we going to teach these children? They need math, they need geometry; what exercises can we given them in biology?" A number of us older students traded off teaching the younger ones until more teachers arrived. By the end of the year university students from the Temuco branches of the National and Catholic universities finally arrived to take over the classes. Then we had history teachers, language teachers, biology teachers—finally we had enough to go around! But still they taught only every other class. For the others they'd just give us the materials and we'd take over the class.

There was an excellent history teacher who arrived at that point, don Manuel. Because he was blind, we had to help him take attendance and record grades. Four of us helped him with these jobs, but in the end he preferred to work with me because the others caused him problems. I learned a lot about discrimination working with him, because my own classmates would stick their legs in the air and do all kinds of things, because they thought he wouldn't notice. But don Manuel told them to put their feet on the floor, as if he could see them. They'd take an apple out of their pockets to eat, and don Manuel would say, "Put the apple away, it's not time to eat." I began to think that maybe don Manuel could see, but in truth he couldn't see a thing.

At the end of that first year, in October 1974, I also began working with Father Francisco Lauschman. We decided to travel to and work with the twenty-eight Christian base communities that had been active in the parish before the coup, but had since stopped meeting. I was assigned the rural communities, both Mapuche and non-Mapuche. My goal was to reach all these communities between Saturday and Sunday, as they were really the only days I could spare during the week. I had a confrontation with my father over this. He said that this was the last straw, that I had no business gallivanting around the countryside organizing Christian communities, and worse yet on a motorcycle! And the truth was, I did fall off once.

F: *What worried your father most? Was it the political situation? Because it was a time of heavy repression, wasn't it?*

My father was worried about the political situation in general, but he was even more worried about the fact that the priest was known as a big UP supporter. They had a big file on him, ah? He was also worried that the people we visited all had disappeared family members: a father, a son, a nephew. This really worried my father. The other thing that bothered him about my organizing was that he wanted his daughter to have a profession. I told him not to worry, that if I wanted to finish I knew how to get good grades. I told him I was very responsible, that for years I'd managed milking the cows and going to school, that I was used to doing several things at once.

When I visited these twenty-eight communities, I began to understand that the old Christian communities described in the parables worked the way Christian communities today should work. They had solidarity, they realized the importance of being united; together they sowed the seeds and cultivated the land. They realized the importance of helping each other. I decided that instead of reading the other parts of the New Testament and the Bible, I would focus exclusively on the parables: the planter of seeds, the prodigal son, and others. And we used these parables to organize in the Christian communities, forming committees to work on roadbuilding, on human and animal health. It was a way of making Christian communities into organizations focused on development and progress. The people called these organizations whatever they liked; I gave them the idea and they put it into practice. The different ways in which communities mobilized to organize made me realize the differences between Mapuche and non-Mapuche traditions.

Even though I'm Catholic, and was baptized very young, I took my First Communion with full use of my adult faith in 1975, when I was a full-grown woman. By then I'd been preaching things I didn't entirely believe, even as I was convinced that, in general, the Church teachings were part of who my people were. The parts that bothered me the most were the bureaucratic, hierarchical dimensions of the Catholic Church. I came to understand, though, that the important thing was to carve out a space for myself within the Church. It was important to gain respect by practicing what I preached. If I'd been saying that Catholicism was good, that it was a part of our community, then didn't I have to make my First Communion? So I did, and I stayed very connected with the Church and I learned a lot. I'm still connected to the Church, but I have many criticisms. I believe this bureaucratic, hierarchical, and administrative Church has some good values; but it's also monstrously powerful in the world and hard to control. That's why we who are members of the Church have to take the initiative. We have to organize the Church instead of letting the Church organize us.

If the Church sets the agenda, it can do what it wants with us. It's the congregation that has to speak up and tell the priests what we like, what we don't like, and why. I've said this, and practiced it, with my Mapuche brothers and sisters; I've said it openly, everywhere. When someone says to me well, you're Catholic, you're a Christian, whatever. I say yes, I'm a

Catholic, but I'm also Mapuche: and I'm Mapuche first, Mapuche second, Mapuche third, and in fourth place I'm Catholic. But to be Mapuche is also to be Catholic. Some disagree and say that the Mapuche haven't participated in the revelation of Christ. But I say that it depends on what you call a revelation: is it only forty days, forty hours in the desert? Maybe we don't have a desert like the one in the Bible, but we have a different kind of desert, one that we've lived through, made our pilgrimage through, the Mapuche people have done this! Among many Mapuche brothers and sisters we've talked about alternative understandings of the Bible and Mapuche religiosity. There's still much to be done on this topic, and I hope to focus more on it in the future, once there's many more women participating on gender issues.

With the help of the Church's Rural Mission (*Pastoral Rural*), we organized a seminar for leaders of Christian base communities, both Mapuche and non-Mapuche. In terms of lifestyle the rural populations were basically the same, but they brought very different understandings of the Bible to this meeting. A brother who lived near Toltén asked me, "Why do the wigkas (non-Mapuches) always have an image of Christ nailed to the cross if they believe he rose from the dead? Why do these ignorant wigkas have him hanging there dead, if he was resurrected, eh?" He thought Christ should be sitting up, gazing out at the world. And the way he said it, in Mapuche, came across very strong, emphatic. And I thought to myself, it's true. We Mapuche believe in a God who's good, who helps us, who gives us strength and courage. He's in the water, He's with the birds, He's on the road, He's everywhere. Why isn't this belief equivalent or superior to the wigka belief? The wigkas say we're all brothers. Well, this isn't a new concept to the Mapuche, we've said it for a long time. So what do the wigkas think they're doing, and why do they come and take advantage of us? So when people asked these questions at the meeting, it set me to thinking and I began to grow spiritually.

I didn't know how to speak Mapuche, I struggled with the language. My parents didn't speak to us in Mapuche even though both my mother and father knew how to speak it. They didn't want us to have problems and to be discriminated against in school, the way they had been. In this sense I learned a lot working with the Christian base communities and in the seminars. Afterwards in Temuco, I began to work with a group of young

Mapuche, some university students and some not. It was a political group, a committee in solidarity with political prisoners. We put together a whole team and a lot of people joined us. But later we began to pull away, thinking we'd like to do something specifically for the Mapuche. We realized that, no matter how you cut it, the Mapuche always got the short end of the stick. Most didn't even have a bar of soap to call their own. The wigkas, no matter what their political leanings, got help somehow. The Mapuche were the worst off because they received no solidarity whatsoever. So when we were doing this work, an idea also came from a group of anthropologists led by Mireya Zambrano, who worked at the university and wanted to investigate how the Mapuche would be affected by the new land law Pinochet had promised.

The Mapuche Land Law of March 29, 1979, still hadn't been issued, but the regime had indicated that it would fit within its general policy of modernization. In 1978 there'd been a lot of talk about ending land tenure problems once and for all. What exactly was going to happen no one could say, but we'd heard that all kinds of professionals—scientists, anthropologists, and lawyers who were specialists on Mapuche issues—were carrying out studies. I went to a Christian meeting in Cañete where I talked to a friend of someone I'd recently met. "Look," he told me, "the Mapuche Law's going to have four basic points." When I asked him if he could lend me the list of the four points so I could make a copy, he said, "No, don't worry, I've got several copies, I can give you one." So he gave me an official copy as a present, it had an official seal and everything. I brought it back to Temuco and we photocopied it and circulated it to everyone.

That's when the Archbishop of Temuco, don Sergio Contreras, and the Archbishop of Araucanía, don Sixto Patzinger, decided we had to do something about this. From the office of the Archbishop of Araucanía we issued an invitation to all the leaders from Christian base communities to attend a meeting to talk about the Mapuche land question and the law. We spent most of 1978 talking about the situation and having meetings. In September the Indigenous Institute, which was part of the Archdiocese, was formally charged with calling the principal meeting, but with the Archbishop's approval. It was don Sergio himself who held the public press conference.

At that meeting I was elected General Secretary, supposedly for six months, from September to December, or possibly until March. It was temporary, in the meantime. I think they elected me because, from among all the organizers, I seemed to know best how to write. Also because I greeted them at the door and was very nice to everyone, saying *"Mari mari, lamñen, chen zuqu fauple* (Hello, brother, sister, how are you)," which was one of the first phrases I'd learned in mapunzugun. So we all went in, we registered and began to talk. Melillán Painemal was the last to arrive, he walked in around three-thirty or four, near the end of the meeting. From that day I haven't stopped organizing. It's like an indigenous bug that's awakened within me, and has awakened me at the same time. That meeting initiated the process of the Mapuche Cultural Centers, which lasted from 1978 until 1980. In March of 1980 we received legal recognition not as the Mapuche Cultural Centers, but as the Ad-Mapu Association of Artisans and Small Farmers.

If I were to tell you all the things I went through in the Mapuche Cultural Centers, the discrimination I felt from my Mapuche brothers and sisters who spoke the Mapuche language when I didn't. The fact I spoke Spanish well, that I was self-confident in front of a group and willing to call things by their names, this bothered a lot of people. Some criticized me quietly, others sang or shouted their disapproval. Some criticisms hit me hard, like when people asked how I could be the secretary of the Mapuche movement if I didn't speak the Mapuche language. Or how I could be the daughter of a cacique if I had no knowledge of the culture. It was very hard, and I had to dig deep inside myself to deal with it. I was very open-minded when it came to politics, culture, or religion. I didn't have this idea that some were Catholic, some Evangelical, some Christian Democrats, or Communists, or whatever. I still believe we're all part of one world, and that ideological divisions do more harm than good to all of us, especially to the Mapuche people. I understood then, as I understand now, that political parties are important; certainly they're necessary and sometimes they accomplish things. But my experience back then taught me that the Mapuche should take advantage of political parties, rather than the other way around. I've developed lots of doubts and questions about political parties, but I don't see the point of fighting with them. I've learned that all backbiting, whether political, cultural, or religious, can come back to haunt you.

Well, as I was telling you, in 1978 we created the Mapuche movement of southern Chile, and the first formal organization, known as the Mapuche

Cultural Centers of Chile, was founded on September 12, 1978. The project took root and grew until it encompassed 1,500 communities, each one with its own steering committee, engaged in concrete local work that was funded mainly from within the communities and sometimes from external sources. The movement was very, very strong, from Arauco to Chiloé. I could count for you the strongly organized communities in Arauco: Lebu, Sara de Lebu, Cayucupil, San Ramón, Mequihue, Tirúa—areas where seven, eleven, up to fifteen communities met and worked together. At the school in Huape, also in Arauco, more than five hundred people attended our meeting, the same in Mequihue. Once in Malleco, on the other side of Lake Lanalhue toward Capitán Pastene, in Huayepén, the weather was really bad. The road was dark, it was freezing, and we got stuck. But so many came and met with us anyway, talking, organizing, asking tons of questions. We all had lots of questions back then: about when and why we were losing our language and our identity; about what was our culture and what was not; about how and when we'd allowed external influences into our communities and our lives.

What happened in Arauco, happened in Malleco, Cautín, Valdivia, Osorno, Chiloé. Luckily, as I was Secretary General, I got to tour the majority of the organized communities. I got to know so many parts of Mapuche territory and met so many people. I felt solidarity and support from the various Mapuche communities as well as from the Catholic religious orders that were involved, both nuns and priests. Because I had an identity card, a piece of paper the Archdiocese had made up for me on their typewriter, signed and sealed by the Archbishop of Araucanía, as well as a letter of recommendation from the Archbishop of Temuco, Sergio Contreras, it was easy for me to sleep in convents and parish houses. These documents protected me, and on more than one occasion they saved me from problems with the police. They also made it easier for me to say in my talks with Mapuche communities, look, the Church is involved, there are people involved who aren't Mapuche. We need to be strong, to speak out, to say what we need and how to get it. The Church protects us, it fights for our rights. I think this provided an opportunity and an opening.

I'll tell you an anecdote that illustrates the role of the Catholic Church in our movement. There was this old priest who lived in Cañete, his nickname was Father *Monedero* (change purse). I never did find out his real name, but the people in Arauco would know. He said to me, "Look, you can stay with

those little Franciscan nuns and I'll lend you a room for your meeting." And
he made gestures with his hands, like this. "But I won't be caught dead at
your meeting. These little Mapuche Indians killed my hero Pedro de Valdivia,[1] and you want me to be happy with them? And on top of it, this
gentleman the Archbishop wants me to lend you my church?" Because I had
the identification card, like I just told you. I answered humbly. "But Father,"
I said, "we just want to meet, a meeting for us as Mapuches"; I gave him the
whole explanation. "All right, all right," he said. "You already have the room
you want. Isn't that enough?"

We met many times in that room. Then we moved on and stayed with the
nuns at Los Alamos, the Sisters of the Child Jesus. These nuns were more
open and showed us more solidarity. Obviously their attitude was different
from the priest's. He was one of the priests who made plain, let's say, that he
didn't approve of such meetings, even under the umbrella of the Church.
There were others who'd say, "Look, I'll lend you the place just this once, but
after that you'll have to find a different space." And they didn't say another
word to us. They'd give me a place to sleep, some wouldn't even ask why; but
at least I'd have a place to stay, that was the important thing. Later I could
always figure out where to meet.

It wasn't like that when we asked people in the communities or neighborhoods to put us up. We'd talk through the night. When dawn broke we'd still
be talking. People had a lot of questions: Why are we meeting? What's the
goal of the movement? They'd also tell us the history of the place: the land-
grant titles, the fights with the neighbors, nearby wigka farmers or other
Mapuches; how water from the river or the lake would swallow up the land.
Where there were no land problems, they'd tell tales of the night, about local
customs, local lore. They told us the stories of the Manquián spirit; of the
girl with golden hair who appeared in different places; of how their machi
became a machi, about her dreams. The people gave us a real education.

For me, these experiences were the best education I ever had. I learned
about the differences between the regions of Arauco, Malleco, Cautín, and
Osorno; the different ways palin was played, the gillatun, the stories people
told. In Chiloé, for example, they'll tell you the story of the Trauco or of
other mythological beings who are part of traditional indigenous literature.
Then in other places they'd tell you the same stories, except with different
names. These are fables that teach indigenous concepts of courage and

moral behavior to future generations. The people along the coast, from Arauco to Chiloé, have similar stories about having respect for the water, or explaining when they can fish, when they'll catch more, and when less. The story of the Caleuche is told in many forms, each one in its own environment. Messages of respect for nature—for rocks, inlets, sunsets. All these stories had many things in common, even with their different details. At bottom they were the same.

F: *Were people scared at that time?*

Yes, people were scared, very scared. The fear was alive, you could almost touch it. "My dear," they'd say, "don't talk to that one, because look, that one was a Communist, he had a red identification card." Or they'd say, "Look, that one's a snitch for the cops, this policeman always visits and he tells him everything." When I'd stay with someone, they'd usually tell me the next day, "Don't tell anyone you slept here, don't mention me, don't write my name down anywhere." But later I'd go back and stay with them again, and I'd say, "Don't worry, you have to be strong, don't be afraid." So people began to take a stand, a lot of people started with us and many of them dropped out along the way. Often, when some people stand up to be counted, it's others who find the strength to continue later on. Those who'd been leftists were especially scared. I remember one such leader, from whom I learned a lot, Melillán Painemal. He really liked to be involved in the ceremonies, but he never did the background work or the local organizing, because he'd been a well-known Communist leader. He told me it was better if he didn't go, because instead of helping he'd only scare people. You go, he'd tell me. That's also why I was given the opportunity to travel everywhere and organize. The male leaders urged me on, because I wasn't burned politically and wouldn't call attention to myself the way they would.

F: *Don Mellilán Painemal was marked by the police after 1973?*

Of course! He was one of the thirteen leaders we selected in the offices of the Archdiocese, when we formed our organization. I'll tell you the names I can remember from the original 1978 steering committee: Mario Curihuentro Quintulén, president; Rosa Isolde Reuque Paillalef, secretary; Melillán Painemal Gallardo, treasurer; Honorinda Painén Panchillo, prosecretary; and Antonia Painequeo, from Lumaco, protreasurer. The director was José

Luis Huilcamán, Aucán's father.[2] Rosamel Millamán Reinao, from Pitruf-quén on the way to Villarrica, was also there but wasn't initially selected on the twelfth of September. Also present were Cecilia Aburto, from Panguipulli; Fabriciano Catalán, also from Valdivia; Carlos Peñipil, from Galvarino; Pedro Huañaco, from Ercilla; Manuel Cheuque Huenulaf, from Victoria; and Irenio Huaiquinao, from Labranza, who served as our first treasurer but never came back; and another man from Huinpil. In 1979 a brother was elected from Padre Las Casas, but we never saw him again after the election.

Obviously we had people from all the political parties, and the first to leave our organization—the ones from Labranza, Padre Las Casas, and Huinpil Galvarino—were the ones with conservative or rightist tendencies. Everyone worked on this project, not only the steering committee; but of the thirteen who made up the leadership council, we—that is, the president, the secretary, and the treasurer—worked the hardest. The others worked at the grassroots, and I think their dedication to the movement gave us energy. We knew they were depending on us. We three didn't organize the meetings and get people to come. The others did that. We only came when the people had already gathered. So the people without official positions became the catalysts in the communities, at the local level.

In 1979, when we were still known as the Mapuche Cultural Centers, we participated in Temuco's centennial celebration. We asked ourselves, what should we do? We were invited to dance, and we accepted, but we didn't just want to dance. Between 1980 and 1981 we worked in communities organizing and planning, a whole year and a half in advance. The idea was to organize a chain of local ceremonies that would culminate on Conun Hueno hill in December 1981. Where people did gillatun, we asked them to make a gillatun. Where people played palin, that's what we asked them to do. In some communities people didn't want to make a gillatun because they said their ritual wasn't a spectacle and couldn't be used for political purposes. They said, "We'll organize a cultural event, it'll have spiritual content, but not a gillatun like the one we only do for the community." We said that was fine, that was what we wanted, we meant no disrespect. And we simply explained our objectives.

People really got into the idea. On Huapi Island Héctor Painequeo organized storytelling sessions called *epeu*. In other regions people played palin.

In Tragua Tragua, also on Huapi but in another community called Piedra Alta, they organized a palin tournament and exchanged teams with Cholchol. It was a lot of fun! We organized matches between Lumaco and a Cholchol community called Coigüe, where the Painemal family is from. Launache played Piedra Alta, different communities in Freire and Pitrufquén played each other, also in Malleco. But the farthest that anyone traveled to participate was when people from Lumaco traveled to play in Cholchol, and when the community of Piedra Alta played in Cholchol. The other matches were closer, between communities where you could go and come back in a day, by bus, on foot, or on horseback. People held gillatun, they played palin, and they had cultural events, storytelling competitions, even traditional cooking contests.

F: *Can you describe the game of palin a bit for me?*

I always describe palin as hockey without skates so people will understand me! You use sticks, just like in hockey. Fifteen to seventeen people play on each team and the field is two hundred meters long. The game begins at center field, and the players have their positions, just like in soccer, they each have a role to play. The idea is to shoot the little ball into the goal to make points.

Palin also measures a player's physical strength, his knowledge of the game, the speed of his reactions, and his talent. The players have to jump over the sticks or go under them so that they won't be hit, understand? They swing the sticks hard and the little wooden ball just takes off. Some are the size of tennis balls, others like ping-pong balls. If one of those balls hits you in the head, it can split the scalp wide open. I've seen people bleeding badly after getting hit by one of those balls. They can also break people's legs. That's because after a ball is hit hard by one of those sticks, it moves really fast.

F: *So reacting quickly is very important, because if they don't have good reflexes the players wind up badly wounded.*

Exactly! The game measures a series of things: knowledge, strength, wisdom, and the general ability of the person. But the community also takes part by supporting and cheering its players, running to the corners of the field and shouting encouragement to the players. The communities size each other up, too, gauging how well they've kept up their traditions, what customs they've let in from the outside. They appraise each other's food, overall presentation, level of play, even the cheers, because you can't just yell any old thing at your players. You have to say things that fit with the sport's traditions. There's also dancing and music along the sidelines. It's a lively, dynamic event. So a tournament is part religious meditation, part sport, part social gathering, and the hospitality of a shared meal. Communities measure each others' participation at all these levels. But in any case, we were talking about the chain of ceremonies and events we organized between 1979 and 1980. It extended throughout the region.

F: *From what I've read in the newspapers, the dictatorship adopted a folkloric, almost tourist-oriented approach when dealing with the Mapuche, obviously discriminatory since the dictatorship did not consider the Mapuche political equals. But I wonder to what extent this might ironically have facilitated your efforts to organize? In a sense, you could use these paternalistic assumptions as a cover to hide your deeper goals. Did people think about this, or discuss it, when you began mobilizing?*

We did recognize this, and used the opening a bit; but our goal was not to be "folkloric." We weren't going to make a spectacle of our culture, turning it into a photo opportunity or using it for commercial gain. We weren't interested in making the dictatorship look good.

Our movement wasn't like those famous "cultural weeks" in Villarrica, which were later called artisan fairs. No, our goals were very different; from the beginning our discourse was about struggle, rediscovering our roots, and making up for lost time. We had a vision toward the future based on our continual, historic struggle for the land.

F: *But in a purely strategic sense, didn't you take advantage of the dictatorship's "folkloric" approach in some way?*

Strategically speaking, perhaps, we might have been seen as "folkloric," even if that wasn't our goal. And truth be told, we were trying to confuse the enemy, and we succeeded very well at that. For example, at the palin tournaments we organized—like the one near Eusebio Painemal's house, in Carreriñe—you could have forty teams at a single gathering, with people from Lumaco and Cholchol, and have only a pair of policemen assigned to monitor the event. Let me tell you that under no other government have we been able to have so many people, so many teams, gathered in one place. In Lumaco we had over forty teams, two days of competition. We had to limit play to ten minutes per side, on four or five fields, because we simply didn't have the time or space to have everyone play as long as they wanted. We had to impose wigka time limits so all the teams could show their skills, and sing and play their instruments as well. And the speeches people gave were truly militant! "Look," they said, "it's time to rise up and face the common enemy: the dictatorship, on the one hand, and what it's brought us; and on the other hand, the law that's supposed to end all land problems but in reality means a death sentence for our communities." All of this was said in Mapuche.

Then I'd talk in Spanish, about development, participation, the importance of unity and solidarity. That was the facade for the wigkas, especially the cops. I remember when we were in Cholchol, and Miguel Landero and Melillán Painemal called out "*akuy epu pakarwa*," which means two toads have arrived, because two policemen were arriving on horseback.[3] Miguel and Melillán told us to go on with our activities, to continue with whatever we were doing. They even suggested that if someone hosted the policemen at their wagon, it would be a great help because it would keep them occupied and out of our hair. Some women took charge of the toads—sorry, I mean the policemen—and they took a turn around the grounds and understood nothing. With time, though, in a year or two, as our movement kept growing, it became enough of a problem for the police that some of them began to take basic classes in mapunzugun. By the time of our big event on Conun Hueno hill, they'd learned how to say "good morning" and "good afternoon." We strongly criticized the people who taught the policemen to speak our language, because it was like working against your own people.

I wouldn't call our movement folkloric, we were against all that. We spoke out against the cultural week at Villarrica immediately: in 1978, 1979, 1980, and 1981. In 1979 I had problems when I went to Villarrica to hear a musical group from Lumaco. José Railef had invited José Luis Huilcamán to come and perform, and he'd arrived with his whole community, including the machis. And what happened? They built a traditional *ruka* (family dwelling) in front of the plaza and someone burned it down. I got accused of doing it! They said that a well-known Mapuche leader who opposed the government had passed through and that surely she had burned the ruka. It came out in the newspapers and everything. Funny thing, though, they built the ruka every year, and every year it was mysteriously burned down!

Our organization made strong public statements. I remember once we were invited to a dialogue with General Mendoza.[4] José Luis Huilcaman said to him, "Look, General, through my veins runs the blood of the indomitable Araucanian. What kind of blood runs through your veins?" He said this because the General was putting on airs, pretending that the government was really trying to address the issues of land tenure, public health, education, and culture that we were raising. We had big discussions with important government officials like General Mendoza. Shortly thereafter the Villarrica cultural week began to change. It became an artisans' fair and was transformed from a folkloric festival into a tourist attraction. There was dancing and music, and machis participated, but they were paid for performing. Those who attended were mainly tourists; you could see blond hair all over the place but few people from around here. This kind of activity contrasted strongly with our movement.

At the same time, the progovernment organization, the Regional Mapuche Council, couldn't play the indigenous identity card, because we'd already played it! We'd taken over the claim to our identity, and done it strongly and militantly, with all the local organizations. So the Council had no influence in the communities; all their events were in Spanish. This was one of their greatest failures.

F: *So we could say that one of your greatest strengths as a movement was cultural revival?*

What was most essential for me was the chain of ceremonies—religious, cultural, and athletic—because they occurred in practically all the communities. Some were gillatun or palin, but there were also storytelling sessions, or epeu, and singing events, known as *ilkantun*. At these singing events people would improvise on the spot, and compete to see who could come up with the best song. Some would record their songs and then listen to their own voices. Many times they laughed and joked during these competitions, other times it was more serious. This whole chain of events really left a strong impression on me, and I wasn't the only one. Many people who participated at the time felt the same way. And having this cycle culminate in a gillatun on Conun Hueno hill to mark Temuco's centennial meant a great deal more because it was a strong show of Mapuche solidarity at the precise moment when the city was remembering the destruction of the border between the Mapuche people and Chilean national society.

But the strength of the movement really came from the fact that the communities used their own cultural practices to rebuild solidarity and pride. The gillatun, palin, the burial rites specific to each place—all events had a double meaning, both cultural and political. It helped us get in touch with our roots, and we said it loud and clear: our culture gives us pride and self-esteem. You said a while ago that maybe the dictatorship created a space we could use, and in this sense you're right. If the dictatorship had any positive effect, it was to reawaken our culture. I think in times of great repression people look for ways to connect to each other and to unify. When the repression was greatest, the Mapuche movement was strongest: with militant revivals of our language, our traditions, our traditional organizations. People respected the logko and the machi; they looked to the traditional leaders of the communities. Our greatest strength was that the younger generation was able to rekindle our identity as a people.

F: *And this kind of organizing also fell outside the usual categories of politics, and thus protected you from repression, right?*

Yes, to some extent you're right. Because our methods were different we could get away with organizing a palin tournament with more than forty communities in Lumaco. Everyone arrived playing the *kulkul*, the *xuxuka*, and the *kulxun*. We paraded through town beginning at five in the morning, one community after another. It was really beautiful. Wagons, horses, and people carrying their community and team flags paraded until ten in the morning. Before, during these parades, people marched with the Chilean flag and the community flag. This time they marched with the community flag and another flag called the *weñufolle*, which was specific to the ramada built by each participating group. According to the stories people tell in the communities, this special flag had a man's head in it, which was carried secretly in order to give the community's team special power to defeat the enemy. I never saw the man's head, I can't tell you that I saw it with my own eyes, but everyone will tell you the same story. In any case, it was a beautiful procession, with everyone playing the kulkul. And our leaders took the liberty of saying, in mapunzugun and in the very face of the police, "Here are two toads who have come to watch us, to try to see what strategy we are using against them." And people served the cops *mote* with chilies, saying, "We have to feed the *pakarwas* (toads)." And they'd say this over the loudspeakers, and the leaders used the microphones to damn these policemen to hell and back. The police had no idea what was going on; they smiled and clapped like everyone else. But they must have figured out something was up, because they began to send Mapuche officers who spoke mapunzugun. They'd send a team of two policemen, one Mapuche and one non-Mapuche.

F: *So it's clear that at some point the dictatorship began to take the Mapuche movement seriously as a form of opposition.*

The government always knew we were against them, but in 1979 they saw us more as pawns of the Church. After 1980 the government realized that we had our own project, our own goals and demands. We worried a lot of people, with the huge numbers we were mobilizing. In 1980 more than a thousand communities were working with us. The government became very wary of us. "These Indians," they must have thought. "Something happens to one of them and they all gang up on you."

Given all the ceremonies and events taking place in so many communities, people began to realize that, well, it couldn't be that Isolde was in Cholchol, in Arauco, and in Lumaco all on the same day, right? Not even God or the devil could do that. And people spoke out, they stood up to the police, whether the agents were in uniform or undercover. Because in the countryside the cops would pose as wine merchants, or they'd peddle clothing, jam, plastics, whatever. These guys weren't dumb, and they'd find a way to penetrate the communities. They'd try anything; sometimes the person who bought mutton from you was really a security agent. The police could really get around; one would be here, another would be over there, and a third one a few miles down the road. And everywhere they turned someone was hosting an event. So it couldn't be that just a few of us were everywhere at once.

People were demanding land, fences, scholarships, improved medical services, a solution to soil erosion. Some of the medical posts did get fixed up. Before people were lucky to get one medical visit a month, but now some had a permanent health official stationed in their community. Not that these people did much, but at least someone was there in case of an emergency. Schools were painted and fixed up, roads repaired, and bridges rebuilt. What I really liked was that people didn't just hold political meetings, they also worked on concrete projects. They developed communal gardens, built community tubs to bathe their sheep, erected bridges and chapels. These chapels, both Catholic and Evangelical, weren't numerous; but they got used for meetings as well as religious services. They also cleared out the *murra* and the *pica pica* weeds native to this region, which can take over a field in no time! To do these jobs, people didn't sit around and wait for some outsider to come up with the money. No, they just agreed which part each person would clear; pooled their axes, pitchforks, and other tools; and set to work. If they wanted to widen a canal, they studied it together and said, "OK, we need this many shovels and pickaxes, we'll dig this deep, and these are the days we'll work." They knew exactly how to do things. When they wanted to teach the kids how to play palin, the old guys said, "OK, Saturday afternoon we play." All these little old men would arrive. I remember one elderly man from Launache: he was ancient, but boy could he move! Honorinda, the woman I told you about who was a leader, her father was very old. Honorinda herself must be more than fifty now, so her father was obviously well over fifty back then. He died just a few months ago. He was one of the runners who began the game, and he'd tell the kids what to do in Mapuche. All the kids attended. They had to jump and prove themselves physically. All the instructions were in mapunzugun. People showed up to watch. The women were on the sidelines, watching the smaller children to make sure they didn't get in the way. The feeling of respect among community members, the cultural knowledge the older people had, how everyone listened—it just took my breath away.

In March 1980 we got legal recognition as Ad-Mapu. The Mapuche Cultural Centers had been organized under the umbrella of the Catholic Church, initially limited to the IX Region and under the protection of the Bishops of Temuco and Araucanía. But as the movement grew, it spread beyond these jurisdictions to the VIII, X, and Metropolitan regions, and this was too much. So five Bishops from the southern regions, starting with the VIII, or Bío-Bío, got together in Temuco and issued a joint pastoral letter to the indigenous peoples of Chile. At the same time that they issued their letter, essentially setting us free, we got our legal recognition, and all of a sudden we were all grown up, flying on our own.

So in 1980 we became independent, legally recognized by the Ministry of Economy, Development, and Reconstruction. According to the rules of the dictatorship, any group consisting of more than twenty-five people could become a social organization. We dropped the name Cultural Centers because, according to the Interior Ministry's rules during Pinochet's regime, a cultural center could only exist within the confines of a specific municipality, and this would have fragmented our organization. So we looked for a rubric that allowed us to stay large, and the only one was the trade association (*gremio*), through which we could represent all the Mapuche of Chile. Our new name was the Association of Artisans and Small Farmers Ad-Mapu (*Asociación Gremial de Pequeños Agricultores y Artesanos Ad-Mapu*).

This name change marked our movement from 1980 to 1983, because even though we still functioned as the same cultural centers, our new name had vital significance for us. "Ad-Mapu" meant "with the land," or "part of the land"; it's a guiding principle of life for the Mapuche people that unifies living and inanimate things, that represents the balance between people and the world. When the elders explained Ad-Mapu, they said it was the whole life process, from birth to death; it included balance and reciprocity in all kinds of relationships—among humans, between humans and nature, with animals, birds, and the water—even the way a person was buried. Ad-Mapu was the whole cycle of life of people in relation to the land. For those who speak Mapuche, who understand it well, Ad-Mapu was a very inspirational name. So we abandoned the old name, and all the local cultural centers became branches of the Association of Artisans and Small Farmers Ad-Mapu.

That's how we presented ourselves to the Ministry of Economics, Development, and Reconstruction, and as a legally recognized organization we had to keep books, design a basic administrative procedure, and pay dues, all in a form agreed to by the membership. We ran our own organization, but we did enter into an agreement with the Indigenous Institute (*Fundación Instituto Indígena*), part of the Temuco Diocese. They agreed to provide us with training, all the way from the most elementary organizational issues to more technical, productive know-how. Now the Diocese did count on some international funding, and we benefited from that, too. We took courses in leadership development; methods for keeping minutes of meetings and financial records; how to record financial information in a notebook; why the secretaries needed to take notes at each meeting, including the main points discussed, the people who attended, and number present; why the leaders needed to sign in. In addition we ran sewing, bee-keeping, and artisanry workshops. People in the communities had done artisanry all their lives, and we already had the boxes for keeping bees, so it was expanding on what we already knew. With sewing, we learned how to use machines for the basic tasks, like mending or remaking garments, sewing skirts, shirts, and blouses. It wasn't fancy stitching, just basic. And we also learned to prune fruit trees, when and why it was necessary; and animal husbandry—how and why to kill parasites, when and why to castrate or dehorn our animals.

So that was more or less the gist of it. But like I told you, now that we were on our own, we couldn't keep depending on the Church, so we branched out and began to receive international support. Our first grant as an independent organization came from the Ecumenical Scholarships Program. They financed one hundred scholarships for our students, which was a lot at the time. With other grants we were finally able to buy a property at 1635 Cautín Street, 230 square meters, and we had enough money to buy the place and maintain it. The house had four rooms, a dining room, and a kitchen. We added on two meeting halls, built with low-quality materials, but at least it was our own place. In back there was a kind of lean-to we converted into a sleeping area for people who came in from the countryside. That was our place, and it was one of the main pieces of property we owned as an independent organization. Later, a grant from Canada allowed us to buy thirty sewing machines that we distributed in the communities.

This was Ad-Mapu, we all worked to create it. Each local branch took the name and added it to their place name: Ad-Mapu Lumaco, Ad-Mapu Imperial, Ad-Mapu Freire, Ad-Mapu Pitrufquén. After people found out we'd become legal, the local branches multiplied and there wasn't much turnover until 1983, when the same 1,500 communities made it to our January congress.

Another thing that made us stand out in 1980 was that we issued a statement reacting to the plebiscite the dictatorship had called in order to approve its new constitution. *El Diario Austral* printed the entire document just as we'd presented it, with the ten reasons why we disagreed with the whole exercise. And they didn't just print it in normal type, they emphasized the letters by setting them off in bold type on a gray background. It was a way of calling attention to the article. After reading it, some people said hey, you might have to go into exile! And in truth we were scared, wondering if some of us might not return from one of the many activities we were participating in.

At about the same time we also organized another event that appeared in the newspaper, around the visit of an international human rights delegation. We tried to invite people from other parts of the world, but had to ask them to pay for their own transportation. The Argentinian Nobel Prize winner Adolfo Pérez Esquivel came, as did Salvador Palomino, the Peruvian Quechua leader who headed the South American Indian Council (*Consejo Indio Sudamericano*, or CISA), an organization based in Peru that depended on the World Council of Indigenous Peoples (*Consejo Mundial de Pueblos Indígenas*). Also present was George Emmanuel, a Canadian, who was president of the World Council of Indigenous Peoples, and John Ilvo, from the Methodist Church. They were all well-known figures who weren't usually allowed to enter Chile during that period, but they were allowed in for the conference and watched by the authorities. They had the opportunity to speak with many Chileans, because many people came from Santiago for the conference, including Domingo Namuncura, a young Mapuche who led the SERPAJ, a human rights group Pérez Esquivel helped set up. We met at ANECAP, at a house belonging to the Temuco organization of domestic workers. My friend Aurora, who was here the other day, belongs to that group. All kinds of leaders attended, community leaders, people from NGOs, and many others opposed to the military government. Priests also came, and people like you, folks who wanted to learn about the situation and help publicize it. So we had a public event that combined religious, sporting, and political activities, and that transcended the boundaries of Temuco and of Chile. People came from as far away as Arauco and Chiloé, paying their own bus fares to come and participate in the event. Sometimes the authorities stopped the buses and didn't let people through. Once the Bishop himself had to intervene when the authorities didn't let a bus get through. Was that ever a story!

This event resulted in our leaders' being persecuted by the military authorities, especially by the Intendant, who saw the human rights conference as a clear case of outside meddling in Chile's internal politics. So they really began to keep track of us, we began to feel threatened, we felt watched. It wasn't fear that cut to the bone, because they didn't say anything to you or bother you directly, but when you'd get on a bus, for example, someone would get on behind you. When you got off the bus, the person would also get off right there, or maybe on the next block, sort of casually, if you know what I mean. These men who followed us were always eating ice cream, drinking endless cups of coffee, or reading the newspaper for hours. They were everywhere. It got so we had a number of them clearly identified.

When I traveled to help with local activities, or when I went to find cultural information at the Regional Museum—we didn't have access to that kind of material in those days, nor many supporters who could provide it— I'd keep seeing the same guy who'd been seated near me on the bus. When I worked in the museum, there he'd be, sitting two tables away. When I left the museum, I'd turn in the doorway and see him following me out. This kind of thing kept happening to the president, the secretary, and the treasurer of our organization.

Some of these spies ended up trying to become our friends, searching for an effective way to talk with us and get information. Sometimes they'd end up drinking wine with some of our leaders, which wasn't the best thing, but was probably the furthest they managed to get. I only had official conversations, interviews with the police, the Intendant's office, officials from the local government. They'd ask me direct questions, and I'd answer them. I don't think they believed everything I said, that was pretty clear to me, but at least they weren't yet interested in too many of the things we were doing.

F: *And all this began to happen around 1980?*

Yes, but we saw it coming earlier on, not just because of what we said about the 1980 plebiscite on the constitution, but also because of the 1979 Land Division Law.

F: *It's clear from reading* El Diario Austral *that around this time the regime increasingly identified you as political opponents. And it's around the same time that the official indigenous organization—the Regional Indigenous*

Council (Consejo Regional Indígena), right?—began getting a lot of publicity. It depended on the Intendancy and, according to some, was specifically created to implement the Land Division Law.

Yes, the Regional Indigenous Council depended directly on the Intendant's office. They had offices in the Intendancy, and they used state resources to run their organization. The Council was created at the end of 1978, because in 1979 it was needed to facilitate the implementation of Pinochet's law. They were the speakers in Villarrica, when the law was signed.

F: *And from that point on, your organization began to get marginalized in the press, and all the attention was turned on . . .*

On the Regional Indigenous Council. We saw all this and knew it was a strategy to discredit all the work we had been doing, and thus allow the smooth implementation of Pinochet's Law 2568.

F: *And the more they saw you as the opposition . . .*

The more the Regional Indigenous Council was featured in the press saying it was a good law.

F: *The newspapers wrote a lot about rural subsidies for the Mapuche, about the fact that Araucanian blood should not be a source of shame; they discussed the number of scholarships and new health posts being provided by the regime. All of this was part of the government's campaign against you.*

I think the campaign focused on us indirectly, by trying to prove that what we said wasn't true. They tried to discredit our position, which was to tell people look, if you receive an individual property title, you're really accepting a death sentence for your community, because the community as such is liquidated by this law. The law said in its first article that the Mapuche will no longer be legally considered Indians. So if we stopped being Indians, what were we all? Equals? That's what the regime wanted people to think. The authorities said, look, you have your land title now, just like everybody else. And if people didn't have fences, they'd give you wire and stakes to mark off your property, even zinc for a new roof. It was a way of pressuring people in the communities to accept the Land Division Law.

F: *So the Regional Indigenous Council served as the regime's shock troops in the countryside, helping the dictatorship implement its land law while discrediting your movement.*

Yes, that's exactly what happened. More than once we ran into these people in the field, in the communities. There were arguments, because they had one point of view and we had a different one. We suggested that if this was really an indigenous land division law, then if a family had ten hectares and five brothers, each of them should receive two hectares, whether or not they lived in the community. But the others said no, that according to the law, only people actually living in the community could receive land. We replied that their law was a land to the occupant law, not an indigenous law benefitting the community. Because if it were an indigenous law, then all indigenous people would be included. But they said that only the people who were living in the community, whether they were indigenous or not, would receive land titles. In many places they gave out titles for land to schools, churches, or outsiders renting land in the communities. It was a real mess in many places, because most communities have people like that, outsiders who receive hospitality in the form of rentals, but then abundantly overstay their welcome.

F: *Let's see if I understand things so far. Beginning in 1980, the military government identified your movement as part of the opposition and began a countercampaign using the Regional Indigenous Council as its shock troops. You confronted each other in the communities, and your leaders began to be followed and spied upon. What effect did the regime's new strategies have on your organization?*

At first, I think these tactics had a positive effect on us because we only became more dedicated and committed to our goals. Even more communities joined the movement, until we reached a membership of 1,500 communities. When the organization got that big, we restructured and developed local branches based on many different criteria—sectoral, territorial, municipal. We developed leadership committees at the national, regional, provincial, and local levels. Many of the smaller communities, like my community of Chanco, joined forces with their immediate neighbors and formed a nucleus. In our case there were several of us on the same side of the railroad tracks, then further down another group formed their own nucleus. Everywhere people got together and they dared to speak up. They were convinced that the only way they'd leave their land was in a coffin. So people let loose, they spoke their minds, they stayed united. And this made us the biggest movement in southern Chile, nobody could stop us! Leaders inside and outside the government tried to co-opt us, going to communities, trying to negotiate, giving out wire and stakes, anything to split the movement. Proof of how far they'd go is the fact that one of the first communities whose land was divided up was in Huilío, in the same general area where the president of the Mapuche Cultural Centers lived. After that happened they told us look, you denounce the land division law, and yet the community of your organization's president accepted it, and everyone agreed it was a good idea, they even had a big fiesta. The authorities contributed a horse to be eaten at the fiesta, and of course people ate it.

F: *I imagine that this countercampaign had to affect your organization in the long run, no?*

We were really united, we really dug in our heels. From Santiago to Chiloé we were very united. This began in 1978 and only intensified in 1980 and 1981. But by the end of 1981, after the gillatun at Conun Hueno hill, the movement began to falter. Rodolfo Seguel's workers' assembly took to the streets and a different kind of politics began to emerge. People in Temuco, too, began to speak a different language. The language of the left, people calling each other *compañero* (comrade), which had been hidden for a long time, came out into the open. It was a political opening, and groups that had been afraid to be seen began to come out in public. In earlier years some of these folks had approached our organization and suggested that we all march on May Day. We'd agreed, but on the day we'd be the only ones showing our faces. The folks who'd earlier used the Mapuche organization as a facade in order to say they were doing something, the ones who'd stood on the sidelines while we marched in the street—they were the ones who began to claim a central role.

For example, on May Day in 1980, 1981, 1982, even 1983, when we took to the streets to march, the students and other so-called political leaders who'd suggested we march together were nowhere to be seen. They'd be standing at a safe distance, a block, two blocks away, or even looking through a second-floor office window to see how many people were in the street.

Sometimes one or two would show up with a banner that read "retired railroad workers," or maybe "discharged for political reasons (*exonerados*), from such and such a workplace." But they'd only stay long enough for the photo. Often they didn't even walk a block with us. So tense situations developed, because some of these people had friends in our organization. We also began to have problems with the NGOs, many of which existed in this period. The NGOs had been doing really good work supporting and providing technical assistance to the Mapuche movement, but in this period, because they, too, were grouped according to ideological preference, they began to play favorites in the communities. People who didn't belong to the preferred political party, or didn't click with existing political sensibilities, started to be viewed as enemies. These were the changes that began to fracture the Mapuche movement.

F: *Do you think the movement was also weakened when the Regional Indigenous Council went into high gear, appealing to Mapuche unity, arguing that people no longer wanted to live in the communities, that they wanted the division of the land, individual land titles, and each family working on its own account? And did the economic crisis also play a role, because the CRAV (Viña del Mar Sugar Refining Company) was investing quite a bit in small beet production in the region, right?*

Yes, in Temuco, with the credits provided by IANSA . . .

F: *Quite a few Mapuches were involved with beet production . . .*

They still are. Orfelina Manque, a well-known leader, and the whole sector of Roble Huacho; there are also many commercial beet farmers near Quepe. Since many people were only producing beets, with the crisis they ended up having to throw tons of beets out on the street, or feed them to their animals. It was a huge loss.

F: *Another factor that surfaced in a conversation I had with Pepe Bengoa, and which also comes out in an article by José Marimán, is that people in a number of Mapuche communities actually seem to have supported the division of community lands.[5] They thought that maybe it wouldn't be so bad to divide up the lands, and that this was a pretty big factor in weakening Ad-Mapu. What do you think?*

I think it's a valid interpretation, because we can't deny that, today as in the past, there's a strong collective desire among indigenous people to know and to define what belongs to them. This private property bug eats away at the insides of many indigenous people, those who live in communities and those who don't. So there were many people who wanted their individual title. But how did they want to receive that title? This ended up being a real problem. In reality, a number of communities requested the division of their lands, they wanted their individual titles; and this also helped divide our movement. But because the law was a land to the occupant law, rather than a law to divide the land among all community members, problems just began to multiply. Some people were in favor, others against. Some wanted the division, but only according to their personal criteria. Some family members wanted or claimed more land than others. And political divisions and political parties began to get involved as well, causing further fragmentation in a movement that had begun with the attempt to unify all political currents.

Our organization changed dramatically as a result of all this. We'd begun as a movement whose core demand was the land, and while it continued to be important, it was no longer the only central point. We began to discuss other social movements, we became more conscious of what was going on in other parts of civil society. We talked about broader participation, about making alliances with universities or labor unions, making common cause with other organizations that were struggling and suffering, because in some small way our suffering was shared, even though it was different. We shared the experience of injustice and struggle with hospital workers, railroad employees, university students, and even if we were different, in the end, we all suffered and struggled, right? So we began to search for a common denominator, which turned out to be the return to democracy. But the strategy for returning to democracy that the organization adopted wasn't shared by everybody.

F: *Let's try to expand a bit on this point, because it seems to me that there's a lot of background to your comments that we may want to make explicit. As you said, there were many positions within Ad-Mapu about the return to democracy. I'm thinking in particular of the personal testimony of José Santos Millao that we've both read.[6] In his testimony, Millao describes how, when he first joined Ad-Mapu, he had a conversation with Melillán Painemal.*

Santos's interpretation of the conversation was that Melillán didn't want to get the organization mixed up in politics; but that Santos couldn't understand how Ad-Mapu could continue to exist without getting mixed up in politics.

Let's see. Even though interpretations might vary, I think what the original leaders of Ad-Mapu were suggesting was that we shouldn't introduce the kinds of differences or problems that existed in the political parties into our organization. Even if some of our members belonged to political parties, we wanted Ad-Mapu to remain independent of party structures, so what we meant by "apolitical" was simply without party affiliation.

F: *But to what extent could an organization without party affiliation, like yours, seek alliances with other groups and be part of a broad movement against the dictatorship? Wouldn't it be contradictory, in a sense, for a group like Ad-Mapu to participate in a larger united front, since such a front was made up of political parties?*

I still think it was possible to participate as Mapuche without first looking for a godfather, or becoming the clients of a particular political party. The demands of the Mapuche people are not the province of a single political party. Rather, they should be taken into account by all political parties. If we associated our movement with just one party line, it would make us a much smaller organization, with a much narrower view of things, and some of our members would simply leave. It was much better to be a Mapuchista, an *Indianista* or a syndicalist (*gremialista*), however you wished to call it, because it was much broader.[7] It allowed you to respect differences and to maintain a more diverse membership, which could include people from the Catholic Church, like me, and people who had a history of involvement in political parties, like Melillán. Mario Curihuentro, our president, might not be a card-carrying Christian Democrat, but everyone knew that, when he got drunk, he'd just say Frei, Frei, Frei. There were others who were more conservative, and some of those left after the first intense discussion. But there were many who would have stayed, I think, if our positions hadn't become so politicized. We started out a very, very broad movement. And yet we always recognized that our most important friends and allies had to be the university students and trade unionists who struggled for workers' rights, and for the right to subsistence that was the most fundamental human right for all.

F: *What was Melillán Painemal's role in all this? As we've seen, Santos Millao thought that Painemal didn't want to get Ad-Mapu mixed up in politics, but according to what you've told me, Painemal was a member of the Communist Party.*

Mellilán Necul Painemal Gallardo was a schoolteacher, a very charismatic and clear-thinking political leader. He had to face many things in his life because he was Mapuche, both in his career as a secondary school teacher and as a political leader. He knew what it was like, for example, to have the rug pulled out from under him by members of his own party, to not have the support of his own political comrades, to have politics consume most of his youth and what little he earned as a teacher. He pretty much abandoned his family, choosing instead to be an apostle for social change. I think he believed more in social change than he did in the Communist Party. He was in the Communist Party because he saw a better reception for his ideas there, and because he had good friends in the party. But he also had friends who were on the right. He rubbed shoulders with national-level leaders from the conservatives and the National Party, and even though he wasn't one of them, he was friends with them because he learned a lot from them, and they learned a lot from him, too. Domingo Durán, for example, was one of his friends. They fought a lot, but they also respected each other. Melillán knew how to gain people's respect.

In 1980 Melillán and I attended the Third World Congress of Indigenous Peoples in Canberra, Australia. What clarity of thought he had! He was the consummate diplomat, an ambassador for the indigenous cause who worked equally well with all of us indigenous peoples attending from around the world, and with the nonindigenous people. On that trip I learned from him that you need to be very precise about identifying your audience and the context for each event. I remember that he gave an excellent speech in Sydney, Australia, to a union of transportation workers, I forget whether they were naval or airport workers. Then he gave a speech to the Parliament in Canberra, saying exactly the same thing, but with very different words, and turned around and gave yet another variation to a group of Chilean exiles. The same message all three times, the same goal; but he tailored the language and direction of each speech to fit the audience. It was then that I realized the importance of Painemal's gift of speech and the facility he had with language. Don't get me wrong, it's not like I worshiped him or anything, but I think it's important to recognize his talent for reaching people. He could talk to you about the Bible and the Communist Manifesto; he understood the bureaucratic structure and policies of the Catholic Church; he'd become an Anglican activist. This versatility and depth of knowledge gave him the facility to make contact with many different people, and to feel comfortable in many different environments. Having been around for more than fifty years also gave him the right to say, look, I have a history, I can tell you these things because I've been there, I know, I have experience. He had a lot of clarity. To be honest, sometimes I'd look at him and think, he's just an old codger, he thinks he knows everything, and he doesn't listen to us younger folks. And that was true, too. But even with the doubts I had, I ended up learning a lot from him.

F: *Is there anything else about this first stage of organizing that stands out for you?*

We accomplished a lot. But in addition to what we've already discussed, I'd say that our international contacts were truly essential. It was crucial that some of us Mapuche leaders were able to travel outside of Chile. Those of us who managed to travel used to joke and say it was like getting an advanced degree. We got to know the experiences of other people, situations worse than ours, better than ours; we saw how other people lived, how they experienced poverty. We learned about other political experiences, about other religions; we observed how others formulated strategies to deal with their problems. I can't exaggerate how valuable this was. It seasoned us as leaders.

Now, these contacts, and the visits we received from World Council representatives, members of churches, representatives of other indigenous nations, also helped us develop a closer connection with the Chilean Commission on Human Rights. They also helped us gain respect from the leaders of the main Chilean labor association (*Central Unica de Trabajadores*, or CUT). The CUT originally wanted us to be part of their organization, and they wouldn't recognize or respect us as a distinct group. They always told us it was okay to have our own issues, but that we should really be part of them. They never said, "Hey, it's really good that you're fighting there in the South. We're working here in Santiago, sort of camouflaged, but surviving;

let's work together." No, they never took us into account. And yet, when one of us would travel, people from the international solidarity movements would invariably send something for the CUT. We'd ask, "But what if we're caught?" The answer was always that it was better to send things with us than with someone else.

Once we waited half a day for Manuel Bustos in the Church labor office (*Vicaría del Trabajo*) in Santiago. It was located in the Vicariate of Solidarity (*Vicaría de la Solidaridad*), and Monsignor Alfonso Baeza had his office on one side, and Manuel Bustos and his people had their office on the other side. We waited a whole half day to give Bustos a letter and some money. Bustos gave himself the satisfaction of walking back and forth, never even acknowledging our presence. I didn't know him, but one of the many times he walked by I just reached out and grabbed him, and demanded to know if he was Manuel Bustos. "Let go of me!" he said. "No," I replied, "we've been waiting here half a day and it's about time you talked with us." Melillán was with me and he said, "There's no point in begging guys like him. Let's go, he can come to Temuco to pick up his stuff." I let Bustos go, but I walked after him, fuming, and told him, "Who do you think you are? I'm carrying things for you, bringing them to your house, to line your pockets and fill your stomach, and on top of it I'm supposed to stick around to beg you to take them? I'm Mapuche, all right," I told him, "but that doesn't mean I have to beg. Better you come to Temuco to get your letters from Australia, I wouldn't dream of giving them to you now." Well, Bustos turned around and got Monsignor Baeza on his side; they apologized left and right. "Out of respect for you and your office, Eminence," I said, "and because I don't want my temperature rising any further, I'm going to ask my partner here if he's willing to turn over the package." During this whole time I was carrying the money, dollars in cash, and Melillán had the letter. So I couldn't let Melillán get away without turning over the letter, because in the envelope there was a receipt Bustos had to sign and return to us, so we could send it back. It was a real mess. On top of it all I was carrying the money in special pockets I'd sewn in the lining of my pants, up and down both legs, and I was walking around trying to cover it all up with a huge sweatshirt. It was a good bit of money. The Union of Naval Workers, or something like that, had sent him the cash from Sydney.

This is an example of how non-Mapuche workers and peasants—because the national peasant organization (*Confederación Nacional Campesina*, or CNC) and the Ránquil association both belonged to the CUT—didn't take us into account at all. At most they came when we invited them to one of our conferences, but only to impose their own line. "This is what you need to do," they said. "You little Indians have to obey us because we're from Santiago." And when we told them no, and stood firm, they got mad and told us to go to hell. So our international connections also helped prove to these people, who should have been our allies from the start, that they could form a coalition with us and not demand that we do exactly what they did. Afterward it also helped us get a representative on the national board of the Assembly of Civility (*Asamblea de la Civilidad*),[8] and to send someone to the various national meetings of the democracy movement. Now of course they tended to call us and ask for someone with the same political stripes, but that's to be expected.

F: *But as Ad-Mapu gained visibility and respect, there was also more interest in trying to co-opt you, right?*

Yes, lots of people were interested in that. We also became the recipients of international solidarity, which was offered, I've always thought, with the best intentions in the world. Our organization was able to fund a series of small projects and some bigger ones; we trained leaders and technical experts, learned about administration, organization, and even the bureaucratic details of how to write a business letter. We Mapuche are good at talking, we know how to use words in an oral setting, but we have little practice with reading and writing. It's hard for a Mapuche to develop a taste for the written language. We don't often get the chance to do it, and there's only a few of us who even understand how important it is. Most of us pick up a book, and in no time we're asleep. We're bad at reading. But the long and passionate speeches Mapuche leaders gave impressed the people in the NGOs, formed mainly by people who opposed the military regime. Today we can look back and see that so-and-so was a Christian Democrat, the other a Socialist, maybe a member of the Radical Party. But in those days we were all a part of the opposition to the dictatorship, even though some of us knew better than others how to place people politically, and many of the NGOs had a connection to the Church. These organizations were good at funneling money, and looking back I can see why they were the main mediators. It would be interesting to sit down and figure out how the moneys from international solidarity arrived and got distributed, and how much of it really ended up in the communities. Because I can tell you that the Mapuche organizations received about thirty percent of what the NGOs got. The NGOs received a lot of money, and they worked with us, but maybe around ten percent of the money ever got to the countryside. The rest of it got skimmed off in paying for offices, salaries, cars, and trucks, and then folks would drive into the countryside to meet with people in the communities.

F: *Last week, when I was attending a meeting for Mapuche leaders in Puerto Saavedra, at one point someone brought up the topic of the NGOs. There was general laughter, and one of the logkos from the Isla Huapi said, "Ah, yes, the NGOs; the ones who steal the money."*

That's pretty much the idea people have of the NGOs. They're the big piranhas who gobble up all the funding; very little of the money ever reaches the communities. When the NGOs gave out credit, it was usually with their famous system of rotating funds, where they'd give you a loan, but you had to return it so they could pass it on to the next person, and so on down the line. You always ended up having to give back more than you put in! The way people explained it was, say you get a kilo of salt in December that costs one hundred pesos, but when you have to give back the money in March, that same bag of salt costs more, so you have to give back one hundred and twenty pesos. People in the countryside resented this. They'd say sure, the gringos sent the money for us, but the NGO guys keep it for themselves, to pay their salaries and buy those huge pickup trucks, and those jeeps!

I tell you, the NGOs helped us out a lot, and we have to admit it. But we also have to admit that many people in the NGOs got big salaries, started businesses, made a good living on the backs of the Mapuche people. The anthropologists and social scientists from CAPIDE, for example, the Center for the Training, Research, and Development of the Mapuche People, bought a piece of land where they set up a development and training center. When you go to Europe, people tell you CAPIDE is a Mapuche organization. It works with the Mapuche, and we gave them this much to do thus and so. The Dutch said they financed this center, that it was only for the Mapuche. Now, I've been to this training center several times. I've been invited to give talks on several topics, but I've never been paid. The first time I went, it was to see how the building looked. The second time, because we were going to rent the place for one of our meetings, thinking it would be cheaper than another location. But it ended up being more expensive, because we also had to pay for the bus fares, food and lodging, everything. It was as expensive as renting a place here in Temuco. The only good thing was that, because we were out in the countryside, people couldn't go out drinking, and we were spared the constant interruptions of the telephone and other distractions. So that's more or less the size of it.

Still, if you have the chance you should go see Mireya Zambrano and let her tell you her story. She's my friend, and most people will tell you she knows a lot about indigenous issues. She's a smart woman, forceful, who knows how to make her way in the world and has strong values. I've gotten to know her pretty well. She's also an emotional person, which gives us something in common!

F: *So the NGOs really were a double-edged sword. While they supported projects that benefited the Mapuche people, they also made a good living off the funds intended for the Mapuche communities. As I understand it, and please correct me if I'm wrong, once Ad-Mapu was formed through Mapuche initiative and managed to gain recognition, NGOs became interested and started to move in. Even with the best and most humane motivations in the world, the result of this was that the Mapuches got taken advantage of, and that what they themselves had created got co-opted by others.*

That's exactly how it's often seen. If we try to step back and look at the whole picture, we see that the NGOs have provided a great deal of technical support for Mapuche organizations. At the same time they've also fostered divisions, supporting some factions or leaders over others, taking a paternalistic position, telling people they should be grateful because of the help and education they've received. When a Mapuche group wanted autonomy, they were told they were wrong, that if you didn't do things the way the NGO wanted them done, they'd pull out completely and abandon you. I'm telling you the truth, often it really was like this. But it's also true that most people got involved for good motives, because they really wanted to help. I don't want to condemn them, because in many cases the NGOs were the only place where people who opposed the dictatorship could train for a technical career, many of them were famous political dissidents or were the children of someone who had been burned politically. Some were motivated by party loyalties or nostalgia for the past and managed to form an NGO and, with the best of intentions, went out into the countryside to help people.

But these same people ended up trying to figure out how to make things more efficient, more businesslike. With the new world economy, things had to be quick, modern, advanced. You had to have a vehicle, because otherwise things took longer and you did less. And then obviously you had to have money to maintain the vehicle. If you needed two or three people on staff, they needed to be paid. And if anyone had a professional degree, well, then they wouldn't be satisfied with a small salary, they'd have to get a big salary. And who ended up with the small salaries? The Mapuche agricultural technicians, young guys who'd only finished high school or some other sort of secondary technical training. These were the ones who really did the work in the countryside, who moved the agricultural, sewing, weaving, and artisanal projects. They went to the countryside and stayed there, these young technicians, whether Mapuche or non-Mapuche. And they were paid the least. The fancy professionals stayed mainly in their city offices and, when they came to the countryside from time to time, they arrived kicking up dust with their powerful jeeps.

For all these reasons, by 1985 people were already skeptical of the NGOs. The Mapuche wanted more say inside the NGOs, they wanted to share equally in the work, the administration, the development of broader plans and ideas. And some of the NGOs said, "OK, we'll open up, we want your input and if you tell us what you want we'll do what you say." But in reality they could never do that. They never got beyond asking for our opinion. Not the state, and not the NGOs—neither of them could really change their plans. They had to listen to their financial backers, who had distinct plans and objectives. So they'd say one thing, and do another once they got to the countryside. That's why the NGOs have such a bad reputation in the communities.

All this is said in the spirit of constructive criticism. I've said the same things within the NGOs themselves, when we were invited to offer our opinions. Maybe I took my cue from Melillán Painemal, and sugarcoated the pill just a bit; but I've said what I think. And it's ironic that, with the return to democracy, when Patricio Aylwin finally became president, many people in the NGOS said, "Uh-oh, once democracy arrives, our cash cow's gone. We won't have any more work, we'll get paid less." They went to work for the state, politically that gave you a certain status, a few perks; but boy did they have to take in their belts a few notches! And I haven't heard this from just one person, but from several people, here in the IX Region as well as in Santiago, and it's really gotten my attention. You can't make the kind of money working for the state that you could make working for an NGO. Isn't that interesting?

F: *So could we say that the NGOS grew and flourished alongside the Mapuche movement, taking their strength, energy, and resources from the Mapuche organizations?*

Look, when our organization was born on September 12, 1978, immediately new NGOS were formed and already existing ones got stronger. CAPIDE, for example, which prior to 1978 was just a group of anthropologists without legal recognition, became a training center, achieved legal status, and received a lot more funding. The Indigenous Institute Foundation (*Fundación Instituto Indígena*), which was run by the Temuco and Araucanía dioceses, was a Church institution with a tiny budget. They'd borrowed a vehicle from the Maryknoll priests, and their whole staff consisted of Eugenio Teicel and, after a while, Francisco Velex, who now lives in Valparaíso. They had one agricultural technician who specialized in bees—systems of pollination and honey—and she'd distribute bees to the communities. I tell you, that was all there was, and they had their office in this old house, where today there's the San José building, all big and modern. This old rambling house somehow managed to contain all the different organizations: Caritas, the Indigenous Institute, the Solidarity Committee, the Committee of Relatives of Political Prisoners, the youth organizations, the soup kitchens. We were all in there together, like a pot full of crickets, but the sounds we all made somehow went well together; all those little crickets managed to sing in harmony! Then the organizations began to grow and expand, like a balloon when you fill it with hot air. Directors with secretaries, large staffs for each; technicians and lots of money to pay for them; legal departments, training departments, social departments, public relations departments, technical departments. At least five departments each, and I'm not even counting the missionary department, ah? And they formed an interdisciplinary board, headed up by the Bishops of Temuco and Araucanía, the director of the Indigenous Institute, plus experts from this and that university, you know how they're always asked to be part of boards like this. And since our organization was so big, they also invited us to send a representative to the advisory board. I remember that Melillán, Mario, and I got together to decide whom we should send, and everyone said well, let's send Isolde, after all, she's a Catholic, she's the right person. So I served on the board, I don't know for how many years, from 1979 until 1986, I think, until I criticized something. My criticism must have been very big, because they threw me off! That institution is still very big, and it receives a lot of financial support from churches and lay organizations from around the world.

A number of other organizations broke off from the trunk of the Indigenous Institute. At one point a problem developed in the Indigenous Institute between the Mapuche technicians and their wigka bosses, because whenever the Mapuches would make signs of advancing or taking on more independence, their supervisors would rein them in. So the Mapuche technicians decided to leave the organization, and to do so in a friendly way, not causing resentment but simply finding a way to work on their own projects. That's how the *Logko Kilapán* was born, headed by Mauricio Huenchulaf, today an important national leader who was trained as an agricultural engineer at the Temuco campus of the Universidad de Chile, what is today called the Universidad de la Frontera. Logko Kilapán was a big success. It grew to be even bigger than the Indigenous Institute, in part because it was the only NGO run for and by indigenous people. The leaders and technicians were all Mapuche with strong links to Ad-Mapu; they were dynamic and politically committed. The organization received a lot of money and became a huge NGO, a really strong and exciting group composed exclusively of Mapuches.

Among the many Mapuche organizations whose focus was technical or productive—and there are many more that I can't even mention now—there was one with a more intellectual orientation that called itself Liwen. Their idea was to collect books, manuscripts, historical documents, the writings of activists and technicians, in general to make an archive and a documentation center. It was really a good idea. A few kids who'd graduated from the local university, mainly in history, language arts, and accounting, had the idea first, but others took it on as well, from music, art, and other departments, and they created the Liwen society. Well, that's just to give you a basic idea of the kinds of NGOs, both Mapuche and non-Mapuche, that dealt with indigenous issues, because we could spend a whole day talking about them all! Here in the IX Region there was a moment when there were seventy-two NGOs. I've only talked about some of the ones that dealt with the Mapuche; there were others who worked with peasants or other groups that I haven't mentioned.

F: *What was your personal experience with all these organizations as they grew and expanded?*

Like I told you before, at a personal level I was much too naive. I was open and clean-minded, moral in a Christian sort of way, gullible and idealistic really. I didn't question other people's motives. If someone said he'd bring me five pieces of bread, that's what I thought he meant. I didn't look for a hidden meaning. If a person said she'd arrive at one o'clock, I'd expect her at one o'clock. But I learned the hard way that people didn't mean what they said, they didn't bring bread and they didn't arrive on time. They said they loved me when in truth they hated me.

To illustrate what happened in our own organization: I was the General Secretary from 1978 until 1983, and I did a bit of everything. We got funded for a lot of little projects. Money came from Canada for a sewing project that was run by the women's branch of our organization, directed by Cecilia Aburto and Antonia Painequeo; the Inter-American Foundation funded a leadership training project; the German Ecumenical Scholarships Program put up money especially for student fellowships; the Santiago Quakers cooperated with the United States Embassy on a donation of three hundred books. We also had other types of projects dealing with agricultural production and animal husbandry, such as an animal health program funded by Lil Hoffman, from the German part of Switzerland; and others to deal with animal parasites, castration and dehorning, pigpens, and the planting and pruning of fruit trees. Like I said, these were all small. The biggest project we had was the purchase of our house, and we did that in conjunction with CAPIDE and the Indigenous Institute. The money was received by CAPIDE and then coadministered with us. The rest of the moneys came through the NGOs, especially the Indigenous Institute, with which we signed an agree-

ment to provide technical assistance and leadership training. So the money
we received to hire lawyers, defend the major court cases, and take care of all
the most important legal questions was funneled through the Indigenous
Institute and helped create their legal department.

With all the projects that came through our offices, there was always a
small surplus that served to cover administrative costs. For example, when
we bought the house there were a few pesos left over which we used to fix
the windows, to buy a two-burner stove, because we didn't have enough for
a bigger one; and to buy the wood we needed to make a table and benches.
There'd always be a little extra to pay for transportation, to get people from
one place to another. So the national leaders—we were the ones who moved
around the most—could put aside a bit for daily expenses, to help us get
around. So at some point, I don't remember how, the people on the steering
committee decided that each of us would get one thousand pesos for expenses. We'd started out with five hundred each, but then it rose to one
thousand. And that's what I got from 1980 until 1983, with one thousand
pesos a month, I got nothing else.

When I left Ad-Mapu, a gringo who really liked me invited me to Europe.
I was just married, and here I went to Switzerland, on my honeymoon
without my husband! While I was there, I met Mapuches in exile who had
helped support several of our projects, and also the Europeans who'd
helped us out. You know how the gringos are really open, well, they just
came out and asked me why I'd left the organization. "How are things," they
asked. "We've heard that the Communist Party took over Ad-Mapu, that
you're a spy for the CNI (Center for National Intelligence), that you answer
to the Catholic Church." It was in Europe that I found out that the Bishop
had supposedly married me and my husband, and saw a lot of other things
from a different angle. When I talked to Lil Hoffman, an elderly lady, she
showed me the records of our animal health projects. "Look," she said,
"here's how much we gave for the breeding stock, both sheep and cattle." I
went to another funding agency, and they showed me the records of the
scholarships they'd given us, so many scholarships! I visited another office,
and they showed me the books for the women's training project, including
what I had supposedly been earning all this time! When I saw all of this, I
wanted to die! And it was all signed by our own president, treasurer, and
protreasurer! Sure, we'd discussed these projects. Melillán had reported on

them, and I'd signed the reports he'd presented at our meetings, but not the version he'd sent out to Europe. The accounting in both was totally different. So it was in Europe that I first found out that I wasn't making the one thousand pesos I thought I made, but six thousand pesos, just like the other leaders. Only I'd never seen a peso of those other five thousand. I just wanted to go home. I cried a lot in Europe, alone at night.

Of course when I went back, I went straight to the leaders. I told them I'd found, for example, a project destined for Ad-Mapu in which people from CAPIDE would teach us to take pictures. CAPIDE had given cameras to Ad-Mapu, but they'd given us these terrible super-cheap ones, where you just open the lens and shoot. They were really popular here for a while; they gave out one per neighborhood. And what would have been the point of giving out more, they were so awful! So I told CAPIDE that I knew what they were doing.

Earlier in 1981 when I'd gone to Geneva with Melillán, we'd found out about the misuse of project funds and we'd talked to CAPIDE and the Indigenous Institute about it. What we'd agreed to in our conversations was not the accounting that ended up on paper and sent to international organizations. What ended up happening, though, was that I was blamed for blowing the whistle, and beyond my one thousand pesos a month the NGOs didn't give me a cent more. Somehow Melillán kept getting his salary of six thousand pesos, plus a commission from each project that came through the NGOs, all the new ones that kept forming. And meanwhile I didn't receive a peso from the Church, from the NGOs, or from any political party. I was personally very frustrated by this, I felt that I'd been betrayed. Why didn't they just tell me to my face why they'd all decided to treat me this way?

I still carry around the wounds from these experiences. If I left Nehuen-Mapu, it's not because I don't agree with their principles, since the statutes and mission of Ad-Mapu and Nehuen-Mapu are part of what I know, of my political goals, and of what I want for my people. But is it fair that some people should take advantage? Let me tell you, I have a lot of resentment toward my Mapuche brothers who've led Mapuche organizations, because they exploit women, both sexually and economically, and take advantage of their fellow leaders. And also because they discriminate ideologically and politically.

They said I was a Christian Democrat, but I wasn't. The Bishop didn't marry me and my husband, and in fact we lived together for quite a while, from March 3, 1983, before we got married in a civil ceremony in 1986. Supposedly we'd been married by the Bishop at the Diocese, and he'd given us an apartment in a new urban development, Villa las Estrellas, as a gift. I didn't even know if this place existed, but I decided to investigate. After more than a month of looking around I found it. It was a series of unfinished buildings on España Street that did indeed belong to the Diocese. One building was completed and there were people living in it; the other building was sold still unfinished. And the Bishop got mad at me, because he thought I'd spread the rumor that he'd married us, supposedly to cover up the mistake I'd made, the sin I'd committed by living with and then marrying a guy so much younger than I, with no professional degree, no future, and not very Christian to boot. So I requested a meeting with the Bishop, and told him that it wasn't true that I'd been spreading rumors, that they were all lies, and that I hoped he'd listen to me. We talked for about an hour, and happily, in the end, the Bishop said he understood, though he'd been very upset. And in my opinion, he certainly had good reason to be upset.

I'll tell you, I've gotten badly burnt out twice in my life, and both times it was because I cared about things, I wanted things to work out for my people, and then a few individuals came along and took advantage, using the money for themselves and not for the communities. The only help Juan and I ever got was from the godfather who'd stood up for us when we got married, the husband from an exiled couple who, unfortunately, recently separated. Because they lived in exile they couldn't even come to the marriage ceremony. They helped us from a distance. But it was my Swiss friend who reminded me that I had to look out for myself. "It's good to do so much solidarity work," he said, "it's good you got married, and that you work so hard for your people. But you also need to think about yourself, take care of yourself." It took me a long time to accept that I'd have to charge for the work I did for my people. And it was then that I began to understand and to remember that my father had told me the same thing all those years, even if with different words.

I had to learn the value of the work I did. I had to be firm and say this I can do, that I can't. Many times I took in compañeros who were on the left, not knowing if they were Communists or from the MIR (Movement of the Revolutionary Left). They came from Santiago to do a job, and someone would ask me to put them up for a night. I'd take them in, but I was really tense. In the morning we'd eat breakfast, I'd take the person to a predetermined place, then return home. But when I'd get home and could finally relax, I'd sit and try to figure out who the person had been. Geez, could it have been so-and-so, or someone else, was it his name, was it her alias, who really stayed in my house? The only thing you ever really knew for sure was if your guest was a man or a woman.

I've had to develop a thick skin. Many times I've thought that, as a leader, I have a double, no, even a triple, personality. First I'm my parents' daughter; then I'm my husband's wife; and finally I'm the leader who must answer to her people. But maybe there's yet a fourth identity, that of the Mapuche woman who has to live in a non-Mapuche society that demands many things of you that aren't part of your culture, things for which you're not prepared and don't have the resources. Sometimes you feel powerless. You have to overcome obstacles, prove yourself all the time, be better than the men and better than the non-Mapuche, or you aren't anyone. It's like being a fish out of water, constantly challenged to know more than the rest, to behave differently from the rest, you don't have a private life anymore. You're a public woman, everyone looks you over and points at you. They judge you for the good things and the bad things. Everyone feels they have the right to evaluate you, whether it's with good or bad intentions; you're constantly on public display.

Yet whenever I've been tempted to leave all this behind, when because of all the pressure from my family, from other people, I've thought, that's enough, I can't take it any more, it's the people themselves who've pushed me to stay on, to continue with this so-called career of being a leader. And it's not only the people who support me who've told me to stay, it's also the people who don't share my same ideals. Some have told me, "Look, you're a good adversary, I like our discussions, I know what you want, not like this other guy who's a crazy fireman putting out fires where they don't exist." When I've heard things like that, I've thought, "Wow, and I was so sure this one couldn't stand the sight of me. All the times I've fought with them, said mean things, and here they are telling me they need me to stay." Sure, there's a double motive there, but I've also realized that some people need me because they work best reacting to my suggestions. Once I make one they can react to it, turn it around, and offer it back as their own. So that's how folks from other political parties, from other Mapuche organizations, people who work in groups that aren't the ones I've chosen to belong to, have shown they need me. And then I've had to stay. Because I've realized that if I falter, even if it's another woman who takes my place, there'll be a missing link in the chain.

Right now I think there's a lot of links in our chain that, if they're not missing, they're certainly loose. People are really frustrated by the shortcomings of the political process we've lived as Mapuches. They feel duped and deceived after having had such high hopes for the Indigenous Law 19253, a law we'd worked for from 1978 until 1992, when Aylwin listened to us and made good on the promise he'd signed in Imperial. At that point, I think the leaders thought to themselves, "Finally! We're finally going to have a voice, a space in this government; our time has finally come and all our hard work's going to pay off." But in the years that followed it's become clear that it's much harder than we thought, that it isn't so easy to solve problems, that we have to do what we can, not what we want to do. That's why I think a leader gets frustrated sometimes, and decides simply to stay home. That's the way it is today for many of the more experienced Mapuche leaders, women and men, and for our relatives, who ask us, "What did you gain by sacrificing so much? Weren't you just wasting your time?" I never finished my degree, for example; and I was fired from the school where I was teaching, at Molco and Los Galpones, because I belonged to an organization that defended Mapuche rights. I was lumped in with leaders of leftist political parties, at a time when I didn't even understand what the left was, when I didn't even know what the Communist Party stood for, ah? It never crossed my mind to think if it was good or bad, they were all people who worked with me, we struggled together because we were all Mapuche.[9]

Look, this is my own personal opinion, I haven't discussed it with anyone, not even with my husband. I think the political parties definitely wanted to impose their will on us, to manipulate the Mapuche movement. They went about it in a very personal way, going after the leaders in our organization who showed promise or potential. People from the Communist Party, the Christian Democrats, and the Socialists would show up and they'd give you individual gifts. When I say gifts, I mean documents you might need, or money. They'd give you cash as an incentive, telling you it was a way to help you fight for the cause, because they knew you were a good leader, that you had talent. And they'd praise you, puff up your ego, invite you out to eat. It was a total brainwashing session, they'd make you feel chosen and special. And depending on how the dinner conversation went, you were either in or out. So with all these folks making inroads, our leaders—who, like all human beings, needed money, right?—began to become clients of specific political parties.

And truth be told, we were all vulnerable because we got paid so little. Like I've told you, there was often a little money left over from the grants we got, and we each got a monthly salary, which in my case was one thousand pesos. This didn't even cover the rent for my room! So where did I get the rest of the money to make ends meet? Well, I had to find other work, and you might say I had friends in high places! Father Francisco Lauschman, the priest who'd been my teacher, became my friend because he helped me out a lot when I got pregnant. He was like a father to me, a father and a friend, he was always there when I needed him. He died recently, he suffered a lot near the end; I still miss him terribly. Father Pancho was a part of my personal network of friends who supported me, people I knew from before I became involved in the movement. But not everyone was so lucky, and the political parties took advantage of that to increase their influence.

In addition to the political parties, the NGOs used the same strategy—and here we go again with the NGOs! They'd also latch onto individual leaders, so by the time we all arrived at the annual congress, we looked around and realized that, whether it was an NGO, a political party, a respectable human rights organization, a church group, everyone had a godfather! As gossip would have it, my godfather was the Bishop of Temuco. Funny, everyone knew except for us. Juan and I were the last to know! Anyway, this was the kind of thing that got out there on the grapevine, and many rumors weren't even half true. Still, because this was the way parties and organizations began to function, and because many leaders really did take on godfathers, it was easy to believe things and a lot of people got confused.

F: *During which congress were all these rumors circulating?*

The turning point was the 1983 congress. It became perfectly clear at that point that things were changing and the old style was gone. Before, people addressed each other using the Mapuche terms for brother and sister, *peñi* or *lamñen*. At this congress, once the new steering committee got elected, all of a sudden the slogan they shouted was "We will win (*Venceremos*), compañeros!" From that moment on there was no more peñi, no more lamñen; we were all just compañeros. And the people who were still afraid, or who were uncomfortable with this old leftist vocabulary, simply left the organization. The new style was like a strainer separating the wheat from the chaff.

JUAN: *At that moment—and we can be open about it, since it's already a part of history—I believe the Communist Party invaded and took over the Mapuche movement. That's when the social movement ground to a halt, because everything became more ideological. While the movement had been autonomous, its leaders were more fully able to visualize new political strategies that were in keeping with Mapuche principles and philosophy. Once everyone took on a more ideologically driven position, the earlier efforts were left hanging because everyone said geez, now that we're all together we'd better find our place in the right movement and on the political spectrum. At this point the Christian Democrats were also waiting for the right moment to get involved, not because they were particularly dedicated to the Mapuche cause, but because, like everyone else, they were raising their banner of struggle and wanting to expand their social base for the future. So when the Christian Democrats got involved, they competed with the Communist Party for Mapuche membership and the situation got really complicated.*

That was in 1985.

JUAN: *But already in 1983, when Ad-Mapu had its annual congress, the Christian Democrats had a meeting as well where they announced that they planned to create their own Mapuche organization, not with a Mapuche agenda, but with a Christian Democratic ideology.*

The Socialist Party also had a meeting, remember?

JUAN: *Of course, but at bottom it was the Communist Party that began this whole strategy of trying to co-opt the Mapuche social movement. That was the beginning of the end. And when I reflect on that period, and ask myself why did they take over our movement? For what purpose? I don't think there's an answer to that.*

F: *Well, maybe there's an answer if we look at the Party's internal logic, since at the time it was generally trying to expand its social base and the Mapuche movement was attractive because of its size, strength, and dynamism. But there's another aspect to your question, which is, how? Exactly how were they able to take it over? In any such process you can't just decide to take over. First you have to get your foot in the door, and that means that someone on the inside has to open the door at least a crack.*

That's true, and it's important to admit that our movement was both very strong and very weak at the same time. We were strong because our culture was reawakening, but also because people supported a long list of demands we'd drawn up, which mainly dealt with economic issues such as health care, the quality of education, more scholarships, housing subsidies, easier credit, dignified employment, all those kinds of things. These demands were shared by all the leaders, and had been taken up enthusiastically by the many local activists from the communities who came to the training sessions we offered in conjunction with the Indigenous Institute, CAPIDE, and the other NGOs who worked closely with us. These local activists interpreted our demands through their own agendas and economic situation. They, too, wanted to work, to get ahead, to travel. People had huge expectations and many dreams. In addition to fantasizing about a unified Mapuche movement, people fantasized about touring Europe. At one point rumor had it that anyone who traveled, to Europe or anywhere else, came back with their suitcases overflowing with money.

JUAN: *Yes, that was a discourse, a series of beliefs that political institutions were able to manipulate. And that's the answer to the "how" question, it's in the manipulations by the political institutions.*

They say that money can't buy you happiness, but boy does it help! This thing called money really helped, and continues to help, a great deal. But I believe that the Mapuche, as a group, just didn't know how to manage the little money they were given. We began accusing each other of taking more than our share; this or that one cut a deal; they saw a leader walking around drunk, or maybe he showed up wearing a new tie. The NGOs fueled the fire, saying, yes, Melillán left the country, he's in such and such place; Mario Curihuentro went over here, Isolde Reuque over there. And everyone would weave their own little strand into the story. The sad truth is that in comparison with what a single NGO received, the money we got amounted to little more than zero. We'd fight each other for the right to buy two or three sows for a particular community, so that they'd all be able to participate in a pig-raising project, or else over ideas to improve animal health. We fought over little projects, most of them under two thousand dollars; five thousand was considered a lot. Five thousand dollars was peanuts for an NGO; they'd get ten, twenty, thirty thousand dollars a shot, and they had several projects going at the same time.

F: *It would seem, then, that these tendencies were already present within the Mapuche movement, and that they came to a head with the January 1983 Congress. How did this happen? How and when did the political parties begin to infiltrate Ad-Mapu?*

As we've already discussed, several of our original leaders were already members of political parties. Melillán Painemal, for example, was a well-known Communist leader in the region until the 1973 coup forced him to take a back seat. Now, just because he was forced to break his connection to the Party didn't mean he stopped being a Communist. Don't get me wrong: if you asked him, he'd give you a very critical evaluation of his participation and his life in the Communist Party. Because he was so pro-Mapuche, the Party discriminated against him, that's well-known. But nothing could erase the label, the stamp he had engraved on his forehead, that read "Communist Party." Still, he was there from the beginning, as was this man from Galvarino who was a well-known Conservative, a right-wing leader. From the Christian Democrats we had a retired policeman, Manuel Cheuque Huenulaf. Another of our original leaders was also a Christian Democrat. Another well-known leader was José Luis Huilcamán Huaiquil, from Lumaco, who'd run for a municipal council seat on the National Party (*Partido Nacional*) ticket during the Popular Unity government, but made an agreement with the Socialists so they'd also vote for him. But then the right didn't want him anymore, because after being elected by them he'd switched sides and joined the Popular Unity coalition. That's why, even though he was a prominent and well-known leader, his nickname was "the Fox."

F: *So initially, were these leaders who'd already been active in political parties still committed to the unity of the Mapuche movement regardless of party labels? What was different about the leaders who arrived around 1983?*

For those of us who started out in 1978 and kept at it until January 1983, it was really different. We were committed to unifying the communities, strengthening and promoting Mapuche culture, rediscovering our identity and getting back to our roots. Ad-Mapu ran smoothly, with no internal divisions, from 1980 to 1983. Sure, there were arguments, doubts, disagreements, but not along party lines. We had people from every political tendency, Christians and non-Christians, a bit of everything. Beginning in 1983 things moved in the direction of class struggle. Instead of focusing on our demands as an oppressed nation (pueblo), we got swept up in the social demands of the broader society. And that's when Ad-Mapu began to fragment, with smaller groups splintering off to form their own movements.

In January 1983, the so-called syndicalists (gremialistas) lost the election. We gave it everything we had, but the odds were stacked against us. According to our statutes, an outside observer had to be present at each local election for delegates to the national congress, and the person designated to play this role in the statutes was the General Secretary. This meant that I should have been present at every local election, not to decide who the delegates were, but to act as an official observer. Given the number of local branches in our organization, however, obviously we had to form teams that would play this role. We decided that all the national leaders, plus a few provincial leaders, would serve as observers, and up to this point everything was going fine. But then we began to notice that everywhere I went to preside over the elections, or when Melillán Painemal was the observer, right behind us came folks who were not official observers, people like Santos Millao, Domingo Jineo, and Lucy Traipe. Or José Huilcamán's son Aucán would show up, or Eusebio Painemal or Jorge Pichiñual, and they'd talk with the people who'd been elected. If the delegates refused to cooperate with them, they'd simply name new ones.

When we arrived at the Congress that year, we found that a lot of delegates had been replaced. When these shadow teams hadn't been able to move the delegates to their side, they'd told them the date had been changed, that the Congress had been postponed until March. Then they'd go to their hand-picked supporters and say, "You go, and when you get there tell them that you're the alternate." Our Congress that year was made up of sixty percent alternates! Some of these people who caused problems in the communities had received support from NGOS, or perhaps it was from individuals who worked for specific NGOS, because when I confronted the NGO directors they insisted they had no idea what was going on. But they thought some people had requested assistance through their agricultural technicians. They'd said they had to get to meetings, and the cars had been loaned out as a show of solidarity.

Our unity as Mapuche ended with this Congress. The new steering committee elected at that point, headed by José Santos Millao Palacios, put an end to our earlier strategy of fostering autonomy in Mapuche communities and substituted a strategy of political and social struggle. This new line involved confrontation and class conflict, not the cultural strategies we'd used when we'd helped organize palin, gillatun, epeu, and music festivals. Street marches and demonstrations took the place of cultural events; the organization's resolutions were now presented as social demands. What before had been community needs became nonnegotiable social rights. Phrases like "we request" were replaced by the harsh bark "we demand." So from that moment, our way of facing non-Mapuche society was transformed into clash and confrontation. It didn't matter that some of our fifteen-hundred member communities might pull out; and in fact, some communities did pull out of the organization when we were no longer part of the steering committee. Many leaders left, and entire communities were left wondering what the future would bring.

Despite all the rumors, accusations, and manipulations, I have to say that a lot of people still voted for me. The nine people who received the highest percentage of votes became part of the national leadership, and the president, secretary general, treasurer, and other national posts were distributed among them. I received the tenth highest number of votes, which to me seemed pretty impressive after all the public criticism I'd received at the Congress. My annual report, for example, had been thrown out because they said it was a term paper rather than a political-administrative document. They said it had been individually produced by me, as secretary, and was not the collective product of the steering committee. Some of the people who'd worked with me on the old steering committee agreed with this position, and were in favor of the political changes going on. Among these were José Luis Huilcamán, Aucán's father; Miguel Landero, whom I understood to be very good friends with Melillán Painemal; and Rosamel Millamán, a young Mapuche anthropology student. Rosamel was really combative, he had a confrontational political style. But he wasn't a good street fighter, if you know what I mean. He was at his best in the meetings, writing up documents, signing declarations once positions had already been worked out. He wasn't the kind of guy who did grassroots work in the communities. He was more of an armchair intellectual.

F: *Now, this change in Ad-Mapu must have been a very painful, frustrating, and bitter experience for those who left the organization at this point, no?*

For me it was absolutely horrible. It was a real blow in the sense that the dream I'd nurtured, that I'd yearned to share with so many of my people, of the Mapuche people I'd gotten to know and to love since 1978, was suddenly shattered. All the faith and hard work people had put into our broad and inclusive organization, into that movement that accepted them unconditionally, was blocked. For me, accepting this was a long, painful, and difficult childbirth that lasted a couple of years. I left the organization, pretty much automatically, in March 1983. To go to the office and talk with the new leaders was terrible, because they'd make fun of me and say sarcastic things. "So," they'd say, "you thought you'd still be here but you're not. So you got a few sympathy votes, so what?" Because of my high vote percentage I ended up on the accounting and discipline committee, but I only managed to draft one report before I just had to leave for good.

Having moved in with my husband in March 1983 gave me a convenient pretext to stop participating in the organization, but the whole experience was psychologically so hard on me that I had to seek professional help. Within Ad-Mapu two defense groups had formed, trained paramilitary brigades that could handle chains, clubs, Molotov cocktails, and other weapons. These brigades were intended as bodyguards and were trained by leftists who had experience in these things. Personally, I never had anything to do with these groups, but one of them actually interrogated my husband. It was a truly baffling, terrible time, and it's important that this information finally become public. Then the harassment and persecution began, and I was attacked for being a woman close to the Church and to the Christian Democrats. They branded me a Christian Democrat, even though at the time I had no idea what that actually meant. So much so that I'd received the written platforms of the Socialist Convergence and of the Socialists before I ever saw the Christian Democratic platform. And in fact I didn't join any of them!

I tell you, this experience cost me so much suffering. I'm a romantic woman, full of hope. I have a lot of guts, but I've also felt a lot of frustration. In fact, my greatest frustration in my struggles for my people was this, the destruction of the organization I'd helped build. And I think I blamed the political parties, some of which I had deeply respected, even though I didn't know them well. I always said, I won't be a Communist. I can respect their views, but I'll never join them. I said the same about the National Party. The others, I didn't feel I really understood. I liked the Socialist Party—the Party for Democracy (PPD) didn't yet exist—and the Christian Democrats attracted me because of their humanist and Christian values. But I didn't really feel a part of any of them. So it was very discouraging.

Though my distress wasn't the same as what my brothers and sisters felt in the communities, theirs was also very great because, when I resigned, many of them also pulled out of the organization. I had a really close relationship with many of them, a strong mutual commitment, and they helped me stay connected to the movement. The community of Llamuco, for example, in Cajón, left with me. Part of Licanco, our local branch in Boyeco; Launache, located in Cholchol; in Freire, the whole district of Huilío, twenty-three communities—all of these locals resigned when I did. I think it shook us all up.

I kept talking with the leaders in these communities; I stayed in touch with them, and I lived my daily routine in my own community. I was trying to be a housewife, but I still traveled around to the communities. It was hard for me to stay home, you would've had to tie me down! Besides, even if my husband Juan and I were no longer in Ad-Mapu, we couldn't distance ourselves from the communities. Sometimes I think we worked harder than any of the leaders who'd stayed in the organization. We were already living on this lot, in Temuco, in an old house that was here before and that served as the headquarters for meetings and as a refuge. People arrived and slept over if they had to go to the hospital. They'd stay up talking to us, telling us their problems, and about how the organization was declining in their communities. We also went out into the countryside, to Boyeco, Licanco, Cajón, and planted apple, peach, and plum trees, cherry trees, too. The cherry trees we took from around my parents' house, about a hundred saplings. The rest we ordered and paid for, mainly from the Angol nursery, in order to maintain our ties. We worked with bees and set up training programs. We got there on foot or hitched a ride when we could.

Working with the Church's family program we also got paid for transportation and had connections with local church people, and we got to talk to people about their right to participate. We connected to the Church human rights movement, to the National Institute of Rural Missions (*Instituto Nacional de Pastoral Rural*). We found a television and an electric generator and toured the communities showing movies and talking about people's rights in the countryside, about participation, the right to vote, about respect. One thing a lot of people wanted to talk about was the problems they'd had selling pine trees. Outsiders would come and buy pine trees in the Mapuche communities, and they'd say, "Look, I'll take the first truckload and the second, and I'll pay you when I come for the third load." So they'd take the first bunch, and with the second load maybe they'd pay for half the first, but they wouldn't show up to pick up the third or fourth, and they'd never pay. They'd leave people with a few branches scattered on the ground. All kinds of injustices were going on in the countryside, and we'd encourage people to do something about it, to present complaints. So we kept a close connection to the communities in that period. My brother-in-law and Juan made connections through the sports clubs. They'd go to almost all the tournaments because there they'd talk to people about human rights. Or else the communities themselves would send us a message, telling us we absolutely had to go to such and such a place on a given day. Every event was an opportunity to talk about the return to democracy, that democracy we all yearned for and which, as someone recently said, was like a beautiful but elusive woman who continues to evade us still today.

Can you imagine the responsibility resting on my shoulders, as a woman, as a young woman? I'd been the youngest member of the *Centros Culturales'* original steering committee, the same in Ad-Mapu. I was a Christian woman who believed in a Supreme Being who loved us all, but the crisis of 1983 even made me doubt the existence of God. I began to reflect on the road I'd taken that day, back in September 1978, without having sought it out, but willing to accept it because of the longings I was feeling for my people. At first I said I'd only stay a short while. On September 12, 1978, I asked the plenary to appoint me Secretary General only until the end of the year. I thought I wouldn't be necessary after that point. But things turned out differently, and the road that opened up before me took me to places and experiences I would have never known had I continued to study elementary education, which was my goal before I got involved in the Mapuche movement. As a result I got to know my own country, practically the entire VII, IX and X regions—their communities, their roads, their people. I got to know the indigenous peoples of northern Chile, when in 1980 our Mapuche steering committee traveled north to motivate and to express our solidarity with our Aymara brothers and sisters.

As my knowledge of the Mapuche people and of other indigenous peoples in Chile expanded, taking me even to Easter Island, it opened doors for me I never even dreamed were there. I gave presentations at the country's most important universities and institutions, exchanging ideas on an equal basis, even if we were different, with many scholars and well-known people. We discussed topics as diverse as economics, religion, literature, mathematics, and ecology. I got to travel internationally. First I went to Argentina—to Zapala, Neuquén, Cipoletti, and Río Negro. My second trip, in September 1979, was to Bogotá, Colombia, where I participated in a conference of international jurists on the issue of human rights among Andean communities. The topic was closer to the experience of the peoples further to the north than it was to us, but nonetheless I was able to learn a lot about the rights of indigenous peoples throughout South and Central America, and about other countries as well. It turned out we had many issues in common, diverse strategies, and lived in a variety of distinct climates and environments.

After Colombia, I went to Australia via Temuco, Santiago, Easter Island, Tahiti, Papeete; then Fiji to Sydney, and from there to Canberra. To be in Canberra, the capital of Australia, to meet with the university students and with the government; to be in Sydney, where they make so many famous movies—these were experiences I never even dreamed of having. To spend time with Australian native peoples, to learn about the ways in which our Australian brothers and sisters struggled for their right to the land, and used their art and their writing to further their cause. I learned how the mining industry was destroying indigenous lands and how, when the government relocated the native people who still lived a simple life, walking around half-naked, even though their new houses were pretty and had kitchens and other modern conveniences, our brothers and sisters couldn't adapt because they felt trapped outside their habitat. To be in Australia's government palace in 1980, with our brothers and sisters from other parts of South

America at the Third World Conference of Indigenous Peoples, was a once-in-a-lifetime experience. Now obviously, we all tend to gravitate toward the people we have most in common with, and that meant people from countries near our own. But we also shared with others from all over, and we took a tour through Queensland, Darwin, Wood, and other places I can't remember, and got to know more about the struggles and strategies of the local native peoples. We visited the government offices that had been established to assist our native brothers and sisters in their social, political, and legal battles. We were able to see how, despite very different life experiences, we had many problems in common, like defending our rights to the land, to our languages and styles of dress; and that our ways of seeing the world, our spirituality, our art had more in common than we might have thought.

I returned to Chile in March, only to get back on a plane in September and fly to Geneva to take part in a discussion of indigenous land rights at the United Nations, as part of a working group that included people of all colors, languages, and political inclinations. To sit there and make a statement, to talk and carry out interviews with people—the learning involved was truly amazing. As a distinguished visitor from Chile, I gave presentations to unions, cultural centers, theater groups. I met with Chilean exiles, with activists from youth groups, solidarity organizations, students, clergy. The rooms were always full, never less than fifty people; it was a world I had never imagined. After Geneva and Zurich, I went back to Chile thinking, as always, that it would be the last and most beautiful trip I'd ever take as a representative of the Mapuche cause. But this was only 1980.

In 1981 I had the chance to travel again, this time to Peru and Bolivia. These trips were my best school, because I got to know so many of my indigenous brothers and sisters and to understand their struggles. It was wonderful to see how other peoples lived, but it was also sad when you realized how much they lacked and how hard they had to fight. Afterwards I went back to Chile and toured the universities one more time, realizing that times were changing and the political climate was changing, too. Then in 1983 I thought my dream had ended, everything I'd learned and the things I'd fought for. I knew that what I had inside me no one could take away, but I was sure I'd never again travel outside Chile because I'd left the organization. Yet suddenly, unpredictably, an invitation fell into my lap.

I'd written a letter to Ramón Daubón, who worked for the Inter-American

Foundation, telling him more or less what I'm telling you now, how frustrated I felt. "You met me," I wrote. "You know I'm defiant and full of spunk, but I feel like a big, fat zero. I'm on the verge of saying that I never want to be involved in a Mapuche organization again. After all the effort I put in, learning the language, understanding the world of the communities and Mapuche views of the cosmos, it's all come down to this. Democracy is still so far away." I'd abandoned my university education, against the wishes of my parents, and it was terrible to think this was all I'd gotten in return. Ramón Daubón answered my letter, and told me that they were planning a conference, that he'd try to get me a ticket to Santa Fe, New Mexico, for that conference of the OAS. Leaders from many places were going to attend, but I had no idea who else had received an invitation.

It was 1985 when I received the invitation to New Mexico, sponsored by the OAS, the Interamerican Indigenous Institute, and the Inter-American Foundation. I went with the idea of talking with Rolando Ramírez, who worked at the University of Saskatchewan, Canada, and telling him my version of what had happened. I thought for sure he'd be mad at me, that he'd have heard the rumor that I'd been thrown out of Ad-Mapu for being a snitch. I wanted to tell him my side of the story. We met in New Mexico, with Ramón, Rolando, and many others, and they all listened to my story. They told me that I'd confirmed what they already thought, that I'd been invited so that they could hear my version of events. You're a trustworthy woman, they said; you helped us a lot. The first letters from the south of Chile that we received during the dictatorship were signed by you. Suddenly I realized that I shouldn't stop organizing, and all that emotion I was carrying around inside me, hardening into a huge ball of frustration, could come out and become positive again.

I stayed in the United States for about a month. I was able to visit some indigenous communities, called reservations in the United States, getting to know the Navajos and the Hopis, traveling to the very edge of Colorado. I saw things I'd only seen before in movies, from Albuquerque to Santa Fe, the University of New Mexico. It was beautiful. I climbed a long set of stairs up to an old church that had been restored, a church from the time when all of that land belonged to Mexico and folks spoke Spanish, back when they were Catholics. I even visited some old movie sets! We drove into the Grand Canyon. People were selling jewelry there, necklaces, all kinds of things. I did everything I could on that trip, I didn't hold back or try to limit myself.

We spent a lot of time joking and laughing. Once, when we were driving along, we saw a machine digging out potatoes and another one picking and piling beans. I stood up on the bus and shouted, "Hey, guys, look! That's exactly how they pick 'em, how they beat 'em, where I live!" Of course everyone laughed, because obviously they knew we didn't even have machines like that in Chile. When we had to go to the bathroom, when we'd stop to pee, I'd say, "Here we are in Pichilemu, pretty soon we'll have to get to Chicago." Most of the indigenous brothers, whether from North or South America, didn't quite get what I meant, but they laughed like crazy when our translator, a young man from the Inter-American Foundation, translated for them. He must have embellished it, and no doubt something got lost in the translation; but I tried to explain to him that *si cago* in Spanish meant to have to poop; and that *pichi* meant to pee. And of course, to make it more fun, I combined the name of a city in the United States with one from Chile.

Everyone commented on what a zest for life I had. I think it was one of the very best trips I ever took, visiting in Colorado with my Hopi and Navajo brothers and sisters; touring a hydroelectric plant that was run cooperatively by both indigenous and nonindigenous people; visiting day-care centers. What impressed me the most when I visited the hospital was that the indigenous doctors wore their hair long. Native people in the United States wear their hair very long, in thick braids decorated with lots of artisanry. I also saw how many local offices and projects, from hydroelectric power to nuclear-waste facilities, hospitals to day-care centers, were co-administered by indigenous and nonindigenous people. I also heard my indigenous brothers and sisters express their grief over the loss of their wealth, of what was once theirs—of what was once ours. Because the government gives them subsidies, there's this place they have to go once a week, where they're on display like museum pieces. And yet somehow they maintain a sense of identity in the midst of such a crazy world, if only in the length of the hair or the cut and look of the clothes.

Letting go of all this, thinking I'd never be back, or maybe someday I would return—it was really hard. I asked myself over and over what I'd done to deserve such a wonderful trip. You've told me I'm a romantic, well maybe you're right, because in my mind I kept seeing the trailer trucks from the movies set in Colorado or New Mexico, the adobe houses. I'd heard so much about the Chicanos, and I got to stay overnight at the house of a

Chicano. I had the privilege of sharing the house of a Native North American. Walking up the adobe staircase to where the movie *Geronimo* was filmed, you felt a special energy when you got to the top. To come across medicinal herbs growing wild, and realize that we use some of the same ones. I had that feeling of discovery when, all of a sudden, I looked and thought, hey, this is rosemary!

At a very lively dance, where people were dressed in clothing full of colors, I met a Hopi woman whose whole family were silversmiths. In months past, at demonstrations protesting the placement of a nuclear-waste dump in her community, she'd spoken of the dreams she'd had, that winds from the south would bring new things, good news. We went to the ceremony where she presented the mural she'd painted, based on her dreams, to her community. It was a huge painting, about three feet wide and over five and half feet tall. It was taller than I am. When she uncovered it, I saw myself! Small details were different, for example, the woman in the picture wore a *xarilogko* with three flowers in front, whereas my xarilogko has only one. It was scary, but also moving. My Hopi sister talked about her painting, and obviously I didn't understand a thing, since she spoke in her language. The translation was first into English, then into Spanish, so I got it third hand; but it was clear she was very moved.

We were so much alike. The dress, the chamal she wore, was a lot like ours, only the ribbons we wrap around our head they let hang down their backs. They're the same color, though, even the same width. We measured them to make sure! The *xariwe* they use, the belt; many of the things and the colors are a lot like what we wear. She was a short Hopi woman with a broad, weathered face and a wide, stocky body. So we understood each other very well! There she was, at the front of her community, all gathered to receive us with tacos. That was really the week of the taco. We ate tacos everywhere for ten days, even though at first I had no idea what a taco was. With so many tacos, we'll end up like pancakes, all battered up, I said jokingly; but they were delicious.[10]

My Hopi sister's grandmother had given her a ring when she got married, and she gave that ring to me. She didn't give it to her sons, because they were all silversmiths. She had intended to give the ring to her daughter upon her death, but her daughter had died first. She had only sons and grandchildren left. She told me it was better that the ring ride with the southern winds, so she gave it to me. Since then I've hardly ever taken it off my finger. And in truth our whole relationship was very emotionally charged. She took me to the nuclear-waste dump and told me about all the horrible effects it had on her people. Of the fourteen of us from South America—among the Peruvians, Argentines, Colombians, Ecuadorans, and Bolivians, I was the only Chilean Mapuche—and among the Canadians, Guatemalans, and Mexicans who rounded out our group, almost no one wanted to go the dump. We all signed a collective protest, but everyone preferred to visit the hydroelectric plant, the hospital, the university, or the day-care center. Our Hopi sister really wanted us to see it, though; I think she needed our support. So I said I'd go, and a Peruvian brother went too.

This trip in 1985 gave me hope, and helped me believe that our movement had to go on, that it couldn't die just because people disagreed. Believing in diversity means learning to live with it, learning to respect other ways of doing things, other opinions, other strategies for living in the world. The trip helped reinforce that part of me, which had begun to weaken, the part that believed in the right to differ, the right to disagree. And at a personal level, it was especially powerful to have met this Hopi elder, a leader, artisan, and fighter who had walked all the way to Washington, D.C., to support indigenous people's rights in the United States. When she gave me her ring, one of her greatest treasures, or at least a favorite that she was wearing when we met, she told me publicly the story behind it. It was an emotional, powerful, meaningful, and painful moment.

Here we were, two women, leaders in our communities, both on the verge of desperation because we felt there was nothing more we could do. She was struggling against the nuclear-waste dump, but felt that nobody was listening anymore. Even other folks in her own community had stopped caring about the nuclear-waste dump. They were tired of struggling; she was the only one who kept speaking out. As for me, I was so frustrated because my organization, the unitary movement, the most beautiful movement I'd dreamed and struggled for, had broken up. I grieved and yearned for my movement, the one I'd always said had to remain above political parties— not in the sense that people couldn't have party affiliations, but that the movement itself had to stay above the fray. Maybe people hadn't understood what I was saying, or maybe my political immaturity kept me from expressing myself clearly. Whatever the explanation, I felt desperate. And this woman, my Hopi sister, was herself so desperate that when she welcomed me—my visit, my support, my strength—even though she was seventy-some years old she gave me back much more than I could ever have given her. I thought to myself, "I'm still young, forty's still a long way off for me. Why do I despair, if this woman standing next to me is pushing eighty, she's more than twice my age, and here she is telling me there's still so much to do."

When I returned to Chile, about a month and a half later, everyone was organizing. So I returned with the idea of starting a new organization. It was a time when lots of people were leaving Ad-Mapu, and as they left they formed new organizations. Melillán Painemal, for example, formed his own group in 1985 and preserved the name of the Mapuche Cultural Centers. The Rewe Association, a socialist group, and the *Choinfolilche*, led by our old president Mario Curihuentro and José Luis Levi, were both formed at this point. As exiles began returning, they formed new organizations that tended to follow one of the Socialist lines, renovated and traditionalist, I think they called themselves back then: the *Lautaro Ñi Ailla Rewe*, led by Juventino Velásquez and Ramón Chanqueo; and the *Kallfulikan*, led by Camilo Quilamán. By the end of that year José Luis Malequeo and don Juan Conejero also founded another Rehue Association, this one in Lautaro.

Given how much was going on, Juan and I talked it over and decided we, too, should start an organization. The Christian Democrats had also announced that year that they were beginning an organization called *Pehuen-Mapu* that would gather up leaders of Christian base communities, people like us who had stronger connections with the Catholic movement. I waffled back and forth about it, but it seemed a good place to be since we already had strong connections in a number of communities. So we talked with some of the politicians in Santiago, and they said they'd discuss the idea with some of the party faithful in the South, specifically with Francisco Huenchumilla, one of Temuco's more prestigious lawyers, and see if they could start something with a clearer Christian Democratic stamp. So they came south to meet with the Institute for Free Labor Development (*Centro de Desarrollo del Trabajador*, or CDT), to a series of meetings sponsored by the U.S.-based trade union, the AFL-CIO.[11] They ran some workshops and met with union and Christian Democratic leaders and, initially without much enthusiasm, they decided to begin organizing a group with the Mapuche folks who were already in the Christian Democratic Party.

Isolde in 1991, while visiting a friend in Santiago. *Courtesy of Isolde Reuque.*

Isolde's parents, doña Martina Paillalef and don Ernesto Reuque, in their garden in Chanco, their community, in about 1979. *Courtesy of Isolde Reuque.*

Isolde in 1979 at the Pastoral Center attached to the Temuco dioceses, participating in a meeting of Mapuche leaders of Christian base communities. The leaders are reading *Solidarity*, a human rights publication put out by the Vicariate of Solidarity, which Isolde was distributing. The cover story of the issue they are reading concerns the recent discovery of a mass grave of peasants from the central region at Lonquén. Sitting next to her is José Luis Huilcamán, leader of Ad-Mapu in the 1980s and father of Aucan Huilcamán, today the leader of the *Consejo de Todas las Tierras*. *Courtesy of Isolde Reuque.*

The founding leaders of the first social and ethnic movement created by the Mapuche people during the dictatorship, known first as the *Centros Culturales Mapuches de Chile* (1978–1980) and then as Ad-Mapu (1980–1987). Sitting in front is Mario Curihuentro, President; to his left, Melillán Painemal, Treasurer and Vice-President of the World Council of Indigenous Peoples; to Painemal's right, Isolde Reuque, Secretary. *Courtesy of Isolde Reuque.*

Isolde in Sydney, Australia, at the Third Congress of the World Council of Indigenous Peoples (1980), with an Otavaleño member of the Ecuadorian delegation. *Courtesy of Isolde Reuque.*

Isolde and Melillán Painemal posing with friends they made in Fiji during their return from the Third Congress of the World Council of Indigenous Peoples. *Courtesy of Isolde Reuque.*

Isolde during one of her visits to indigenous communities in Galvarino county in 1981. *Courtesy of Isolde Reuque.*

Isolde and Melillán Painemal at the National Congress of Ad-Mapu in January 1983, when they relinquished the leadership of the organization to a new political faction. *Courtesy of Isolde Reuque.*

Isolde and Juan Sánchez Curihuentro at their wedding, June 21, 1983. To Juan's right stands his mother, doña Graciela Curihuentro Turra. *Courtesy of Isolde Reuque.*

Isolde and Juan dancing at the reception the night of their wedding. *Courtesy of Isolde Reuque.*

Isolde, months after her wedding in June 1983, at a meeting of Fotem Mapu, an organization of Mapuche migrants to Santiago. *Courtesy of Isolde Reuque.*

The 1986 National Congress of Nehuen-Mapu, the Christian Democratic Mapuche organization. Isolde sits to the right of the speaker and President of the organization, the late Mario Millapi. *Courtesy of Isolde Reuque.*

Meeting of the National Congress of Indigenous Peoples, Temuco 1991, on the last day before submitting the conclusions that would become the basis for the Indigenous Law. In the first row, straightening his badge, is Isolde's brother Lionel. Isolde is sitting in the aisle seat of the second row, and her sister Elvira, wearing a hat, is directly behind Lionel. *Courtesy of Lily Reuque.*

Around the same time, in November, the various university student federations began to discuss their yearly summer work projects. The Confederation of Chilean Students (*Confederación de Estudiantes de Chile*, or CONFECH) was made up of people from all the political parties, but the president and the secretary were Christian Democrats. The president and vice-president of the Catholic University branch, Tomás Jocelyn-Holt and Delia Del Gatto, were also leaders of the Christian Democratic youth. So we decided, OK, the CONFECH's summer work project will be in the IX Region, and it will be with Mapuche peasants. Isolde can contribute her connections in the communities. In December, before the whole of CONFECH was to arrive in Temuco, we got together to plan it all out.

In the last days of December 1985 the CONFECH appeared in Temuco to plan for the arrival of three thousand students, more or less, who'd get here in January. That was a huge number, it was going to be a flood of university students. People from CONFECH arrived with the names of contact people written on little slips of paper, and one of those papers had my name on it. They came to give talks explaining the program and purpose of the summer work projects, and why the CONFECH had decided to come here and establish links with the region's Mapuche population.

In the first days of January 1986 a big meeting was held in the Temuco Diocese. Ad-Mapu showed up, represented by Santos Millao, who arrived carrying a spear, a xuxuka, and with an animal horn draped on a sash across his chest, ah? The only thing he lacked was a headband with feathers. He arrived at the head of his group, flanked by a flock of women and a group of young warriors who served as bodyguards. In those days he never went anywhere with less than six women, and four to six warriors carrying palin sticks, well-fed young specimens of Mapuche masculinity! He'd arrive dressed in regular street clothes, but he'd be carrying a suitcase. Right before things got going he'd stand up. Somebody would hold the suitcase open for him, and between him and his helpers they'd push and pull and tie on his get-up. It was a real show, a spectacle, a triumphal parade. Everyone turned around in their seats and stared.

Juan and I came in afterwards. A well-known friend of ours, René Inostroza, who worked at the Cooperative radio station (*Radio Cooperativa*) and later became a popular singer, was sitting there and I slid in beside him. We sat there gossiping. Hey look, and these people are going to host the students from CONFECH? I told him, "Hey, did you hear that the kids asked me to cooperate with them, they came to Temuco and with Juan we agreed we'd help them in any way we could." I guess I was naive, as usual. Juan insists he wasn't taken in, but we'd both agreed to work with them. Silly me, I thought I'd just help them out with a few things, the food, contacts in the communities, whatever. And that's what I told René as we sat there watching everyone and commenting, "Look, I've never seen these people in action, aren't they good-looking, sharp-talking, really political kids."

And then suddenly Francisco Huenchumilla, today a congressman, stood up and said, "It's fine for Ad-Mapu to help host the CONFECH, but we Mapuche with Christian sensibilities have an organization of our own, called Nehuen-Mapu. And our person in charge of hosting the summer work project is Isolde Reuque, one of Nehuen-Mapu's national leaders." Can you believe it? I broke into a cold sweat and René kept saying to me, "Get yourself together, woman, you look like you're about to faint. Get a grip, or I swear I'll pinch you." I didn't know what the hell to do. And Juan was over in the other corner, talking with the kids from the other organization we were supposedly going to join.

JUAN: *At that point, to top it all off, I was trying to work with José Luis Levi.*

That's right, the plan had been to join José Luis Levi's new organization that was also forming at that moment. I was so mad, I nearly peed in my pants! Truth was, I'd gone to one of Nehuen-Mapu's meetings, a conversation we'd had in Francisco Huenchumilla's office. Juan had been there, too. Huenchumilla had told us we should really consider joining Nehuen-Mapu, and we'd said we'd think about it. That was it. I never said I'd join. But now I couldn't do anything or say anything, because as René was telling me, if I spoke then and said no, I'd be dead in the water. It would be the end of my political career, because they'd start saying women couldn't be trusted. René even said that if I said no, I'd make him look bad, too! But I told him I'd never been a part of Nehuen-Mapu. "Be quiet," he told me, "this is going to be a really important political activity. The arrival of all the students is going to have an impact at the national level." "It could be," I said, "but I'll be burned if I'm branded a Christian Democrat!" "Details, details," he answered.

What could I do but leave the meeting and go to Huenchumilla's office, with every intention of giving him a good scolding. I went to Pancho's office immediately. Juan went with me and one or two more people, I don't remember who. I told him I wasn't a member of Nehuen-Mapu, that I never had been, etc., etc. He protested that, when the president of the CONFECH went to my house to ask if we'd help with the summer work project, we'd said yes. Now I had agreed to work with them, but working with the CONFECH was not working with Nehuen-Mapu. At least that was my naive impression. From that moment on I had a sign pasted on my forehead, another on my back, a pair of huge antennae coming out of my head, all screaming "Christian Democrat!" What could I do? I was a Christian, that was true. Everyone said the Bishop was my godfather, and all that garbage. I'd never denied that I got my start in the rural base communities. Every time someone threw it up in my face, used it as a joke or to hurt my feelings, I'd say, "Yes, it's true, and I'm proud of it. I consider it an honor to have started in the Christian communities." So I didn't have a problem with that part.

So I ended up staying. I became a member of Nehuen-Mapu and served as the director of the student work project that summer. I turned up on the national steering committee of a group that hardly existed, except in the minds of a few intellectuals. At the same time you couldn't say it didn't exist, since a number of well-known and prestigious regional leaders were involved, including Francisco Huenchumilla, Víctor Hugo Painemal, and O'Higgins Cachaña. In addition, grassroots community leaders were trying to form Pehuen-Mapu, also associated with the Christian Democratic Party but following the "pot-bellied" line (*línea guatona*) instead of the "long-haired" tendency (*línea chascona*) that Nehuen-Mapu followed. So I stayed with Nehuen-Mapu. I appeared in the newspaper and in the public statements that Francisco Huenchumilla or the CONFECH leaders made. There was no turning back. And in a way I belonged there, since I, too, was and am still inspired by the humanistic and Christian principles the party espouses. And, of course, all our supporters in the communities immediately joined Nehuen-Mapu as well. Within a week we had popular bases of support all over the region.

JUAN: *It was a grassroots base, solid and strong, with lots of people. It became the second Mapuche organization with a large social base, and this cut Ad-Mapu's ego down to size, because until then they hadn't allowed political or social activity outside their control. But with the rise of Nehuen-Mapu, Ad-Mapu could no longer claim to be the only, the genuine, the authentic organization, and they had to give space to others. Santos Millao and company were forced to recognize the existence of another Mapuche movement, not because it was called Nehuen-Mapu or was Christian Democrat, but because it had broad grassroots support. So, for example, when the three thousand students arrived to work with us for the summer, we said to Santos, OK, let's split 'em right down the middle, fifteen hundred each, eh? We began talking from that position, though sometimes it was hard to find places for so many students in the communities because you had to talk to the people first. But in the end it worked out really well, because the groups we placed—and at that point they stayed two weeks—were always well-received and well-fed, and we came out better in the final evaluation the kids did.*

Because, in fact, our grassroots supporters were more closely tied to the cultural politics that formed a part of the Mapuche movement. At this point Ad-Mapu chose to take a much more ideologically correct line, less action and more politics. Our effectiveness at the local level was proved when the mayors in Gorbea and Freire, uninvited, tried to take advantage of the summer work project and manipulate it to their own advantage. We stepped in, with the kids' support, and carried the day. So folks in Ad-Mapu saw we meant business and had strong local support, and its reputation began to go down while ours began to rise. This was really positive for Nehuen-Mapu as an organization, because until then people perceived our community work in personalistic terms. The community of Boyeco, they'd say, that's controlled by Isolde Reuque; Cajón, Launache, and Llaullamen—all Isolde Reuque's. That's exactly the way people used to talk about Melillán Painemal. But with the summer work project it stopped being that way. When people mentioned Llaullamen, Launache, and others—Nehuen-Mapu, they'd say.

People got to know what Nehuen-Mapu stood for because we put out a leaflet. We didn't have the wonders of computers back then, just a small typewriter I punched on with two fingers. This leaflet had sort of the platform of Nehuen-Mapu, which served us until the by-laws, which Juan and I mainly wrote in any case. Most of the people who made Nehuen-Mapu, who initially joined it, were Juan's and my families, and our closest friends from the city and the communities. So even though Nehuen-Mapu initially took shape and was branded as a Christian Democratic organization, it was our presence that gave it strength, clarity, dynamism, and direction. People usually say, oh, that was Isolde. But it wasn't so much me, it was me and Juan. We'd worked together in the countryside, in the Catholic family groups; in all the work we did together we had a strong bond.

JUAN: *But at the same time we were fairly naive . . .*

I'd say we were just plain stupid, because I had this well-scrubbed, shiny-faced attitude, you know. I didn't think there was a double meaning behind every tree. I didn't think about corruption, I thought people were honest. I'll be straight with you. Do you know why I got so frustrated with Ad-Mapu? Because people lied, because part of the steering committee played both ends against the middle. I was there from 1978 to 1983, a national leader, General Secretary of the organization; and in the end, I had to do everything. Our President—now I'm going to dump on our President, such a nice man he was, really—but he liked to drink, and preferred to go out romancing the ladies rather than doing what he needed to do. And our

Treasurer, Melillán Painemal, was a gentleman who expected to have the room full and waiting for him when he arrived at a meeting, the table set. And who do you think cleaned up afterward?

When I was still Secretary General, Ad-Mapu had a project funded by the Inter-American Foundation, and it went really well the year I ran it, said the show-off. But the truth is that when I left and Santos Millao and company took over, no one knew where that money ended up. Lots of money got lost in Ad-Mapu; from the German Ecumenical Scholarships Program, one million eight thousand pesos vanished, which was tons of money! Our young kids who were studying were left in the lurch, without a cent. The Inter-American Foundation had set up a fund to run training workshops, some two million pesos, and that disappeared, too. Ad-Mapu's cash register was like a sieve! To top it off, remember that house we were able to buy? Whose name do you think appeared on the title? Not Ad-Mapu, but Mario Curihuentro and Antonia Painequeo, who were the President and the Pro-treasurer back then. They appeared on the deed as the private owners.

After I left in 1983 we started getting letters from Europe, saying that when I was on the steering committee they'd get letters telling them what was going on, but later all they got were requests for money, money, and more money. But the fact was that all kinds of rumors were circulating in Europe in the Chilean exile community, Mapuche and non-Mapuche, tales about me, about Melillán. People from the NGOs wrote that the Mapuche movement was falling apart, and that the NGOs were the only organizations working for a return to democracy so that all the exiles could return. It was a rumor mill, a competition to see who could do whom the most harm. It was a horribly difficult time for the Mapuche movement, especially for those of us who were leaders. People kept trying to yank the rug out from under each other.

The fragmentation was tremendous. Everyone's speeches kept claiming Mapuche unity as their goal, but in fact the Mapuche people as such no longer struggled together. Ad-Mapu fell into the hands of the leftist faction of the Communist Party, along with extremists from the MIR, which had been very strong in this region, especially among the Mapuche. It really scared me! With everyone breaking apart for ideological reasons, many Mapuche felt deceived and disappointed. After having wanted something different, something unified, people felt frustrated with the same old thing.

This was true in the countryside, too. I know because later on I got a chance to talk it over with people.

What we lost in this period was our ability to cooperate across political differences, our respect for diversity. It's something we'd managed to express in this or that demonstration, this or that meeting, but we weren't able to maintain it in the long run. It's something we still lack. This happened to us in the Mapuche movement. We weren't able to nurture our commitment to diversity within our own organization. Knowing that our neighbor was Mapuche, even if his thinking was different; even if she was more conservative or more progressive, or simply on the extreme within our own faction— somehow we didn't know how to give space to different positions. When people arrived with a possessive, sectarian mentality, they capitalized on a sense of discontent that was beginning to grow, because community lands were being divided and people were getting tired of fighting. They pushed the idea of party-oriented politics and ideological preferences as the new panacea. A workshop with the Socialist Convergence, a seminar with the Communist Party, a leadership training session with the Ránquil peasant association, today called Surco, another for our brothers and sisters from Arauco, Cañete, and Tirúa communities, run by militants from the Lota coal miners' union. And since each NGO had a different angle on the return to democracy, they also contributed to this general climate of factionalism, as during 1985 and 1986 more and more organizations broke off from our main trunk, which had begun as the Mapuche Cultural Centers and then became Ad-Mapu.

I don't know, maybe because of all these divisions and problems it was hard for me to commit to a political party. Nonetheless, I did stay with Nehuen-Mapu as an organization, and worked very hard with the 1986 summer work project. Between January and February we placed over three thousand students in the communities, students of all backgrounds and ideological stripes who came from all the political parties. Some of them went hungry, some more than others; they all had a great time. Temuco was flooded with students, shaggy-haired and bald, tremendously strong and full of energy. We worked hard that month and a half to put our organization on the national map, to make real something that had essentially started on paper. And the person who put meat on its bones, who made that summer project work, was once again Isolde Reuque. My dedication knew no limits—of time, money, or family—because when I put my mind to a task, I give it my all. When the students arrived by train at seven in the morning, it was I who greeted them at the station. I was also in charge of the speeches when the kids were distributed to the communities. As our organization grew stronger, we also began to make speeches in the street.

When the students left in mid-February, I also gave the good-bye speech in the name of Nehuen-Mapu. Any of the five leaders who were well-known, including Pancho Huenchumilla and Víctor Hugo Painemal, could have given the speech. But during our discussion—and I remember that, in those days, there were only a few of us but we discussed everything—Pancho pointed out that I was the one spending time in the countryside, in the communities, doing the work. "It wouldn't be fair," he said, "for one of us who has stayed in Temuco the whole time to give the speech." So I gave the speech in the Plaza Teodoro Schmidt, which we renamed the Plaza Lautaro. It's still called Plaza Lautaro today.[12]

Unfortunately, I didn't tape that farewell speech, because I felt deeply inspired by the moment. "Many of you," I began—as I looked out at the sea of faces, students sitting on their backpacks or resting in the grass—"will tomorrow be the ones who decide the destiny of this country. You'll be the politicians, doctors, teachers, engineers. You'll be in charge of the nation's public and private institutions. And when you get to a position of power, don't forget the time you spent among the Mapuche people, don't forget about our needs." When I think about that speech, I remember people who have since served in ministries and government offices, human rights and feminist organizations, even headed offices of indigenous organizations. They were all student leaders who participated with us that summer.

F: *It seems, then, from what you're telling me, that between 1983 and 1986 the opposition to the dictatorship became more radical, more divisive, and more violent.*

In all of Chile, not only in the Mapuche movement but also in the labor and social movements more generally, these were the most intense and difficult years. Unions formed, coalitions came together only to divide again. As one grew another fragmented; some tried to divide and conquer, others to bring more people together. The peasant movement revitalized over these years as well, expanding and becoming more active. What happened in the Mapuche movement was similar to what was going on in the rest of Chilean society. I think this was a period when people were searching to define their objectives and to unite around them. And it finally got to the point that people were so divided that they began to look around and say, hey, we'd better find a way to work together. It doesn't matter that you have your organization, I have mine and he has his. We need to pull together if we're ever going to reach democracy.

People began to think about this, so much so that, within a year of the summer work project, we were all prepared to find common ground. Around that time all of us leaders, including Melillán, Santos, Levi, Mario Curihuentro, and the people in Santiago who had followings, like Sofía Painequeo and Haroldo Cayún, couldn't look each other in the face. We saw each other as enemies! That was also the time when the *Consejo de Todas las Tierras* was forming, out of frustration, I think, in the face of all the divisions. So we decided to get together and talk. Nehuen-Mapu extended the invitation, and the Union of Domestic Workers (*Trabajadoras de Casa Particular*) kindly lent us their house. The idea was just to get together, talk a bit, look at each others' faces and accept each other, eat lunch together. We sought out funds so that no one would have to spring for the food, and we set a tentative agenda that included a discussion of autonomy, culture, unity, and land. The idea was to take stock of what had happened: how many communities had been divided, how many had not. We drew up a document to serve as a basis for discussion; if people agreed to its points, fine; if not, no problem, at least we'd gotten together. We gave the meeting a name, and from all the suggestions put on the table we chose to call it *Futa Trawn Kiñewam pu Mapuche*, which means "a big meeting for one Mapuche people."

We all sat together. I have the pictures to prove it! I had all my energy back by then, so I took pictures, talked, and taped conversations. At first people just looked at each other sideways, out of the corners of their eyes, almost without wanting to. They seemed to be saying, hey, don't ask me to sit next to that one. Then people began to talk, and out of this came a larger conversation that yielded a technical commission, including representatives from most Mapuche groups here and in Santiago. They got together with the already-existing Human Rights Commission to draw up a document. Ad-Mapu and Nehuen-Mapu didn't send representatives to this meeting, because as the largest organizations we felt we could come up with our own documents. Ad-Mapu worked with the Mapuche Cultural Centers to produce a single document, and Nehuen-Mapu also produced a single document. The rest got together in this technical commission and produced a draft document to be studied and presented in Imperial to presidential candidate Patricio Aylwin. This would later serve as the basis for the discussion around the Indigenous Law.

For those of us leaders who had been working since 1978, I think this was a very constructive period of reflection when we were once again able to assume the vision of unity we had started with, that sense of commitment to the demands, needs, and proposals that emerged from the Mapuche people as a whole. Our movement has grown a lot, and today the people in our various organizations—*Kallfulikan, Choinfolilche, Lautaro Ñi Aiña Rewe, Rehue de Lautaro, Keyukleayñ Pu Zomo,* or the Coalition of Mapuche Institutions (*Coordinadora de Instituciones Mapuches*)—go all the way from the original group of students who studied with the help of the German Ecumenical Scholarships Program I talked to you about to kids who over the years have gotten scholarships from the Ministry of Education, where today we've managed to increase the total to more than five thousand for Mapuche students. But there's something special about those of us who started in that first movement. We carry a mark, we take our identity very seriously. Even if for some of us it started out being skin-deep, over time our Mapuche identity became ingrained in the most profound part of our being, and we have this in common wherever it is that we work and struggle today. We are the ones who most passionately support the existence of a Mapuche nation, and who struggle for its formal recognition in the Chilean Constitution.

CHAPTER THREE

The Transition to Democracy

F: *Let's start with the plebiscite. How did you live the process in the region, and what did it mean that this was the only region in the country where the "Yes" won?*

Well, the plebiscite has already taken on the quality of a historical myth in Chile. But I think it was a great challenge for the Mapuche population. The population in general was contaminated by the military government's successful distortion of a series of concepts. The clearest example of this was how people thought about "politics." Through the municipalities and other public service institutions, the dictatorship made people think that the word "politics" was synonymous with Communist, terrorist, or extremist. Peasant folk in general, Mapuche and non-Mapuche, as well as people in the cities, developed a kind of fear of the concept of politics. So it was very difficult for people to open up politically.

On the other hand, the people who worked for organizations outside the government and the public service sector, like NGOs formed by churches, technicians, or professionals with common ideological or religious principles, did not do deep or unified political work in the countryside. Instead they worked on specific projects and training programs—orchards, vegetable gardens, chicken coops, some craft work, what people already knew. The truth is it wasn't new, it was telling people who already did artisanry, look you can market it over here. With orchards and vegetable gardens it was the same thing: the ones the community already had were enlarged or collectivized, and they would offer better marketing information, where the fairs were, where the goods moved better, where they moved worse. If a community had a tradition of singing, if they'd preserved the Mapuche language, then the NGO would provide motivation and assistance so people could express themselves culturally and artistically through dance and music. But there wasn't what you might call a sociopolitical commitment, in the sense of strongly supporting local grassroots organizations, and in some cases traditional community structures were not respected. Besides being oriented toward more practical matters, and doing a somewhat superficial job at that, NGOs competed for clients in the different neighborhoods, because this community was better organized, or that neighborhood had a leader who was more favorable to their ideological tendency or party line. Political, ideological, philosophical, even religious affinities helped determine who helped whom, who worked with whom. And that's why in places which were well organized, where people of different political tendencies and beliefs participated together, unity was quickly eroded when the NGOs arrived. They brought new things, I remember: what became really famous were water pumps and student scholarships. Besides that, plastic-covered vegetable gardens became popular. With new seeds you could promote intensive production all year round, it wasn't seasonal any more. They would bring sewing machines, an average of two machines per community, and would teach the women how to operate them. Then the machines, that were initially for the community as a whole, would be left for the one or two people who had the closest political connections with the NGO people. This type of selective assistance helped divide our Mapuche organization and produced divisions among those of us who were participating in an organized way against the dictatorship. Different currents of opinion began to emerge in the communities, and those of us who opposed Pinochet's Land Division Law found that our opposition to its promulgation began to weaken.

If it's true that the NGOs fractured the communities politically, it's also true that they counted out their funds peso by peso, and therefore picked their spots. They tended to prefer the easy-access communities, where costs were lower and where there already was a high level of organization, rather than those with an incipient level of organization and where the political challenge was often greater. Nobody went to the neighborhoods and communities where physical and political access was harder.

F: *Then the NGOs would not go to, say, Curarrehue.*

As a matter of fact, that's right; they didn't reach Curarrehue. They didn't reach Curarrehue, they didn't reach Lonquimay, these NGOs did not go to the farthest reaches of Villarrica and Panguipulli. Or Neltume, for example, a place off the beaten track in the foothills of the Andes mountains; these NGOs didn't go there, not a one.[1]

F: *Maybe the most adventurous ones would reach Puerto Saavedra.*

Well, yes, they reached Puerto Saavedra, Lumaco, Cholchol, Imperial. Why did they go there? Because people were better organized, they had a longer history of participation, and they had preserved traditional forms of Mapuche cultural organization that were different from other areas. On Isla Huapi, for example, or nearby in Puerto Saavedra, around there it was easy to find a palin team, and you could tell people, look, let's hold a palin tournament, we'll contribute the prize. It was easy, because there people play palin. You could tell people in Cholchol that you'd pay for transportation from Lumaco to Cholchol, to get a group of communities together, because in Lumaco all the communities play palin and each community has a team. Personally, let me tell you, I'll probably die before I get to see another tournament like the 1979 *chueca* competition in Lumaco, where more than forty teams participated and they all arrived with their machis, wagons, and wives, it was huge. Everybody was impressed, and there were speeches, vehement speeches in Mapuche, with the police right there and all.

So that's what I mean when I say the NGOs took the easy way out. Look, right around here near Temuco, if you go out Pedro de Valdivia Avenue, no one dared to organize. Why? Because it's too close to the city, access is too easy, people don't do gillatun anymore, they don't play palin, they don't want to dress traditionally. People no longer have a collective indigenous identity they can show publicly.

F: *What specific places are you referring to, what are their names?*

Well, Reloncoyán, Los Copihues, Chanquín, for example. Yet down the same road, some kilometers further along, in places like Boyeco, Conoco Alto, Conoco Bajo, Mapuche Catholic base communities had revived mapunzugun and traditions of solidarity, such as kelluwun. They built houses together, one helping the other, they'd teach newlyweds how to build. So this was a different, more culturally interesting, type of participation. And the NGOs arrived, three or four at a time. Facing Boyeco, on the other hand, where the Temuco garbage dump is, you'll find Tromén Alto. And no NGOs went to Tromén Alto even though it's right there, facing Boyeco. Contrast that again with Cajón, here where the highway by-pass goes through today, there's Cajón, Pidilliguin, Truf Truf, Tres Cerros, Llamuco, and these communities have certain characteristics. Lots of women artisans who do beautiful work, the *xarihue*, blankets, ponchos, many kinds of weaving. They practice intensive agriculture on a small scale and they're quite successful, plus they've kept their traditional horse-drawn wagons to travel to the city to sell firewood and buy supplies. These carts or wagons would arrive in the city in rows of ten, twenty, thirty at a time; they'd put on an interesting show when they pulled in. So these places, you see, have their own particularity, people don't have to be told look, why don't you get together, go back to using carts, go to town on horseback. They do it on a daily basis, it's how they live. So this is the kind of thing the organizations were looking for, that's why they ended up in these places.

Nobody went to Melipeuco, over there past Cunco, because people there were too scared. People migrated in search of work. Fifty percent of the men went to work in Argentina and the women were left alone with the children. Thirty percent went to work in the VII Region and in Santiago and came home once in a while. So there wasn't a sense of community, whether political, cultural, or emotional, and everyone looked out only for themselves.

So given all this, why did the "Yes" win in the region? Because the regime—with the help of television, which had reached most communities if only in battery-operated form; radio, which obviously did the same; with the special ceremonies they organized in every school, both urban and rural—had instilled a false patriotism, ah? Formal education was definitely under their control, and they imbued it with a hidden message full of *chilenidad*, patriotism, and I don't know what else, that was especially strong because it was hidden. So we could speak of formal education, but also, and very clearly, of a hidden education implicit within the formal education.

F: *But I'm still confused about the role of the NGOs in the plebiscite. Did the NGOs work for the "Yes," for the "No," or since they reached only certain areas, it didn't really matter what they did?*

The truth is I don't think the NGOs tipped the scales in either direction, because many weren't interested in winning votes one way or the other. Some did indeed work hard to influence the vote, but others never touched the subject. They were more interested in maintaining their presence in the community, their role as technical advisors, their friendship with people, and they weren't about to convert that friendship into a "No" vote, or try to explain the meaning of the vote. When push came to shove, neither the NGOs nor the Mapuche organizations could influence the vote in places where we had little presence and low levels of organization. That's why there were entire counties in which the "Yes" won.

Now, if you look at the first plebiscite in 1978, about the United Nations declaration concerning Chile's human rights record, we called that the "Yes or Yes" plebiscite, and not surprisingly the "Yes" won by a great majority. That's because a lot of people said, look, when you go to vote, there's a camera on the ceiling. If you vote "No," or if you deface your ballot, the cameras will catch you in the act. So in this second plebiscite it really was a "Yes" or "No" vote, people took it more seriously, you did have a choice. And that's why in some places it was very close, and even when the "Yes" won, it won by a hair. And more people talked up the "No" and acted as if they'd vote "No," than were actually able to vote for the "No."

F: *Well, the "No" won in Temuco.*

That's right. Now, just because the "Yes" won in the IX Region doesn't necessarily mean that it was primarily or exclusively the Mapuche who voted that way, because many non-Mapuches had received absolutely no information as to what the "No" meant. Of course there's a high percentage of indigenous population in the region, but there's also a large pocket of what I would call wealthy people, and many others work for them on their estates. They all voted "Yes," because it was preferable to losing their jobs.

F: *This would include the wigka poor (wigkas pobres)?*

That's right, but also the Mapuches who were working in that sector, they'd have to do the same thing. Today there are many people who recognize that this was the case. But to get to the point, I think the NGOs had real limitations, and the best proof of this is that, after the transition, many people who worked for the NGOs have said that they were better off economically during the dictatorship. The international support, the salaries they could make, were better than what they're able to get these days. Some of these folks are working in the public sector, for the regime in power, and they complain that they're not doing well. I've heard this from more than one person, and it startles and worries me at the same time.

F: *Perhaps we can talk a bit about the transition itself, if that's OK. Let's start with the accords the indigenous movement reached with the nascent Con-certación. I've heard people say that the agreements signed in Nueva Impe-rial are very important because they represent a new way of seeing the relationship between indigenous people and the Chilean state, and that the only reason they were signed was that the Mapuche movement demanded from the opposition groups who were managing the transition a new kind of voice and political space. What do you think?*

Let's see. The Nueva Imperial Agreement was a visionary political docu-ment that brought together all the indigenous peoples of Chile, which wasn't easy. Reaching agreement on all the points was extremely difficult within the indigenous movement. It took us a good couple of months, and even hours before the formal signing at Imperial, heated discussions were still going on.

F: *How did you make it to Imperial, then, what was the process?*

If you remember, we'd had that meeting in Temuco to try to achieve unity among all the different organizations with distinct political affinities, and out of that a working group was formed that collaborated with the Chilean Human Rights Commission. That happened after the plebiscite, because once it was clear that a transition was coming, we knew we'd have to do something. If the political parties were uniting at the national level, why shouldn't we be able to join our efforts? We, too, had to consolidate forces. So we had our meeting in Temuco, *Futa Trawn Kiñewam pu Mapuche,* a great assembly for one Mapuche people. At the first meeting we all shook hands for the first time in a while, because by that time we no longer considered each other brothers and sisters, not even adversaries, but ene-mies. In total we met about three or four times and even produced agree-ments on the usual issues—the fight for land, culture, autonomy, and par-ticipation. Once reminded that we had those points in common, we decided to move ahead.

We started communicating with the indigenous people of the north through the working group of the Human Rights Commission. José Bengoa and others who supported the movement offered their contacts as social scientists to help us communicate with the people up north, with whom we'd already been in touch since 1980, as well as with folks on Easter Island and further south. We reached a basic agreement at a first meeting held in Santiago, with everybody; and then we held conversations in Santiago with Patricio Aylwin, Enrique Correa, and others with diverse political positions from the Group of 24.[2] And we agreed to hold a ceremony here in the region, in Temuco or someplace nearby. Given that Temuco had recently hosted a very large women's demonstration (*mujerazo*), we thought we'd spread the wealth around a bit, though the place chosen definitely had to have a high concentration of Mapuche population. Imperial was chosen because it's one of the counties with the highest Mapuche population density, and besides it's connected by good road to Puerto Saavedra, Carahue, Cholchol, Lumaco, and Galvarino, so people could arrive without major transportation problems.

F: *Now, two questions about that. Reading* Nütram[3] *I found a public declaration of unity. Was that the result of the first meeting, a document in which the problem of unification was revisited? Then in another issue I also found a document in which the same organizations that signed the first one declared that the first meetings with the Human Rights Commission, regarding the discussion of an indigenous law, were not representative of the Mapuche organizations. Can you explain what happened there?*

Well, to begin with, that first document, the public declaration of unity, came out of our first meeting in Temuco. And the second declaration you mention was also made jointly, signed by all of us, because the Human Rights Commission had done something which was very common, and well, it's still very common, no? They seemed to have a hidden agenda, and had hand-picked the people they wanted to participate in their workshop. With this group of people they put out a document to serve as the basis for discussion of the Indigenous Law, and they wanted to present it to the united opposition parties in Santiago, what is today called the *Concertación*. Missing from the discussion were Ad-Mapu, Nehuen-Mapu, and the Mapuche Cultural Centers; participating were the Socialists who had left Ad-Mapu to form the Party for Land and Identity (*Partido de la Tierra y la Identidad*). So we rejected the document because it was not representative, it didn't come from all of us. And the people who'd worked with the Human Rights Commission agreed with us and also signed the declaration. They didn't take responsibility for the document, although they admitted they'd worked on it and put their stamp on it; and we were able to make them see that we didn't feel represented by it nor did we identify with it. Of course, we hadn't been able to see the document, and it wasn't possible to make it public before it was formally accepted. That document was nonetheless presented to the united opposition because it had good sponsors: José Aylwin, Eduardo Castillo, Enrique Besnier, plus one or two people from the Santiago human rights movement. These people were celebrities of a sort, whatever piece of paper they laid down would be received. We made up a document anyway. A very consistent one, too, as Nehuen-Mapu, with a much more polished narrative than theirs, so much so that they were forced to reincorporate our ideas and Ad-Mapu's ideas, and ultimately to revise their narrative to make it consistent with all of our suggestions. The final product took into account all the declarations we'd produced, and reflected the fact that we'd all participated.

F: *And that final document, which somehow managed to weave in all these different threads, was that the one presented in Nueva Imperial?*

It was indeed, and resulted in the first draft of the Indigenous Law, a little green book that still circulates here and there. This was in 1989 and, for better or worse, at that moment I headed the Coalition of Mapuche Organizations for the IX Region. Each organization and each leader wanted to sign the agreement, and they did. But because as head of the Mapuche Coalition it was my job to coordinate the event, I was also put in charge of security, with a team from the *Concertación*, the nonindigenous *Concertación*, obviously; and me representing the indigenous *Concertación*. There were four days of work surrounding the event, day and night, and it was very hard, because the leaders were still debating and arguing hours before the document was to be signed. But ultimately it led to the first commitment to the indigenous peoples of Chile, made with a presidential candidate who later became President, that was actually fulfilled.

Initially there were five major objectives. The first was for the President to study, plan, and submit to the Chamber of Deputies a law favoring indigenous peoples. The second was to create, with broad participation from the indigenous social movement and from all the indigenous peoples of Chile, an institution that listened to them and respected their rights and values. A third objective was the constitutional recognition of indigenous peoples. Another was to submit ILO's Convention 169 to Congress for approval. Patricio Aylwin attempted to fulfill all five objectives. That's why if today you speak to any Mapuche, they will all say look, the only president who has known how to listen to us and understand us is Patricio Aylwin.

F: *When I was in René Ailío's house yesterday, I noticed there's a picture of Patricio Aylwin on the wall.*

Sure. He appeals to the left, the center, and the right. Any Mapuche who's involved enough in politics to have a favorite president will speak very well of Aylwin when it comes to the indigenous issue. The same doesn't happen when folks discuss members of Congress, because it was not Aylwin's fault that the Indigenous Law came out the way it did. That was the result of negotiations. No thanks to the Congress if the Law's still good, recognizing the existence of the indigenous populations and peoples of Chile, because in truth when it was sent to Congress, it was Congress who cut it, and people are definitely aware of this. Like I said on several occasions, these members of Congress had very good scissors, machetes, and knives, and they can cut to the marrow whatever gets there. And what they left, as a result of their trimming, was the development fund, the land and water fund; what they left as a whole is not entirely good, because they cut off some of the most interesting articles in the original Law.

THE REUQUE-PAILLALEF FAMILY

F: *It seems to me, personally, that there are in fact two good things about the Indigenous Law. One, that it originated from an organized indigenous movement that demanded from the transition government a law; and two, that despite all the problems suffered in the past and the problems at that time, indigenous people participated in the discussion and formulation of the law. And that has great symbolic importance in my view . . .*

LIONEL: *Of course, it was a personal commitment made by don Patricio.*

F: *Well, I think . . .*

LIONEL: *As one of the most outstanding lawmakers at the national level, he set a challenge for himself as a person to inspire and include the Mapuche people, and in the end the Mapuches—and I include myself here—were unable to meet his challenge. I have a speech I'd like you to hear, in which I said good-bye to the citizens of Pitrufquén when I concluded my period as member of the municipal council, in which I say that the efforts of don Patricio Aylwin on one side, and the great efforts of the cacique Paillalef on the other, have fallen into the void. This has happened because people have not been capable of understanding their message, and have not known how to respond to the great effort these two men have made to benefit the community. Don Patricio did it on a national level, contributing in a way to the efforts being made on behalf of indigenous people throughout Latin America. He involved the people from Easter Island, didn't he; he involved the Atacameños; he even gave priority to those folks to the south, the ones who are almost extinct down there, who're only . . .*

LILIANA: *The Kawaskar.*

LIONEL: *The Kawaskar. He gave so many opportunities . . .*

LILIANA: *Well, that's what it's about, an indigenous law is for all the indigenous peoples.*

LIONEL: *. . . he gave his all on the issue, but then the Mapuche somehow couldn't understand him and we distorted things. Because we aren't immune to corruption, either. Mapuches are corrupt. They are corrupted by envy, there is envy among the Mapuches, they look down on one another. When a Mapuche manages to get ahead, whether through education or other means, other Mapuches, unconsciously perhaps, vow to bring him down and don't support him. In other cultures or races, when a person gets ahead others support him and encourage him to keep working. Here it's the opposite, I don't know where it comes from, I've tried somehow to look for an explanation, to understand where this envy comes from, this disdain . . .*

LILIANA: *We are not immune . . .*

F: *I don't think there's a group of people in the world who's immune . . .*

LIONEL: *Then why is it such a big deal, I don't know, I just don't understand . . .*

F: *Well, I see the relationship between indigenous peoples and don Patricio Aylwin a little differently. I have a lot of respect for don Patricio Aylwin, I*

*think he did very important things during his presidency, but I don't think
that even don Patricio Aylwin would have thought of an indigenous law if it
hadn't been . . .*

LILIANA: *If it hadn't been for the organization.*

ELVIRA: *Yes, for the movement.*

F: *. . . and besides, ultimately they did unite, didn't they? There was coordination, and all the indigenous peoples of the country were represented, although of course the Mapuche were the majority group, because numerically
they are the largest. But I don't know what you think. I think there really was
a kind of pressure . . .*

LIONEL: *I participated . . .*

ELVIRA: *The Law was the product of the indigenous movement, but after all
that participation the movement dwindled, it disappeared.*

LIONEL: *There was a lot of foreign influence. I participated in the work in the
communities, at the county and regional levels, and in the congresses that
were held in Temuco. I participated quite a lot in the discussions of the
Indigenous Law and I saw groups from other places conspiring and trying to
influence, maybe they were from the Latin American indigenous movement,
and maybe not just from Latin America, but from other places, too. So there
was a lot, a lot, of foreign stuff.*

F: *The other thing that I think is important about the Law is a recognition, at
the national level, that the whole country must respect and support the
existence of indigenous cultures and identities.*

ELVIRA: *Yes, in education the Law has served a lot.*

LIONEL: *The principles are there, it's true, but how to do it, how . . . That's
where you need directives, and those just aren't clear in the Law.*

F: *When reaching Nueva Imperial, when reaching the agreement that the
indigenous organizations signed with Patricio Aylwin that led to the Indigenous Law, did all of the movement's leaders agree?*

That same day, when we got together at the Methodist Educational Center, which was our rendezvous before proceeding to the ceremony itself,
Aucán Huilcamán arrived with a group of people who were still part of Ad-
Mapu. At the time, Aucán was still one of the national leaders of Ad-Mapu
and he was the only one who did not favor signing the agreement. Accord-

ing to him it was a pact of surrender, it was unclear; and so he left the discussion hours before the rest of us signed that visionary compact formulated by our leaders. From then on that fraction of Ad-Mapu became the *Consejo de Todas las Tierras.*

F: *According to an essay by José Marimán, the* Consejo de Todas las Tierras *is born from a disagreement about the plebiscite between the Socialists who had remained in Ad-Mapu—who were in fact Aucán's followers—and the Communist Party.*[4]

I really don't think so. Aucán Huilcamán was a national leader of Ad-Mapu, and when he left he held a national office in the organization, something like the head of Education and Development, I think. It's true that he left with the *Comandante* faction of the Socialists and a fraction of the Mapuche Communist Party, but it wasn't only or exclusively with the Socialists who'd remained inside. Because others who weren't active in Ad-Mapu became active in the *Consejo,* the so-called *Comanche* Socialists, and part of the MIR broke off from the main organization and joined the Consejo. Later on, the folks from the MIR broke off again and formed a new faction within Ad-Mapu. So Aucán was left with people who were mostly Comanche, and individuals from all over, folks who'd been at loose ends, unattached, dissatisfied with all the previous organizations, who then said, I'll stay with this one because it's more confrontational. And indeed the Consejo was more confrontational, its shock troops were a force to contend with.

F: *I'm still unclear on the reason for Aucán Huilcamán's exit from Ad-Mapu. According to Marimán, Aucán doesn't want to participate because of differences over the plebiscite. Just as the Communists in Ad-Mapu are in the process of affirming electoral participation, Aucán says that participating in a plebiscite that will be fixed is not the way to struggle against the dictatorship. This, then, would be the reason for the split.*

I think that's right. They were against the registration of political parties as well. They said no to registration, no to the plebiscite, they felt everything was fixed. They were against all forms of negotiation, they favored armed struggle against Pinochet. Let's not forget that this was a decisive period when people said all forms of struggle are possible, and armed rebellion was one of these possibilities. The *Consejo* chose rebellion and confrontation, and they've stuck to that same strategy. Now they were lucky to get a lot of good advice and technical assistance, as well as access to historical documentation, from Mapuche and non-Mapuche anthropologists, history professors, and others. They were able to document the treaties the Mapuche had signed with the Spanish government, starting with the famous Pact of Quilín. They got help from lawyers and researchers able to search the indigenous archives, held by INDAP-DASIN in those days, for all kinds of historical documents such as land-grant titles (*titulos de merced*).[5] They'd take these land titles to the communities that had suffered land usurpation, and they'd make militant presentations, agitating and calling for confrontation in the city and in the countryside, managing to elicit strong international support. With this strong international support they had the financing to transport machis and logkos, people in traditional dress who would appear here, there, and everywhere. And they'd come out against everything.

Around that same time the King and Queen of Spain came to Chile, and even though they stopped near Valdivia, we decided not to speak with the Queen, because we had nothing to say to them. This was even though the Mapuche people had been taken into account by the Spanish, for Spain had recognized the existence of the first peoples in the south of Chile and, when it could not dominate them, recognized their sovereignty. Speaking with them could have been a nice gesture and, after reminding them of our common history, we could have asked for their help with the difficult challenges we were facing at that point. But the interview with the king was declined. When we said no, however, the Consejo said yes. Of course later on we also agreed to the interview and went to Valdivia, and there the Consejo was, with bells on! When the King and Queen arrived they held interviews in their hotel. We barely got to see them from a distance. Aucán took the liberty of speaking with the King, shaking his hand, going in without an appointment, without asking permission. We had a scheduled interview and everything, and Aucán had nothing; but he had the presence of mind, the strength simply to show up and do whatever he had to do to talk to the King, even if it meant taking over the office of the hotel.

F: *Didn't the Consejo also boycott the negotiations around the Indigenous Law?*

Yes, it did. The Consejo disagreed with the compromise we made with don "Pato" Aylwin, that if he were elected President, as reciprocity he would create an institution to struggle for the rights of the indigenous peoples of Chile. The Consejo strengthened itself by criticizing Aylwin, saying he was just like any other wigka and wouldn't keep his promise to the indigenous people. After they refused to sign at Imperial, they wanted no further discussion. When we held two thousand and some odd meetings to discuss the content of the Law, the Consejo said they were not really discussions, that all we did was to present information to people, because in one or two hours you couldn't debate all the points to be included in the Law. I agree that we didn't discuss the document as a whole at every meeting, and often all that people did was to provide general information; but some meetings went on for two, even three days, even if the majority of the discussions lasted only two hours. I don't dispute the truth of their criticism, but the point is that the Consejo was never in favor of negotiations, never.

They didn't participate in the discussions, they contributed no information, even though José Bengoa met with them to talk about it—they were good friends—but still they didn't formulate a proposal. They boycotted the whole process: they weren't present at the signing; they weren't present during the first part of the Law's formulation. And yet the Law was drafted and signed without them, and afterward they questioned it again, saying that it did not represent them, and didn't grant constitutional recognition, which is something we question as well.

F: *Now, after Aylwin was elected, I read in the newspapers of the time about the Consejo's attempted land occupations, I think they were in 1991, right? One thing that really struck me, even more than Enrique Krauss's declarations as Minister of the Interior, which were particularly harsh . . .*

That they were going to cut off their hands as had been done to Galvarino,[6] and that they weren't going to cut off just one, they were going to cut off both . . .

F: *Yeah, but even beyond those things, probably said in the heat of the moment, what caught my attention was that a series of Mapuche organizations signed a public declaration supporting the human rights of the members of the* Consejo de Todas las Tierras, *and protesting the way they were being treated, kept in jail, in solitary, and all that. The declaration said something like, it's possible that we don't agree with the Consejo's methods, but we believe they must be granted the same respect accorded to any political leader. And this unitary document was signed by many Mapuche groups.*

Yes, we signed that document.

F: *How did that work? How did people decide to support an organization that, from the very beginning, had pulled in the opposite direction from the rest of you?*

I think we felt a certain complicity, like brothers who fight a lot among themselves but then come together against outsiders. We didn't agree with the means they were using, but our ends were similar. The big difference was that we wanted to follow the path of negotiation to reach our common goals. If forced to choose, we felt a bird in the hand was better than three in the bush. We wanted some security, an institution that could represent us and fight for our rights, and to follow through on the process that had already begun. If this Law allowed for a deepening recognition of the indigenous communities and populations of Chile, if it allowed us to legally recover lands we had historically lost, then we, too, could respect the rights of those who thought differently.

Let me tell you, if this Law has had a positive impact, it's been on the issue of land. Even if Aucán has not wanted to participate, his county has recovered five hundred hectares of land under the Law, something they would never have accomplished through confrontation. With the kind of strategies used by the Consejo, they could not have obtained what they now have in the swamps, in Ranquilco, in Lumaco; over a hundred hectares on one side and over two hundred on the other. And that's what happens when, complicitly, people use diverse strategies, and follow different paths to reach a common goal, because the struggle for land is the same. So are the struggles of culture, identity, bilingual education. Perhaps in the case of bilingual, intercultural education the strategies of implementation are different, but the general goal is still the same.

We also saw that, even if these brothers thought differently, their declarations helped us in our negotiations. Maybe ironically, but precisely because they waged war from the trenches, they made us look good with the state and helped us reach an agreement. So our actions complemented each other, in a way, and this brotherly complicity wouldn't let us rest if we didn't speak out against what was happening. When one is negotiating firmly, it's always helpful to have a counterpart in direct action.

F: *Let's move on to a different topic. Can you explain a bit how Patricio Aylwin implemented the Nueva Imperial agreement once he became president? When was the CEPI created, what was the transition from CEPI to CONADI like, and what was your role in all of this?*

Let's see. I've always been a leader. The CEPI, the Special Commission of Indigenous Peoples (*Comisión Especial de Pueblos Indígenas*), was the first institution created by the *Concertación* government as a response to the demands of indigenous peoples. Born in Nueva Imperial, it was created by Presidential Decree on May 17, 1990. I worked in CEPI as an indigenous leader and member of Nehuen-Mapu. My role was mostly in promoting discussions of the Indigenous Law, elaborating the first-draft law and then organizing discussions in the communities. We went to many communities and held many meetings in this region. I also participated in the Coalition of Mapuche Organizations, which grouped all the Mapuche organizations here in the IX Region and whose main task was to coordinate the work of the various members. Leaders from the various groups took turns heading the Coalition, and as luck would have it my turns came at very interesting and difficult moments: during the signing of the 1989 agreement; and when the Law itself was signed, on September 28, 1993.

F: *Was the Law also signed in Imperial?*

Yes, and it was published in the *Diario Oficial* on October 5th. I was one of the leaders who spoke in Nueva Imperial on September 28, the last speaker of all. There was a lot of hope, a lot of interest in those days. People had put a lot of energy into the creation and discussion of this Law. And even though we were already yelling to the four corners of the earth that the Law had emerged from Congress in stunted form, people still felt the Law was a part of them because they'd participated in discussions with us or with other organizations, they'd contributed to it. The desire to be in Imperial that September 28th was intense. People came from everywhere, as members of organizations, as individuals; somehow they all got there.

A complex process got us to Imperial that September 1993. The CEPI, special institution that it was, created under such special circumstances, was the forum where we studied and negotiated the last parts of the Law. Created directly by the President of the Republic, the CEPI was placed under the authority of the Secretary General of Government, in that ministry, with a very small staff and offices in Santiago, Temuco, and Iquique. These three headquarters, which together constituted CEPI, rented office space, bought a few sticks of furniture, and operated with a secretary and a maximum of three other people in each office. In Santiago CEPI was a little bigger, it had an Executive Council similar to the one CONADI has now. This Council was constituted by an indigenous majority and a nonindigenous minority, and presided over by CEPI's national director, José Bengoa. José Aylwin also participated, there was somebody from the Secretary General's office, and then the rest of the Council was composed of leaders representing the different indigenous groups who'd participated the most in the process: the Rapa Nui of Easter Island, the Mapuche, the Aymara, the Atacameños. The Huilliche from the X Region had a representative from Osorno, and the indigenous people from Santiago, who were obviously Mapuche, were also represented. In addition to the members, other people participated in the Council for various reasons: lawyers, students, and researchers formed a team that collaborated with the Council, and they were all present at the meetings as well.

The council members were elected through the different indigenous organizations, each of which sent a name through José Bengoa, as CEPI director, to the President of the Republic, who then approved a list of Council members from among the nominees. Nehuen-Mapu chose me, and my name was sent to Santiago along with the rest of the nominees. It couldn't have been more than an hour after the fax was sent, the registered letter, that a group of brothers in the organization said that I couldn't represent Nehuen-Mapu on the CEPI's Executive Council because I was not a registered member of the Christian Democratic Party, and because I was a woman. Because of these questions I was placed at a disadvantage, and José Santos Millao from Ad-Mapu and Camilo Quilamán from Kallfulikan were named the Mapuche representatives from the IX Region. Now, the Mapuche with a more Christian sensibility also needed a representative, and Nehuen-Mapu had an incipient base in Santiago through which Juan Queupán, leader of the Commission for Juvenile Rights (CODEJU), was named as Nehuen-Mapu's council member.

The CEPI did pretty well at the level of popular participation. More than two thousand meetings were held to discuss the draft law, and I participated actively in many of them. You might ask me why I did this, even though they didn't name me to the Council and essentially hung me out to dry. And my answer is because there was a greater goal, the Indigenous Law, that would affect practically every aspect of indigenous people's daily lives. So that had to be more important. And maybe it was more interesting to work in the communities, with local groups, discussing the draft law, instead of spending my time traveling to Santiago. Of course that would have been fun, too, the negotiations, talking with the politicians and everything. But each person has a particular role to fulfill at any given moment. Mine was playing it out in the communities of the IX and part of the X regions. And I went everywhere, I did as much as I could, without resentment, without bad feelings. The experience of rejection was filed away as just another anecdote in my personal political history.

F: *What were the meetings in the communities like, how were they done?*

I would have wanted the meetings to be more like workshops, so that people could have participated more than they did. But the document itself was a little green book full of concepts, principles, and objectives; it had a section on customary law, another on the objectives of ethnodevelopment, yet another on land recuperation; so it was like a finished law. It was a lot of material, more content than we could cover in an afternoon meeting in a community. Most meetings were prepared in advance at the local level. Only in a few places did we have to meet first with community leaders in order to promote the idea, a small meeting in preparation for the larger, more formal one. But in most places people did the preparations themselves and agreed on what to do. Here in Temuco we formed many teams with the people from CEPI, in collaboration with the Institute for Agrarian and Livestock Development (INDAP), with folks from the NGOs, and with leaders from many of the members of the Coalition of Mapuche Organizations. There were ten organizations at that time: the Mapuche Cultural Centers, Ad-Mapu, Nehuen-Mapu, Lautaro Ñi Ailla Rewe, Choinfolilche, Kallfulikan, the Lautaro Rehue Association, Keyukleayñ pu Zomo, Raquiduam, and the Lonquimay Pehuenche Association, who participated from afar.

But even with all these organizations it was still difficult to cover all the communities, all the places where people petitioned for meetings. Between Kallfulikan—who had the largest number of people going out into the field—Lautaro, Nehuen-Mapu, and Ad-Mapu, we had approximately one hundred organizers. That meant fifty teams, two per team. And when it came time to leave there wouldn't be enough vehicles, the meetings would overlap, one would be here and the other way over there. There'd be meetings that went on for a whole day, for half a day, because that's how people wanted them; and there'd also be meetings that lasted only for an hour or two.

It was a beautiful moment, very different from what happened under the dictatorship, very different. People really wanted to participate. People would talk a lot about customary law (*derecho consuetudinario*), and you could explain what it meant, but you also went out into the countryside to learn. I remember that in Galvarino, a Mapuche brother stood up and said, "Speaking of customary law, what is customary law?" When we explained it to him, he said, "I ask that customary law be respected, especially the customary law tied to land rights, but also relating to our wives and children. Because many Mapuches have more than one wife, and more than one child with different women, and these children are not ours under the law." And he talked about his own experience, that he'd recognized all of his children as the children of the woman he'd been forced to marry according to civil law, because that was the only available option. But when it came time for his children to divide their inheritance, they'd only get his and his legal wife's land. Many of his children would have no right to the land of their biological mothers. The other women remained single before the law. They had no rights as wives, not even to their children, since legally their children were no longer theirs. So this man was desperately asking for help: he had three wives, and he was legally married to one. He wanted his children by the other wives to inherit the land that belonged to their mothers. Though he would have liked to give them another piece somewhere else, he couldn't. By trying to do them a favor and recognize them as his legal wife's children, he'd also done them a disservice.

I was really struck by this case, and I spoke with a lawyer about it, also with José Aylwin and Eduardo Castillo, and others as well, to see if something could be done in this particular case. To this day an NGO is helping sort out the legal rights of the mothers in this case. In similar instances they've sometimes tried legally to return the child to the original mother, who bore and raised the child, since the other relationship exists merely on paper. In some of these cases, our original meetings were only the start of a broader discussion.

F: *Was customary law a major topic of discussion in most places, or did topics change depending on the meeting?*

Topics varied, depending on the level of participation. To be realistic, sometimes people simply listened to us as we presented the information contained in the document, and provided minimal feedback. They might ask for clarification on certain points, but they didn't contribute anything of their own. In other places, though, people contributed a lot, especially on subjects like the right to the land, to the soil and subsoil, to territory more broadly defined. Why aren't we Mapuches owners of the land in all of its dimensions, as it should be? These were the kinds of questions people had. They talked a lot about the fact that, one and a half meters under the surface, where the groundwaters are and there could be mineral deposits, the land no longer belonged to the individual owner, but to the State. That was a controversial topic. So was the legal code that governs water rights, which states that the ownership of water must be registered, and that there-fore the owner of a particular body of water is not necessarily the person living there, but the person who registered it. According to this water code, someone in Santiago, in Arica, in Temuco can buy the rights to water anywhere in the country, that's what the law says; like everything else, water is subject to the free market. Initially people saw this as absurd. How could indigenous people conceive of a spring, or the origin of the river that passed through their land, as something to be bought and sold? That someone could own it and even change its course—to slap away the river's arm, they said—surely this meant the end of the world was near. There were a lot of opinions about that. The restitution of usurped lands was an obligatory topic everywhere. Also the division of community lands, which people wanted done in equal parts: if there were ten hectares and four brothers, then each should receive two and a half hectares. This had not been done under Law 2568, because the Pinochet Law legalized only the occupant's rights, so whoever was occupying the land at the moment got it. If somebody was holding seven hectares and someone else half a hectare, that's how it stayed and there was no right to complain.

So the topics were, as I said, diverse. People who lived at the water's edge also wondered about the boundary between their property and the river, lake, or ocean: how many meters away from the water belonged to you or didn't. We'd say to people that the uppermost point the water reached, the crest of the wave, marked the limit between what was yours and what was the river's, the lake's, the ocean's; from there in it's not yours, from here out it is. And they'd say that one year, the waters crest here, next year they may crest there, and some years they may crest in my backyard; so then none of that is mine? And then more doubts and questions would arise. So the discussions really varied by place, by people's ideas and needs, and by the interest they had in what the Law should be.

Where people had a long history of participation and were more political, they'd talk about constitutional recognition, the right to particular kinds of organizations, the fund for ethnodevelopment. People wanted this fund to be like a bank, to have the autonomy of a Ministry instead of being INDAP's puppet on a string. There's no reason to depend on INDAP, they said. We aren't just small producers, we're a people, and we should be recognized as such. Other topics that were never missing anywhere were the right to scholarships, to education, to centers for warehousing and marketing goods, to long-term credit without high interest rates. No one asked for handouts or subsidies, nobody. But they did ask for access to low-interest credit. They also asked that INDAP revoke the debts they'd carried since 1970, because once people can't repay their debts they lose the right to further credit with INDAP. They'd gone into arrears on a debt of five hundred, a thousand, maybe fifty thousand pesos they had back then, and today they owed millions. So people say no, that wasn't my debt, I can't pay that. If I owed fifty thousand pesos, maybe I could pay five hundred, and even that's too much already.

Women's participation was also a theme, but it generated much less interest. Besides, everybody took for granted that the paragraph in the Law recognizing equal rights for women and their right to wear traditional clothing would remain in the final draft. In the CEPI we talked a lot about that paragraph and how it was written, but in the countryside people didn't give it much importance. They didn't seem to care that much whether women had the right to participate in the programs and projects sponsored by the indigenous institution the Law was going to create. People cared more about education, about recognition as a distinct people, about the land, subsoil rights, and customary law.

F: *And how did people get from* CEPI *to* CONADI?

Well, the transition from CEPI to CONADI was part of a normal process, anticipated by everybody, questioned by some. Those who were more political, who had participated in the upper echelons of the different organizations, questioned that 20 percent of the personnel from INDAP-DASIN was transferred to CONADI. One fifth of the personnel, as well as the infrastructure left over on what used to be the Trianón estate, specifically Lot 10 of the Trianón estate—a huge green barn left there had become the offices of INDAP-DASIN—was passed on to CONADI.[7]

F: *Today those are the offices of* CONADI's *National Deputy Director* (Subdirección Nacional), *right?*

Exactly. All that was passed from INDAP-DASIN to CONADI, along with a contingent of people already working there. The transition was a bit difficult, and questions did emerge, but in the end it wasn't so hard and nobody protested, because they kept their jobs, and they had to keep working, better now than before, because they'd be given more resources and be accompanied by new people who were going to come work with them. In addition to elements from INDAP-DASIN, CEPI's property was also transferred to CONADI. Santiago, Temuco, Osorno, and Iquique had received some furniture and infrastructure from INDAP, but not so the other offices. In Santiago the furniture actually came from the Secretary General's office, a few things that had already been replaced by new purchases. Here in Temuco and in Osorno they had to make do with whatever sticks of furniture they inherited from INDAP. In Cañete they had to buy everything.

Then they had to hire personnel, a stable office staff for CONADI as a whole. It's important to note that more than a thousand qualified indigenous and nonindigenous applicants, mostly indigenous, presented their résumés. There were only eighty-eight positions total, of which twenty were filled by transfers from INDAP-DASIN; so in reality there were only sixty-eight vacancies, you couldn't hire any more. Add to this the need to maintain a political equilibrium among the political parties of the *Concertación*, and you get a sense of the long and difficult process this entailed, a process that was questioned, but silently. For some positions the choice was clear and easy, but for others there was blood on the floor, in the sense that it was very hard to make a decision and leave everybody else out.

Mauricio Huenchulaf—if you remember, he helped found the first Mapuche NGO during the dictatorship—received a piece of paper saying he was CONADI's National Director, nothing more. That first month I decided to help out in his office, we started with absolutely nothing. We began by buying a pencil, a file folder, a piece of furniture; then a combined fax and phone. That was the first thing we needed in order to communicate with the outside world, we said. We rented an office on the sixth floor of a building, not easily accessible, the stairs were closed off. It was hard to receive visitors, there weren't comfortable places to talk and to communicate with all the folks who came by to say hello, to congratulate you, as well as the Mapuche brothers who came to say, peñi, you have to be on my side, I need this and that, they'd list their demands. There were so many things to do in the first sixty, ninety days, the first month was terrible. The second month was a bit more relaxed, because we had bought some office supplies. By the third month we had a small Xerox machine, furniture, it was more like an office; the head of the Land Department (*Jefe de Tierras*) had already joined the staff, then the Head Prosecutor, then the Head of Development. We were all packed in together, two or three desks to an office; we had to do cartwheels in those first ninety days to get things moving! And the council members had no office space, there simply was none; we'd meet with people on the stairs, in the hallways. We just had to do our work under those conditions.

F: *What were the council members doing at that point?*

What they still do today. The only difference is that we were appointed for a year, until the new Council was elected a year and a half later. In the meantime, having started with nothing, no infrastructure, we had to make things up as we went along. The Law is the law, but to apply the Law you must have guidelines, you must have regulations. So we drew the map along the way, we learned through doing, the entire staff, everybody. And that's why, when I think of CONADI's first three years, I say that the only reason we managed to do what we did was because indigenous people were leading it. Not because they are my brothers and sisters, but because their work knew no schedule, it was around the clock. It was a full commitment, we all pulled more than our weight and worked with single-minded devotion. And we did what we could, not what we wanted to do, because we started from nothing.

We had no regulations for how to deal with land issues, for example. If we began applying the Law to a specific land issue, suddenly it was no, stop, you can't apply the Law because you have to wait for the guidelines to arrive from the National Budget Office (*Contraloría*) in Santiago. Then they had to be approved by the Ministry of Planning (MIDEPLAN), and MIDEPLAN had to present the revised guidelines back to the Budget Office for approval before they could be applied. One month, two more months, ninety days. Even to buy furniture we had to call a meeting, write a resolution, send it to MIDEPLAN, then elaborate a more technical version to send to the Budget Office. The bureaucracy made your skin crawl! Not because people wanted it that way, but because that was the way it was done, and since we didn't understand the system, we didn't know how to use it effectively. We ran up against so many brick walls because we lacked the necessary skills and information. We had to learn everything from scratch: decrees governing administrative procedures, decrees determining the behavior of public servants, what was considered appropriate behavior for a state agency like ours. We learned we had to follow the political rules of the regime in power, but also that as a state agency we depended on the Budget Office, over which members of Congress had a huge say. And the pressure and demands from members of Congress were really intense, not only from the right-wing opposition, but from the *concertacionistas* who'd worked on the Law and now wanted their constituents to see the results. All right already, they'd say, when will the land-subsidy program be operational, when will usurped lands be recovered, how about the plans for education, development, cultural revival? Amongst ourselves and in hallway conversation we'd say geez, this guy thinks the subsidies are like a pork barrel project for his district, right? I don't know, it was a wonderful and extremely difficult time for me. It was a time when we were constantly negotiating, trying to reconcile different positions and ideas, making deals and reaching agreements. If I vote for your project today, you'll vote for mine tomorrow, that's how it had to be because the unwritten rule was that only one development project would get approved per county. So if today I defended hers, tomorrow she'll defend mine.

F: *Do you miss those days?*

I think I remember them very well, and fondly. But I also remember how we began to uncover the limits of the Law as we applied it, because the Law just didn't come out as we expected. CONADI, for instance, is the agency created by the Indigenous Law No. 19,523 to carry out its policies and is thus empowered to grant legal status to the indigenous communities formed and recognized according to the Law's statutes. But unfortunately, when you look a little closer, you realize that it's not always the reconstitution of the original communities, which is what we had envisioned. Under the provisions of the Law, a single community can divide into two or three over political differences, because the Law says that where ten Mapuches share an objective, a Mapuche community can be constituted. So there are cases where one community has divided into two, three, even four.

Among the articles Congress cut from the original Law were articles about political participation. In its final form the Law limits certain kinds of participation. It makes it harder to organize more broadly, to develop organizations with broader constituencies, because it privileges local organizing by communities. This broke with the practices we had under the dictatorship, because now a single community has more political weight than a trade association, or a regional or national organization. I don't know, it's another form of divide and conquer, because it also limits the power of Mapuche organizations to demand things from the state. As the main institution empowered to represent the Mapuche in all situations, the community nevertheless has problems getting credit. It's not valid before INDAP or the State Bank, or any other state agency except for CONADI, and it has no broader claim to representation beyond the small group that makes up the community. So in the end, from my perspective, the Law has lowered the profile of broader indigenous organizations, because there's no legal difference between an indigenous association and an indigenous community, since either one can be formed with a minimum of twenty-five people over eighteen years old, and as we know there are communities with more than one hundred people over eighteen. As a result, the broader repercussions of Mapuche political activity have been significantly lowered.

F: *So even if it wasn't the Law's original intention, does it seem that in practice
the process of constituting indigenous communities through the Indigenous
Law has actually promoted disorganization and division among different
sectors of the indigenous population, who earlier were more united through
regional or national-level organizations?*

This is definitely the case, so much so that the leaders of legally constituted communities, as well as the so-called indigenous associations at the
county, regional, or national levels, are disillusioned with the present state
of affairs. Because the broader associations don't carry weight outside the
community, the Law, whether unintentionally or intentionally at the congressional level, has in effect castrated, so to speak, the Mapuche social
movement that existed between 1978 and 1990. Why do I say this? Because
on October 5th of this year (1997) the Law will be four years old, and the
indigenous movement is in a state of lethargy and disenchantment, society
in general is less receptive, and discrimination is alive and well. And despite
all the energy put into the discussion of the Law, despite all the energy
Patricio Aylwin's government put into promulgating it, we didn't get constitutional recognition and the articles didn't get written the way people
wanted them.[8]

The Law has succeeded in recognizing the indigenous population. All of
the indigenous peoples, no matter how small, even if there's only a few
families left, are recognized. And it has succeeded in returning indigenous
lands, with a fund specifically for this every year. On the issue of development, of creating special ethnodevelopment areas, the government still
hasn't formulated a policy that is clear and understandable to most people.
The people in the government who participate in the *Concertación*, and the
Concertación as an organic political entity, have to share the blame for this.
Once the Law came out they washed their hands of the whole issue and
stopped funding Mapuche organizations. The same has happened with the
NGOs, which no longer finance Mapuche leaders because doing so wouldn't
give them the passport into the communities that it did in the past. Because
no one is financing the leaders, they can't have the critical presence they had
before. The only leader who's always funded, and has the resources to go
wherever he wants, inside and outside the country, with international financing, of course, is Aucán Huilcamán. The Chilean government has no

policy to strengthen Mapuche or other forms of social organization, and is in fact not interested in doing so.

THE REUQUE-PAILLALEF FAMILY

LIONEL: *The Indigenous Law is there, but the directives aren't clear or specific, so this makes it hard to follow.*

ELVIRA: *People see the Law but they pass it by just like that, thinking there's nothing to it, it's just another unimportant law.*

LIONEL: *That's because within the existing judicial system, the Law practically does not work.*

F: *Besides, I've spent a lot of time lately reading the Law for work-related reasons, and it seems very contradictory to me. Some parts say one thing and other parts say the opposite. I was commenting on this to someone who was on the Commission that wrote the Law, José Aylwin . . .*

LIONEL: *Ah, you mean Pepe . . .*

F: *. . . yes, and he told me it's true, that he agreed, because during the congressional debate the rightist senators and representatives were very opposed. So there were points where they just closed ranks and said no, this is not going to pass; or they changed it; or one part was modified when both sides cut a deal. So I think there are parts where the Law came out wobbly or crooked, with one leg shorter than the other. It doesn't work as a whole, and you can see that, right?*

ELVIRA: *When private lands, larger farms, are purchased as restitution to communities, they don't become indigenous lands and don't have the same privileges.*

F: *Exactly . . .*

LIONEL: *Then, for you at least, the Law partially works?*

F: *Well, I think . . .*

ELVIRA: *But lots of things have been done as a result of the Law; for example, lands have been bought, and they will become indigenous later; some scholarships have been given . . . What else has been done?*

LILIANA: *Another example is what we were talking about earlier, remember? That family members who were absent when the lands in their community were divided up now have the right to be paid compensation. But when they get paid, suddenly they find out that the land's been appraised according to what is was worth years ago, and instead of getting millions of pesos, they get paid a hundred and twenty thousand.*

ELVIRA: *And the Law doesn't give* CONADI *any autonomy, either. Suppose that one day* CONADI *decided to set up an agricultural and livestock bank, so that when people came in they could trade their products and open up a government retirement account at the same time, because people are always talking about having one of those for their old age. The Law doesn't allow* CONADI *to do that.* CONADI *has the power to do things, but its hands are always tied behind its back because it depends on others and is responsible to others. That's the problem. And agencies like* INDAP *don't like to work with* CONADI *because of all the paperwork, all the hoops they have to jump through, that it's better to not even try.*

LIONEL: *The problem is not* INDAP*'s, the problem is that the Law doesn't work. I've studied the Law extensively, not because I wanted to, but because as an alderman I felt it was my duty and my obligation to at least understand it, and I've discussed it with some five friends of mine, who are lawyers with vast experience, and I've reached the conclusion that the Law doesn't work. And the Law doesn't work because, for example, even if a community is legally recognized on paper, this doesn't give it the right independently to compete for an agricultural improvement grant. Its rights are limited. I've been told the lack of guidelines is the problem, that the Law is there but not the regulations to put it into effect, and those guidelines that do exist aren't clear. And this just reproduces the forms of discrimination the Mapuche have always experienced. So there's a lot to be done, a lot. The way things are now, what does a Mapuche group have to do to work within the Law? Organize a cooperative, a corporation, a limited liability company, and then the state can grant resources; but the state will not provide resources to indigenous communities, even if they're legally constituted. Because the Law lacks guidelines, communities are neither fish nor fowl. That's why the Law doesn't work.*

ELVIRA: *That's why until now the only thing indigenous communities can do is petition* CONADI.

LIONEL: *But* CONADI *has the same kinds of limitations. It's true that it recently received more resources, but what will these funds be used for? Too much is missing from the plan.*

F: *There are people who say, for example, that if the Ralco hydroelectric project*[9] *reached the Supreme Court, the Indigenous Law would be in trouble as a law, because there'd be a conflict over which law was more important, the Electricity Law or the Indigenous Law. And with divisions in Congress reproducing those in the society at large, who gets to decide which will be constitutionally more important, electricity or indigenous identity?*

LIONEL: *Electricity.*

LILIANA: *And the government also gives more importance to electricity, that's already decided, because there's a technological improvement.*

LIONEL: *The indigenous question is important at a community level, and it's localized in a particular part of the country, but electricity concerns the well-being of all the people, including the Mapuche. It's related to the common good and to the progress and development of the whole country, in other words it's a national question. The national interest is above everything else, you have to accept that. The same happens with the right to private property, if you have to build a school or install an important health facility, it overrides private property, which is why there's such a thing as expropriation. For me that's clear, crystal clear. Now, when a road is supposed to pass through a cemetery, where a lot of people have been buried for a long time, then the road has priority, because a cemetery is a cemetery, while the other thing . . .*

LILIANA: *Is for the living.*

LIONEL: *. . . and the country must move forward . . .*

LILIANA: *Over the bodies of the dead.*

LIONEL: *Over the bodies of the dead. I mean, I put myself in the situation, if they had to go over me and I'm dead, then go ahead, over the few bones I have left, because the country must move on. We're talking about an international system here; in other words, progress and development must continue, modernization must go forward. You can't stop the country's progress and development for a couple of hundred dead people. And that's fine with me.*

F: *But from such a position . . .*

LIONEL: *I could get killed . . .*

LILIANA: *It's sort of anti-indigenist.*

F: *You do away with diversity, with all values that aren't strictly materialistic . . .*

LILIANA: *Exactly, cultural.*

F: *. . . cultural values . . .*

LILIANA: *Especially cultural values . . .*

F: *. . . human values.*

ELVIRA: *And with what is sacred, because even the Catholics would get mad if you built a road, say, over a Catholic cemetery.*

F: *And besides, we beg the question of modernization, for whom? Progress, for what? Because obviously there are, I would say, important benefits to progress and modernization. I think it's good if everybody has electricity, if everybody has running water, if the roads are in good shape . . .*

LILIANA: *You can get around more easily, have easier access . . .*

F: *Of course, a whole series of things . . .*

ELVIRA: *Supermarkets, health care, schools . . .*

LILIANA: *It's good to have all that, but it doesn't have to trample the rights of the living or the dead.*

ELVIRA: *So whatever's in the way, I mean, a dead person, a sacred place, can change the road's course?*

LILIANA: *Exactly.*

F: *For me, the problem starts when you put modernization above all other values. In my opinion, you end up with a modernization that loses all sense of direction because it takes priority over anything of human value. That's too high a price to pay for modernity.*

ELVIRA: *Yeah, that reminds me of the technological innovations that hurt rural people and cut off their alternatives.*

F: *Because, for example, the price of industrial products goes up and the price of agricultural products goes down . . .*

ELVIRA: *In response to that there've been a lot of attempts at training and technology transfers. But it's all been piecemeal, no systematic efforts to do something big so that agriculture can improve again instead of deteriorating. Many country people go to school, but what use is it if they can't apply what they learn on their land? No matter how much you learn, you still end up having to get a job elsewhere. It doesn't matter how much you love the countryside, how much you love your family, like that beautiful saying, "Bloom where you're planted," but how can we bloom?*

LILIANA: *And with this drought we can't even water the plants. (Laughter.) So they dry up before the flowers even bud.*

ELVIRA: *These are the changes going on from day to day. You walk around in the countryside and you see lots of abandoned homes, women living alone, men living without their families, or old people, really old, alone or with a little grandchild that they've been left to raise, long after they've past the age of parents . . .*

LILIANA: *The child of an unwed mother . . .*

ELVIRA: *You see this in all the communities. Here (in Chanco) at least you can see more people, and you can hear children, because we're close to town. If we were further away we'd be equally abandoned. Loica's like that, solitary, you don't hear little kids. Besides, there's a whole generation that didn't marry, so the countryside doesn't produce people, either. New people show up in the city every day, but not in the countryside. In many families, once the old man dies, that's it. The kids prefer to live in town, all bunched together, in shantytowns, but never in the countryside. For them that's a step back.*

LILIANA: *People give priority to everything that's technology and modernization, but when you accept that kind of modernization you lose what's culturally yours.*

ELVIRA: *And people lose their humanity. Because I remember saying once that true modernity should combine what's new with the good parts of the old, taking things from each culture and combining them. In education, for example, modernity would be if kids learned Mapuche history and mapuzungun as subjects in school. Before teaching Japanese history and culture, honoring their parents' own traditions in the classroom. That, for me, is modernity, because it brings to light the things about ourselves that aren't well known, and it works from what we already have.*

F: *And I'd say it's also sharing what we have with others, so everyone can learn to respect diversity. In my own case, for example, I'd love it if my two sons' school in Santiago had a class on Mapuche history. Their school is one hundred percent wigka, but a class in Mapuche history would help kids understand and be more sensitive to the cultural diversity in the country. Because right now my sons' schoolmates say things like, "Why don't the Mapuche just get educated once and for all and integrate into society, and stop bothering us?" And that position comes from ignorance, from an absolute lack of respect for other traditions and other ways of being, right?*

LIONEL: *I think it's also because the media only show the conflictual moments, and not the constructive aspects, of our reality. They never report, for example, about a Mapuche academic teaching at a national university, or an eminent Mapuche doctor working at one of the more distinguished hospitals in the country. They don't show that. But whenever the famous Aucán Huilcamán is out protesting, reporters fall over each other to cover the story, and they generalize about the Mapuche people as a whole.*

LILIANA: *The truth is, the Mapuche people are very divided, but that never gets covered in the media. Whenever Aucán is at a demonstration, he ends up as our representative, and even though there are other groups that disagree completely with what he's doing, no one understands that because the media is bunching everyone together. That's why the public ends up thinking that all the Mapuche are alike, they're all up to the same thing.*

LIONEL: *When I threw Aucán Huilcamán out of Pitrufquén nobody interviewed me, I didn't appear on TV, but I kicked him out of Pitrufquén, with my legs as you see them. So that's how it works. The same thing happens when there's a conflict in a particular county, the mayors and aldermen come out in the newspapers and on television. And where people are working peacefully, elaborating projects, contributing to the development of their locale, no one knows about it. So it's really more of a problem with the media.*

ELVIRA: *Yes, that's true.*

F: *But I also think there's a problem with education in the long run, no?*

ELVIRA: *Yes.*

LILIANA: *Education—more than anything else, it's education.*

ELVIRA: *Besides, in the media, whether it's the written press, the radio, or television, there's an underlying economic motive, they're looking for what's going to sell. Sometimes, no matter how decent a journalist's coverage can be, his newspaper or television station takes advantage of him, because that's how it is.*

F: *Or they don't give someone a front-page story, because what he or she is reporting isn't going to sell newspapers. So they put it on page six, seven, or eight, and how's a journalist going to make a career of it when they're always on page twelve?*

ELVIRA: *Or they change it. Don Sergio Prenafeta, a science reporter, one of the first, he was on* Mundo *on Channel 13 with the late Hernán Olguín, he said that even a serious newspaper like . . .*

LILIANA: La Cuarta[10] *(laughter)...*

ELVIRA: ... El Mercurio, *or* Qué Pasa *magazine, where he wrote, or* Ercilla, *the editor changed the headline, distorted the article. So the news gets misrepresented, because the editor changes the story. The reporter can write well-researched, well-documented articles, with a broad perspective, but the editors will always emphasize what's going to sell. When don Sergio wrote about a new disease, they put a big headline, to scare people into buying the paper, when it could be happening in South Africa and not in Chile. So it was turned into more of a commercial question rather than a scientific question. Some companies, like the kids who report for the show* Al Sur del Mundo *(South of the World), have no editors; instead they produce shows as entrepreneurs and then try to sell them to the* TV *stations. If the station likes it, they like it, and that's that. But even these guys end up having to censor themselves so that their show doesn't get cut, and also to recover the money they invested.*

F: *All this talk about the transition makes me wonder how, over time, the relationship between political strategies and ethnic strategies changed in the Mapuche movement. With all its internal differences, in the '80's the Mapuche movement had a very strong ethnic profile, and yet you've said at various points that this changes with the transition. What happened?*

To some extent the transition coincides with a very intense moment in the Latin American indigenous movement as a whole, which is 1992. That year I took part in a walking tour of Europe whose last stop was Assisi, Italy, where St. Francis is buried. We started off in Germany, then we went to France and to Strasbourg; from Strasbourg we went to Florence and then on to Assisi, where we were hosted by the Christian youth. In between we stopped in other cities and towns, and in each place we discussed the present-day reality of indigenous peoples faced with commemorating five hundred years of conquest.

Each of us specialized in a particular topic, and of course mine related to women, and the land. Our delegation was made up of Rigoberta Menchú, Nobel Prize candidate, and by brothers and sisters from Peru, Bolivia, Colombia, Ecuador, Costa Rica, the Dominican Republic, and Mexico. We were a very compact group, most of us had seen each other before and it seemed as if we'd always known each other. It was a beautiful trip we shared.

We'd split into groups of two, three, or four in order to attend all the activities to which we were invited. Antonia Agrega and I were the most daring. We'd take the train alone, without a translator or anything, and manage to get off at the right stops in order to give talks in the little towns where they were waiting for us. They'd tell us if you're one minute late you'll miss the train. We liked getting to the terminal five minutes early, so we could be there on time, because the trains leave exactly every three minutes, and if you don't know what you're doing, even if you're there the train can pass you by and that's it. And it's the same thing getting off, you have to get off in a flash and know exactly which way to go.

The last event in Assisi was really special. I have the speech I gave written down somewhere. In Assisi, I symbolically gave back the ships Columbus sailed in to discover America. They were in a painting. I told the young people, more than five hundred of them, that they had to be like a swarm of bees to produce the sweetness the earth needed; that they must go where people no longer knew how to taste the many flavors of life, where they'd lost all connection to the natural world. Because a real connection to the natural world doesn't allow us to accept polluted rivers and eroded lands, or to overexploit our lands, trees, birds, animals, and mineral wealth. So that's where you should all be, I told them, making the honey that will sweeten the future of the world. I think it was one of my most romantic and emotional speeches, full of faith and hope. I was congratulated by many people. There was some tension with Rigoberta Menchú because she was supposed to be the main speaker.

But her speech didn't reach the young people, that was the difference. She had the podium at the culminating moment, for the event's closure, and her speech didn't reach the audience. Mine was different, the language was different, and I was able to reach the European youth. Standing among them was a Chilean priest who was traveling, and when I finished my speech, in a downpour that started toward the end, he came up to me and said, "I know you." "And you speak Spanish," I answered. "That's because I'm Father so-and-so, from Santiago." "And what are you doing here," I asked him, "leaving your congregation all alone in Santiago?" "I'm resting," he answered, "and your speech made me feel very happy." I think my speech was the best that day, and of the entire pilgrimage.

I also really liked Ana María Huachu's speech in Strasbourg, France. Her speech was delivered before a lot of politically influential people, including members of the European Parliament. On that occasion my speech was before a small group, but Ana María was given the opportunity to talk in the big hall. A beam of light coming through the window really bothered her, but she's a woman who never takes off her hat, a white hat. She said, "Gentlemen, respected politicians: don't pretend you can cover the sun with a finger so as not to see all the indigenous peoples of the world, and especially us South Americans, Latin Americans, whom Columbus tried to colonize. Did Columbus, who sailed those three ships, really think he'd killed off the Indians? What a lie, gentlemen, because here we are!" It was a strong harangue, very forceful, very political, that really got to people. I think it was one of Ana María Huachu's most overwhelming speeches.

Another speech I liked a lot was by Colombian senator Gabriel Mullui, a very young man, who was my travel companion on that trip. Speaking at the ethnology department of the University of Munich, he said that in the relationship indigenous people maintain with the land lies the future hope of the world. Even though nonindigenous peoples have cut down the forests and destroyed nature, they haven't been able to completely destroy indigenous peoples or Mother Earth, and that's why we still have some hope left. And he entreated the students and social scientists who were present to write the truth and take indigenous people into account, so that their writing would influence policymakers in the direction of true development and growth for the world, rather than toward destruction. He said they shouldn't use their data to build factories and fortresses, which are not beneficial to our planet.

Among so many, these were the speeches that made a mark on me during that trip. There was another young guy named Carlos, from Peru, who was from the village patrols (*rondas*) that defended their communities against Shining Path. A really sharp kid, very bright, who got barbs from all sides because apparently the exiled Peruvians who came to our events were in some way connected to, or had gone into exile as part of, Shining Path.

F: *Or at least they were the ones organized enough to speak out.*

Right. So this brother from the peasant rondas was the target of all these barbs, and no one seemed to understand why the rondas were against Shining Path, against the massacres of entire villages, and why they developed a system of sentries and carried out education in their communities. Every once in a while we had to throw him a life preserver, so we never left him alone during his speeches. I was with him several times when he needed a lifeline, and usually we'd bring up the fact that extremists used the indigenous problem for their own ends, but they were never really serious about addressing it. He was very nice, very enthusiastic, that *rondero*. I hope he's alive, I really hope to God he's alive.

There was also our indigenous brother Serafín Ajuacho, a Bolivian Methodist, a guy with an immense faith. He was interested in revindicating indigenous religion. He thought indigenous people had the true religion, not Methodists, Catholics, Orthodox Christians, or Lutherans; and therefore indigenous people deserved the respect of all the rest. He also believed that Catholics and Methodists had to recognize how much they owed indigenous peoples, who had welcomed them into their lives. "It's like someone who invites you to their house," he argued; "if I invite Catholics or Evangelicals into my home, that doesn't mean they're welcome to snoop around in all the corners. I need my privacy, and that involves respect for my way of seeing and understanding the world, it means being able to practice my autonomous, autochthonous, original religion." Even though he was Methodist, he was strong and mystical; today he's a pastor. I recently heard from him, and he's extremely active. His topic, religion, is seldom discussed in Chile in relation to the indigenous question. I've discussed it in Ecuador, Colombia, and in correspondence with Bolivia, but here in Chile there was only one opportunity last year, I think. I think here in Chile we're afraid of confronting it, which is why it's one of the least explored topics and there's so much to do.

F: *So in a sense, Chile's political transition parallels the culminating moment of Latin America's indigenous mobilization. This seems ironic, because apparently, when politics in Chile are again governed by parties and their strategies, that's when the indigenous movement itself begins to dissipate. Is there a necessary contradiction between party politics and the Mapuche movement?*

I think this contradiction is inevitable, and that it's also important to say so publicly. In the difficult first stage of the transition to democracy, those challenging times don Patricio Aylwin was forced to live through, the indigenous movement gave him much support. During the dictatorship the Mapuche movement had confronted the military, which is more than the nonindigenous people in the south were capable of doing. There are many who tell tragic stories of persecution and suffering, and I don't mean to imply that they're lying. But in this region we never, never heard them speak out in public. When we held demonstrations on May 1st and October 12th, they never joined us. In the conversations leading up to the events, for example, the railroad, industrial, manufacturers', and construction unions all said they'd be there, and their organizers would show up a week or two in advance to plan and support the May 1st march. But then May 1st would come along and we'd march down the street alone. The closest they'd get was a block away, half a block away, where the organizer who had been with us stood watching what was happening, eh? Only when the Assembly for Civility (*Asamblea de la Civilidad*) gets formed do the professional associations join in—doctors, architects, accountants—and that's when we start to feel supported, because we, too, were part of the Assembly for Civility and that's when we were part of a larger group. Only then do the nonindigenous people start to show their faces, so to speak, because between 1978 and 1980 I saw no one. Forgive me, all you respected gentlemen in politics, but I saw no one else in the streets during those early years. They might have been writing very eloquently, because, oh yes, paper can stand up to whatever you put on it; and one-on-one conversations are pretty safe, too. But you had to be seen on the streets, you had to be willing to lay it all out in the streets for the good of others, which is what we indigenous leaders did.

Many of us were professionally stunted, because we sacrificed everything for the indigenous movement. Personally I sacrificed everything, against my family's wishes I didn't finish my degree, and others did the same, eh? We faced conflict and opposition from our families, our communities, everything. But the movement had no schedule, there wasn't a day, from Sunday to Sunday, where you could rest. No schedules, no hours, without salary, with occasional support from solidarity groups here and there. And this wasn't the kind of work you did for the money, anyway; no amount of money could repay what we put in; I never received a salary in the movement, and no one can say otherwise.

F: *So how did you manage?*

I had a friend and godfather in exile, Humberto, who'd been a professor in Valdivia; he lives in Zurich. With his family he's somehow managed to help me stay on my feet, I'd say, up to this very day. Because our new democracy hasn't been capable of finding a way to help people who were left without degrees. Whenever there's a technical position open the first thing they look at is the degree, the title, or diploma; only afterward do they consider the skill or capacity of the applicant. Another person who supported me was Father Pancho, who unfortunately died a few months after I got married. I got married in 1983 and he died in early 1984. So I wasn't able to share with him that I'd found what he had wanted for me.

I owe him a lot as a Christian woman and as a Mapuche leader. You know, it's one of the ironies of life that some people say you can't be Christian and Mapuche at the same time, because simply by being a Christian you already have a colonized mentality. But for me that isn't true; instead, it's something that's given me strength. Father Pancho, Pancho Lauschman, with whom I worked since before 1973, always helped me to go on. He said to me that when you know yourself, when you see yourself as Mapuche and look for your roots, when you understand your people and see yourself as an indigenous woman who thinks and acts, you do what's right for you and for your people.

I hope that his strength, energy, and firm faith continue to live inside me as a reflection of what he meant to me. Time after time, when I'd go to him in tears, saying, "That's it, Father, I can't go on, I don't have money, I want to finish my degree, I have to think of my daughter, my family," he'd always say, "First things first. You're Mapuche and you have to finish what you started." "But I don't even have a pair of shoes," I'd answer. "It doesn't matter," he'd say, "I just got a package of clothes from Caritas, let's pick out a pair of shoes for you." From 1978 to 1983 shoes came in from Germany or other parts of Europe, along with parkas, sweaters, all kinds of things. The only thing I never took from these packages was underwear, you know, bras or panties. But the rest of what I had were clothes that people gave me; even now I hardly buy clothes on my own.

I got married, but I can't say my husband supports me financially, because he's still a student and, since we got married, hasn't had a stable job. Now, you might ask, why do you stay with him? It's because we're different, because we're like the black sheep who stand out from the herd, always saying what we feel, what's on our mind. That binds us. Before the plebiscite, we used to tell the NGOS that they were not acting right. After the plebiscite we continued to tell them the same thing, that they used 70 percent, 80 percent of their money on salaries, vehicles, and personal amenities, instead of reaching the communities. We told them what we thought, and that closed many doors for us. Even though I'm a Christian Democrat, a concertacionista interested in negotiation and understanding, both Juan and I are still capable of telling the *Concertación* and the present government, which today is Frei's, that it's acting badly. That closes many doors, and even if you were about to get a job, suddenly they say no. Even if they've said look, I guarantee you my support, I'm with you, you'll get a job at CONADI, it was enough for me to say no to a few things they wanted me to do for them to turn around and say sorry, we had to give the job to someone else.

F: *Is this just the way the political party system works, or do you think there are other reasons to explain this type of . . .*

I think it's the way political parties operate, that if you don't obey the party line, don't keep to their objectives, then you're not one of them and you become dangerous, if not an enemy, then at least dangerous, not trustworthy. So then you stop being an insider and they throw you in a pile with the rest, saying don't call us, we'll call you. Supposedly they still take you into account, you're still a member of the party, but little by little you realize they're only using you. I've seen this happen in the Party for Democracy (*Partido por la Democracia*, or PPD), I've seen it among the Socialists, I've seen it among the Christian Democrats. I can't say I've seen it in the National Party, because I'm not very close to them, but I'm pretty sure the Communist Party does the same thing with my people, meaning the Mapuche who participate in politics.

I remember a moment here in the IX Region when a number of us discussed the possibility of fielding a Mapuche unity slate for the congressional elections. All our parties called us and told us we couldn't do that. I remember the calls to Ramón Chanqueo, José Luis Levi, Isolde Reuque, and José Santos Millao, who were the viable candidates here in the region. And when the time comes to choose candidates they put another on your same initial slate, both to show they're not against fielding a Mapuche candidate, but at the same time making sure they've padded the list so the Mapuche doesn't get the top vote count. Because the nonindigenous candidate has the money, resources, and contacts, and because his friends help him, he always wins.

Let me tell you, I've been asked to run many times; most recently I received the second offer to run for city council. Twice I've said no, even though I wanted to run, out of fear of coming in second, because I'm a woman, because I don't have money, because I couldn't reach all the out-of-the-way places the other candidates would get to in their fancy cars. At the county level you have to visit everybody, people expect you to get there and talk to them, to make promises; and they like you best if you get there first, eh? Or if you're last you better know how to make your entrance. So I said no, simply because I didn't have five million pesos and a luxurious pickup truck with an extended cabin, which is what you need. This may not be pleasant, but it's the truth: not everyone can be a candidate. A candidate must be able to move around, and even if it's not your own money, you need people to lend you the vehicles and the money, for a minimum of three months, which is the length of the campaign season. And you have to make posters, calendars; people expect you to distribute all the little knick-knacks they like.

F: *And the party doesn't contribute any of these?*

The party gives you the minimum, the absolute minimum. It gives you the name, the label. The Christian Democratic Party gives you the use of their symbol, the little red arrow with the two crossbars symbolizing its main principles. And maybe they make you a little pocket calendar, which is what they've made for all the candidates; and perhaps a poster no bigger than eleven by fourteen, in color, on nice cardboard, that may or may not arrive in the last two weeks.

F: *Given all of this, I can't help but ask, why are you still in the party?*

Good question. I'm a Christian Democrat, and will continue in the Christian Democratic Party, only as long as I think it's useful to me. I think that, being within the party structure, it's easier to meet people and get to know them. But it's important to point out, quite honestly, that I've only been a card-carrying Christian Democrat since 1994, late 1994, which isn't that long.

F: *In all the previous years, when everybody said you were a Christian Democrat, you weren't actually a member of the party.*

I never was before, and I never wanted to be. After 1994 I became a Christian Democrat because, as a Mapuche, I believe deeply in humanism and social justice. And, obviously, I'm democratic, too. At the same time I can work well with people from all political parties, without exception, whether I like them or not. I've sat down with *Miristas*, Communists, members of the National Renovation Party (*Renovación Nacional*).[11] If there's a job to be done, a clear goal to meet, I can do it, no problem; I don't put up roadblocks when there's a truly multicultural, multiparty, or multidisciplinary vision. I don't have misgivings about that, and I think it's a gift, because it's easy to be sectarian when you've been discriminated against over and over again. Yet if that's the way you react you end up being no different than the racists who've discriminated against you. Now it's true that I'm sometimes racist or discriminatory in my thoughts, but in practice, in terms of working with people, I'm not.

Being in the Christian Democratic Party and getting to know it from the inside has given me a new perspective, a new understanding of how party structures work, in relation to my people, in relation to the neediest people in society, or to put it bluntly, in relation to the marginal classes of this country. This has been a particularly intense time for the Christian Democratic Party, and therefore a good time for me to participate actively. I've learned how the structures work, what the fight is like from the inside, those fights that I never understood before, when people would call you "long-hair" (*chascón*), "visionary" (*iluminado*), "pot-bellied" (*guatón*), "singleton" or "stray" (*huacho/a*). Each group has its own line or sensibility within the party. I'd always said heck, I'm just a Christian Democrat. Hey pot-belly, how can you associate with that long-hair! And I'd look at the guy and there'd be nothing long-haired about him, good haircut, well groomed and all.[12]

As a matter of fact, one of the reasons I joined the Christian Democratic Party is that people in the Mapuche organizations respect you more if they see that you belong to a party. Whether they nominate you for a particular position or not, they take you into account if they know you're in a political party. But when people don't know where you belong, they think, well, she's not beholden to anybody and she's not going to get support from anybody, so why talk with her or invite her, it won't make any difference. Let's invite this other guy who's in a party structure. It matters less what you think, what your ideas are, than the fact you're in a party; that's when they'll always invite you.

The reason I didn't serve on the CEPI's council, even though I was elected by Nehuen-Mapu, was that I was not a card-carrying Christian Democrat. I was elected, seventy people voted for me. Because I received the highest vote count over several other candidates, my name was sent to President Patricio Aylwin and to José Bengoa, who directed CEPI, in the document that listed all the nominees from our region. Each organization sent President Aylwin a name and he was going to choose from that list. Everyone said someone would be picked from the left, and someone who's a Christian Democrat would have to be picked. But I wasn't a Christian Democrat. I was in Nehuen-Mapu, which clearly followed a Christian Democratic vision, supported and guided by folks from the Christian Democratic Party, but I was not a party member. So I could not be on the CEPI council, and instead Juan Queupán, who wasn't even a member of Nehuen-Mapu, got picked. I'm not saying he's a bad person, he's not, he's a good person, hardworking and everything. But he hadn't yet committed to his indigenous identity, he hadn't yet assumed the full responsibility of being Huilliche. He was more a Christian Democrat, an activist in defense of human rights who'd served on CODEJU, the Commission for Juvenile Rights. And since he was in Santiago, he was better positioned to influence people; it was easier for folks to say, OK, this comrade's in.

F: *So here we have a very deep contradiction, and if you see a solution perhaps you can tell me what it is. Political parties operate with an internal discipline that demands giving priority to party interests over all others, and if you don't agree you end up marginalized. In Ad-Mapu, for example, this has caused a lot of problems, because people pushed their parties' interests inside the organization, otherwise they couldn't advance in their party, right?*

This doesn't just happen in Ad-Mapu, it happens in all the organizations.

F: *Let's just take Ad-Mapu as an example.*

Yes, definitely.

F: *If party dynamics divide social organizations, it would seem that as a Mapuche and as a feminist, you'd have a double reason for opposing a party system that weakens the very movements you care about so much. But on the other hand, if you don't have a political party identity and don't understand their internal workings, you can't have influence and weight in this country's social organizations and political system. So what do you do? Do you think there's a way this could change in the future, or do you think it's just the way it is?*

Well, I don't think there's a way to change this soon, because we indigenous people don't have the kind of solid unity we'd need in order to move forward. There are possibilities for change, though, and I'm one of those who believes that we can use laws—whether the Constitution or the Electoral Law, I'm not quite sure yet—to change the way political representation works, especially here in the IX Region where we have districts with a highly concentrated indigenous population. In those districts, I think that if two deputies are sent to Congress, one of them should be indigenous, elected by the Mapuches. This would increase indigenous sociopolitical participation and organizational activity and imply a legal recognition by the state, thereby paving the way for the constitutional recognition of indigenous people. And within this we Mapuche women might also consider the possibility of having our own candidate, even knowing that men vote mostly for men, but we could field a man and a woman and see who gets elected. It's an idea, a possible solution; it's something we still need to consider further.

I don't think the political party system is going to generate a lot more Huenchumillas. Francisco Huenchumilla is an excellent legislator, but I don't think he emphasizes his Mapuche origin. He doesn't participate in any of the basic structures of Mapuche society: he doesn't participate in the gillatun or attend palin games; if people lack something in the communities, he's not the first one who shows up. Now, he is someone who came up through a community structure, he has his roots there, he has family there; but he doesn't participate at the grassroots. And when he was elected, he said something that's true even though it's hard to hear: he said he'd been elected by the people of Temuco and not by the Mapuche, that he represented a district with very few indigenous communities. There are some, but not many. So obviously the majority of his constituency is not Mapuche, that's true; but if he wants to be senator, he should work with the communities, with their leaders, be with them and talk with them, and share his knowledge with them. And that means inviting not only the Christian Democrats who are Mapuche, but also the Mapuche leaders of other persuasions to talk with him.[13]

F: *You mean from the communities, from the organizations.*

From the communities and the organizations. Then one could say that he was responding to the concerns of his people, because we're always trying to increase the number of scholarships for our young people so they can give back the knowledge to their communities. He went to school on a state scholarship; it wasn't on my watch, because I'm a lot younger than he is. But he's a good example of what the elders and today's leaders have hoped and dreamed for: an educated and successful Mapuche able to give back to the communities. Now what he's managed to do, as a Mapuche, to get elected to Congress from a mostly wigka district, is extremely difficult and not just anyone can do it.

F: *After the recent municipal elections, in a seminar for Mapuche leaders in Puerto Saavedra, I witnessed a discussion of why, with more than 50 percent Mapuche voters, none of the Mapuche candidates were elected. One of the most frequent explanations people gave was envy. This made me wonder if it's possible to further an ethnic agenda through electoral and party politics, because there seems to be a missing link between Mapuche organizational and community politics, and the electoral process. While the Mapuche participate actively in elections, they seem to do so as individuals rather than applying their sense of Mapuche identity, their feelings of belonging to a Mapuche organization, culture, or community, to the electoral process itself. It seems that elections and Mapuche identity are two different, almost contradictory, things. What's been your experience, and how do you see it?*

It's very complicated, because at first glance you really do see a lot of envy, selfishness, and suspicion. Mapuches in the parties obey their leaders, people who are not party members listen to their friends. Mapuches express their dislike silently, in the voting booth. They like to listen to everyone, say yes to everyone, and keep their votes to themselves. One thing I've seen happen in the countryside, in both municipal and congressional elections, is that when a candidate arrives people will say yes, yes, we'll vote for you. But then you fix the road from here to there, you bring paint for our school or health care center; or else we need this or that, a roof for the community center, there's always something they need. And once they feel taken into account, the creative people in the communities will make things for you, for the election, for this other thing. So I think there's a lack of political culture, wigka political culture, in the communities.

And on the other hand there's absolute disillusionment; people don't see their elected officials responding to their concerns. Why? Because people don't see what their congressman does over there, in Valparaíso, it isn't tangible. They don't say, look, so-and-so got this law passed, he collaborated with this other guy and the law was passed, he did something good for our district. If the congressman does something concrete for the community, it doesn't matter if he's terrible in the Chamber of Deputies. If he builds a school or community center, if he donates machinery—like, for example, a well-equipped tractor—it doesn't matter if he never shows his face in the Chamber.

Let me give you an example. There's a senator from Malleco who's really loved and respected by people in the countryside. Now, you might say that's because he spends time in the countryside. Congresspeople have two, three days a week, I think, two or three days to be in their districts, and he uses his very well, visiting both urban and rural areas. So he's capable of buying and delivering soccer balls, improving roads, and blaming others for the problems that crop up. "Look," he'll say, "it's not my fault, I asked for that, but the bureaucrat in that office just sits on his hands, and here's the letter to prove it." Because his staff does their homework, he usually has the answer in his hand.

This guy wasn't even there when the Indigenous Law came up for the vote, he didn't even show up! That really caught my attention. But he's really well-loved in the communities, because for the palines, for the soccer games, he'll be there with the nets, the balls. Very astute, this guy, a real populist. So these kinds of things make you wonder if the congressional system we have here in

Chile really allows us to elect the best representatives. The ones who get elected are already well positioned to climb on the congressional train, they have the money, the resources; they're given easy access to everything. Some times they can be the best representatives, but often it's the worst possible representatives who make up our honorable Congress. Now this makes clear to me that, whether we start by reforming the parties or the electoral system, something has to change.

F: *The other option is to reform the organizations, to begin from the bottom up.*

That's probably the most urgent thing right now. Personally I'd like to start reforming the organizations by renovating the leaders, because there's no point in canonizing Santos Millao just because his name means "saint." Unless the organizations move quickly and encourage the emergence of new and capable leaders, the state and the political party structures will continue referring to and depending on people like José Santos Millao. But the organizations will mobilize only to the degree that they get financial, social, and political support. Without support people can do little in the broader society, because their needs are great and that means they must begin by working in their communities. And this easily becomes a vicious circle, because renewing the organizations and their leaders can only happen with the support of political parties, there's no alternative. And I worry that this will yield future indigenous leaders who, from the very beginning, are cut in the mold of this or that party. I see it happening already, I see it coming. Fewer and fewer leaders have an autonomous mission. Fewer of them will be capable of saying, "Look, first I was born Mapuche, then I became a Christian, and finally a Democrat, and if I put these three concepts together I am a Mapuche Christian Democrat." I think that instead they'll say, "My name is so-and-so and I belong to such and such a party; and by the way, I'm Mapuche."

F: *I'm puzzled by what seems to be a vicious circle between grassroots movements and political parties, and not just because I'm working on Mapuche history. It's also confusing at a more general political level, because it doesn't matter on which end you try to break the cycle, you end up going around in circles again, right? Do you know what I mean?*

Yes, yes. For me, a very emotional woman, it's been especially frustrating. Many times I've been tempted to just abandon everything, for that very same reason. I don't see a way out, I don't see a way to channel all this energy and hope that blossoms, that you can hear in the speeches but is missing in practice. We say we want autonomy, and we fight for it. How beautiful it would be if the Mapuche people had autonomy! We want organizational and political autonomy; but in order to have these we also need economic autonomy, and we don't have that. And we're not willing to pay even monthly dues, because we don't have the means to pay them, to pay rigorously set quotas like the tithe the Evangelicals are required to pay, that they pay no matter what. We don't have that custom, we aren't willing to do this, and personally, I couldn't do it, because as it is I have difficulty paying 1 percent to the Catholic Church. In fact, given my negative income, the Catholic Church ends up paying me more than I pay them! But seriously, it's very difficult in this sense, I think, and in these times. I don't want to force my perspective on you, and maybe I'm confusing you even more with my own insecurities and internal conflicts. But I insist there should be a set percentage of Mapuche representatives in Congress and Mapuche aldermen in the region, elected by popular vote, with a binomial electoral system, or whatever you want to call it. But unless there's some way to require that some of us be elected, we'll never be elected.

F: *What you seem to be suggesting is that any in-depth reform needs to follow different paths at once. On one side, the party structures need to represent the diversity of the population. But on the other side, the mass movements need to be renovated, the electoral districts reorganized, and the election processes reformed, all taking into account the same population diversity.*

Yes, that about sums it up.

F: *A little ambitious, don't you think?*

Maybe so, but I believe that it's our hopes, dreams, and ambitions that move the world. If we dream, we can't just leave it at that. We have to try and make our dreams a reality.

F: *And in the meantime, you'll keep learning within the party system?*

I think so, at least for now. I've learned a lot, I've understood a lot. But I think you've seen that my greatest school has not been the Christian Democratic Party, but the Mapuche movement, the communities, and the different problems people face in the communities. The years I yearn for, the years I cry for, are the five initial ones of the Mapuche movement, 1978 to 1983. I lose sleep when I think of them, but they also give me joy and happiness, they dignify me, they exhilarate me and provoke me each day to continue working.

For me, between 1978 and 1983, our struggle had teeth. We battled furiously, with intensity and conviction, and we didn't seek personal advantages of any kind. Our main objective was to elevate, to honor, and to increase the participation of the Mapuche people. We were also helping to say good-bye to the General and to reach democracy, a stable democracy for Chile. We were all in it together, and we were many. With the arrival of democracy we entered a slump, I don't know if it was more from exhaustion, relief, disenchantment, or disillusionment. But the great majority of those who fought, Mapuches and non-Mapuches, accepted positions in the government. And that produces a downturn, because those who didn't get government positions feel resentful, while the ones who did get positions expect the excluded ones to help them and support them. So you get this rupture between government officials and movement leaders, deeper for some than for others, which instead of facilitating cooperation between the two groups makes them into adversaries, even enemies, because if you're not with me, you're against me. I think this helps explain the divisions and lack of dynamism in the Mapuche movement today,[14] because the great majority of the people who participated between 1978 and 1990 today hold jobs in different public offices, not only in CONADI, but in other agencies as well. So the movement was shorn of leaders and members. And those who stayed, unfortunately, tended to be those who had nowhere else to go.

CHAPTER FOUR

The Mapuche Movement under Democracy, 1990–1998

The first Mapuche women's organization was born on September 24, 1991, with the transition to democracy; it was born with twenty-five women. That date's an accident, the truth is it should've been sooner, fifteen days earlier more or less, when we'd actually decided to hold our first meeting. I don't remember exactly when that first date was, but we'd contacted each other and said let's meet, let's create a women's organization. So what happened? Men as well as women who found out about it started saying, hey, the date's been changed, there's no such meeting, it's been canceled. These men and women got together to abort the very idea of a women's organization. So we tried a second time, and the 24th of September was chosen because that's when all the women could attend. So the day has little meaning in itself. The meaning lies in what happened, that it was the day we got together, the day we decided to create this organization, to follow through on our original idea.

We chose the name that day, too. We brought four names to choose from, and the one that stuck was *Keyukleayñ pu Zomo*—women helping each other. Depending on the context, *"keyukleayñ pu zomo"* can mean women in action, solidarity among women, or women helping each other. Personally I prefer women in action, but what we usually say is solidarity among women. At that first meeting we also talked about the different reasons it was important for women to unite: that women were the majority; that women generally did the majority of the work, both productive and domestic; that we worked the most to preserve customs and traditions; that we were the essential educators and the givers of life. So these were the things we discussed at the first meeting. This was the beginning, let's say, of the women's organization.

F: *So did the women in this organization come from all points on the political spectrum?*

From all political tendencies. Then and now, they belonged to sociopolitical organizations outside the communities, as well as to traditional organizations inside the communities.

Our objective was and is to dignify women. We were born precisely because Mapuche women were not given prominent roles in any Mapuche organization. They always occupied secondary positions, as secretaries, treasurers, in charge of this or that thing in the communities, or in the city they'd set the table, serve the food. They'd provide the pretty face, they were the flower arrangements.

A good example is Ana Llao, a prominent Mapuche leader who received a secondary school scholarship from Ad-Mapu when I was still a leader. Later on she became a leader in Ad-Mapu, National President for two years. But no one remembers that part; nobody points out that Ana Llao was one of the leaders who signed the agreement in Imperial; nobody says that she is one of the most principled and visionary leaders of the Mapuche left. She's a member of the Communist Party, but first and foremost she's a socially committed militant for the Mapuche cause with a clear grasp of gender issues. She's now working full time, because she has to feed her son. She's a single mother. She had a partner but he left, so now her own and her son's survival depend exclusively on her. She's working in a polyclinic that's part of the Health Department of Araucanía, in a program called *Amulzungun*. It's an orientation program to help the Mapuche who use these facilities, especially the Miraflores office. I'm very glad she has a job, because without it she'd have no income; but the Mapuche movement has lost in her a visionary woman. When she was president of Ad-Mapu she received international support, so she could survive. But here in Chile nobody values her. To this very day her merit hasn't been recognized, not by her fellow organizers, not even by the man who was her partner, another Ad-Mapu leader. I think she deserves better. She should be encouraged to advance to higher positions of leadership and responsibility.

F: *Do you think this happened to her because she's a woman?*

I think it happened because she's a woman, but also because she doesn't have a professional title or a technical degree, so there are positions she can't fill. She finished high school, but beyond that she's self-taught, like most of us, autodidactic. She has obviously participated in meetings, seminars, international forums, in courses and workshops that last three months, maybe a year, but nothing more. So you can take these computer classes for a year, maybe a class on indigenous rights for six months; and that's not a degree. At most you get a certificate of participation and regular attendance.

F: *And you think this same kind of problem confronts the majority of Mapuche women who are leaders?*

I think that's right, and it's especially difficult for women who've been leaders in the Mapuche movement. It happens less to NGO functionaries, because they get the chance to study. Perhaps the greatest advantage the NGOs who hired indigenous people were able to offer was a chance to study. Some universities held Saturday classes in some specialties, like social planning or administration. Or else people studied at night while they worked during the day, because you have to pay for a professional degree. It's not so much the lack of time as the lack of money, because careers aren't cheap; they can cost between thirty thousand and fifty thousand pesos a month.[1] So it isn't that you're unable to study, it's that you can't afford to study; that's the catch. What happened in my household was that Juan and I decided that one of us would study, and we decided Juan should study first. He was eligible for an indigenous scholarship, which I wasn't because I was already over thirty. For me to study I'd have to pay it all out of pocket, and someone needed to hold down a stable job in order to do that. So the only solution was for him to get his accounting degree and then he could eventually pay for my studies.

F: *Has Lucy Traipe had an experience similar to yours and Ana's? She's the main receptionist at the offices of CONADI's National Deputy Director, and it seems to me she hasn't had the opportunity to continue studying, either.*

What happened to Lucy, to Elisa Avendaño, and to other women is that they worked in NGOs that gave them the opportunity to study. When CEPI was created, Lucy Traipe spoke with José Bengoa. She was facing a very critical economic situation, and she was a leader in Ad-Mapu, so she talked with José Bengoa and he told her she could work in the CEPI's Temuco office. She began in CEPI Temuco doing the cleaning, and she always complained that, despite being a movement leader and having finished high school, she had to clean the floors, the bathrooms, the offices. So Bengoa himself told her, "Look, what I can do is have CEPI pay for a secretarial degree for you in addition to your salary," which wasn't much. So she studied two years at the *Instituto de las Americas*, completing the typing and keyboarding course. Since she was studying keyboarding, Víctor Hugo Painemal, who was the CEPI Director in Temuco, let her use the machines and the computer they had at CEPI, so she could learn more and do well in the course. Lucy's a dedicated woman, a hard worker, and Víctor Hugo would tell her, "Come with me to this meeting at such and such a place, because most people talk in Mapuche there so I need you to translate." Lucy would go, she'd translate for him, help him out. She'd explain to people in Mapuche what CEPI was, and so in effect she became a leader in CEPI.

F: *So then she studied keyboarding after high school, but she didn't get a professional title, like in engineering or something like that . . .*

No, no, nothing like that. She completed keyboarding, which includes typing and a course as executive secretary, that's the basic course she completed. She's a good secretary and with practice she can handle a computer. She can manage all that, she's already done it in the past.

F: *So far we've been talking about the experience of different Mapuche women leaders, who face discrimination partly because they're women, and partly because they can't study. Are these two problems related?*

Very much so, because if a family in a community can afford to send only one of five children to school, it will most probably be the son and not the daughter. The reasons people give are that it's better to send a man out to study, that nothing can happen to him. A daughter is more likely to end up with problems, by which people usually mean an unwanted pregnancy, or else she won't finish her career, or she'll have more problems finding a place to live. A son is easier to set up with room and board. He can sleep anywhere and is less responsibility for the person running the boarding house. Plus you don't often find special boarding houses for indigenous students; here in the IX Region there's only one. Besides, women can find work more easily without an education. They can be domestic workers, or else serve at a coffee shop, in the kitchen of a restaurant, a dining hall, whatever. Whatever it is they can work at something, usually in the service sector, but hardly ever specialized work, not even in a kitchen. Many years have to pass before a woman even gets to be head cook, that's just the way it goes. So women have historically found it easy to get work taking care of children, cleaning, cooking. Though lately, with all this talk of modernity and everything, some people are actually requiring that their nannies have high school diplomas, just to raise their kids.

F: *We've already spoken a bit about this, but what motivated you most deeply to begin thinking of a women's movement, of a women's organization?*

What motivated me the most was the lack of recognition, the devaluation, of women in the communities. Even though they did everything, it seemed as if they did nothing, and they generally were relegated to second-class positions as secretaries, treasurers, or program directors. Though women are in charge of all traditional Mapuche ceremonial activities—appropriate food and dress, the formalities of each situation, how to do things—and even though machis are well-respected in the communities, as great leaders and important women who have crucial knowledge and wisdom, women in general aren't fully appreciated. Respected, yes, and also loved; but they're not valued for their strength and dignity. In the broader organizations, the more sociopolitical ones whose structures have more wigka influence, trade and professional associations, for example, women don't hold the influential positions, either. Except for Ana Llao, who was President of Ad-Mapu, the rest of us haven't held those kinds of positions. And not because we didn't have the ability, but because we never got the number of votes men got in order to be elected.

I was also motivated by personal experiences with discrimination, things that happened to me along the way. I'd been left out or passed over because I didn't commit to one specific political party; or didn't come out unconditionally in favor of certain people; or because I looked at situations critically, always looking for other alternatives, other possibilities, even if I agreed with the one being presented. I've always felt that there isn't one unique solution to a problem, there're always more than one. And I think people don't like that, especially when it's a woman who speaks. Men in general, Mapuche men, don't like it when a woman speaks. They want women to serve them, half-guessing at what they need. They want women to do everything, accept everything, without the smallest complaint. And this applies to my father, my brothers, the leaders I've met, even my husband. There are no exceptions: they all expect you to be docile, submissive, never questioning what they do. And the moment you question, they intimidate you in public, or else they say well yes, that's a very good idea. But if it wasn't their idea, they push it to the side; and maybe twenty minutes later they retake it, change the wording, and present it as their own. Then it's valid, then it's worthy. So that really gets under my skin.

Another thing that motivated me to form a women's organization was more personal, if you will, related to my own sensibility and identity as a woman. The male leaders in our movement thought nothing of disrespecting and making fun of their own Mapuche sisters. What I mean is that they went to bed with the women, taking advantage of their status as leaders. They'd promise the women marriage, but their only objective was the sexual act. Many of the women ended up pregnant and the men never assumed their responsibilities as fathers. So when men criticize women in the movement, I believe their criticism has no moral authority.

When I say it has no moral authority, they ask me what morality am I talking about: Mapuche, Christian, or Chilean morality. And I tell them, real-life morality, the kind that's decent and doesn't discriminate, and in this sense I believe caciques aren't morally justifiable anymore. Caciques used to have a dozen, half a dozen women, but today the conditions just aren't the same. When our people faced a condition of permanent war, the women themselves decided that their duty was to procreate children in order to defend the people. Today we don't have the land or the healthy environment we used to have, we can't sustain life in the same way anymore. People don't have the economic means, so if a man has one, two, three, four, five, six women, they end up supporting him instead of the other way around. And already I'm thinking badly of him, because he's acting like a pimp, an opportunist. We talked about this among several women, and I said, "Look, a Mapuche leader who has six children in one year is not a man, he's an animal, and his word is absolutely worthless. And to top it off, he never takes responsibility for any of them? How nice, they all carry his last name, but what does he give them? Not even a crumb." So I insist that men like these don't deserve to be valued or recognized as leaders. But unfortunately, from 1983 to the present, different Mapuche leaders have behaved this way. And I think it's time to say so. It may be that today I choose not to name names, but those who know, know; and if this reaches the hands of a guilty party, he'll hopefully see it as a clear indication of why these women formed a women's organization.

I was also motivated by my own pain. I think that when you're deeply touched by something, your everyday life and actions are affected. In personal conversations with other Mapuche women we've told each other many things, from the most personal, intimate confidences to our perspectives on external, political issues. And I've felt touched politically and sentimentally, as well as in my Mapuche identity. I thank my sisters, my *lamñen*, who with great effort managed to tell me, to share with me details I don't think they've told anyone else. This gave me the hope that we could form a women's organization, and that it would be respected. And we've survived to this day, although it's true we have no funding, but we've continued working. Many of the women are community leaders in Launache, Cholchol, Cullinco, and other places. Heading the communities, or heading concrete projects within the communities, they're willing to participate in their own way, as dictated by their specific situations. And one thing we've found is that you can't organize effectively by saying hey, only women here, men don't count. Because that style of claiming equality only pits us against fathers, brothers, uncles, grandfathers, and husbands. So we've had to find a way to show how human beings, be they men or women, must complement each other in all aspects of life, not only in some spheres or activities. So this is how we were born September 24, 1991, at first only a de facto organization, but once CONADI began advocating the inscription of indigenous associations, we registered our name and received legal recognition.

F: *Does this same organization still exist today, and do you still participate in it?*

This year we hold a congress to elect a new steering committee.[2] We're still very active, there's thirty of us from different places. Ten of us are from the city, from here in Temuco. The others are from rural communities, mostly from Cholchol, Imperial, Freire, and Pitrufquén. I think that in September we'll elect a new steering committee.

F: *And what kind of work have you done?*

Initially we began with workshops of various kinds, especially leadership training. We've participated in the constitution of communities, in the legal recognition and reestablishment of indigenous communities in different regions. We've participated in seminars, in concrete projects related to adult education, what is called Fundamental Adult Education (*Educación Fundamental de Adulto*, or EFA). Our goal has always been to carry out specific tasks in each of the communities and neighborhoods involved, according to people's needs and interests. In the end, we've found that participation always involves both men and women. Women drag along their husbands, sons, and fathers to many of the activities. Generally we've agreed that, when we finish something, we invite the entire community, as well as issuing some special invitations, to a final celebration. But the community often begins attending long before we reach the closing event. And it's been wonderful, learning how to write projects, training leaders, teaching women to read and write—which is not often emphasized in the communities. We've also helped people with marketing techniques, buying and selling products, things like that. And we've had discussions about the Indigenous Law, what's good, what's bad, what can be improved, what we'd like to change. Each of these activities has been done in different places.

F: *I remember that the first time I came to visit you at your home you were with a friend of yours who worked in an organization for domestic workers.*

Aurora. Yes, Aurora is vice-president of our organization. She's a domestic worker; she used to hold a leadership position in the organization for domestic workers, but now she's just a member there and vice-president of our women's organization.

F: *So you also collaborate with other women's organizations?*

Yes, we're an active member of the Coalition of Mapuche Organizations in the IX Region. With several other women's organizations we worked on training and preparing for the 1996 Beijing International Women's Conference, and on the follow-up after Beijing. Now, other women's organizations, like the *Casa de la Mujer Mapuche* (House of the Mapuche Woman), for example, are not sociopolitical organizations but have a more specific objective. The *Casa de la Mujer Mapuche* is an NGO with the sole purpose of buying and selling crafts and artisanal products. Through them as an NGO you can participate in training programs, but not in political issues.

At the local level women have formed organizations in their communities, but they haven't received the publicity, the recognition, you might say, that we have. I think the women who are in the organization I presently lead are guaranteed a certain public presence through me because, with all due modesty, I'm pretty well known. The organizations of women artisans, or of women from the communities—in Boyeco, or the *Ñimen Rayen*[3] that's here close to Temuco—they're also women's associations. There are a number of them in different places, but they don't have public recognition. They also haven't had the finesse to insert themselves in the mass media or in the sociopolitical arena, be it indigenous or nonindigenous. So they're not part of the wider political discussions.

F: *Have you communicated with these other organizations, and found out what they do? Has your organization developed a relationship with them, helped them reach out to other areas, or has this not yet been part of your project?*

Part of our work has involved contacting them and meeting with them. But when they depend on NGOs, as is the case with *Ñimen Rayen*, which depends exclusively on *Logko Kilapán*, then they don't have the autonomy or flexibility to work with us and share activities. The *Casa de la Mujer Mapuche* is also an NGO, and in both cases communication needs to go through the NGO. When one organization depends on another, when they have specific, more technical or health-related goals, they will tend to focus on the particular project for which they've received assistance and funding. Not so in our case, since our organization wasn't born with a specific, grant-generating project; and this has given us greater independence and the ability to survive from 1991 to the present. By contrast, the organizations that are born with an economic project, with well-planned and carefully defined goals and activities, tend to die when their technocrats move on. That's happened to a number of them already.

F: *There's a widespread debate in women's movements over how important it is to remain autonomous from other organizations. One of the the arguments in favor is what you just said, that if a women's organization depends on another political party or association, it stops existing the moment the priorities of that party or organization no longer include it. But at the same time, your group doesn't keep men from participating in your activities. So how do you see, in the case of your organization, the relationship between an autonomous space for women and the inclusion of other social groups?*

I think we must always be autonomous, in the sense that we make autonomous decisions about when and how others can participate. If men understand clearly that we are an autonomous organization, and that they'll never be able to occupy leadership positions, if they understand this fully and still want to participate under a woman's direction, then they are very welcome. But we won't allow them to join if they think they can become leaders and make decisions. Women must be the ones in charge of the decisions, the planning process, and the activities themselves; they'll invite the participation of others. Just as the men have their organizations and they make the decisions, sign the agreements, and then have us participate, we have to do the same with them.

Let me give you a few examples of why we need an autonomous space. I've already explained the strong criticisms I have of male leaders in the Mapuche movement, and I'm going to tie their stale, outdated machismo to the need for an independent women's organization. We announced our existence in 1990, to be precise, informally at first; we were legally constituted in 1992. Listen to what the leaders said, both male and female: that we were lesbians, that we were incompetent, that we had narrow minds, that we broke with our Mapuche culture, that we were frustrated, and I'm only mentioning the less colorful taunts they threw at us. Women listen to the same kinds of sneers in any part of the world when they organize to do something! And yet these gibes hurt us much more when they were directed at us by men who abused women, or by women who'd had a child, maybe two, with a leader they knew had children elsewhere. As I see it, these reactions demonstrate why women need their own space.

Now, in traditional Mapuche communities I think that women's dignity and participation has always received the utmost respect. The machi carries ancestral knowledge, knowledge about nature; your average Mapuche mother who lives in a community is the one who knows the herbs, the foods, the crafts; she knows the customs, the traditions. She's the one who strategizes subsistence, the home economist; she's learned to live in harmony with nature, she knows the legends and the stories and she teaches the children. It's the mother, not the father. The father is the one who says look, go talk with her; he can make the pretty speeches (*weupin*), but he listens, and he sits next to the fire and says, yes, that's how it is, and he learns from his wife about the proper behavior and language of the Mapuche.

Somehow, when this kind of participation—in local religious rites, sports events, solidarity work in the community organization itself or in traditional organizations—gets integrated into the sociopolitical organizations of today, into a broader political framework, women get marginalized. You know, if in the communities men and women have a more equal public presence, in these broader Mapuche social and political organizations, which are more in the wigka style, women take a back seat. Women aren't capable of transcending the boundaries of their own homes, the borders of their own community, because their husbands don't let them, because their brothers don't let them, or simply because the men in the community don't allow them to go any further. This happens even though women have a different perspective, a different vision; they're more politically aware.

Men have a narrower view of reality. They're colder, more calculating; they're always thinking about how much they'll produce, what they'll sell, how long they'll stay. I'm talking about the present, eh? They think about political gain, they say let's go to this event because so-and-so will be there, and it'll be to my advantage. So the leader has to arrive surrounded by his retinue of women, and that's when women are very welcome if they're all decked out in full costume. Oh, she looked pretty, how beautiful she was, I want her at my side. But they don't give you the floor when it's time to speak. It's the men who deliver the speeches, who discuss what's happening, not the women. And who are the secretaries, who does the cleaning, who does the work, who does the thinking, who designs the projects? Generally, almost always, it's the women. In Ad-Mapu, Nehuen-Mapu, Choinfolilche, Kallfulikan, Roble Huacho, Rehue: it's women who do it all. They're the secretaries, the treasurers, the program directors; they make the proposals and the projections; they write and they transcribe. And men show off presenting the projects and reading the proposals.

So this is where our questions, criticisms, and misgivings came from, because we knew we weren't second-class citizens and we were no longer willing to be the flower arrangements. As women, we demanded recognition for our ability to think, and for the practical work we do every day. In this sense our struggle to participate, to stand up and be counted, to be a part of the social and political structures of the Mapuche movement has been fruitful. Initially I began this struggle with a group of sisters, of lamñen, and many dropped out along the way. But I understand them, and I admire them for having had the courage to start. In some cases they left because they had to preserve their family, because if they continued in the group they would lose part of their family. Obviously, in cases like that, they needed to use their strength to keep their family together, and inside that family they could teach our values and highlight the importance of the work women do.

I've traveled around to countless places, and I've always said that if a man doesn't recognize the importance of what women do, then he's denying value to his mother, his wife, his daughter. If a man isn't capable of making the smallest changes in the household, like learning to wash his own laundry, sew his own buttons, helping with things, then he also loses. Let me give you only one example: the Mapuches who join the army are the ones who get kicked around the most, they suffer the most abuse and punishment. Why? Sometimes, Mapuche recruits even die. Why? Because they don't know how to wash clothes, sew on buttons, iron clothes; they don't know how to do anything, not even set the table. That's why they suffer, that's why they're punished. If they did even one of these things once a week in their homes, they'd learn to understand their mothers.

You know, these things I'm telling you here, I've said them throughout the countryside. I've told people that the man who does laundry, hangs the clothes out to dry, goes with his mother to the clinic when she takes his little brother, goes with his wife when she takes the baby to the clinic or to the children's school meetings, doesn't stop being a man. He grows and becomes stronger as a man. He's recovering a part of himself that he's lost, unlearning a lesson that unfortunately he's learned from the wigkas. Why do we learn the bad things, instead of the good things? Men were shocked at first. They'd tell me, "Look, friend, you've got style, you've got courage, clarity, and everything; but don't come stirring up my henhouse." And yet these very same men support me now, and they say, "Isolde, go to my community, speak to the men and the women about what women's participation is." I've won a space inside the communities and the organizations because I've stuck to my principles and haven't given up.

I have to admit that, at one point, I was left alone. And even though Juan and I have had plenty of problems communicating, he was still my best cheering section. He told me, "don't give up, you have to go on, you can do it." And he'd show me how right I was by analyzing the relationship between my mother and father, or his father and mother, who were the closest people we had. "Look," he'd say, "look at what your father says, the gestures he makes toward your mother." I hadn't even noticed most of it, because after all, it was my own father. You love him, you know him, he's there every day, you don't really question his behavior, you see it as normal. But my husband would say, "look, my father does this and my mother says nothing; or else she says this or does that." Don't get me wrong; my husband is not a saint. We've had plenty of ups and downs in our relationship; he's younger than I am, for one thing, and also his work isn't going well, he hasn't found stability, and obviously that stresses him out. He's decided to study, and he has a lot on his plate between his studies and not finding a job, then suddenly finding work in this or that small project, which is always short-term, but you have to be serious about working on it. He and I have always criticized others for not taking their projects seriously, so when it's our turn we have to take them seriously and work hard. So with all these pressures it's been difficult for me, for us both. But I think it's given me strength, and I've learned a lot. I've learned that suffering and hard knocks can help you get ahead.

So in the end I think there's two kinds of discrimination against women. One is the abuse of women by social and political leaders in the Mapuche movement. The other is the general misunderstanding of women by the men in the communities, the abuse of single mothers in the communities or by other men. Now when there's a palin, a gillatun, you'll see the machi, the mothers; it'll be the women who work the most. Women are the real engine of the community, and they work shoulder to shoulder with their men. But in the organizations that, if I had to classify them I'd say they have a more wigka style . . .

F: *Or maybe it's in the leadership positions that serve to mediate with the rest of society?*

That's it. The leadership structures that mediate with the rest of society carry an ideological weight that's more political, different from the ideological weight of the culture. It's there that women's participation gets subordinated, and that leadership gets seen as superior. That's it exactly.

F: *Now, this mediating leadership that handles relations toward the outside, and that ends up marginalizing women's participation, is it related somehow to the dynamics of caciquismo, of men thinking that they have more privileges simply because they are men, and that's why they can do these things?*

Let me explain. There are customs that got started at the moment when the Mapuche confronted the Spanish and lives were lost. At that moment Mapuche men stopped being peaceful, coexisting and sharing with nature, and became warriors. During this transformation, when peaceful fishermen and gatherers became warriors, the women of the time decided that they would bear children to ensure the survival of their people. If one died, ten would take his place. And that's also when the custom known as *ñukekurre* begins: if my husband dies, I can become his older brother's wife. My husband's older brother automatically makes me his because I'm of childbearing age, I'm still able to produce human beings, crops, crafts, doing everything that's generally useful for my people. From that moment on everyone shared in these beliefs, including the women, and that's why they didn't fight. The men who became caciques didn't exercise raw power, but instead emphasized strategy and daring in protecting their family. There was respect and people shared and took care of each other. If I became a widow and my brother-in-law took me in, nobody else would even try to talk to me, because they knew to whom I belonged. They knew what was allowed. Now if that brother-in-law didn't want me, then somebody else could step forward, but even then there was respect, conversation, a previous arrangement. So I think that, in a sense, European sexism converged and blended with Mapuche sexism, with the specific way the Mapuche had of facing reality, and a new sexism was born that today has penetrated the very marrow of the Mapuche people.

This sexism with a Mapuche label takes on a zealous intensity, it's reflected in the arrogant way men order women around, that superiority of the male before the female, in the fields, at the dances, after a few drinks, at sports events, when there's a visitor in the household. When company arrives the lady of the house says good morning, and she takes care of everything. And the man says, bring me that *chem*, and his wife brings it, even though she has to guess, because chem means thing, any old thing. And she has to think, what could he mean. If you say to me bring me that chem I have to guess, in the context of what you're doing, what it is you're referring to: a hammer, a saw, a glass of water, a plate; I have to guess. Maybe there aren't any chili peppers on the table, but he doesn't say *merken xapi* (bring the chili peppers). It's hey you, or else your name, bring the chem. She turns halfway around and she has to guess right away, almost on the run. And hitting women has also become accepted.

Today, after the very popular finding in our last census, that there are seven women for every man, the guys go around saying, hey, now each of us can have seven women. The respect, the mutual respect between women and men that formed a part of our culture, between food preparation, our own ways of dressing, our values—it was there in the past, but it's gone today. Ever since I came into awareness, and since I became fully integrated into the indigenous movement in 1978, I've had the impression that men relate to women in a slick, opportunistic way, with little or no feeling. There's a lack of responsibility, a permanent abuse toward women, toward the wife, the daughters, the closest relatives.

ELVIRA: *But there's also injustice between brothers and sisters. Because the men always get to keep the land and the women have to get married, they have to go to other communities or out to work. In the countryside, if the family needs provisions, the things you buy at the store, it's always the woman who has to help the family by going out to work as a domestic servant somewhere. That's why there's always a supply of domestic workers, because women are the ones who have to worry about buying everything, from the sugar and the mate leaves, to the table, chairs, and beds. She's in charge of everything that's inside the house. Always, in the countryside, if a house gets fixed up it's because of the woman. All the tasks inside the house belong to the woman. When there's a table, when there's a tablecloth, some-thing to eat, whatever is wigka, it's all women's work. Whatever comes from Western culture, up to this very moment, comes from the work women do. Men don't contribute to any of that.*

Starting a while ago, women who live in the countryside became the ones who support the household. How so? Well, if you have three, four chickens, you take a couple of dozen eggs to town, sell them, and come home with sugar, with detergent, maybe Omo or Rinso, or Popeye, which is the cheapest soap; you bring salt, which is a daily necessity in the countryside; mate leaves, candles . . .

ELVIRA: *Pots or buckets to carry water; all the things that might seem insignificant to the non-Mapuche; a jar, a plastic container to carry water from the well; all these things the woman brings. It's the woman who's up early, carrying water from the well so her husband can wash, so the children can wash. Or the sisters carry the water so the brothers wash. The man only worries about the fields, the animals and the fields, and he thinks that if he works all day in the fields, in the orchard, only his work has value. And what about the work the woman does, in the vegetable garden, raising the smaller animals, cleaning, sweeping the ruka and the other house people keep for when they have company. Because there's always the ruka for daily use, where the kitchen is; and the other building where the bedrooms are. And even though today people have houses like this one, wigka houses, they still follow the same custom with the ruka. But the man doesn't care about what the woman does.*

Women raise the hens, pigs, and sheep; they tend the vegetable garden and sell the fruits, vegetables, and animal products. They do artisanry, including the spinning, dyeing, braiding and weaving of the wool, and they sell their goods in the market. Here around Temuco, the men you see in the market, they're guys who buy and resell. And in many cases these guys are employed by wigkas, who make a percentage of what is sold each day. That's what you see here in the marketplace.

In addition, people often think that the difference between men and women, the superiority of men, lies in the practical, everyday work they do. But the man only focuses on one big activity, like plowing, that takes up the whole day. He wakes up, right, he'll have breakfast, he'll take out the yoke, he'll harness the oxen, he'll take the plow, and he'll start plowing. And all day he'll go up and down, up and down, plowing away. And in the meantime, while he's thinking about that one activity, the woman's thinking about ten, twelve, fifteen different things. She's fetching water, sweeping, cooking, watching the kids, planning dinner, making and baking the bread, setting the table, sewing. And she doesn't sweep only once, she sweeps the house a couple of times. She has to fetch firewood, which is also a woman's task. In the city the men bring in the firewood and chop it, but in the countryside it's the women who do that kind of thing. Women also milk the cows, though in the big dairy farms the men do it, and if the Mapuche man works at a dairy farm, then he can milk the cows. But he can't do it in his own home, ah?

Beyond issues of work and workload, there's another kind of abuse toward women that's become quite common in the countryside. From what different men and women have told me, at least from the 1960s, and probably before then as well, there's been widespread abuse of young Mapuche women by Mapuche and non-Mapuche men. There are many unwed mothers, single mothers who as domestic servants in the cities become the victims of their bosses' sons when these boys are learning about sex. Other times it's the boss himself, though he'd never admit it. Or it can even be a young Mapuche man, as a result of a sports event, a palin game, or a family celebration. The girls are left pregnant and their children go unrecognized. I have to say that this is very, very common in the countryside.

And I think it's even worse, a much graver error, when the abusers are male leaders in the Mapuche movement. Leaders, I think, should be like mirrors in which the people can see their own reflection. The people should be able to look at us as examples of good and moral behavior. And yet almost all the male Mapuche leaders I've met have more than one child out of wedlock, either with a woman other than their wife or before marrying. They abuse their own Mapuche sisters. I see it as abuse. Maybe they do it because of a momentary crush, maybe the girl was madly in love, I don't know. Most of the girls must have thought they were in love, because I don't think they just wanted to sleep with the guy because he was a leader, and get pregnant. But from the man's perspective, I think we have to question his motives and see his actions as morally quite grave.

ELVIRA: *It's also psychological abuse. The leaders see the girls who are just entering adolescence and they begin insinuating things, they begin destroying all the beautiful expectations the girls might have had about sexuality. They distort the sexual message. It's like a perverse ritual among some Mapuche leaders, who think that when the girl reaches fifteen they have the right of the first night. You see this now, among girls fifteen, sixteen, seventeen years old, that a leader's already put his mark on them.*

Since these sexual issues haven't been addressed by the leadership, the male Mapuche leaders go on as if nothing were happening. This harms

Mapuche culture, because before the Spanish arrived the question of sexual initiation was handled with a lot of care and concern. There was an almost mystical teaching about what was natural, and this has been distorted; now we have a clash among the Mapuche themselves.

What happened before, rather than being mystical was more of a religious process. Young girls got engaged eight days after their first menstrual period. The sash you wore, the xariwe, marked you. The designs on the xariwe meant something, the length, the width. A woman's xariwe revealed many things about her. So you were part of a process. If the *ülmen*, who was the son of a logko from a different place with lots of land and children, wanted to marry the daughter of this other logko, he could go and bring the girl home with him when she was twelve. But the girl had to sleep with a sister or the mother, not with him, until her parents gave their permission. So he had the right to raise her, to have her living in his house for a year or two, but she didn't have to sleep with him. He had to say that she was his, that she was going to be his wife, his fiancée, his partner. If she was twelve, thirteen, fourteen, she didn't sleep with him, they didn't abuse women like that. Now, it's just a matter of going straight to bed, a morbid utilitarianism.

F: *OK. We've talked a lot about the experience of Mapuche women, we'e documented quite extensively the need for a Mapuche women's organization. In your opinion, were there any other reasons for creating a women's organization?*

As a participant in the *Concertación*'s electoral coalition, I was also interested in creating the National Women's Service (*Servicio Nacional de la Mujer*, or SERNAM). During the dictatorship, *Mujeres por la Vida*, the group known as Women for Life, proved politically quite inclusive here in Temuco. We organized one in the series of demonstrations sponsored by Women for Life, known as the mujerazos, here in the city that went from the extreme left to *Renovación Nacional*, with flags and banners and everything. I think that's an example of how, when we're inspired by a common gender interest, we can get beyond party structures and sensibilities.

F: *Now, does the idea of* Mujeres por la Vida, *of a broader front that left party hatreds behind, have a parallel in a wider vision for the Mapuche movement, with room for all political tendencies within an agenda that's specifically Mapuche? Is there a lesson here somewhere for the political parties?*

Well, I think the women made a beautiful gesture in the mujerazo, which here in Temuco, in the middle of the dictatorship, brought *Renovación Nacional* and MIR flags together in the Bernardo O'Higgins gym. The building was filled to capacity with more than three thousand women; many more were left outside. The flag of the Mapuche people was there, too, in addition to the flags of all the parties. After talking with a lot of people, I'm convinced that our rally here in Temuco was broader and more inclusive than those held in other parts of the country. I think our mujerazo dramatized the need for tolerance and coexistence, for a return to democracy, for women's participation, and for respecting diversity and the existence of the parties themselves. I think we went far beyond what the men could have done. Men are more categorical, they're centered in a party or in a union, they're always looking to define their political faction. For us, Mapuche and non-Mapuche women, the mujerazo represented the greatest and most diverse range of the region's women. And yet this effort born from *Mujeres por la Vida,* but with help from the Church, civil society, private institutions, and a variety of individuals and groups, over time was dissipated as people paid more attention to short-term goals. So even though we've come a long way, achieving a transition to democracy with don Patricio Aylwin, the women's movement has languished and the mujerazo has become no more than a symbolic recognition of the need to respect diversity. At that large demonstration, and at smaller ones as well, we expressed this respect for diversity; but we didn't continue building it politically. That continuity is missing, and I think the same thing happened in the Mapuche movement. We weren't able to keep respecting difference inside the movement, even knowing the other was Mapuche, when he had a different ideology, she was more conservative or progressive, or someone was simply at the extreme of our own political tendency.

F: *I'm hearing you say that, despite the lack of continuity, gender is an issue that can really unify people across the political spectrum. To what extent do you think that seriously addressing gender within the Mapuche organizations could also unify them across political differences?*

I think an in-depth look at gender issues is a definite necessity, and it would give vitality and strength to families, communities, and broader organizations. I think it would unify the movement. In the Coalition of Mapuche Women (*Coordinadora de Mujeres Mapuches*) of the IX Region, for example, we meet and hold workshops, with or without money, it doesn't matter. But the men's organizations have to wait for CONADI to call them, or until they get connected to a funding agency that can assemble a particular group of people. We women, on the other hand, are out there, we don't wait for the money to come to us, we're in the Chile Initiative (*Iniciativa Chile*), which is a national program; we're here, we're in Santiago, whatever it takes. Ana Llao and Elisa Avendaño are part of our group, there's women from all religious and political tendencies and we don't have a problem with that. No problem, in the sense that we leave certain topics off the table, and if we do talk about them, it's half-joking, half-serious, laughing, and that's it.

Women can say anything to each other, as long as they find the right way to say it. I get told all kinds of things and I laugh, I accept it, I counter it, I say, hey, it's not like that, I clear things up when I think they shouldn't remain in the air. And I respect different ways of doing things, because it's the only way people can bring what they're doing into their own context. At one point, I remember people began gossiping back and forth, this one did this, that one went there. I said, "Look, if we're going to have a women's gossiping organization, then we're going to have to pull out all the stops. You know what the men have been saying about me, and some of the women, too, they've said I'm harder than a man." Among the women who were there one asked me, "And what exactly did they say about you?" So I gave them the list, all sorts of things: that I was frustrated, that I was incompetent, that I was a lesbian, I don't remember what else, that I received money from some group in Europe, etc., etc. I repeated everything they'd said about me. And I knew some of the women present had also repeated those things. But I said, "Forget all that. It's come to nothing, because I've opened up a space for myself; and through that you've all won a space, too." Before they'd all worked in Mapuche institutions, small groups of women working on particular projects. But when my organization was born we got involved in something bigger, and besides they didn't want to let me escape. And I had no problem in saying well, OK, let's work together. So we started working together, and the results have been good in the sense that they're permanent, and they're better than what the men have been able to do.

F: *What kind of future do you foresee for the Chilean women's movement, Mapuche and non-Mapuche?*

Despite its many successes, I think the women's movement is asleep. I think the transition taught us that significant concessions come only when negotiation is accompanied by direct action. It's that direct action component, which we had with the mujerazo as an opposition movement to the dictatorship, that's missing today, and that's why we're going so slowly on the gender issue in Chile. Our feminist fury has died down. It doesn't exist anymore, even though the urgency of addressing gender grows day by day. Without a strong counterpart in action, in confrontation; without, in a word, an uncompromising feminist movement, you have nothing to negotiate, and the other side is not motivated to search for consensus or a mutually acceptable way out. Because if everyone is for equality of opportunities, for balance and rationality, gender means both man and woman and they complement each other in practice, taking on different roles and tasks; then, to be perfectly honest, we're all getting too soft. Even if I personally might not like it, I think it's necessary for Chile to have a strong and confrontational feminist movement, at least for a while, like the one we had during the transition. That one helped create SERNAM, and it helped put into place the equal opportunity plan which, quite frankly, seems nowadays to have been transformed into a quality management team.

The same thing is happening with the indigenous movement. During the transition our direct action component was the *Consejo de Todas las Tierras,* but today CONADI has no confrontational counterpart.[4] The indigenous movement is asleep, lethargic; CONADI has in fact demobilized us because it's assumed tasks the movement used to carry out, and has also taken responsibility for Mapuche welfare more generally. There's no money in the CONADI budget earmarked for the Mapuche movement, and in any case we weren't ready to write grant proposals, to carry out research or formulate projects through FOSIS, CONADI itself, universities, or invite bids from other institutions. We weren't prepared for that.

F: *Recently, when I was talking with Lucy Traipe, she told me that at CONADI, if today there was an indigenous movement like the one in the 1980s, they'd have to provide a much better service. She is referring to the same thing, right? That an active and organized mass movement facilitates negotiation.*

Definitely, because let me tell you, clarity facilitates negotiation. I've learned this in practice, and to cite one of the most recent examples, when

SERNAM set up its working group on rural issues, no one thought to incorporate, with full status and equality, an indigenous peasant woman. There was no woman present from Temuco who would go to the wall on the issue, getting other women involved to push for a discussion of the topic. Luckily, the Center for Women's Development (*Centro de Desarrollo de la Mujer*, or CEDEM) in Santiago, took it on. I might disagree with CEDEM on many things, but thank God that, as an NGO, they have resources and were willing to argue that, if no institution supports peasant women, we'll remain one hundred years behind, as it's been until now. So thanks to CEDEM, indigenous peasant women earned a space to sit down and talk with SERNAM.

F: *In a sense,* CONADI *plays the role for the Mapuche movement that* SERNAM *plays for the women's movement: as an institution that channels popular demands into the state, it can sometimes actually demobilize the mass movement. Can you talk a bit more about how this has worked in the case of* CONADI?

Well, we've talked many times about the fact that CONADI hasn't contributed to reviving the indigenous movement. Even when it has finally taken a strong position, as in the case of the Ralco hydroelectric project in the Upper Bío Bío Valley, it's turned out to be very complicated. I've told you a little about what Ralco means to me: it raises so many emotions, from impotence and desperation to disillusion, disappointment, devastation. When I think of it, I see cash and bills on parade instead of people. I see ambition, money, power. It's disgusting! NGO upon NGO, institutions both national and foreign, have all made the climb up into the valley, so much so that the people there have washed their hands of everybody and they'll say yes to whoever goes there at this point. There are only three or four people, two women and one man, who are still standing strong, like a wall, a concrete wall I don't know how thick. And you look at all of this and say, geez, who am I, less than nothing when compared to this so-called modernity that's trampling us. And the political parties stand in the distance, screaming; they have strength, they don't have strength; they can do it, and yet they can't. They have everything at their fingertips and they're not capable of doing anything! There are vested interests in the way. And what are these interests, if not economic growth, so-called progress, and the daily race for money, money, and more money?

That's a summary of what Ralco means to me, and it's like saying leave me out of it, enough already. I remember when I went to the Upper Bío Bío Valley in 1980. From Ad-Mapu we issued a declaration about the situation; I've looked for a copy of it and unfortunately I can't find it, I had it here somewhere; the declaration had ten points. In 1980 I visited the communities of Pitril, Malla Malla, and Callaqui in the Upper Bío Bío, and Cauñicú was the other place, the nuns of Cauñicú gave me a place to sleep. There's a copper mine in Cauñicú, according to the local people there's also gold underneath. That's possible, but it seems to be copper and silver. The deposits haven't matured yet, with time the mineral will develop a certain grade, I think they call it, and it'll be ready to be exploited. So in the Upper Bío Bío you have a road that was built by the people from the communities, using brute force, during the dictatorship; you have the hydroelectric dams; and then the mineral will be ready to be exploited. If the communities leave, they lose their rights to the land, water, and mineral deposits, though because the Indigenous Law doesn't mention subsoil rights—something we've already talked about, right?—they probably didn't have those to begin with, anyway.

The people lose everything! It's not simply a matter of saying, hey, let's move 'em, take 'em to Mulchén or wherever, they'll have more access to the means of communication, the cities, education; they can spend more money. You can discuss the probabilities, play with the possibilities around a table, but if you stop and take a good look, you realize it's not an easy problem with a quick solution. It's not as easy building it or not building it, eh? Building it would mark a negative precedent for the Indigenous Law, which would be negative not only for the folks in the Upper Bío Bío Valley, who in numbers are not many, but for all of the indigenous peoples of Chile. This is an opinion I share with the people who are most vehemently opposed to Ralco, because I think that historically it'll set a precedent, it'll say that it's all right to disrespect, violate, and trample a special law that was passed to respect and protect indigenous peoples. On the other hand, the jurists have said that the Indigenous Law cannot be ignored, and the studies done so far suggest that, if the case went to court, the Indigenous Law could not be violated, and at least that's a good thing.

F: *For a time, it seemed that the people who most strongly opposed the construction of the dam were a coalition of environmentalist groups with sectors of the Upper Bío Bío Mapuche-Pehuenche Cultural Center (Centro Cul-*

tural Mapuche Pehuenche del Alto Bío Bío). *But recently a new coalition has taken a more public anti-dam position, right? The Coalition in Defense of our Territory* (Coalición en Defensa del Territorio) *has people who oppose the Temuco by-pass, the coastal highway, the paper factory, the sale of the southern territories, and Ralco*[5]*—these are the five. And it seems that Ad-Mapu is leading the group?*

Only in part, because there really are many other people behind it, especially several Mapuche NGOS—*Sociedad Nehuen, Liwen,* the *Xen Xen Center,* the *Casa de la Mujer Mapuche,* and the *Logko Kilapán.* These institutions can take charge of the public demonstrations because, in contrast to the organizations without outside money, they have the contacts and the funds to move people around. And I think what they're doing is good, though I haven't been involved in their strategy sessions. I think it's great that some people dare to show their faces and negotiate the best possible outcome for the Upper Bío Bío. But I don't think that a group of people screaming and demonstrating in the streets will decide whether or not to build Ralco. That kind of decision will be made through other channels, in conversation and negotiation. I agree with most of their demands, at least on a theoretical level, and consider them legitimate; but as I told you before, the Upper Bío Bío for me is a terrible disappointment. In 1980, when I presented ten points in our first public declaration, none of those who are out demonstrating today said you're right, Isolde, that could happen. In 1980 no dam was being built. In 1980 they were just finishing the road with workers from the dictatorship's Minimum Employment programs, the POJH and the PEM, local people at hard labor, with pickaxes and dynamite, blowing up the rocks and moving the earth that stood in the way of the road.

F: *What was the situation like in 1980? What did you say in the declaration?*

Well, we said that, according to what could be seen in the conversations appearing in the news, that in time they would build dams in the Upper Bío Bío Valley. We predicted that the Nitrao thermal springs, which belonged to the Mapuche—there were wooden canoes, very well maintained, I bathed in the Nitrao thermal springs more than once—were going to be turned over to the municipality. They were the first thing that passed to municipal

control. By 1981 the Nitrao thermal springs were in the hands of the municipality of Los Angeles. We'd foreseen this, that if until that day the thermal
springs had belonged to the Mapuche, for their own use and for nobody
else, if they passed to the municipality the indigenous people of the locality
would no longer be able to administer them. Besides, if the municipality
took them over, I was sure they would build restaurants and hotels, because
a lot more outsiders would come to the place. Another point in the declaration was to get rid of the alcohol trade. It was customary for trucks to drive
up into the valley to trade goats for wine; they'd drive up with truckloads of
wine and come back down full of goats. So the first five points warned about
the hydroelectric dam, the Nitrao thermal springs, and how the expansion
of commerce and tourism would affect people. Beyond that we came out in
favor of more schools, for child welfare, and expanded health care. It was a
mix of old and new demands.

F: *So that was part of what Ad-Mapu did.*

When I was in Ad-Mapu, yes.

F: *And you looked for a copy of the document, but you couldn't find it.*

No, I haven't found it yet. Somebody must have a copy, but I even asked in
Ad-Mapu and they didn't have it.

F: *So given this background, your position on the recent* CONADI *crisis with the
replacement of Mauricio Huenchulaf by Domingo Namuncura, the public
demonstrations and all that, has understandably been a bit cautious. What's
been your experience with all these recent events?*

Mauricio's replacement has nothing to do with Ralco, nor does my lack of
participation in the march to Santiago.[6] I think we have to separate things
out here, and if we do we can see that the march to Santiago was about a lot
of different things. Had it been only about Ralco, or about Ralco and the
rest of the present-day conflicts over territory and development, I would
have been there or gone anywhere else. But by mixing these bigger issues
with a more sectarian political disagreement over who should be the new
Director of CONADI—a nomination, incidentally, that the President of the
Republic has the legitimate right to make—I think the Mapuche confused a

much more complex problem with questions pertaining to the structure of the state. CONADI is a state agency, controlled and funded by the state. Its only innovation is that eight indigenous members sit on its National Council, as a form of direct participation by indigenous peoples in this institution created to carry on their work and their way of life.

F: *I get your point. But according to the press, Mauricio Huenchulaf said he was removed because of Ralco.*

I don't see it that way. Begging my brother's forgiveness from a distance, but I don't see it like that. I think the removal of Mauricio Huenchulaf was for strictly administrative reasons; his tenure had ended and so had a particular stage of CONADI's development. It's inevitable that CONADI go through different stages, because as an institution it represents the different phases of the government's policy toward indigenous peoples. I'm not saying yet if this will be good or bad, just that there are different chapters to the story and we'd just finished the first one, which was to get the offices running. I think being in charge of that first phase, when you get an institution running, was actually a privilege for Mauricio Huenchulaf, a young Mapuche professional who had no experience with public administration. He had three years to inaugurate a national institution and become familiar with how it worked. Now Mauricio is a resource that the Mapuche people must know how to appreciate: his knowledge, the work he's done, all of that. I don't think he did a bad job. There are many things he could have done, but you have to do the things you can, not the things you want to do. Besides, the team he had—his administrative staff, the people he had to rely on while developing the rhythm and policies of the institution—was not the most creative. It seems that they were too attached to the letter of the law when there was room for interpretation, and other times they perhaps bent the rules when they shouldn't have. That's an administrative question, a question of how people understand political structures.

Rather than criticizing Mauricio Huenchulaf's administration of CONADI, we have to recognize his bravery, tranquility, and ingenuity in establishing good relations with the public sector, the mass organizations, and international institutions. Those of us who stood with him from the beginning could see that he had to start out buying the first pencil, the first chair. From there he was in charge of hiring all the personnel while striking a balance among the different political parties that, as a part of the new governing coalition, wanted to put their people in the institution. This was not an easy stream to ford at the beginning. And he faced the same challenge in the northern and southern deputy directors' offices and in each local branch, where he had to hire functionaries, keep a balance among the political parties, and somehow develop good rapport with the indigenous people in each place. I think CONADI is now up and running: it's working, it has a physical plant, an administrative structure, all of that, and it has an important contribution to make. As it enters a new stage the focus must be on further development, and I hope the new director is able to coordinate policy with the different public and private institutions that exist in Chile. He should also look outside national borders, something you can't do when you're building something from nothing, not because you don't want to, but because you can't.[7]

F: *By going outside national borders, do you mean making direct connections with institutions abroad?*

I mean connecting directly to outside public, private, and international institutions that can help further the goals of Chile's indigenous peoples. And sadly, it also means going beyond the goals set by the Chilean state. Why? Because if the next Chilean government is not run by the *Concertación*—and I don't care who, as long as they're from the *Concertación*—if it's somebody from the opposition, we indigenous people stand to lose a lot, a lot. So the new director has to make the kind of international contacts that, over time, can help support us; he has to find a hook where we can hang our hats, a way to demand our rights that doesn't depend exclusively on the Chilean state. This is where I share some opinions with Santos Millao when he says that CONADI must be ours, a pure and totally autonomous institution. Because this one we have now, we must recognize that it belongs to the state.

F: *Today in CONADI, do you think Domingo Namuncura is the right person to make the necessary changes?*

Look, personally I have my doubts as to whether Domingo Namuncura will be able to respond to the needs, dreams, and the hopes of our indigenous peoples. In order for his administration to succeed, he'd have to emphasize teamwork and inject new dynamism and creativity into a group of CONADI functionaries who are very depressed and lethargic. In addition, he'll have to coordinate his efforts with the indigenous organizations and the indigenous movement, as well as with the state in general. He's a young man, and it's possible that he has a dose of strength and motivation large enough to get all this on track. But it's very hard to do this right now. I recognize that inside and outside CONADI, politically it's a very difficult moment. But it's also possible that Domingo will only take CONADI through a transition from one process to the next and, if so, he might be in CONADI only for a couple of months. He's a strong and dedicated human rights leader, but he hasn't been too involved with the indigenous question.

F: *The impression I have is that he's very much a political party activist who came up through the general social movement. Do you know where he's from? Did he grow up in Santiago?*

He was born in Valparaíso and grew up in Santiago. His father is from here, from the IX Region, the Namuncura community of Loncoche. But Domingo's never had direct contact with the community, not even with his closest kin there. I think becoming CONADI's Director might give him the opportunity to go to his community and meet his relatives. At the same time, given his commitment to human rights and to the principles of Christianity, you can be certain that he has all the best intentions. In this sense, you don't have to practice indigenous culture or dress in indigenous clothes to think and work for indigenous peoples. I might be going out on a limb here, but I believe that even a nonindigenous person who is willing to work for indigenous people would be a good Director. So I think Domingo Namuncura should be given a chance, to see if he is up to the task, and not only because the President of the Republic chose him. He's well placed within the structure of the current government, well-loved by President Frei's most influential ministers, always helpful and cooperative. Like you said, he's definitely a political party man and very much an urban man. But he's a principled and committed Christian, and at least on that score we need to give him a chance.[8]

He'll let us know—at least I hope he does—whether he can meet the challenge or not, before the Mapuche movement ends up telling him we told you so, we warned you, we asked you to think about it and you didn't react before. And if he doesn't have what it takes, he should say this is as far as I go; I'm out of here. But I don't think his goal is to build the Ralco dam. In fact, CONADI's Council should focus on convincing him to fiercely oppose the construction of the dam. Domingo Namuncura's vote is one more that can be added to the opposition, or else it could be the tie-breaking vote, since the rules of the CONADI Council are perfectly clear on this point: if after voting there's a tie, the Director breaks it. The Council has eight indigenous members and eight nonindigenous members, plus the Director; so if there's a tie and he says that Ralco goes, then it goes.

F: *I'm not really clear on how the new Director was named. In the newspapers it said that neither the organized Mapuche movement nor the Council of CONADI were consulted. What did that mean here in Temuco?*

Here what they said was that it was totally on the spur of the moment, they just tore in here and imposed him from one day to the next. They dropped him on our heads just like that and we didn't even have time to react. Look, I think the government received some very bad advice. There had been talk for quite a while that the Director would be changed, or that he'd quit. Especially after Mauricio Huenchulaf's October 5th speech on Conun Hueno hill, where he harangued and challenged the government, saying he'd quit if they built Ralco, our more politically connected people were sure that Mauricio would be asked to quit before December, but that didn't happen. It's also important to point out that CONADI's Council, especially the indigenous representatives, had asked Mauricio Huenchulaf for his resignation not once, but many times. They'd asked for his resignation as well as those of the Deputy Director and the main CONADI legal counsel. In their minutes there's a clear record that they'd been asking for a change for quite a long time. But then the government did it overnight, in less time than it takes a rooster to crow, with very bad advice. In a blink of an eye the Director and Deputy Director were decapitated. CONADI was left ungovernable, because the people who supported Mauricio had a very different view of what happened than did the people who were less involved and just doing their job.

Those who'd arrived at CONADI as Mauricio's inner circle, or who in the three years that transpired developed a close affinity with him, started screaming, proclaiming loudly that Mauricio had been thrown out overnight, that he'd only been given a week's notice, that in no other public institution had something like this ever happened. Generally people get thirty, forty-five days to clear out their desks, so his people started questioning and looking for laws to support their claims. And Mauricio himself took offense at the process, being asked for his resignation on a Friday and told he had until the 30th to clear out, and the 30th was Wednesday. He had only three days to hand over the office. He took it personally, as an offense against a Mapuche who'd given his all in public service.

Of course this affected CONADI's work and daily routine, because people inside and outside the organization weren't pleased with the way the changes were made, including people in the Mapuche NGOs that had received financial support during Mauricio Huenchulaf's tenure. The leaders closest to Mauricio considered it an attack on the indigenous members of the CONADI Council, the Mapuche leadership, and the Mapuche people in general. Now some of us who were close to the events didn't see it quite that way, but certainly the methods used were all wrong. I participated in the first takeover of the CONADI offices, on the first day, because I thought the way the government had acted, having decapitated CONADI overnight like that, was simply wrong.

F: *What was the takeover like?*

Initially the takeover was in solidarity with Mauricio Huenchulaf, to show that indigenous people felt trampled and that we wanted the state to renew its commitment to us. We felt we needed to renew the commitment Aylwin had made to us in Imperial. It seemed to us that the spirit, the essence of the commitment was still there with the *Concertación*, but that Congress had blocked an important part of Aylwin's agenda. So we had to reactivate the part of the agenda that was still missing, protesting the government's actions that we saw as an affront against indigenous people. That's what it looked like to us, that we'd been trampled. Any change in a public office is done with thirty days' notice, so that the person coming in has time to adapt, and at least a week to learn things and be shown around.

And CONADI wasn't any old institution, that's the other thing. It wasn't the Registry of Births, Marriages, and Deaths; it wasn't a hospital, a school, or a department in a municipality. They weren't changing a school principal, but the National Director of CONADI, an institution with a bipartite Council, evenly divided between indigenous and nonindigenous members, between the state and organizations from civil society. So the very least the state should have done was to respect this uniqueness and grant it the recognition it deserved by calling a meeting of the Council right away, so that the Council could meet and approve the new Director first. Government representatives could have introduced the candidate and said we want this person to be the director for this and that reason. Domingo could have said, I come with the best intentions, with all the will and energy in the world, and I ask that you give me two or three months to get my bearings and then we can make policy and move forward. But this didn't happen. Instead we were angered and disillusioned because our rights were trampled. Domingo Namuncura was imposed on us, as a leader he was shoved down our throats. Now, that the President of the Republic had the right to name him is not something I've made up, or the *Concertación* got out of the blue. The Mapuche also recognize this. The Indigenous Law says it, and as a people we're very legalistic, we accept it. But the way it was done, the disrespect, the trampling of all sensibilities and alternatives. . . . Santos and all the other people who are out protesting knew the Director would be from the PPD, it's not that they didn't know. But nobody imagined that Mauricio would be asked for his resignation on Friday, and on Monday Domingo would be in the office. That's what nobody knew.

F: *How many days did you take part in the takeover, and how many days did it last?*

I was there the first two days, and the takeover lasted three days. Why did some of us leave? We had presented a list of fifteen demands, some of which we saw as negotiable, as talking points. But when Roberto Pizarro, the Minister of MIDEPLAN, arrived he was so eager to reach an agreement that he immediately accepted all fifteen points! He said, "I accept the fifteen points, let's draw up a formal Act of Agreement, but Domingo Namuncura stays as Director. The decree has been signed, and as a government we can't go back on that." This caught the negotiators by surprise, the indigenous members of CONADI's Council plus two indigenous leaders, and they weren't able to rearticulate their demands quickly and thus became divided. That was the result, because they insisted on flogging a dead horse when they refused to accept Domingo Namuncura. And what Santos and the NGO representatives said was that Pizarro had tried to bribe them.

F: *The newspapers said that he offered them a car, or some kind of vehicle.*

Yes, yes, a truck, a new office, everything they'd asked for. Because that was part of what they'd asked for, they'd requested better accommodations for the Council members, an office apart from the National Office, and the Minister had agreed. A truck so that they could move around and get out to the communities, and the Minister said sure. That was all part of the fifteen points. They'd asked for more money for CONADI, and the Minister said yes.

So in the end we really didn't handle the situation very well, because the fifteen points included funding and implementing the indigenous development areas, resolving the land conflicts, no to Ralco; they included a provision that all megadevelopment projects had to involve participation by the people who were affected. All that was in the fifteen points.

F: *And Pizarro accepted all that?*

Pizarro had accepted all that, probably at a rather high cost to himself. But he said, "I accept all this, on the condition that Domingo Namuncura is the new Director, no matter what." And that's what the media caught onto: no matter what, Domingo Namuncura is CONADI's new Director. That phrase was in the media, and the marchers to Santiago included it in their letters. Well, that's my perspective in a nutshell, that we didn't know how to take advantage of the situation. Mauricio himself landed the directorship of CONADI because he was a member of the right political party, responding to the PPD and obviously as a Mapuche member of the PPD. He knew he'd last in the position only as long as the President of the Republic kept him there, that was it. After he left he harangued and gave inflamed speeches to the four winds, with the support of many people and NGOs. After signing his settlement with the government he was transformed into an opposition leader; he even said he was reconsidering his membership in the PPD. He questioned the actions of other department heads, thinking perhaps that the people who weren't cheering for him, were against him. I hope that he's able to keep moving forward, because his tenure at CONADI was not bad. But the last things he said and did before he left weren't always the most appropriate.

And that's where we are now. I can tell you that next Tuesday they'll have a press conference here in the offices of CONADI's National Director, to introduce the National Deputy Director for the Southern Region, Mr. Victor Alonqueo Maza, who's the least-mentioned character in this particular story but who still can't be assured of a peaceful arrival.

F: *Why do you think that?*

Because the staff at the Deputy Director's office is made up of people who have been in public service for a long time, people who were, I would say, quite supportive of the military regime. We have, for example, a Mapuche functionary who, even though he's Mapuche, he asks one foot for permission to move the other. He hinders CONADI more than he energizes it. On the other hand you have Mrs. Meyer leading a faction of these functionaries,[9] and you have the people who came in with the previous Deputy Director, Víctor Hugo Painemal, who form a cohort and have a very special style, because instead of facilitating the work of the office they tend to inhibit it. They are very much the bureaucrats, with an eye on the clock. They'll help only if someone knocks on their door, they're not committed or charismatic, they don't work well as a team, they don't leave their own backyards. So I hope that this man, whom I don't know, has the dynamism to give CONADI a vitamin shot, because right now it's drooping.

F: *Why do you think you weren't chosen?*

What?

F: *Why do you think you weren't chosen as Deputy Director?*

Let's see (laughter). . . Why wasn't I chosen . . . Well, the argument I've heard is that I don't have a professional title, at least that's what they say in MIDEPLAN . . .

F: *That's the official argument, then.*

The official argument . . .

F: *And it's true, you don't have . . .*

It's true. I don't have a professional degree.

F: *You gave up your education along the way, out of commitment to the movement . . .*

Yes, that's right. But I think that it's about more than having a degree, because Víctor Hugo didn't have one either, he has a degree in accounting from a technical high school. And there are directors of other government agencies who've also followed a different path. I think the real explanation is that a person who gets close to a good tree is rewarded by bountiful shade (*quien a buen árbol se arrima, buena sombra lo cobija*). The tree I've gotten close to hasn't been the best, I guess; its leaves are still too sparse to give me the shade I need, right?

F: *Now you're talking about Gute . . .*
(*Laughter.*)

Maybe not specifically about Gute,[10] but generally about the different political currents within the Christian Democracy, the favoritism and individualism of some party chiefs who push their own official and extraofficial candidates. Here in the south there were twelve candidates for Deputy Director, and I was the person chosen by the party's regional steering committee in Temuco. I also had a special cheering section in the women's movement. I got support from the women who were with me in the Rural Women's Working Group (*Mesa de la Mujer Rural*) in Santiago. But Alonqueo got chosen because the Frei line, to which he belongs, was stronger in Temuco. So the conditions just weren't there, I guess, and I've resigned myself to thinking that maybe this wasn't the right time for me, and that I have to gather my energies for the future. And if it doesn't work out then either, no matter. Whether inside or outside the state, there's still a lot to do. What I need most are the funds to move around, because one of my major obstacles is that, without a regular income, I have trouble finding the money for transportation. I hope I find the means to continue, because if I don't I'll have to find a job somewhere, just to survive.[11]

And when you're working to survive you're forced, with a heavy heart, to abandon the socially relevant work you were doing unless you connect with a specific program or project that supports the kind of work you want to do. Now I've found some channels through which I can participate; I work easily with teams doing social scientific research, and I usually receive some remuneration for that kind of work. And in those situations you can lower the boom, you know, and say pay me. I'll go if you pay me. And what's your fee? This much if it's an institution, that much if it's an individual, it depends. I'm not one who says, look, this is my fee and that's all there is to it. No, not too much, not too little, but I keep that as a means to make some money. I don't want to tie myself to a particular NGO, which could provide a solution by funneling in some international support, because I've questioned so much the role of NGOs that morally I couldn't work for one. But if it's necessary for economic reasons, I guess I'd even have to do that.

F: *You'll have to wait and see.*

I'll see. Now the work I've been doing for CONADI at the national level has been specifically around gender issues. I'm about to hand the new Director my final report on the Rural Women's Working Group in Santiago, a multi-disciplinary and multisectorial collaboration between the CNC (National Peasant Commission), indigenous organizations, and state agencies. I'm going to hand in my final report and I'm going to say thank you and goodbye, because I think it's time to say it. If they still need my services, then they should pay me. Until now I've been working ad honorem, because I'm a feminist woman in the sense that I struggle for the dignity of women in general, and of Mapuche women in particular, because they're very down-trodden. And that's also why I created the women's organization *Keyukleayñ pu Zomo*, because I think that women's organizations need to demonstrate that women can do a different kind of work from what they've done until now, which even though they're the ones who toil the most, tends to remain silent and invisible.

My organization, when it was created, was created with this vision. A lot of people questioned it, people who participated in traditional organizations, men and women. They criticized us harshly, saying we were showered with money by the whole world. The truth is that no group gave us money, we got nothing. And this is the way women's organizing works, it's one of the things I'm most interested in advancing, even though it's one of the most difficult. I know that in CONADI they're talking about creating a women's department, but I also think that a women's department without a separate budget and some degree of autonomy will be a lost department. Because if all it does is coordinate activities with already existing groups, or with other institutions that already work with women, it won't be productive. And in the end it will be another example people can point to and say you see, women can't do anything. I don't want to participate in something unless it has financial support, because that's the only way women can develop, feel comfortable and confident, and take a more public role. That's the only way women can initiate concrete projects, move around and do things. There are grant competitions through state agencies like FOSIS,

SERNAM, and CONADI, and if a group of women presents a proposal that's successful, then they can carry out their project. But I'd like the funding to be more clearly earmarked to teach men as well as women about the roles, rights, and dignity of indigenous women.

F: *Now, if they had that type of women's department in* CONADI, *with its own funding, administrative autonomy, that type of thing, you'd be interested in participating?*

I would be interested in participating, though perhaps we wouldn't need administrative autonomy, but just like they do with other public agencies, setting a budget for the department with clear priorities. This doesn't mean they'd have to give me all the money and I'd do whatever I wanted with it, no. Just that there be clarity about the role of the department and that it have money, because sometimes a department is created with the salary of the director and nothing more, and all initiatives have to be coordinated with someone else. No. It should have a set budget like the Indigenous Development Fund, the Land Fund, Education and Culture; Gender should also have its own specific budget. And it should be called Gender rather than Women, eh? Because when it's for women you always get a teensy amount, people say oh, sure, it's only for the women. So it should be gender, man and woman, but dealing specifically with gender, so women will be able to express themselves publicly, without problems.

F: *Another part of your experience dealing with the gender issue and the women's movement was at the International Women's Conference in Beijing. How did your organization get to Beijing?*

I went to Beijing as an individual, rather than as a representative of my organization. However, I didn't get to go because I was Isolde Reuque, but because I was president of the women's organization I'd created; because I had the privilege of being a first-round member of CONADI's Council; because I was working with SERNAM on issues and research projects to further women's participation; and because I was a recognized participant in the women's movement. All these things influenced my selection. But the most important was having held leadership positions in social organizations.

F: *Before Beijing there were preparatory meetings in Chile and Argentina, right?*

Well, yes. Beginning in 1995 there were a series of initial meetings in Chile. Some were government-sponsored and others, known as the Chile Initiative (*Iniciativa Chile*), were organized by Chilean NGOs led by CEDEM Santiago, the Women's Institute (*Instituto de la Mujer*), and others. The idea was to encourage participation by many different groups in all the regions of the country, and in each locale working groups were created and called focal points (*puntos focales*). Here in Temuco the focal point was directed by CAPIDE and other NGOs, and women participated broadly from all parts of the political spectrum: through the different political parties, left as well as right; obviously from the *Concertación*; and from social organizations, neighborhood associations, Mapuche organizations. By November 1995 all the focal points came together at a national conference in Santiago and handed the results of their work over to *Iniciativa Chile*, from which a national document was written and sent to Mar del Plata, to the Southern Cone Assembly of NGOs. A Chilean delegation to this assembly would then formally present the final proposal that Chilean women would take to Beijing.

F: *And all of this was part of the NGO conference held parallel to the Beijing governmental meeting?*

Right, but first we had the conference in Mar del Plata. Up to this level you could say that indigenous women participated equally with everyone else, because we'd participated in the focal point meetings of the VIII and IX regions as well as in the national congress in Santiago. *Iniciativa Chile* opened structures for the participation of many professionals, NGOs, and social organizations: the peasant movement, which is concentrated in Santiago, in the CNC, MUCECH and its different organizations; the Coalition of Mapuche Women; the Coalition of Student Organizations (*Coordinadora de Estudiantes*) in Santiago; the Coalition of Professionals (*Coordinadora de Profesionales*); and women's groups more broadly. And this broad inclusion was reflected in Mar del Plata, where from Osorno, Temuco, and Cañete indigenous women arrived representing indigenous organizations. Indigenous women also came from northern Chile, especially from the II and IV regions.

Seven indigenous women from Chile arrived in Mar del Plata, including myself. Each of us followed a different route, we didn't all travel the same road. From Temuco I went representing the indigenous women who were close to the government or to CONADI, whichever way you want to look at it. I was still a member of CONADI's Council at that time, so I went representing that sector. Ana Llao, a prominent leader of Ad-Mapu, went as part of Rigoberta Menchú's working group on indigenous women. Women from the Mapuche NGOs were also there: Rosa Toro from the *Logko Kilapán*; Rosa Rapiman from the *Casa de la Mujer Mapuche*, Elisa Avendaño from the *Sociedad Nehuen*. Lucy Traipe received a personal invitation through her international contacts, because she isn't a member of an organization now, she's a functionary at CONADI. CEDEM also invited a person from the *Casa de la Mujer* and a woman from the north. CONADI paid for the expenses of an indigenous representative from the north and supported the five women who went from the IX Region through different channels.

So you can see that we didn't have a common objective, much less a unified strategy. When we arrived in Mar del Plata we all claimed to represent the indigenous women of Chile. Yet obviously the seven women brought different documents, strategies, and points of view. If there were seven of us, there were seven documents, seven points of view, seven separate strategies. So when we got there we had to confront each other and find a way to present a single document, somehow to combine our ideas into a single message so we'd be listened to rather than overwhelmed. I think this process helped us hammer out a common agenda on the issue of gender, rather than limiting it to women. We didn't arrive in Mar del Plata with a common understanding of what was meant by growth versus development, or women versus gender. It's hard to admit it, and a little sad, but it's part of the story.

We had to lock ourselves in a room, all the indigenous women who'd traveled from Chile, and say all kinds of things to each other. We had to tell each other that the documents we'd brought, the positions we had, were nothing more than the positions of the institutions we came from, and didn't at that moment represent the position of indigenous women. We had to agree on certain key points. Somehow we accomplished that in Mar del Plata, across political divides and despite criticism from NGOs. I don't know, for some reason people always expect religious divisions to be the hardest, some seem to fear religion more than understand it. But over and above parties and religions, as Ana Llao put it, we managed to unite in Mar del Plata.

After that we did a good job with the rest of the indigenous delegations from South America, a very good job. The largest delegations were from Bolivia, Peru, Ecuador. There was a small group from Argentina, a small minority, and from Brazil. The women came en masse, in blocks, with documents. Plus Rigoberta had some institution, I can't remember the name; it was similar to the Chilean Initiative, let's call it the Indigenous Initiative. Her group brought a document, a position paper, that they wanted all the women there to sign and accept. We didn't accept that, especially not me, because it was an already elaborated document in which we hadn't participated. Not even Ana Llao, who was Rigoberta's spokeswoman in Chile, had seen the document before. So to me it was inconceivable, unacceptable, for an indigenous woman to accept an already prepared, ready-to-sign document. So we took the *Iniciativa Indígena*'s document—Rigoberta's sister was there, Rigoberta was not—and we said that because of the history and merit of Rigoberta Menchú, the respect she deserves, we'll use it as a base for discussion. But it won't be the final document, it won't be the assembly's document, because that one will be produced by us here.

That meant we spent all night working, all the South American indigenous leaders together. Rigoberta Menchú's initiative had come equipped with a full team: a psychologist, a Bolivian woman who worked very well; an Ecuadorian sister who was an ace on the computer and had a huge vocabulary, a very interesting woman. And that vocabulary stood us in good stead, because as I'm sure you know, by that point we were fighting over commas, articles, the turn of every phrase. We gave ourselves a full night and the following day. On the day we didn't appear everybody was asking, where are the indigenous women, they're not here yet, nobody knew where we were. But we were just locked away in a room. In that room there were seven beds, I think, and there were about thirty or forty of us: sitting on chairs, tables, beds, on the floor. Luckily there was a desklike table and that's where we installed the computer. Well, we finally reached an agreement and issued a document from that room, a very good document. The nonindigenous Latin American women really praised our document, but it sure cost us a lot of work. And we Mapuche women from this side of the mountains got bruised all right, given the number of positions and documents we'd carried with us to Mar del Plata.

The interesting thing was, that even though each of us had followed such a different path to Mar del Plata, once there we made an agreement that, when we returned to Chile, we'd take up the challenge of organizing a national conference for all the indigenous women of Chile. When we returned we held our press conference in a hall we rented in a hotel around here, not in CONADI or any of the other sponsoring organizations, in order to reinforce our nonpartisan character. That's how traveling on the road to Beijing contributed to unifying and strengthening the Coalition of Mapuche Women, composed of a number of institutions and organizations.

In the context of the Mar del Plata conference it became especially clear to me how ambiguous the role of NGOs can be, within the NGOs themselves, but especially when they also try to work inside the social organizations. NGO functionaries, executives, and technicians sometimes try to take on the role of movement leaders, while leaders sometimes try to give technical advice like the NGOs. And the women from the NGOs don't escape this lack of clarity. They represent the work they do with women in their own NGOs— the *Logko Kilapan*, the *Sociedad Nehuen*, the *Casa de la Mujer Mapuche*, *Auquinko Zomo*—but they don't work on women's issues more generally, even as they try to take leadership on those issues. Other NGOs, like *Liwen* or *Xen Xen*, for example, the women on their teams don't do specific work with women at all, nor do they deal with gender. Despite these problems, we worked well together from that moment on, and managed to organize the National Conference of Indigenous Women. Women came from the north: Aymaras, Atacameñas; two Rapa Nui sisters came from Easter Island; from the south we had one Kawaskar and one Llamana woman. They came from Chiloé, Osorno, Panguipulli, and obviously from Cautín and Malleco, Arauco, Cañete, Bío Bío; a lot of women came from Santiago. I think we had around three hundred women here in Temuco, for two and a half days, two days of very hard work.

F: *When was it held?*

In January 1996, because in November 1995 we went to Mar del Plata, and held the conference here the following January 28 to February 1. We produced a document with many demands, but also very concrete suggestions. CONADI gave us five million pesos, we had no other funding. With the five million we mobilized more than three hundred women with food and lodging. The biggest expense, peso for peso, was bringing the sisters from the extremes of the country: the two Rapa Nui from Easter Island, the sisters from the north, and the Kawaskar. We had to pay their tickets besides paying for their lodging and their food. Those two days were full of dynamism and energy, and lots of people in Temuco helped out by offering lodging in their homes, contributing mate, or providing the drinks for the night of the last day. Our organization made some extra donations, including a lamb. There were a lot of small but significant contributions from women's groups and other organizations, but not from the NGOS, which despite having resources to work with women only used their vehicles to bring in people from the communities. People who lived near Temuco weren't reimbursed for their tickets, nor the people who came from the NGOS, because they had rides in both directions. But we paid for their gas. So you can see what I mean about the NGOS. I'm not saying they didn't contribute anything, because they did and they supported us with their presence, but there were limits.

The most interesting part was that the conference actually took place, and that indigenous women participated from all over. Our conclusions were also important, and the final document included substantive proposals in the areas of health, education, political participation, and development. After that, and as a result of our national conference, the policies we'd outlined were shared with different institutions. We began a sort of pilgrimage, not only me but a group of women who officially handed in the conclusions of our conference and held talks with CONADI and SERNAM as government structures, requesting the necessary funding to go to Beijing. We spoke directly with the Minister in charge of SERNAM, and in addition to SERNAM and CONADI we requested from others that they fund us and help us make the necessary contacts so that indigenous women could go to Beijing. We believed that indigenous women from Chile should be a part of the official or the parallel delegations being sent to Beijing. All of the institutions we contacted thanked us, saying that it was the first time they'd gotten a document like ours, so well presented, and with such good suggestions. They promised to take it into account when formulating policy for their institutions.

But they probably just stuffed our document into the bottom drawers of their desks, because when push came to shove nobody did anything about the specific request we'd made. So we went straight to the First Lady and she said that all the invitations to Beijing had already been sent out through the Ministries, business firms, trade associations, and social and labor organizations. She thought that CONADI and SERNAM would define who among the indigenous women would travel to Beijing. To us it seemed a satisfactory answer, very politically astute, for one thing. But it didn't say, categorically, that an indigenous woman would go no matter what, and that it could be one from the list of ten names we'd presented. The truth is we were told, from the beginning, that ten was too many; and we knew that. But we wanted somebody in the official and in the parallel delegations. So we tried to move our other contacts, through embassies and other institutional channels.

We suspected that Rigoberta Menchú's initiative would fund Ana Llao, and that's exactly what happened. Ana Llao went about a week early to Central America, where they got together to prepare the documents each country's delegation would present in Beijing, specifically in Huairou, where the NGO conference was being held. The road to Huairou was longer, but besides Ana Llao, CEDEM funded a representative from the *Casa de la Mujer Mapuche*, no longer Rosa Rapiman, who'd gone to Mar del Plata, but Carolina Manque. A Dutch solidarity group that works with the *Logko Kilapán* asked them to send the person in charge of women's programming, not only to participate in the Beijing conference, but also to coordinate and evaluate the work they were doing with women in the different South American countries. So Rosa Toro, who had also been in Mar del Plata, was funded by the Dutch to represent the Logko in Beijing, but she also met with other South American women, I don't know in what country.

The Minister of SERNAM requested that the Coalition of Mapuche Women give her two names, and the two that were sent were Elisa Avendaño's and mine. For strategic and political reasons, we women were sure that, when it came time to decide, unfortunately the most important criterion would be membership in a political party. And not because I thought I'd have priority over everyone else, but experience told me the choice wouldn't be Ana Llao or Elisa Avendaño.[12] So I suggested to the women in the Coalition that they put up one candidate, and my name could go as a member of CONADI's Council and as CONADI's representative before the Coalition. I still made it clear that I'd probably have first priority, as a CONADI Council member and its representative on gender issues, and because I was a Christian Democrat.

Among the women we also read the fine print, because whoever went on the official delegation had to pay nearly 1.5 million pesos to get to China. I didn't have them, and CONADI wasn't willing to pay them. But that's not possible, all the women from the Coalition exclaimed. CONADI should be willing to pay that and much more. The people at SERNAM and other institutions agreed. But the truth is CONADI did not pay that amount. They gave a contribution through the Coalition for all the women who went to China, half a million pesos divided equally among Rosa Toro, Ana Llao, Carolina Manque, and myself. Actually, in Santiago they confirmed only ten days before the trip that one of the two women nominated by the Coalition could go. It wasn't clear who that would be until about five days before, when I received an urgent message to go to Santiago immediately to fill out the paperwork and get the passport . . .

F: *Only five days?!*

Only five days. I had my passport, a normal passport, but I didn't know that to go on the official delegation I needed an official passport, with a special authorization. They'd give it to me and then take it back when I returned, as I was leaving the airport. That's how it works. We had an inkling things would turn out this way, that Elisa wouldn't go. I was really disappointed that Elisa Avendaño had to stay. She's a real fighter, from the left, who has one of the clearest visions of what the Mapuche struggle ought to be, and I valued her participation. But if I didn't travel, well, deciding not to go in the end meant losing a seat. So I decided to go to Santiago, to ask for money everywhere I could, making phone calls, writing letters, asking for money from my friends, NGOs, politicians, institutions. But the money was nowhere to be found.

F: *The Christian Democrats didn't help you, either.*

Here in Temuco, I can't say yes or no, because officially nothing happened, but an individual party member, a friend of mine, lent me the money. If I tell you the whole story, I'd have to add that the official document we were taking to China contained nothing on peasant or indigenous women. So the SERNAM Working Group on Rural Women had to meet at the last minute and fight for the inclusion of peasant and indigenous issues. When I participated in that meeting I also discussed my situation, which led to some additional financial support from an anonymous Santiago comrade. It was a significant sum, and it came through hours before the trip, which was lucky for me. Now that last week I spent traveling back and forth between Santiago and Temuco. The first time I went to Santiago I took only enough money for the ticket. I had to come back to Temuco to get the money my friend was lending me and my traditional clothing, my chamal, which I had left behind. And in all that rushing around another friend also lent me a couple of dollars. He said, "Look, I know you need a lot for the trip. You wrote a letter to CONADI but they already gave all their money through the Women's Coalition." That was the first time I knew how much CONADI was giving. So my friend says, "I'll lend you this amount, I don't know when you'll pay me back, but there's always the possibility that you will someday, in dollars or pesos, it's OK." And I told him they were very welcome, because so far I'd only collected nine-hundred-thousand pesos, which I'd been told was only enough for the hotel since we were going to stay at the Sheraton. "I don't know if there's another hotel," I told him, "but they say the only hotel for the Chilean delegation is the Beijing Sheraton. Since I'm part of the official delegation I can't go renting a room any old place or bunking up in a group of two or three. I'm still not sure how this official delegation thing works, either, because it's my first time on an official delegation."

You ask yourself a lot of questions when you're about to take a leap like this one, but on the other hand I didn't want to miss this opportunity. Losing this opportunity meant losing a space, a relevance, a forum the Mapuche women should have. Mapuche women needed to be represented there, with or without me. If I hadn't been chosen I would've accepted it, like I've accepted many other things. The essential thing was for an indigenous woman to be there, and to be clear on what needed to be said. I emphasized this before I left, that what mattered was to contribute to what the Chilean delegation said in China. Before I traveled the Coalition of Mapuche Women, along with other women who had given us suggestions and feedback as we prepared for Beijing, produced another document that summarized our common demands and perspectives.

F: *Was that document part of what you presented in Beijing?*

In China I presented the document agreed upon by the Coalition of Mapuche Women of the IX Region. I think I'm one of the few people who respects an agreement when it's on the table, even if it hurts me personally. If people respect or trust me politically, it's because of that. It doesn't matter what my personal position is, if the agreement was something else, I make it mine. Many times I've done so painfully, but I've still respected it. Everybody knows this and that's why people respect me. But once we got to China, thankfully beyond the problem of funding, of going or not going, in the airport I met the rest of the people who were on the Chilean delegation. We'd traveled with a delegation of sixty people, but in China three more joined us, so we were sixty-three. One of the men was Pedro, a career guy at Foreign Relations, very young, who'd been very much involved in the discussion of indigenous rights. That made it easier to get to know him, because we had a topic in common, including the Declaration of Rights of Indigenous Peoples, the meetings in Geneva and Costa Rica, the different committee meetings at the United Nations. We also shared knowledge on the Chilean indigenous movement, what had happened at CEPI and CONADI; we knew a lot of the same people. So it was familiar territory for me; we felt at home with each other and worked well together.

Even when I have ideas and points of view that are different, I don't usually have problems adapting to a group, Mapuche or non-Mapuche, and that was the case here, too. It was a complex group, made up of people who were very, very different politically, religiously, institutionally. There were representatives from the four branches of the Chilean Armed Forces—the Army, the Navy, the Air Force, the Police; there was somebody from the Bureau of Investigations. All the ministries were represented, congressional representatives from the political parties of the *Concertación*, feminist activists, and women from the political right. I was the only indigenous woman, and interestingly, the only other woman who was not from Santiago was Nenita Díaz, a municipal councilwoman from Concepción.

F: *All the other indigenous representatives went to the parallel conference?*

Of the four indigenous women who went to China, three went to the parallel conference of NGOs, and I was the only one who went to the official conference, on the official delegation. I had the official certification and the passes to go into the various committee meetings where the official work was being done. Not so my other sisters who traveled; they didn't have the same opportunity. We could visit each other, because Beijing was an hour from Huairou. They were very close to the Great Wall and one day we went there together. I had the historic opportunity to walk a short distance along the Great Wall, to look at it, begin to understand why it was built, and how hard it must have been to build it there.

I learned less about gender at the Beijing Conference than I did about a multiplicity of things that entered my consciousness through my eyes. Summertime at the temples, the silk street market, the supermarkets, the pearl market; the amazing work in stone, in china; it's all a dream! I still find it hard to begin when describing this trip to China. At the end of an article I wrote for the Institute of Indigenous Studies[13] I said it was hard to know how to start writing about the Beijing Women's Conference, because the diversity of races, colors, and clothing was already a story in itself. Simply setting foot on Chinese soil was another story. The culture, music, atmosphere, language; the market full of amazing handicrafts, the things people sell on the streets, the food, how they eat on the street.

Among the women there were so many different skin colors, so many colors in the clothing; the hairdos, turbans, hats; all the accessories women wore introduced you to a world outside the more economic or political issues under discussion, or, in my case, the indigenous issue. In the midst of women prime ministers, princesses, heads of state, ministers, and labor leaders, an indigenous woman might seem a mere drop in the bucket, but I didn't want to be a simple decoration in a delegation of sixty-three people. I saw national delegations that brought indigenous women along as flower arrangements rather than participants. The poor things were taken here and there to show them off, they didn't say anything and someone was always at their elbows. So I had to assert myself, I had to go to the committee meetings and participate on an equal basis. Language was already a limitation. The language that dominates these massive governmental meetings is English, hardly ever Spanish. When you translate something from one language to another, first there's a delay, and then it comes across in a language you don't entirely understand. That gives you an idea of the handicap.

More than three hundred meetings were held each day, more than five thousand women; official meetings, the subcommittee of the committee of the general forum; the permanent forum, to which each country sent representatives. Every day there was a plenary session and each country got to present their work, the good and the bad things their country was doing for women. And I heard nothing bad! If you were to believe the ministers, first ladies, or princesses, or whoever were the women representing their countries, everywhere there were wonders being done with gender, with women. The only difference I saw was that some focused on gender and others focused on women. The one who really caught my attention was a princess or countess, a little brunette from Holland. I wrote down what she said. She spoke a lot about the poverty and hunger of women in the Third World, and "Why not admit it," she said, "also in my own country." The other woman who caught my attention, for her strong character and every thing, was Hillary Clinton. These two women's presentations were among the most spectacular, in the sense that they presented critical issues and gave a broader perspective. Because many others simply gave a catalogue of all the wonderful things being done in their countries, when even a simple glance, or later the work being done in committee, made clear it wasn't so. The president of Peru was enthusiastically cheered and booed, he got both sides.

So trying to summarize Beijing is like summarizing the diversity of the world: races, colors, clothing, languages; unique customs and cultures. The history of China itself becomes especially provocative when we're talking about women, because Chinese women can have only one child and they're allowed to have an abortion if they're carrying a girl. Now before jumping to conclusions and condemning China, I think it's important to understand China's history. I personally condemn the idea that you can abort a child just because it's a girl, but it's easy to condemn from a distance, having lived another history. I think you first have to know the history of China and see how people live, and maybe then you'll say look, I understand. Besides, Chinese women themselves don't seem too convinced. There are a lot of little girls walking around in China; it seems the Chinese are very fertile. So there are a lot of things to take into account before we start criticizing Chinese women.

In a similar way we could also begin criticizing our sisters from other Asian countries. Arab women go around all covered up, you can only see their eyes, and when they speak, they defend the harem. They saw it as the perfect venue for women's participation and education. They defended their position by referring to the Koran. They saw their way of life, six or seven women for just one man, as a mutual aid society, a cooperative. They said it made it easier to raise the children, work the land, go shopping. From their own perspective, culture, and customs, they saw it as something good.

I personally saw it as bad, terribly and absolutely bad. And I said so, trying to respect their point of view, but emphasizing that we'd be making a big mistake if we went backward after having taken so many steps forward. Politically and economically conditions aren't ripe for five, six, seven women to depend on one man, because the man would depend on them instead. Men and women have to complement each other.[14]

When we argued, they mixed everything up together: health, traditional medicine, intellectual property rights, political participation. Everything they could do, they saw in relation to the Koran. We'd say, look, those women covered up from head to toe drive us up the wall. But then we'd also say, geez, the lives they lead; and of course they have to defend it all, because a man was always with them, wherever they went. If one of them had said, yes, it's true, we're oppressed, obviously the man there would say, watch out, I'm your husband, or I'm your bodyguard, or whatever it was they were. The women walked around in groups of four, five, or six, always together. Even when they carried a video camera, camera, or tape recorder, they'd still walk around all covered up. And they always had a man with them, dressed in black, brown, or beige. They always stuck together. Their speeches were strong and clear, and they showed real personality in getting across their points. I think this bothered a lot of people; it made others laugh; and some didn't know how to confront them. It's not that they didn't know what to say, it's that they didn't dare disagree with a different culture. And even though I argued with them, I also said that no one transformed a way of life from one day to the next, because everything was a process. The conference itself was a good example, because we'd worked for many years to get to this point.

In addition to the meetings, committees, and caucuses, I also learned a lot in a series of parallel meetings on specific topics, with feminist and anti-feminist groups, including those dealing with Christian issues, family rights and all that. The Vatican was represented there, too, with their Christian reflections and the defense of the family from their own perspective. Sure, it's legitimate in its own sphere, but it represents the hierarchical, dominating Church, the one that follows the Opus Dei line and is tailor-made for the rich, with the poor at best an afterthought. So all of this is why I say that, to understand the Women's Conference, you have to understand the context in which it was held.

I participated in the work of several commissions. The one that interested

me the most was the Health Commission because one of its subcommis-
sions discussed the intellectual property rights of women concerning the
development and application of herbs and medicinal plants. We discussed
indigenous women's right to intellectual property in a broad sense, from
their right to patent traditional medicines and prescriptions and control
how they get marketed, to being recognized as the authors of the handicrafts, art, and literature they produce. So I was very interested in the Health
Commission, whose work lasted two days and one night and really moved
me. The second day we rested from three to five in the afternoon, and then
resumed work in order to reach our final conclusions. Because even if a
subcommission reached an agreement, you had to bring it back to the
commission's plenary because other groups had been dealing with other
issues. When the entire commission got together, everything was subject to
rethinking and rewriting, from broad questions of focus and meaning all
the way down to the last period or comma. Plus it was all going on in
English, Spanish, and French, which changed the meaning of every phrase.
The first three hours of discussion were useless, they didn't go anywhere;
and the next three were only a little better. We finally reached our conclusions in two and a half hours during the night.

So I spent a day and a night straight in this commission, this subcommission of a subcommission of the Health Commission. And when it came
time to clinch the deal late into the night, I had to ask for help. I said I
couldn't do it on my own, that at ten o'clock in such and such a hall, in such
and such a place, I needed somebody who spoke English because the translators were playing me crooked. I could tell they were betraying me at
certain key moments. Fortunately, SERNAM Minister Josefina Bilbao went
with me. She'd worked a lot on the Foreign Relations Commission and
spent a lot of time in the United States. Pedro, who manages English and
indigenous issues very well, also came. I thought Pedro should be there, and
I specifically asked for his presence, but besides him many Chilean women
came. I guess they wanted to see what the little Mapuche was up to in the
commission. When the moment came to defend my position, Pedro translated for me. Since I know a little English I could tell he did the best possible
job, and then he stood behind me to translate what the others said.

F: *From what you're saying, it seems the most fruitful work at the official
conference in Beijing was done by the commissions. In the official speeches, it*

seems people just said everything was great and all the women were de-
lighted. Do you think the commissions in this sense were different, and more
productive?

I think that's exactly right. Obviously the official speeches were important
because you got to know the official vision of each country. And luckily, I
think the official speech given by the Chilean delegation was one of the
richest and strongest. Obviously I'm not talking about how the situation is
in practice, but the speech itself was focused and sharp. I think it clarified
what is meant by gender and it also defined women's participation very well,
especially what was meant by empowerment, that is, that women assume
decision-making roles. It also clarified women's so-called traditional roles
by emphasizing that, even if women alone are naturally endowed with the
capacity to be mothers, it is not the only role all women are called to do.
I think this speech contributed a lot, something commented on by a lot of
people from different countries. It helped clarify issues for some of the
commissions, and for the harder confrontations the Vatican sponsored
around the concept of gender. But definitely the hardest work was done in
the commissions.

It's also important to remember that about sixty percent of the platform
that came out of Beijing had been set before, starting in the previous wom-
en's conference in Nairobi, and continuing in the various meetings held in
different parts of the world, like we had in Latin America. So you could say
that forty percent was left to discuss and work out in the commissions. The
plenary sessions were also interesting, but only because they represented the
positions of the governments in power at that moment. The rest of the work
was more long-term, which is the way work with women must be. That's the
way I saw it, and it's a spectacular experience I'll probably never repeat. And
now people can't threaten to put me on a slow boat to China (¡*Andate a la*
China!), because if they do, I'd just say sure, what port is it leaving from?

F: *Or you could say, been there, done that (*Ya estuve*).*

Right! I think the greatest challenge upon returning from Beijing was to
publicize the platform we agreed on for future action. The convention itself,
and my personal role in it, were already a part of history I wanted to share
with others, but that's different from making known the official agreements
we reached. In fact, when I got back from Beijing I traveled between Con-

cepción and Osorno, something that, with all due respect, the nonindigenous women who went to the conference didn't do even though they could afford to do so. I spoke at a meeting sponsored by a foundation in Coelemu, VIII Region; I talked with women's groups at the University of Concepción. Here in the IX Region, I toured the counties, municipalities, and schools, and held seminars with NGOS. It was a lot of hard work that lasted from September 1996 to approximately March of this year. It was tough, and I'm not saying it's over. But I think the pressure's gone down, bit by bit people's interest in knowing the results of Beijing has calmed down. Partly that's because many institutions have received documents, since the Chile Initiative has sent the material from China to all the focal points. There's a series of documents, including the platform of action and the ten points that answer the question, After Beijing, what? I wrote an article in the Universidad de la Frontera's journal *Pentukun*, and I've also written in other journals about China. So the information has gone out. Besides, when we came back there was a little piece in the newspaper. We also held a conference here in Temuco, at the municipal library, with Lily Pérez, a *Renovación Nacional* municipal councilwoman from Santiago who'd been in Beijing. She came to Temuco to a meeting of her party and we participated together at a round table that gave different perspectives on the Beijing Conference. To my surprise, we worked very well with Lily in Beijing. She's a good friend, very hardworking. It wasn't so with the other women from the right, with whom there were some tough confrontations because they tended to distort what has happening in China.

F: *How so?*

For example, they reported that the concept of gender meant that now there were five sexes, no longer only man and woman, but homosexuals, gays, lesbians, men, and women. This is what we were agreeing to in China, they said in their reports back to Chile through a journalist member of their team who worked for *El Mercurio*, and it was all published. We had very serious conflicts with them.

F: *During the discussions.*

Right there during the discussions, and also in a private meeting of the entire delegation that was held in the Chilean Embassy. At that meeting I said that China was not the place to discuss whether gender meant five sexes or two. I knew of only two, but I also respected other options or variations, depending on the way people were born. If perfect meant being only man or woman, then not all of us were perfect. That this was not a discussion for the convention, where we were culminating more than ten years of work. We had to know why we were there, and that we didn't come to fight about this. We argued a lot, and like I told them, if they didn't learn in school that gender was masculine and feminine,[15] it would be really hard for them to learn it thirty years later.

It wasn't that they didn't understand gender as a cultural concept, as part of human development. They weren't stupid. The thing was that they wanted to define a different position, a strong position in defense of the family, and they decided to attack the gender concept as not defending the family. They predicted it would lead to deviance. Did we want our children leaving home at fifteen, two boys living together, two girls living together, like they did in Europe? With the support of the Vatican folks, who also said that people in Europe were once more realizing the importance of a strong family, they emphasized that Europeans also wanted families to live together again, children with their parents. I would say look, I also know Europe and what Europeans think. But they didn't really want a more general political discussion. Every time we tried to engage the substance of the gender discussion, they'd change the subject. Then they'd say: what's the point of discussing the five sexes when people in the shantytowns need food and education. So we'd have to tell them that women in the shantytowns also needed to participate, that they had the right, the duty, and the responsibility to make decisions in the municipalities and neighborhood associations. And they also had the right to be elected to Congress.

F: *But women in the shantytowns also need to discuss their sexual options, don't you think?*

Of course, but that wasn't a part of their vision. Simply saying that women in the shantytowns also think, and that they want to participate in more than just fulfilling their material needs, raised a lot of eyebrows. They brought up the guidelines the Chilean government had issued on sexual education, what was later known as the *Jocas*, and they said that this encouraged the little girls in the shantytowns to have sexual relations. We said no, what it does is bring the discussion out in the open. Because if you go to a shantytown, the women will teach you more about explaining sex to children than you teach them. It's not a new issue we're taking to them, they often know more than we do. But these rightist women saw the Jocas as a sordid corruption of children. It was a self-serving view; that's how a number of us in our delegation saw it, and I tell you that Lily Pérez mediated this situation very well. Many of us acknowledged this. As a result of this debate I also got to know a number of other members of the delegation, from the Christian Democrats to the left, especially Congresswoman Fanny Pollarolo. I'd never worked with her before. She worked very well on the commissions, in the workshops, as did her colleagues Antonieta Saa and Mariana Aylwin. I really saw that the three of them made an excellent team. I told them that I hoped their complicity of women also worked well in Congress. They said definitely, because without it they wouldn't get anything done.

F: *It seems that you were always defending the more democratic and inclusive positions in the conflicts, arguments, and debates that took place at the official meeting.*

Well, it's important to note that the indigenous issue, maybe because it's a new topic, wasn't handled very well by the other people on the delegation. The only exception was Pedro, from Foreign Relations, who'd participated in a number of events concerning indigenous politics. The rest of the people didn't have a clue as to who we indigenous people were. The only indigenous woman any of them had ever seen was the maid or nanny (*nana*) they had at home, those who had an indigenous nana. With all due respect, I was able to tell the women on the delegation that they had to see beyond the domestic worker they had in their houses, to the family situation that forced her to look for work, and to the kind of work she was forced to do. I told them that indigenous women saw and understood the world differently, and that it would help to try and understand this difference just a bit. At one of the stops we made—and obviously, some of my traveling companions asked me to—I took pleasure in explaining what it meant to be Mapuche and to live in Chile, what it meant to be a domestic servant. You might ask me why I chose to focus it that way, and it's because most of the women traveling with me were most familiar with that particular figure.

I told them that we were first peoples, that we'd lived off the land as gatherers. I gave them the general history of the Mapuche that you already know. So why do we migrate to the cities, I asked them. Because land is scarce and the family is large; and also because we want to better ourselves. So we leave looking for an opportunity to study and to contribute to the family. Never does a Mapuche woman leave her family thinking she won't give back, and even if she returns only once a year she comes back with things for the house and for the whole family. Not only for one or two people, no; with things for the mother, the father, her brothers and sisters, the uncles, the cousins. This is the expectation of all the people in the community. And if it doesn't turn out this way it's because she's had problems in the city. And if she only brings a small gift, but she says I studied, I got this degree, I did this, then the family is satisfied. But if she doesn't bring you anything, or if she doesn't visit, or if she never says things were going well, then people say that she's had problems, and they can conclude that she didn't do well. This is generally the way people see things in the countryside.

I told them that in the countryside you don't have a refrigerator, that the furniture is not the same, things don't have the same names. In the countryside the kitchen cupboard's called *trinche*, or *repisa* (shelf) if you want to sound more modern, right? We don't call our dishes *loza*, we call them *rali*. There's no bathroom like in the cities, where you pull the chain and you have to clean the toilet and put little things next to it so it smells good. In some places in the countryside they don't even have outhouses, and you have to relieve yourself a couple of meters away from the house, in the bushes. Half-jokingly I'd say that communities have to build outhouses because we're running out of trees. I said it half-joking, but also to make them think. Then they would ask all kinds of questions.

F: *So you had this conversation with the Chilean delegation.*

Only with the Chilean delegation and on our way to Beijing, because for them having an indigenous woman on the delegation was a novelty. They were all asking themselves, where is the indigenous woman, who is she. And I had conjunctivitis, I caught it on Bandera Street in Santiago when I was running around getting my passport. I went indoors, and then I walked out again. People said be careful, but the cold wind must have blown something in my eye, so I got an infection. My eye was red, red, red! I was lying down, I had three seats to myself, lying down and putting antibiotic drops in my eye. And they kept asking, who is the indigenous woman, which one is she. But I didn't say anything and no one else said anything, because not everyone knew me. Then in the middle of a conversation I said I was the indigenous woman; it was during a layover when we got off. And I asked them if they had expected to see someone half-naked, with feathers and a weird accent. If that's what they wanted me to do, I said, then I could.

Then Mariana Aylwin and Fanny Pollarolo—let me tell you, do they know how to talk!—well, they started in, saying no, it's really her, and she has quite a history, the fight for democracy and all that. Indigenous people in Chile aren't what they used to be, they've been nearly exterminated or they've assimilated. And I realized that Fanny Pollarolo and Mariana Aylwin knew quite a lot about the issue. The way they talked was similar to us, in the sense that they didn't say that in Chile there were no more Indians because that's how it should be, because we'd gotten beyond the indigenous problem, as others had said. No, they said indigenous people did exist, even if not like before; and there still were communities, despite the pressure to assimilate and a lack of respect for the culture. And they pointed out that Chileans tend to see indigenous people, as well as peasants, shantytowns, and the lower classes in general, as folklore. Their comments made me very happy and helped me a lot.

Well, after that we talked a lot. I became good friends with the woman from the Bureau of Investigations, and the one from the Police. These women were very involved, they knew how to fight for what they believed in. And they defended shantytown women, saying look, they need this and that, and they have rights, too.

F: *The women from the Armed Forces were also from Santiago?*

All of them, except for the one from the Navy, she was from Valparaíso. She was a lawyer; apparently there are no women sailors. The one from the Air Force, let me tell you, she was really cool. The three women—from Investigations, the Air Force, and the major from the Police—were the most involved in women's issues. They knew what SERNAM was, and what *Mujeres por la Vida* and the women's struggle had meant in Chile. You could talk about history with them, from the fight for women's suffrage up to what was happening now, how women were being used. We even spoke about the white slave trade, about how women were taken as prostitutes, to the north or south, or to Peru and Argentina. The woman from the Air Force was also a lawyer, so she understood the situation of women in the Air Force, their families, the right to education, and pay issues. We discussed all the seemingly simple issues women had to deal with when they began to participate, and how when a woman finally breaks through and makes it, after her another woman can come and she can also make it. We talked about how women had to blaze a trail, that our society seemed to be an onion that you have to peel layer by layer. The conversations with them were very interesting, over dinner or at night, when we got together to evaluate the different workshops in which people participated.

Two of them participated in the Disarmament Commission with Minister Bilbao from SERNAM. In Chile this is one of the issues that stirred up the least interest, but according to them it was a key commission that you had to watch out for. They explained that disarmament wasn't related only to war, but to any kind of emergency, and that women were the ones who paid the highest price in any situation. This situation could be a war, a catastrophe, an uprising that occurred from one moment to the next. Whatever the circumstances it was always women and children who were most affected. We must accept this reality, they said, and find a way to protect women. Maybe the best way is to keep things from getting out of hand in the first place. Being against disarmament doesn't mean that we're in a permanent state of war, they said, or that we're prepared to go to war at any moment. That's the perspective they shared with us. And they also shared their view of women who take drugs, have abortions, or work as prostitutes. Theirs was not a discriminatory vision, you know, it was more a vision of reality. It put things in perspective and helped us learn. These were topics that came out in our nightly conversations, when different groups from the delegation got together.

F: *Did the initiative for the SERNAM Working Group on Peasant Women also come from Beijing?*

In the different groups within the delegation we also spoke about agriculture. My roommate was Liliana Barría, who worked for INDAP and was representing the Ministry of Agriculture. We spoke about INDAP and women's participation in their different programs, as well as women's right to

Isolde with part of the 1992 Indigenous Walking Tour of Europe, being hosted by an Evangelical group in Germany. *Courtesy of Isolde Reuque.*

Isolde standing with Rigoberta Menchú and other participants in the 1992 Indigenous Walking Tour of Europe. *Courtesy of Isolde Reuque.*

Isolde reaching the climactic point in her well-received speech in Assisi in 1992. *Courtesy of Isolde Reuque.*

Part of the 1992 Walking Tour of Europe, on their way to Assisi. Isolde is walking directly under the banner, while Rigoberta Menchú is in the next line back. *Courtesy of Isolde Reuque.*

Isolde in 1995, at the National Congress of Indigenous Women on the way to Beijing. To her left are: Rosa Rapiman, leader of a women's NGO; Yolanda Nahuelcheo, activist in Mapuche women's health; Molly Garrido, Aymara leader; and Rosa Paoa, Rapa Nui leader. *Courtesy of Isolde Reuque.*

Isolde giving the opening speech at the National Congress of Indigenous Women. The two women to her left are members of the organizing committee, Yolanda Nahuelcheo and Ana María Llao. *Courtesy of Isolde Reuque.*

Isolde in Iquique in 1996, after her return from Beijing, with her fellow CONADI National Councilmembers, from left to right: Molly Garrido, Aymara; Marcela Llao, Mapuche (Purén); Isolde; an unidentified Aymara leader; José Santos Millao, Mapuche (Purén); Beatriz Painequeo, Mapuche (Santiago); and Aymara leader Cornelio Chipana. *Courtesy of Isolde Reuque.*

Isolde addressing the Chilean House of Representatives two years after the promulgation of the 1993 Indigenous Law, arguing against its proposed modification. *Courtesy of Isolde Reuque.*

Isolde and her mother, doña
Martina Paillalef, standing in
front of their kitchen in Chanco
in 1997. *Courtesy of Florencia
Mallon.*

Doña Martina Paillalef drinking
mate in Lily Reuque's ruka,
Chanco, August 2001. *Courtesy
of Florencia Mallon.*

Isolde's father, don Ernesto Reuque, posing for a photograph, Chanco, 1997. *Courtesy of Florencia Mallon.*

Don Ernesto Reuque working in the fields, Chanco, 1997. *Courtesy of Florencia Mallon.*

Isolde in 1999, posing for a photograph during a visit to Chanco. *Courtesy of Florencia Mallon.*

Isolde's mother, doña Martina Paillalef, returning from a trip to cut firewood, Chanco, 1999. *Courtesy of Florencia Mallon.*

Isolde's daughter, Lily
Reuque, cutting firewood
in Chanco, 1999.
*Courtesy of Florencia
Mallon.*

Isolde's sister, Elvira
Reuque, relaxing during
a visit to Chanco, 1999.
*Courtesy of Florencia
Mallon.*

Isolde in 1999, participating in a series of town meetings with Mapuche community leaders in an effort to reopen lines of communication with the government. *Courtesy of Isolde Reuque.*

One of the campaign signs for Isolde's 1999 run for CONADI's National Council, seen at the terminal for rural buses to Lautaro County. *Courtesy of Isolde Reuque.*

Isolde during her 1999 campaign, stopping to visit her in-laws, don Juan Bautista Sánchez Lincanqueo and doña Graciela Curihuentro Turra, in their community of Huilío. *Courtesy of Isolde Reuque.*

Isolde during her 1999 campaign in Icalma, Lonquimay county, near the border with Argentina. The man on horseback is the President of the Pewenche community of Icalma. *Courtesy of Isolde Reuque.*

Isolde with National Congressional Representative Francisco Huenchu-milla, during the presidential campaign of Ricardo Lagos (1999). *Courtesy of Isolde Reuque.*

Isolde at the Moneda National Palace, May 2000, presenting President Ricardo Lagos with the results of their Working Group's Evaluation of the Situation of Indigenous Peoples after fifty days of his presidency. From left to right: José Santos Millao, CONADI National Councilmember; Beatriz Painequeo; Ariel Burgos, Lay Pastor for the Indigenous Pastoral Group of the Catholic Church; and Isolde. *Courtesy of Isolde Reuque.*

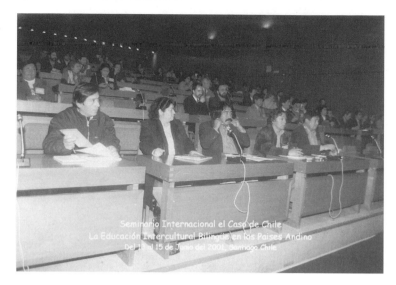

Isolde, participating with her fellow CONADI National Councilmembers in a June 2001 Seminar on Bilingual Education in Santiago. From left to right: Miguel Liguempi, VIII Region; Isolde, Councilmember designated by President Ricardo Lagos; José Santos Millao, IX Region; José Llancapan, Metropolitan Region; Juan Manquel, Huilliche, X Region. *Courtesy of Isolde Reuque.*

credit, to participate in decision making, and all those kinds of things that don't happen so easily. We found the time and space to discuss the pros and cons of these issues. And beyond the delegation, the trip itself, and the platform of action, I think the most interesting thing about Beijing was that, when we returned to Chile, SERNAM coordinated a multidisciplinary and broadly participatory working group on peasant and indigenous women's participation. The idea was born before Beijing, on our way to Mar del Plata, when in December 1994 INDAP held a meeting with SERNAM in which CONADI was also supposed to participate, but it didn't. After this first meeting the idea was discussed more concretely in Mar del Plata, and when we returned we created a study group, for dialogue or negotiation, whatever you want to call it. SERNAM coordinated the participation of INDAP; the ministries of Education, Health, Agriculture; the Armed Forces on a more sporadic basis; the National Peasant Commission; MUCECH; Women of the North (*Mujeres del Norte*); the Coalition of Mapuche Women from the IX

Region; and a few NGOs, especially the NGOs that work with peasant farmers in the central zone.

Generally, in Santiago, the people who participate in studies, policy diagnoses, and political discussions tend to come from the parts of the country between Curicó and Copiapó. I guess that's as far as you can see from Santiago! The reason we formed a part of the study group and the working group in Santiago is because we know how to fight, because more than once we went to SERNAM to speak with the Minister, to tell her that we weren't just anybody, that we were a people. We wanted to sit at that table, and we wanted women from the regions sitting next to us. So we took her a list of the people and organizations we thought should participate, from the I, II, III, VIII, IX, and X regions, and also the V Region because it includes Easter Island. Our list had the names of women and organizations we felt should sit at the table, including the NGOs from the IX Region, Mapuche as well as wigka, because we thought at least one organization from outside Santiago should be present.

So the permanent members of the working group turned out to be IN-DAP, SERNAM, CONADI, the national peasant federations, and some NGOs and cooperatives; then came the Coalition of Mapuche Women from the IX Region, made up of NGOs and two organizations, Ad-Mapu and *Keyuk-leayñ*. So Mapuche women were represented by Ana Llao, for the Coalition, and I was representing CONADI. I have to admit I still haven't handed in my report, but I should do so soon and officially leave my position.

The working group has already published its document, with suggested courses of action or policy for rural women in general, and that includes indigenous women. Someday I hope we'll elaborate a document specifically for rural indigenous women, because this one's more broadly for all women in the countryside. Obviously indigenous women share the experiences of poverty, discrimination, lack of credit and participation, because they really work the land and live off the land. These women are also the seasonal wage-labor force in agriculture, the temporary workers from the shanty-town belt around the cities who work the harvests in the agricultural sector.

Well, in a nutshell this was the work our group did. We formed a good team that included people from the government and from the women's social organizations, and we were able to work together. We've discussed many issues, from handicrafts and agricultural labor to political participation. We talked about people's right to participate in the formulation of health programs, education, credit programs, and agricultural policy. We discussed the difficulties women faced in getting access to credit and succeeded in making the Director of INDAP open up credit applications to women without the husband's or oldest son's signature. We emphasized that women should get direct-access credit, be they single or married, as long as they can prove they can do the work on the land from which they live. And here, in practice, we see little difference between indigenous and nonindigenous law. The great majority of individual land titles are in the hands of men.

We made no bones about this situation. Land titles were held first by the father, and only when the father died did title pass to the mother, and then only if the oldest son wasn't living there. Because if the oldest son was there, neither the mother nor her daughters ever got the land. So women were always dependent on others: first as daughters, then as wives, then as widows. That's more or less the cycle of life, you always end up the same. If not, you're the old maid who lives on the charity of your parents, brothers, or some other relative. You can't be single by personal choice, but instead you must dedicate your life to taking care of the uncle, father, or brother who needs you and thus supports you. This was a little of what we discussed in the working group. We also discussed the lack of a clear agrarian policy that would lead to true development in the countryside, because as it stands economic growth is given priority over development, and over equal participation in policymaking in the field.

F: *Well. And with this we get to the present day? Have we finished?*

Wow. I haven't yet gotten used to the idea of rounding off the book. But at least I've summarized my travels—through the world, through my country, and through the communities belonging to my people. I can't end without telling you that the memories I hold most dear are from my travels through Mapuche communities, through the communities in Chiloé, the communities close to the rivers, the lakes, where I find Günechen (God), where I can communicate directly with that superior being. That's when I find, I don't know what, but I can cry, laugh, sing. My poetry springs forth, my verses, and I can dream and surround myself in reality, all at once. I think there's much in the wind that blows in each one of those places. Where I've most easily been able to find that superior being is in the places where someone says, there's nothing else to be done. There I find something that speaks to me. When a flower is reborn amidst all that filth, it tells you there's still a moment of hope, and that our love for the earth, for nature, for human beings, must open each day toward the world, toward people, toward all of us.

❦ CONCLUSION

F: *I've been very impressed by your parents' story; each of them had such a different experience. Your mom was from a very prosperous family, but with her stepbrother's problems they lost everything. Your father was from a more impoverished family and he had to leave home to find work, among other things as a muledriver (*arriero*). They started living together without courting, and at first faced real economic hardship. Yet your mother's silent strength really kept it all together. What effect did this experience have on you growing up?*

It's really hard to be sure what affected me the most, what guided me or gave me strength, values, or charisma inside my family, because a Mapuche family is a whole. It's true that within that whole my mother came from a family of famous caciques, like they say here in Chile, from the Mapuche aristocracy, the Paillalef. This lineage waged many battles with the Chilean army in 1810, during the Independence wars. Later they gave some of their land to the Chilean state in order to found cities; Pitrufquén is an example. My father's family, on the other hand, the Reuques, are not a cacique lineage. They worked for the caciques, which is why they're called konas. My grandfather was a kona, so obviously my father is a kona. But he came to occupy the position of cacique when nobody else wanted to take it, because he's hardworking, honest, and persevering, and because he's always wanted better for himself and his family. Through his support for his family, his children, he's taught me the value of perseverance and family unity.

In the wealth of night-time conversations, I've learned we're a family that's suffered economically, with very little land. During the time my mother lived in her mother-in-law's house, her relationship with my father's family wasn't the best. I think this happens in every family when wealth marries poverty, and it happened here, too. Even though my mother suffered the most by marrying a kona, her love was stronger than the criticisms of her in-laws. She managed to rise above the blows she suffered each day, being denied the possibility of living on her own land when it was a lot more than what her in-laws had. But as a result, when she was still very young, sixteen or seventeen, she and my father were able to buy a piece of land together. At first it was the quarter part of where we live today. Moving here was an act of bravery! Living for sixty days under a tree, inside a box, few people would do that. But they did, in order to form an independent household and live in peace. What I learned from them is that a couple's relationship grows and gets stronger in good times and in bad.

My mother also suffered what we call domestic violence. She suffered the jealousy of a husband whose wife was seen as superior to him. Besides, according to Mapuche criteria, my mother was a lovely woman. I think she's still lovely. So she suffered the jealousy of a man who loved her, but who loved her selfishly, because he punished her if she greeted or smiled at someone. It got to the point where he actually prohibited her from saying hello to anyone. Not surprisingly, my mother also suffered a lot from loneliness, because she didn't have close relatives nearby with whom she could share what she was going through. She got to choose between staying with my father, or going back to her stepbrother who made her work every hour of the day, where she would be her sister-in-law's servant, answering to the nephews, to everybody. So why not have her own house? My mother is a tower of strength, but she hardly ever tells her story. With you she opened up and shared it. When I got married, she told me go, get married, and live alone. Don't live with a sister-in-law, or with a mother-in-law. Even if all you can do is rent a room, live by yourselves. Although she insisted many times that we should live by ourselves, she never explained why. Knowing her story, though, it makes sense. She wanted something better for us.

Besides, I think my mother is a multifaceted woman, in the sense that she sewed, kept a vegetable garden, built fences; she could do any kind of work. Women in the countryside tend to be this way, but my mother was especially dedicated. She was and is a woman of great determination; she'd stay up late sewing and knitting. If somebody gave her a big dress she'd divide up the material and make us hand-sewn dresses, because we didn't even have a sewing machine. Nowadays you'll find one in every house, but it wasn't like that when I was growing up. Sweaters, hats, pants—everything we wore when we were kids—was made by her hands. She never went to school to learn how to do this; she learned by watching. When she went to the hospital, when she took the bus, when somebody came to the house, the details she saw in other people's sweaters or dresses, she could turn around and make them. I learned that from my mother.

Now, from my father I learned forcefulness and persistence, that sometimes, in order to overcome an obstacle, you have to be bullheaded. You have to be driven. That strength that some focus on revenge, you have to channel for self-betterment. If at first I don't succeed, I'll be better next time. Not that I have to beat the other guy, it's not about looking down on others. It's about improving yourself. My father was tenacious. He always said, I have to be able to do this. He'd say, how can that guy beat me? I have to be better than him! That stubbornness he has. So these are the things I learned from my family, from my parents as a couple, from my brothers who had very strong tempers.

F: *When we began talking, you said that as a child you'd been a man-woman, because after he suffered from polio Lionel couldn't assume his role as the oldest son, plowing the land and all that, so you had to do the hard work. Now hearing you talk about your mom and dad, I can see how you combined your father's stubborn strength with your mother's talent for innovation and her quietly strong and varied presence within your family. Do you think this combination helped you become a leader?*

I think the everyday challenges, those basic things you learn inside the family, remain with you throughout your life even if they take a different form. Learning to harness the oxen without having them run away; to pound in stakes, hammer in nails, cut down trees. Then to make a fire every morning and prepare a broom to sweep the yard—because a Mapuche can't use just any branch to sweep, there's a special branch we use in the communities to make brooms. Today I may not be pounding stakes to fence the pasture, or laying the wire, or making brooms, but sociopolitically I'm hammering down details, defining goals, and making sure the lines are as straight as they can be. Each day, each moment is a challenge, because when you're a kid they don't teach you theoretically, you learn how to do things by watching your mom or dad and then trying it yourself. It's a model I try to follow when I give training sessions for women in the communities. They should learn by doing, because that's how we do it in the communities.

I did the same thing when I started off as a leader and had Melillán Painemal by my side. Even though his training and background had been in the Communist tradition, he was a visionary, a great Mapuche leader. For some, his greatest error was to be a Communist. For others it was not knowing how to guide his people. But he was a man who gave his whole life to the struggle. He was so sharp analytically and had so much vision that you could really learn from him. Personally, I learned an incredible amount from him. He was a man of character, who thought he was better than the rest of us who were younger and had less experience. But I think I was able humbly to discuss issues with him, and to say excuse me, but I think you're wrong about this. I think l learned a lot from him. Just like I learned from my parents, I learned from him. You take from each person what's most useful or relevant, what you want to take. Personally, I don't have one specific ideal politician, I don't have a specific ideal woman activist. But even in women of, say, the more manicured variety, you can find something good if you're looking for it. Observation is a talent that helps you analyze, it helps you in the action of your everyday life.

F: *Since we're talking about the people who've had an effect on your development, let's talk also about Father Francisco Lauschman. He seems to have influenced you a lot, from the time you were in school to the time of his death, shortly after your marriage. Tell me a little more about Father Pancho.*

Wow. I don't know why I always seem to associate my greatest strengths and weaknesses with him. To remember Father Pancho is to remember a friend, a man, a priest. He was the first person who ever told me that I was valuable, that I was capable of doing a lot more than what I was doing. He was the priest who told me, look, your poems have much more meaning than my words ever could. He was the friend who told me I had charisma, the ability to lead others and to take a public role. Things like this mark you deeply when you're trying to figure out who you are, what you'll be able to do; when you're faltering, between quitting your studies, staying at home, working outside the home; when sometimes all you want to do is to disappear from the face of the earth. He was there for me at that moment.

When I had a lot of questions about my life, he was able to see in me what others didn't see.

I still don't understand why or how, on that day, at that time, he knew to tell me look, you have to fight, you have to take this path and not that one. A priest is constantly dealing with people's problems. And yet in my specific moment of weakness, he knew exactly what to say to reach me. He also praised something I did in secret, as if it were a forbidden thing: my poems to Mother Earth and to God. It was something I kept hidden alongside my romanticism, because I thought I was too much of a dreamer; but he helped me believe that, sometimes, your dreams can come true.

When I got married I told him, "Father, I'm going to get married, and these are the characteristics of my future husband." And he said, "Fine, I want to meet him." When he met him he said, "Now just remember: you found, loved, and accepted him. Now it's up to you to preserve your relationship." I think he was the only one who didn't say something against Juan. Unlike my other friends, also Christians, Catholics, deacons, priests, who told me he wasn't the right man, that I was making a mistake, and how was I going to survive living with that snotty-nosed kid. Answers to everything seem to come rolling off my tongue, so I said to one of them, "Look, Father, birds don't farm the land but they live on it. And look at how beautiful the wildflowers are and nobody has planted them. In the same way we'll find a way to live and something to eat." And the priest told me, "Isolde, don't use the word of God to justify your great mistake." This is just one example of what a lot of people told me: academics, Mapuche leaders, many others. Instead Father Pancho said, "No, you found, loved, and accepted him; now it's up to you to preserve the relationship." He never said he's bad, he's good, he's only a kid. No words about him. Instead he emphasized who and what I was. "The day he leaves," Father Pancho also said, "if that's his decision, you were born alone and you've lived alone before. That means you can do it again. We never know for sure when things will begin and when they'll end. But you are capable of surviving in this world and you know how to accept your own reality." That was it. And to Juan he made a gesture, he touched his shoulder lightly and said, "It was a pleasure to meet you." That was it also. After having tea, coffee, there was no long conversation. What stood out to me was how he supported me. And whether he was there or not, I've always felt that I can talk to him about all my problems, even my problems with Juan. Many times I've told Juan, "Look, if Father Pancho were still alive, you wouldn't dare say that to me."

I also think I use him as a shield, a source of strength, because I remember the good things and I can cry and laugh at the same time. It was from him that I learned a joke was a good thing, that pranks could be fun. By example he showed me that, when people were too tense in a group, it was good to be playful, because telling a joke could sometimes touch people more deeply. I learned these things from him. Once we were with a group of farmers. It was Sunday so we were talking about the Gospel, and all of a sudden he starts in on how skinny the cows were! It had nothing to do with the Gospel, but he always took examples from everyday life. If it was too hot or too windy, if there were floods or if the roofs had blown off the houses— everything had a good laugh or a good lesson in it. There are so many things I've learned from him. I remember that when he spoke, I was always left with some doubt or other. He'd ask me, "Did you understand?" Hmmm . . . Yes. "No," he'd say, "you didn't understand everything. You still have questions. The worst question is the one left unasked." That's something I still do when I speak to a group. Ask me, take advantage of the fact that I'm here, I tell them. The worst question is the one left unasked.

F: *To be completely fair, though, you also did something very important for him, since your group was organized enough after the coup to prevent his disappearance, right?*

He had a gift that reached people, he was a charismatic man. There are few priests who can reach all the factions within a parish, but he could. If they were Catholic he reached them. After the coup we young people organized a group that fought for human rights, and we shielded ourselves under the name Civil Defense. We participated in many activities, and I learned to like volunteer work, with pick and shovel, going from house to house. As a group we provided people with medical treatment; we visited them and brought them food and clothes. Our group was quite unusual at that time, not only with our first Commander, Gainú, a retired military man; and then with the priest who became our religious advisor when he joined our team. Many of us started the journey but few were left by the end, as always happens. As Father Pancho always said, many are called but few are chosen.

F: *But he was imprisoned.*

He was imprisoned. He was in jail after September 11, 1973. I don't remember how many days he was in jail, I think it was eight days approximately. When he returned he found that the statue of the Virgin in his
church had been decapitated because supposedly there were weapons hidden inside its plaster frame. The floor had also been torn up, and many
other things that made it look like he'd been involved in something. But I
never thought, I never believed he was involved in anything, not to say that
it would have been a bad thing if he were. What he did was to welcome the
young people who came to the church to talk and discuss what was happening, to talk about democracy, about the responsibilities that came with
being a citizen, about the concerns young dreamers had at the time. Now, as
a man he shared many of these concerns, but that doesn't mean he was
involved in more than he should have been. He wasn't preparing guerrillas
or extremists in the church, none of that; he made that clear many times and
I believe him. Ultimately only God can judge, but what I saw was his
involvement in social work, solidarity, community growth and development. I worked with him in the Christian base communities: doing community work; helping build houses and repair roads; advancing animal
hygiene by teaching people how to detect fever, mange, lice; how to give
injections and prescribe other cures. I never saw him take positions that
didn't call people to action as Christians, in their role as laypeople, in their
own environment. He always said that lay Christians, be they husbands,
wives, children, Mapuche community leaders, peasant leaders, have an important role to play because it's up to them to produce for the family, for
the region, for society. And to do that you must improve the quality of what
you produce, not only by dehorning the cattle, shoeing the horses, and
detecting the parasites, but also pruning and replanting trees and promoting fruit and vegetable production. If that's a revolution, it's a revolution in
human growth, strength, and knowledge.

F: *Was it this kind of community work that inspired you to get involved in
the Mapuche movement during the dictatorship? A phrase that caught my
attention in our conversations was that when you were chosen as General Secretary of the Cultural Centers in the first round, you described it,
a little sarcastically, as "temporary, in the meantime." But four years later*

you were still occupying that position. A very long "meantime," don't you think?

Yes. Look, when I entered the Mapuche movement—like many young people at that time, right?—I entered innocently thinking that the Mapuche problem didn't affect me, that I was not markedly discriminated against. I entered as a Catholic woman, who wanted to fight for the rights of others, and human rights were important for me. And one of the human rights that an indigenous society should have, I thought, was the right to the land. But I thought at the time that it didn't affect me. I hadn't yet learned to give my culture its true value. I didn't know how to speak the Mapuche language, I wasn't practiced in the cultural expressions of my people. No one had demonstrated the value of my indigenous culture to me, with the possible exception of Father Pancho, who had valued my poems and other writings. It was in the Mapuche movement that I came face to face with my roots. Starting from September 12, 1978, already in October I had another vision of reality. I was no longer outside Mapuche problems, I was inside. "In the meantime" had been because I was planning to finish my studies, I was working and studying. So I said in the meantime, until December, when they were going to hold another meeting. Many Mapuche brothers who didn't know me, who met me that very day, said I should be secretary for practical reasons, because I was registering them when they arrived. I asked their names and wrote them down, I was the first face they saw. She can handle a pencil, they said, so she can be the secretary, well, in the meantime, until December.

"In the meantime" turned into four very tough years. First we were thirteen leaders, then nine according to our statutes; but at no point did we all work equally. I stood out from the pack for two reasons: first, I was a woman; and second, I wasn't associated with the political groups on the left that bothered the dictatorship. People on the left—some with clearly discriminatory intentions, others simply wishing to integrate me into their movement—started saying I was a Christian Democrat. I answered that I was Christian, a Catholic, but not a Christian Democrat. Still, this problem got worse with time and marked me as different. I was seen as a young woman who had no overt conflict with the dictatorship, whether apolitical or affiliated with a party that hadn't suffered much repression. In a sense this made me a mediator, someone searching for ways to respect everyone's rights.

During my years as secretary I visited and got to know a majority of the Mapuche communities. Like I said before, I was young with no major family commitments, no husband or children. I had parents who could help me a little economically, and although they would sometimes question what I did or demand explanations, morally they always supported my activities. So I had greater freedom to visit different communities, counties, and regions. And it became a personal process of growth, of learning about the different lifeways of our Mapuche people. I even had to learn what a Mapuche community looks like on the ground, because coming from a Christian community, I really didn't understand the Mapuche definition of community. You have to live it to define it. It's not a Christian base community, nor a community of friends like we are trying to create right now within the Party. A Mapuche community begins from the geographic place it occupies—the topography of the land, the quality of the soil, the nearness of the sea or the mountains, how close it is to the road which is its spinal cord. You have to learn to respect and appreciate these particularities which, by defining community, make up a people.

At the personal level, my first head-on collisions with my culture were in Lumaco, in two very large activities. One was in a church, in the parish auditorium, five hundred people in a place that normally seats about one hundred. The penetrating smell of people who had been walking since four in the morning; a hubbub where everybody spoke in Mapuche, a different mapunzugun than the one you hear near Temuco. Men and women dressed with colorful ribbons and shawls, I don't know; the blankets with designs so different from the ones you see in Cautín. I felt faint, nostalgic in a way. I couldn't tell if I was inside or outside. It was like visiting a different country, a different world. It was one of my great milestones in my personal re-encounter with my people.

The other event was a palin tournament, forty teams, the same people in the same place, but now the focus was on cultural expression through sports. We arrived the day before and got to see how each team celebrated a religious ceremony in their community before setting out so early the next day that they reached the site at dawn, to the sound of *kulkul*, *xuxuka*, *kulxun*, all kinds of instruments, from daybreak until noon. There were four different playing fields—and the food they served! I remember they served mote (stewed corn) with a green chili paste, and eating that hot mote with green chili sauce seemed to scratch me from my teeth all the way down. It was a very emotional experience, but I also think it helped me understand cultural difference. I'd felt strong discrimination when they'd tell me I was *awigkada* (tending toward non-Mapuche, wigka-ish), or *achiñurrada*, which was like saying, in a derogatory way, that I was a stuck-up lady, putting on airs, and thus nonindigenous. They'd say that I wrote and thought like a nonindigenous person. These things really got to me. But in those two events in Lumaco, I understood what they meant. I made a brilliant speech in Spanish, though by this point I'm sure I'd see it as too Christian and politically lukewarm, I guess. Because there were representatives from the military regime there, mayors and everything, and policemen. People clapped, they liked me. But when an indigenous leader from the area delivered a speech in mapunzugun, and when Melillán Painemal also delivered his speech in mapunzugun, people's faces, their gestures, their applause— full of energy, the kind that says yes, that's right, making hand gestures of approval—how different from the wigka-ish applause I received! They clapped for me with their hands, but for them—it was pandemonium! Ah, ya, ya, ya, ya! It was so different. All I understood, through this feeling of being neither fish nor fowl, was that they, the orators who spoke in mapunzugun, said my speech was the speech they all wanted to hear, even the wigkas who were there, but that their speeches were combative, for the Mapuche as a people, and that's why they could use their own language right in front of the pakarwas, in front of the toads. The toads were the mounted policemen and officers, in green uniforms, the agents the government sent to watch. They were also clapping, standing very close to us.

I felt like I didn't fit in, that I was their public face, but that the internal Mapuche process was quite different. I understood more clearly why sometimes people would call me things like that. I understood more clearly that to be Mapuche you had to live it and feel it, not just have Mapuche last names, wear Mapuche clothes, and say, look, I'm a Mapuche leader. It was a terrible challenge for me. On my way back to Temuco that time, I remember thinking well, I guess that's as far as it goes, everything has led to this moment. Yet I wondered at the same time if that was all there was, or if I'd have more to learn.

After that·I traveled through Arauco, the X Region, Chiloé, Panguipulli. I remember that in Chiloé they have a distinct accent, their way of speaking is different from Cautín and Malleco. Everywhere I was welcomed in the same way, openly and with affection. As a matter of fact, those leaders—or the sons of those who've died—still love me today. But my perspective changed after these journeys. I was able to visit fifteen-hundred communities, sometimes five, seven, or eleven grouped together in one place. I was also arrested once, in Malalhue, in the X Region, between Parilanco and Panguipulli, because we held a meeting in a school. The teacher let us use his classroom but he also notified the police, and they said to themselves, this woman must be a political agitator, so let's arrest her. I think back on it now, what bluster I showed, typical ignorance for a young person. In the Malalhue station I insisted on using the phone to call Valdivia, to talk to the regional Police Chief. The officers there let me use the phone, and an hour later the local captain said release her, set her free because this woman's protected by the Bishop, we don't want to get into a bigger mess. But we spent quite a few hours there.

F: *And received quite a fright, too . . .*

Quite a fright, though it wasn't so scary for me, it was more like an honor to have been arrested defending the people's rights. But the people in the community were scared off, the experience made them want to stay home, alone in their own houses. The fear was greater than the desire to stay organized, and not only in the one community but in the ones nearby, so it took a long time to get them going again.

F: *The purpose fear serves, right? Now, if we can return to your experience as an organizer in the Mapuche movement, you describe it as a double experience. On the one hand, you felt very connected, ready to carry on and take responsibility. But you also felt disconnected, not completely integrated in a cultural sense. Did this personal experience affect your vision of how an ethnic movement should be organized? I remember you told me once that we all have to learn how to respect diversity.*

In a complex tapestry like this one there are many threads to follow. If we're talking about respect for diversity we have to begin with the basics, and that means respecting people as individuals. Each person sees the world in a different way, starting from their own experience, so just because we're all indigenous doesn't mean we can or should have the same perspective. We think differently. I think social scientists and researchers make this same mistake; they all learn the same method in their labs, and when they get out into the field they're surprised to find that people are different. I think researchers, too, need to learn respect for human diversity, and that they can't always apply the same theories the same way. The first human right is that when you respect others you have to respect their entirety and their integrity. If you want to be a capable leader you have to start from there.

The second thing I've learned is not to take what others say as the absolute truth. The same people who discriminated against me because I didn't speak mapunzugun had faults I didn't have. Initially I was pretty timid and humble, and I never pointed this out. To my personal satisfaction, time has proven me right. The leaders who most discriminated against me are the ones who have fallen by the wayside. The women got married and didn't continue being leaders. Many of the men who criticized me the most have stayed frozen in their old demands, unable to change with the times. When people don't respect and value those who are different, they also disrespect themselves and can't learn enough to grow. If you respect others while still being able to debate the issues, you can build a community based on mutual growth.

F: *Up to now you've been talking about problems with diversity inside the Mapuche movement. But we've also talked before about the inability of non-Mapuche political movements—the unions, the protest coalitions of the 1980s—to respect or recognize the autonomy of the Mapuche movement as such. That's also a form of discrimination, isn't it? You went through that as well.*

Any differences you might experience personally within the Mapuche movement are even stronger or starker in the national sociopolitical movement. The unions and all other groups interested in restoring and recovering democracy tried to include indigenous people as individuals, to assimilate them into their respective groups, into their objectives, their way of fighting. Not once did they respect indigenous people's own goals or strategies. I think this is one of the great tasks that today remains undone in Chile. Even though the government has recognized the existence of the indigenous peoples of Chile by passing Law 19253, it must also recognize them in the Constitution in order to set an example, one could say, for the nation's citizenry in general. Assimilationism doesn't dignify them, nor does it dignify indigenous peoples. Assimilating us would result in the loss of all the knowledge indigenous people have about the environment, about their own traditions; what the majority society has tended to consider "folkloric." Today I think it's Chilean national identity that's completely distorted. I believe all Chileans should rethink their identity through a recognition of indigenous peoples' contributions to the national community. A large percentage of the Chilean population has indigenous blood, from north to south and east to west. People who have never mixed, pure people don't exist anymore, not among those who came from Europe, or from North America. Mixture is what happens as people join together, and whether they like it or not, the ones with the strongest and deepest roots in this hemisphere are the indigenous peoples. Yet with globalization, today more than ever we're losing our identity. And that's what's happening to the political movement in Chile, too. It doesn't have an identity, it lacks clear objectives. It was different before the fall of the Berlin Wall, before 1973, when there were more or less concrete goals and purposes. Today Chile's political parties share a general ambiguity.

F: *Do you think that this has to do with the transition? We've talked many times about how ironic it was that the dictatorship generated the conditions for a unified Mapuche movement, and later for a general movement against authoritarianism. Ironic that during repression and political closure the strongest and most intense movements took place, and that after the transition they weakened as the state became an octopus, absorbing energy from social movements instead of encouraging them. What do you think?*

I think it's made all the difference that we got rid of the dictatorship without getting rid of the dictator. Neoliberal economics and globalization have given democratization a peculiarly Chilean flavor, so that many elements of the 1980 Constitution, that document written in the very depths of the dictatorship, have remained engraved in the different institutions that govern our country. And if we think and reflect a little deeper, we find that we didn't defeat Pinochet, but instead that he defeated us. He defeated civility and civil society. I don't know if what I'm saying is too strong, but the ironic fact is that he's a designated senator against the people of Chile because he prepared the way. It wasn't our idea. So, paradoxically, Pinochet chose the style and path for our return to democracy, and he feathered his own nest as a senator-for-life. Had circumstances been different, he would have gone home. By now, no longer a general, he should've been judged by the people, which is what's happened to many generals in Latin America. But in our case we have him sitting in Congress, side by side with some of our great fighters for democracy. If this capacity for tolerance can be seen as a virtue of the Chilean people, it's also a weakness. It's what makes political parties today have no identity, no clarity, no strength of purpose. It's also the reason they all have more or less the same economic model, where capitalism rules, the state merely carries out the wishes of the big capital investors, and the indigenous peoples of Chile are once again a minority among minorities. I don't know if this addresses the concern you raised, but I think it's something not all Chileans have yet realized.

F: *So we end up with an orchestrated transition, and the dictator writes the melody.*

And democracy is overprotected.

F: *And too timid to make the necessary changes. In such a context what happens to the relationship between the state and indigenous peoples? Since the transition the government has passed the Indigenous Law, part of whose mandate is the creation of CONADI. With an orchestrated transition and a neoliberal state, do you think the Indigenous Law and the institutions created by it can really serve the indigenous peoples of Chile?*[1]

First I think it's important to say clearly that Law 19253 has represented a giant step forward with respect to the previous laws on the same subject, because it is the first law whose purpose, plainly stated, is to protect indigenous populations. I'd say the law has good points and bad points, and many things in it can be criticized and improved. Still, despite its many good aspects its principles have not prevailed in relation to other laws that are also part of the Chilean legal apparatus, laws that place capitalism above most legal regulations. As a result Law 19253 doesn't mention, in any of its articles, indigenous territorial or subsoil rights; it doesn't recognize customary rights. Nowhere in the Law is there an article that identifies indigenous women's rights. The only thing the Law says is that there has to be coordination with other entities that work with women's issues. I think they say that only so you can't say they left out women's issues entirely! Despite government pressure to increase CONADI's budget and give back more land to indigenous people, the Law is not a legal instrument that entirely responds to indigenous interests. Now, obviously it's a law made by the state, not by the indigenous people themselves, and consequently there will always be questioning. Still, I think it's somehow managed to become one of the greatest strengths, and at the same time one of the greatest weaknesses, in the relationship between the state and the indigenous peoples of Chile.

F: *Do you think the case of the Ralco hydroelectric dam is setting a new benchmark in this sense, because it seems that other laws besides the Indigenous Law will take precedence over the interests of the Pewenche communities in the region?*

Ralco is a good example of what could happen to others, in the north, in the south, anywhere. If the Indigenous Law is helping us recover indigenous lands, through other laws the state is taking away indigenous land—for highways, hydroelectric dams, mining concessions—for whatever it wants. If the state gives with one hand and takes away with the other, how can indigenous people believe that it's democratic? One of the excuses used in the Ralco case is that the Pewenche haven't protested the loss of their culture. Indigenous people don't have to include their culture on a list of demands! Indigenous people live their culture, they don't have to write it down. If Chilean policymakers understood this they couldn't say, "But the indigenous people haven't claimed their right to their cultural practices. There's no paper anywhere that says that the road or the dam in the Alto Bío Bío destroys their culture; all they demand is land." But that's the nonindigenous vision of land, that it's just a good, it's just land. For indigenous people it's much more than just land. It's life itself, it comes with the air, the wind, the water; with animals and birds; with the living and the dead of the community; with all living things.

The Ralco dam has to be seen in broader perspective. There will be a total of five dams along the Alto Bío-Bío, enormous projects. After that come the artificial lakes. They'll surely build a big hotel near each one, with thermal springs, all the other tourist attractions. In the meantime the Indians can just go survive in the mountains, where the snow is more than a meter deep in the winter. And they can spend winter, spring, and summer up there. After all, the people who go up there to ski or visit the thermal springs in the wintertime, or to swim in the lakes in the summer, aren't interested in knowing what happened to the Indians and they don't want to see them, either. I don't know. Besides all that, we have to consider how Law 19253 is being violated, not only in the Ralco case, but for the coastal highway, the Temuco by-pass, the mining projects, the paper factory, just to mention a few examples. It happens in the north, in the south, on Easter Island. In all these cases we have to say, look, the state is responsible. This executive assistant of capital is responsible for the renewed suffering of indigenous people.

F: *You'd also have to add* CONADI, *an institution that has had very dramatic ups and downs. Some people have said all along that* CONADI *has served mainly to silence, slow down, bureaucratize, and politicize, without taking the needs of indigenous people into account. How do you see it now, in 1998, when two different indigenous directors have come and gone?*

Look, I think that CONADI, as a new instrument of the state towards indigenous people, is potentially a good alternative. Unfortunately, CONADI's performance has not lived up to this potential. The people in charge of carrying out policy have done so with no particular vision. CONADI has thus become a bureaucratic instrument, like any other state institution that supposedly serves the public. Whenever there's a competition for funds, whether it's for land, a development project, or any other service, it's like any other state competition. You have to fill out many applications, fulfill complex criteria, present sometimes unpredictable documentation, and all this so they can give you a minuscule part of what you need. I think CONADI's style should've been different. But I also think that to change the style it's not enough to take one person out and put another one in.

In fact, I remember talking at an earlier point about how the departure of Mauricio Huenchulaf might bring change to CONADI. That the arrival of Domingo Namuncura might finally decide the Ralco business, once and for all, either in favor or against the Pewenche families. And things did begin to define themselves, step by step, because Domingo Namuncura listened to the Mapuche organizations. He began to understand that being Mapuche was more than having a Mapuche last name. Still, he wasn't able to negotiate successfully on Ralco. The dam is still moving forward. The negotiations with the Pewenche families have continued on an individual basis and the majority has already agreed to move.

F: *And it seems to me that, even more than in the case of Mauricio Huenchulaf, when Domingo Namuncura was fired it was exclusively because he was resisting Ralco.*

That's right. When Domingo Namuncura arrived, at first we thought he'd try to block CONADI but he didn't. Instead it's been his successor Rodrigo González, CONADI's first nonindigenous director, who despite having the government's full support has fenced CONADI in completely. He's increased the number of people on short-term contracts, and wherever possible he's replaced Mapuche or other indigenous personnel with nonindigenous people close to his own political party. Add to this the fact it's easier to enter a supermarket today than to get into CONADI. At first, when people mentioned to me that they felt pressured going into the office, that they were looked over as if they were suspects, I didn't believe them. But then I went by the office. And it's true, there are guards, they ask you who you're going to see, and it's worse with the people who come in from the countryside.

More than ever, then, it's time to question CONADI's performance and explore new strategies. Despite don Patricio Aylwin's commitment in Imperial, I haven't seen the *Concertación* participate competently in this at all, as the coalition represented by the current government. What I've seen is a scramble for power by certain people who militate in specific parties. So I accuse the *Concertación* of refusing to shape a new instrument with the kind of creativity and efficiency that the historical moment demands, which would mean effective decentralization. There's been none of that.

F: *To make decentralization work in the case of* CONADI, *I imagine you'd also have to reorganize power in general, right? Because the problem still seems to be that everything is centralized in Santiago. If you're trying to create a different kind of institution,* CONADI, *with its national office in Temuco, and you still have to send every document and every request to Santiago, in its very creation are the seeds of its inefficiency, right?*

It's one of the things I've always criticized, that at bottom everything is in Santiago, so Santiago becomes Chile and everything must be managed from there because nothing can be decided in the provinces. CONADI was to have been a new kind of modernizing institution, supposedly one of the pioneers on the path to decentralization, getting closer to people, with less bureaucracy. So far it's hard to tell the difference! Even though decentralization is among the state's present objectives and strategies for development, you still have to find a way to make it a reality and not just so much hot air. It's what has been happening everywhere! Because the old state, the old way of administering the state in Chile, which comes from the time of Portales and I don't know who else, hasn't changed. The Constitution of 1980 has some amendments but in the end it's a copy of the 1925 Constitution. So I don't see any great modernization anywhere. Maybe we've made some advances in the judicial system, but that's because in Chile we were years behind in justice. On modernizing the state in general, though, I think we're about a hundred years behind other countries. Our state still has to take a 180-degree turn to change the way it serves the public.

F: *That also brings up the political parties, whose history is intimately linked to the centralized political system. You've expressed doubts, at various points, about who really speaks for the Mapuche people. Could you explore in more detail, now that your presence in the Christian Democratic Party grows each day in the IX Region, how you see the relationship between the Mapuche people and the political parties?*

In general I think there's an estrangement between indigenous peoples and the state that's reproduced in the political parties. There are times when they get together, in order to pass a law, for specific demands. It's like the estranged couple that comes back together to deal with an inheritance, the children, or any other issue they might share. That's what happens between the state and indigenous peoples, and that's what happens between the political parties and indigenous peoples. Even though most parties have indigenous members, these haven't been able to effect the kind of internal changes all parties need. So the parties continue with their old all-absorbing structures, their domineering and preconceived notions of what politics ought to be, with no respect for cultural differences.

What indigenous people are going through is similar to what women in

Chile have experienced. Despite the great political militancy among women, we are just now opening spaces within the political parties. When men got universal male suffrage, women had a long way to go before they achieved the right to vote. Today, finally, women have entered the parties. Indigenous people also have a long way to go to win a space inside the parties where they will be heard. Despite our great militancy, I insist, within the parties, they still don't listen to us. Although in the Christian Democracy today there is a good number of Mapuches at the county, regional, and national levels, I think it's still insufficient. It's merely a first step, a first step. For the first time in the IX Region we have approximately ten indigenous leaders in party positions, including a Mapuche congressman, three or four leaders at the county level, district leaders, and delegates to the Board. That makes it possible for us to influence decisions in the region, though not yet at the national level. For that we'd need to join forces with leaders in Santiago and in the north. And I think the other parties are going through similar processes. Still, though some innovations will take place, they're still following the same pattern, in the sense that there's one, maybe two, indigenous leaders forming part of a larger team. So they're not the full package, they're only one within a package.

F: *So you're fighting up the chain, link by link.*

Exactly.

F: *Speaking of fighting link by link, could we talk a bit more about Mapuche women? The image you gave me in our conversations was that Mapuche women are not flower arrangements meant to decorate the tables of either the ethnic movement or the feminist movement. Could you reflect a bit more on the present and future of the Mapuche women's movement?*

For me it's not a question of Mapuche pride, but of women's self-esteem. I've always thought women are not simply there for decoration. As women we think and act, and generally we work harder than men. Society in general must recognize our accomplishments. We can't go on thinking that women are inferior to men. I think the Mapuche woman has demonstrated clarity and strength through the hardest times—childbirth, war, land usurpation, accidents, even death. She is the fundamental pillar of knowledge within the family, educating young people from generation to generation, passing down our culture's wisdom about nature in general, but especially about the healing powers of herbs and plants. Given their essential participation, Mapuche women should not occupy an inferior position. They've demonstrated their solidarity, as well as their physical and intellectual capacity. We must recognize the value of all women, but especially indigenous women, who keep alive their traditions, identity, and culture. Mapuche women who are leaders can't be there just for decoration, because even if they wear their culture, they also carry it inside them. They have a special intellectual and spiritual connection with their environment.

When I emphasize these qualities it's precisely to remind the male indigenous leaders that we women are capable of taking care of more than just the practical details, which is what they think. The men always leave women in charge of the practical details, while they make the decisions and the public appearances. So I think it's time to expose this myth that men are superior to women, and show it for what it is: just a myth! The majority of men selfishly think of themselves as super machos and exceptionally capable, whether economically, physically, or intellectually, when in fact they're none of that. They hide their emotional, physical, and intellectual weaknesses behind a veneer of male superiority that, according to them, is based in Mapuche culture. But it's not Mapuche culture, it's their so-called Mapuche culture. They dress themselves up behind this screen, and think they're capable of having ten women in one night, which of course isn't true. Economically, physically, and intellectually, they're hardly able to handle one. When I see how efficient women are—working, raising children, supporting their husbands, keeping a house—I realize how skillfully and ingeniously women struggle to get ahead. When Mapuche women become widows they don't remarry, with a few exceptions; they continue struggling alone. But when men are widowed, not three months go by before they're married again, because they need a woman to take care of them, to serve them. And more or less the same thing happens in the rest of Chilean society. But I've been watching Mapuche men for a long time, and this is how I see it. The great Mapuche leaders of the region have a great many faults when it comes to women and to their own abilities. That's why I compare what they say to what they do, and I question how they justify their behavior by referring to what they call Mapuche culture, which isn't so.

F: *Up to now we've talked about Mapuche women being underestimated and unrecognized in the Mapuche movement. Do you think that the general women's movement in Chile has valued Mapuche women, or do you think there's a long way to go there, too?*

There's a long way to go. Personally, I think I'm one of the few Mapuche women whose work has been recognized within the Chilean women's movement, whether we're talking inside or outside the government. In our work around Beijing at the national level, the *Iniciativa Chile* used the regions as focal points. I've been one of the few women who has traveled throughout the south speaking about indigenous women's rights and the action platform we brought back from Beijing. These are important milestones for a Mapuche woman. But a drop of water in the desert can hardly quench the thirst of an entire country, or even of an entire region. Like they say, a single swallow doesn't make it springtime. In this sense we still need many more women ready to raise their own consciousness. We have a lot of work still to do with the women. As Mapuche we still tend to struggle mainly around our issues as a culture, as a people; but we hesitate to target women specifically. We still need to form a strong women's coalition to fight for indigenous women's rights, in the Mapuche movement and in the feminist movement.

F: *Perhaps this leads us to reflect at a more general level about your trajectory as a leader. What have been your successes, your most important victories? What the wounds, defeats, or sorrows that you have suffered in the political process?*

What a huge question! Let's see. I think what has marked me most profoundly was the time between September 12, 1978, and January 1983. The unity, the strength, the loyalty; the ease with which we Mapuche got together, our common spinal cord in our land, our culture, and our hope for a better future. That moved me deeply. The other thing that marked me deeply was the division of the Mapuche movement in January 1983. Until that point we were united as Mapuches, but then it became more of a class struggle, a popular struggle, a struggle for power. The words peñi, lamñen were substituted by compañero. Even though compañero calls forth a sense of unity, of sharing the same destiny, in this case it meant the advent of ideologies in the indigenous movement, and we divided into Socialists, Communists, factions of all sorts. People were disillusioned, the organization broke up, and a multiplicity of small organizations sprang up in which each leader wanted to have his own movement.

This was a painful and important watershed for me. I think it has been one of the most agonizing moments I've ever been through. The frustration, the dejection of an ingenuous Christian woman, apolitical in the sense of having no party affiliation, but political in the sense of being committed to service. I just wanted to stay home, and I used as pretext the fact I'd gotten married in March of that year. But it was my toughest moment, because I'd always said we Mapuche would stay together no matter what. This movement must be Mapuche, I'd say, above political party differences, above religious differences. It's a movement for everybody. If you're in different parties or churches, discuss those issues elsewhere because here we talk about indigenous issues, Mapuche issues. But there came a time when people told me, OK, it's a good idea, but it didn't work out.

F: *Did this lead you to reconsider the role of Mapuche culture as an inspiration for mobilization? Maybe some would see your experience and that of your community as atypical, but in a sense it's almost emblematic. Sometimes the struggle isn't about maintaining a culture, but instead redeeming or reconstructing it, step by step, tenaciously, even after significant losses in memory or practice. I don't know how you see this. Do you think that moment of unity and vitality, based on a revindicated, reconstructed culture, can be reached again?*

I think many factors need to converge for us to have a united movement once again, but recently, in the conflicts over land and territory in Purén, Traiguén, and other places, we've seen a new generation of leaders. And they've been joined by people of all ages, couples with children, grandparents, entire communities. It's also true that those of us who were leaders between 1978 and 1983—most of us married now if we used to be single, or grandparents if we used to be married—have continued participating through different organizations. And at some point or another we met up with the younger ones and shared some of our experiences, whether in congresses, workshops, or retreats. We're seeing the fruits of those conversations now, there's a continuity. And those who at some point might have thought that the Mapuches who didn't speak the Mapuche language couldn't still be Mapuche have been forced to rethink their position and to realize that all Mapuches are necessary for the struggle and that no one should be marginalized as long as they want to participate in this struggle to develop as a people. More than ever before, people talk today about the creation and recreation of cultural events, of forms of cultural expression. These new leaders are interested in shaking things up, and that's good for Mapuche society and for Chile in general. It does us all good when questions of identity are discussed at a profound level, and that's why I'm convinced that our future struggles will not be over an additional sack of wheat or fertilizer, or about one more bridge here or there. They'll be hard, deep struggles over Mapuche identity, and over what unites indigenous people more generally in their quest for recognition. I believe that indigenous peoples, not only in Chile but in the world, can unite above all differences when something affects all of us.

And yet, if we're going to maintain cultural unity in the long run, we'll need the support of all the social movements in which indigenous people participate. If we succeed, for example, in instituting multicultural and multiethnic education at the national level, even if this means keeping the present educational objectives but respecting indigenous cultures, this could become a backbone that unites us around some common points. To teach about Mapuche culture to indigenous and nonindigenous students, so that those who don't know it can learn part of what the Mapuche culture is in school, would be very positive. What used to be forbidden in the schools can be regained and extended. This kind of educational reform is something we can demand on one hand, and on the other, we can help make it work.

F: *If I'm interpreting you correctly, you're suggesting that one of the great pressures toward assimilation faced by the Mapuche people is that communities and families may not have the capacity to continue building and reproducing Mapuche culture by themselves, without the support of the state through the education system.*

To some extent, I think indigenous people in this country need a catalyst to inspire them to recover their culture. Even if the schools will likely offer their own version of indigenous culture, still a lot of elements will reach people. In that sense it could help spark a process of growth and of recovering what's been lost. That's why I think the state can help through education. At the same time, this is a great challenge that indigenous people themselves must face, independently I insist, and it's a common goal that is shared regardless of political or other loyalties. Because if you speak with people individually, they all talk about land and culture. Autonomy is also a recurring demand, although through different strategies. So even though our organizational divisions have been a source of great disenchantment for me, perhaps my re-enchantment as a leader must begin by believing in the diversity of people's strategies. If you say you believe in diversity, you have to start from respecting the different lines of action that people pursue, and you have to believe and hope that we can unite some day.

F: *When we talk about education and diversity, I'm reminded of the image of the cacique Paillalef, and his call for land and education that's so often discussed in your family. In my conversations with your brother Lionel, he interpreted the Paillalef strategy as a form of selective integration, of accepting Chilean culture while remaining loyal to and proud of Mapuche culture. I don't know how you see this, because it seems to me that your efforts have gone in a different direction.*

Look, for the most part I don't disagree with the Paillalefs. It's part of our history. The Paillalef family migrated south from the VIII Region, as we'd say today, from the Cañete River toward the Cautín River. You can find Paillalefs in different counties throughout the IX Region. They've tended toward integration, which is sometimes confused with assimilation. On the one hand, all Mapuche will recognize that the cacique Paillalef was the man who brought down a hanging wooden bridge in Pitrufquén, a bridge made with natural rope fibers and vines, to finish off the Spanish invaders. On the other hand, he rapidly reached an agreement with the Chilean army during the Wars of Independence instead of joining his brothers who were, let's say, pulling for the other side. There are different visions as to what the Paillalef legacy means, and they're all worthy of respect. I'll stick to the one my great-grandfather, the man who raised my mother, told his family. When faced with the kind of discrimination we Mapuche have faced, there are two important things you must leave to your children. One is the land, no matter how little you have left, because that's where you develop your culture, rituals, religion, and language, and that's where a family remains a family. The other is education, because it allows you participation, development, and integration, and in so doing it gives you much more than a hectare of land can give you. That's all I want to say on this point. I don't want to say that Lionel is wrong. I think I have a different vision of the Paillalef family. But you also have to recognize that the Paillalefs, this aristocratic Mapuche lineage that has taught us so much, has also been among the first to encourage respect for Chilean law and the Chilean courts rather than fighting for the recognition of Mapuche customary law.

F: *Perhaps this Paillalef strategy of integration, combined with the especially early land privatization that occurred in the communities of your sector of Pitrufquén, led to a higher degree of abandonment of Mapuche traditions? Do you think that the desire and the efforts to reclaim these traditions that took place in your community by the end of the '70s, which you describe earlier in this book, are in a sense a kind of nostalgia for what has been lost or pushed to the side? There seems to be an element of this when you mention your desire to have a wedding in the community.*

My experience as a leader who's often been discriminated against by the Mapuche themselves, because I didn't know the culture of my own people, has generated in me both determination and nostalgia for the reconstitution of Mapuche communities in all dimensions, with all their values. Personally I would have loved to get married in traditional Mapuche style, because it doesn't only unite two people, but two communities. In the ceremony, when the couple give themselves to each other, the communities also recount their histories, remembering the values they share as a people and recognizing the specific qualities that distinguish each family and community in their relationship with their natural environment. In a sense I do feel nostalgia for this kind of collective identity when I marshall all my physical, economic, and political energies into celebrating a gillatun in my community, so that the children can sing and make their own instruments, so that they can reclaim part of our lost cultural expression. Perhaps we begin by combining Christianity with Mapuche religion, but from there we gain strength as a group and can say, this part is ours.

F: *Perhaps you found inspiration for this in your connection with your husband Juan's family, since his parents are intellectual leaders in their community.*

More than inspiration, I think I found an answer to my restlessness and the desire I had to learn, to be able to discuss these issues face to face. In that small space called the Sánchez-Curihuentro family I found shared concerns, and this made it possible to talk with my parents-in-law, my brothers-in-law, my husband's other relatives. And I found a gillatun, a religious ceremony in which more than five hundred families participate. Simply seeing that many families together for a ceremony such as this shakes you up, makes you think.

F: *If I remember correctly, in Chanco there are thirty families. The difference between thirty in Chanco, and five hundred in Huilío, is quite large.*

Yes, but to get thirty families to participate from my community is pretty daring in and of itself. It's not that I don't appreciate the numerical difference, it's just that I also appreciate the effort that goes into getting people to participate. And I think both ceremonies share some characteristics, such as trying to emphasize the coming together of individual people with God, with nature, and with the products that nature gives us. We also try to limit outside intervention, whether by people or products, because in both gillatun wine is forbidden. Even the biggest drunk doesn't drink wine those days, which is different from other places where sadly there's more wine than ceremony. So I think these two gillatun have these similarities, even as they also have many differences. Because in Huilío children start participating at a very young age. They have an organization that automatically teaches them; they learn in stages and take on additional duties when they're ready. But in my community of Chanco you have to go after people and say please. You have to really motivate them and help them feel confident enough to participate.

F: *In a sense, your experience in Huilío has given you energy.*

It gives me lots of energy and it helps me find answers to the doubts and questions that come up along the way. The fact I've visited other places and seen other religious ceremonies, even if they all have the same objective, also gives me a unique perspective. And you end up thinking, well, wouldn't it be great if all my people did this. Besides, I'd like it to be more than just the eight days we usually spend, if you take into account the preparations, the two days of full ceremony and massive gathering, and the activities you do afterwards. I'd like the atmosphere to be like that permanently, full of solidarity, friendship, personal reflection. People of all walks of life can mingle together, romances take shape, and you can find the man you've been looking for! But I also see how women's work—their household duties, their daily toil—is multiplied during the ceremony. The burden on women is constant, and one of my concerns is to promote the value and the roles of women beyond their personal, family, and community obligations.

F: *So your reencounter with Mapuche culture has passed through Chanco and Huilío, through your own family and community, and those of your husband. It's also been, I think, an important component in your marriage. Today, with Juan working far away in Chiloé, how do you see this part of your life?*

My emotional life hasn't been easy, because I'm a romantic woman who's fond of sharing and expressing my affection in a family setting. From this point of view my life has been more or less harsh, because I got pregnant very young. Playing around with a schoolmate, a game between uninformed children that suddenly became reality, resulted in my having to change schools and being marked so indelibly that even today, when my daughter is turning twenty-five, one of my uncles still refuses to say hello to me. If even my own flesh and blood, my brothers with whom I share both parents, occasionally throw it up in my face to this day, you can imagine how the larger society has treated me and my family. Under these circumstances, with this terrible mark against me, finding Juan was like a cry for freedom. I'd found my kindred soul and the man I loved was ready to face life's problems with me.

I met Juan in the movement, and we've made a wonderful couple in that we share ideals and political vision. Yet in our emotional life as a couple we've faced many challenges, especially in the discrimination we've suffered from the larger society because I'm older than he is, because I was a single mother, because I've been a leader who moves around a lot from community to community, across the region and across the country, and even internationally. Oftentimes these things make a man feel bad, especially when historically Mapuche men have had such a tendency to express their manhood in an intensely *macho* way. I know it hasn't been easy for him to support me as constantly as he has, at public and private events, meetings, and political discussions.

To marry a woman leader isn't easy, it hasn't been easy for us to live as a couple. As I've said before, we're like black sheep, we did something that was outside the accepted practice in national society and in the political arena where we moved, as well as outside what's customary in Mapuche communities. So he's the man I'm in love with, who's been able to accept me as I am and help me through the hard times. He's been there for me when political enemies, both Mapuche and non-Mapuche, have managed to get me by the throat, to crush me or to question my right to hold a political position of leadership. In the seventeen years we've been together he's been loyal and supportive in all political discussions, when the hard issues are on the table, when debate heats up.

I'll never forget how Juan stood firm when, in Mapuche meetings, people would say to me, "So, you got married." And when I said yes, they'd immediately ask, "And to whom?" "To him," I'd say. And they'd answer, "To *him*? But he's just a kid, he has no future. I was sure you'd marry an anthropologist, a sociologist, a politician, a schoolteacher at the very least." And people tell you this in your own organization, among the people with whom you've worked the closest. They looked at him pejoratively, as if he were inferior, and they were capable of saying directly, "well, I don't know whether to congratulate you, Isolde, or feel sorry for Juan." That was really hard for us as a couple.

I think a lot of people were waiting for me to marry someone who would stop me in my tracks, who'd say Isolde, this is as far as you go. But Juan doesn't boss me around and I don't boss him around. Instead we've both kept a sharp and critical presence as leaders, which has led to a lot of public criticism about our private lives. On that point I have to say that the standard of Christian fidelity, which supposedly many Chileans adhere to, doesn't exist in reality. Among the Mapuche it's much more common and understood for a man to have several women, and to be publicly loyal to these two or three women rather than to pretend fidelity to one while sleeping with many others. Now Juan has been more emotionally loyal to me than he's been physically monogamous, but he's filled a void in my life when it comes to Mapuche culture and politics. We've shared a search for our roots, for the role of nature in our lives. We've worked together in

Mapuche organizations and we've collaborated on research projects about the Mapuche language, traditions, and ritual. I've learned many things with him that I couldn't have learned with someone else.

Even though we're not living together right now, Juan and I still have a lot to share, we have a lot of challenges before us. I'm a woman with a very big heart who knows how to forgive, as Christians say, seven times, though that might not be enough in this case! But I believe love continues through the hard times, through the disagreements. I believe in loyalty and monogamy, a combination Juan doesn't share because he grew up in a community more steeped in traditional Mapuche values whereas I had a Christian education. And even if, over the years, I've criticized Mapuche leaders for not respecting women and for emphasizing short-term relationships, I think permanent relationships have to be based in part on knowing how to forgive. This doesn't mean that I accept being used, no. But I do know how to forgive.

F: *Is there anything you still wish to add before we're done?*

Well, to finish up, I'd like to say that, for a long time, I've wanted to write from my own point of view about all that's been happening, because I think each person writes according to their own origins, feelings, strategies, and ideological perspective on Mapuche reality. There are many points of entry into the indigenous question, as some like to call it. I've learned a lot since 1978 and many of those things have remained unsaid. But sitting down to remember all the things that have happened to me, especially in the years since the transition, has made me see more maturely, or perhaps more clearly, what can be achieved through an organization. I've also been impressed by the unity of indigenous reality, and how false it is when we separate indigenous issues into culture, health, religiosity, or whatever. As a people we are a whole; and we have to keep this whole in mind when we search for ways to meet the multiple needs we have today.

These multiple needs, this economic poverty we're living in, point to the urgency of a new negotiation with the state. Even though then-presidential candidate Patricio Aylwin signed an agreement with indigenous peoples at Imperial, and some of whose points were transformed into CEPI and then CONADI through Law 19253, it's not enough. The Chilean state must still pay back its historic debt to indigenous peoples, and how to do this still isn't clear. More than a question of land, of adding to the fifty-thousand hectares that have been returned, it's about the air, the subsoil, everything. Everything must be given back to indigenous people! For this to happen the state and the indigenous organizations must sit down at the table, face to face, with all their cards in full view. No more generalities, because at a general level everything is promised and nothing gets accomplished. It's preferable to define goals and set time limits—three years, five years—with clear responsibilities. So when something doesn't get done you can't just pass the blame back and forth.

If this is going to work, those who represent the Mapuche people need to respect all the political sensibilities our people have. The Mapuche people don't have only one sensibility, they have many. Traditionally our forms of organization have obeyed as many logics as have been coherent with our culture. Until today, the representatives who've mediated Mapuche issues, who've dealt with the indigenous problem in Chile, haven't always been the best. We've accepted them nevertheless, because we Mapuche are always respectful of formalities. Yet we've always questioned who appointed them, and why those individuals have represented only this or that political sensibility. Why does the state recognize those who make the most noise, those who occupy the most public space, instead of those who are recognized in the communities? Why not take the time to look for representatives with far more legitimacy and responsibility towards the community, and who don't just dress up for the cameras. Because those who do parade for the media end up, one way or another, supporting solutions that might be the hardest or the easiest, but never the ones the majority wants.

What's been happening for the past fifty years is that the ones who fight the hardest and yell the loudest; the ones who, being a small group, always show up; they get listened to instead of taking into account people's more general needs. In part that's because the majority of indigenous people are not in the political parties, and therefore parties sometimes question indigenous participation. But parties should examine their own internal situations. Who have been the most loyal? The indigenous members. And who have left the parties, because of disenchantment, because they were not welcome? Also the indigenous members. I would say that from left to right and from right to left, the majority of indigenous people are outside the parties, because we aren't willing to give ourselves, body and soul, to any one of them. And where in the political spectrum are the Mapuche people?

I would say either closer to the left or closer to the right, near the extremes. I'm not too sure why that is so, but I think if parties don't recognize indigenous values and culture, which are present and alive today, there won't be serious, responsible, and respectful participation by indigenous people in the parties.

That's why I think we should have constitutional recognition, which would facilitate the recognition of our territory. We should also have a great indigenous Congress that represents the regions, a Congress respected and recognized by the Chilean state. We would vote for our own elected representatives, and they would be our own parliament. Some people get scared when one refers to the territory south of the Bío Bío River, or talks about an indigenous Congress. They say it's like having autonomy, a separate country, but it isn't. It's having our own representation, making representation much wider and rewarding the work, the effort, and the sacrifice of our people. And it doesn't mean kicking out the non-Mapuche who live here.

In these alternatives there could be true participation, and with that comes development, but development with growth rather than alienation and usurpation. Maybe it's a utopia, an illusion, to think that we could someday have true development, an autonomous movement, and an economy with real participation that's sustainable over time. Yes, it's a utopia, but it's a possible utopia if there's political willingness on the part of the Chilean state. It depends a lot on that.

But true development also depends on the full participation of women. Women are around fifty percent of the population. We're half the people, in some cases more than that. Mapuche people have a cyclical perspective on the world, we believe that all stages come full circle, all cycles are completed. Looked at this way, women are only half a cycle, a half-moon, because the other half is the man. So we can't close the circle or complete the cycle if women don't participate. It remains truncated. And so does the cycle of Mother Earth, who is a woman and the mother of all human beings, of all indigenous people, and obviously of the whole planet.

I've already gone through one cycle of work with the organizations. I was a founding member of the Mapuche Cultural Centers of Chile, I spent five years as General Secretary of Ad-Mapu. Then I participated in creating Nehuen-Mapu, even though it followed the Christian Democratic line, because I saw that those who had left the movement, as well as others who wanted to participate, should have a place from which to help negotiate the transition. I was there for a while. But I left, just like I left Ad-Mapu, to look for another road. I created the women's organization. I think I'll be in that organization one or two more years, maybe not leading it but always working. In the last few years I've also participated in the structure of the Christian Democratic Party because I want to make the indigenous issue a national issue. The Christian Democracy is an attractive forum because it's part of the governing coalition. And if it's in the places of power and decision making, it must be capable of recognizing the existence of indigenous peoples, their demands, their revindication, their distinct vision as a people.

Speaking personally, but as a sociopolitical leader, I would also like to occupy a public office from which I could demonstrate my personal capacity, and through which other indigenous leaders could also believe in themselves, that they, too, are capable of occupying positions that have previously been closed to indigenous people. I want to challenge my people and show what we are capable of. I always say our challenge is a permanent one: for women, for leaders, for people who want to produce change. And the final piece in this permanent challenge is religiosity. I'd like to help create a group of people who believe in Mapuche religiosity as a spiritual inspiration, an inspiration for life and personal development in today's world. Because it's lacking. These are materialistic times, but they should also be spiritual times. I think the Mapuche people could be leaders in this regard, and I consider it a personal challenge to help bring that about.

So there are many things left to learn, and I have many goals left in front of me. Yet when I look back, I can also see all the things I've lived through and already done. First, going into the Christian communities, then getting into what was the Commission of Human Rights, the Political Committee for the Disappeared, the Mapuche organized movement, the women's struggle. These are steps you take in life, and in the end they all come back to the same place: a love for family, participation in your broader community, and respecting the rights of others. So I hope that when you come back to visit, next year and the years after that, you'll find me still reaching for new things and seeking out new experiences. But you'll always find me in this same place that's my home, because I have all my good and bad memories right here. So I'm staying here, where I can say with pride, if not without some sadness, that in the forty-plus years of my life I've planted a tree, given birth to a daughter, and been married to the same man for seventeen years. And now I'm writing a book that will soon see the light of day and be read by many people.

❀ AFTERWORD

F: *In my introduction I explain what was going through my head the first time we talked. Now it's your turn: at first, what did you think of our collaboration?*

When we first got together, I wasn't sure exactly what we'd be doing. But I had a premonition, one of those feelings you get, that we were going to get along well. The first time, when we met at the Café Raíces, I don't know, I felt a kind of empathy. Even though I'm pretty critical of researchers, especially political scientists, who've worked with indigenous peoples, I felt a "click" with you, I don't know how else to describe it, and that was interesting to me. You seemed different, at least in that first conversation. Even though you tried to come off as really informed and secure on the topic we were discussing, I glimpsed the fact that you didn't know everything and that you really wanted to learn. That interested me.

Second, from the beginning it was really clear that we'd be working together. You didn't begin by demanding that we do it your way, which is what I've generally seen with other Chilean and foreign researchers. They come in with their hypothesis, it's preconceived, and all they want to do is prove it. This was something different I saw in you that first time. Still, I consulted with others about you. I remember telling you at one point that I'd talked with José Aylwin. I also talked with Fresia Manquilef, with my husband, with my sisters, and I told them, look, there's something about this lady, I'm not sure what, but she seems different. And I began to have confidence in you, not in the sense of proving my hypothesis that you were a different kind of researcher, but more because I felt an affinity with you.

To that must be added the fact that I'd been thinking about writing for a long time. In fact I had a lot of things written down, a piece here and there, one or two more polished things, a lot of ideas in my head. I'd already written a series of shorter essays that had been published in journals or edited books, twelve to fifteen pages each, on practical topics like culture, women and the land, the Quincentenary, Mapuche organizations, the role of women. But even though I wrote these pieces, I didn't feel they ended up being mine, because they'd end up in a bigger publication with a lot of other articles, some of which were similar and some that disagreed entirely with me. So I wanted to write something better, and I thought that working on a personal testimony, something not often found in Chile, would be easier, because it involved a collaboration with someone else. So that's how I see that first process. It allowed me to say to you, look, we have a common goal here, to be able to write, and I'll be able to realize my dream of writing something different.

F: *Did you wonder at any point, well, what's her motive in all of this?*

Well, yes. What interest did you have, what was your goal, why did you keep coming back. And in the meantime I got to know your Chilean half, and your North American half, and you told me that your husband wasn't fully North American, either. We began to find common themes, like the disappeared, and what had happened before and after the 1973 coup. These were issues that still concerned me, that made me think, when already many people in Chile were saying that we'd discussed them enough during the dictatorship and now it was time to move on. In the meantime others said no, that these issues couldn't be forgotten, that in fact they had to be addressed even more forcefully, that demands had to be presented, including compensation for the victims. As a Mapuche woman, I felt my position was different from both these groups. Through our conversations on these topics I felt able to analyze the period and its history, as well as the personalities involved, in ways that hadn't been possible for a long time—among Mapuches or between Mapuches and non-Mapuches—at both the regional and national levels.

F: *I was really surprised the day you told me that you'd never taken researchers, as researchers, to your community. We were on the bus coming back to Temuco, one day we'd gone to visit your family. I was surprised because, by that point, you'd talked to me about a number of other people you'd worked with, researchers who'd then returned to Germany and other countries, and how you'd taken many of them to meet your family.*

I think one always wants to keep something back, to keep something private. Besides, my community was a very difficult case for researchers who, like I said before, usually arrived with a preconceived notion of what they were looking for or wanted to find. My community, as I've told you, is not typical, because the land was already privatized by 1940. Distinct families, with diverse last names, had been trying to rebuild a collective unit, first as a Christian base community and then as a reconstituted indigenous community with several family trees. In this sense it wasn't the kind of place anthropologists wanted to study. What they wanted was easier to find in Cholchol: the Mapuche language; traditional dress; people sitting around an ancestral hearth (fogón) on pieces of leather; a form of religion which, if it was Christian, wasn't the church-going kind; ritual knowledge that included everything connected to palin and a gillatun every year. You could find all of that in some places, but not in my community. So the people I worked with were obviously looking for these things, or else they were interested in finding a community that had longstanding conflicts with a great estate, and where a number of Mapuches were fighting to defend their land. My community didn't have that, either.

The other possibility would have been someone who was interested in studying the situation of the Mapuche who lived near the cities, but usually these studies are centered closer to Temuco. Even though Pitrufquén is only twenty to twenty-five miles from Temuco, that's not close enough for students who are trying to do research. And Chanco's not a community with lots of hills, or some other unusual characteristic; it's flat, with good vegetation and good-quality soil. It's true we don't have a lot of land, but what we have is good. And without a river we still have subterranean water that allows us to irrigate and to have good wells. So that's why I hadn't taken researchers to Chanco. Now gringo friends, I'd taken several, the kind who visit and take pictures. But I didn't do a specific study with them, of the community or in my community.

Now, already in 1978 and 1979 John Hilbord came by my community, with the idea of visiting me and my family and getting an idea of who was behind this leader. John Hilbord was a Methodist minister interested in human rights, a member of the World Council of Churches and I don't know what else. He'd served as England's ambassador to Chile. He and his wife were very nice, and they both spent a whole day in my house in Chanco. Her name was Pamela, and it turned out that we had a young calf by the same name. And Pamela fell into the irrigation ditch . . .

F: *Which one?*

The calf. Well, Pamela's husband also made a lot of jokes about her name being the same, no? But a lot of other young people went by my house, without ever looking to begin a research project, whether anthropological, historical, scientific, or whatever. So to finish with this topic I think it's pretty clear why it worked out with you and not with other researchers, even though I had previously invited one other person, José Aylwin, to work with me on a project in my community. My friendship with José began around issues of human rights, and we set ourselves the challenge of doing a study of my community, precisely because it was atypical. But we were never able to carry it out because he never found the funding to do it, and since all researchers need funds to carry out their work, it never got beyond the planning stage. I still consider it an interesting challenge, and maybe when José comes back from Canada we can take it up again.

F: *I think it would be a good idea, because as you know one of the things that attracted me to your community was precisely the fact that it was atypical. I thought it was very important to record the experiences people had with the reconstitution of community forms. Because that's what you did, really, you rebuilt a community, and it's one of the things that caught my attention during our first interview. Rather than bother me, or make me think it wasn't a good case to study, it attracted me and interested me even more.*

Do you remember if there was a moment during our work together when you said to yourself, OK, now I can tell that things are going to work out? Or, yes, now I can see we're getting to know each other and I'm confident this is going to work out?

I think so. It was a moment when we were in my house, drinking mate and gossiping (*pelando*).[1] The conversation seemed very frank and serious and it flowed freely, and I felt my hunch (*tincada*) had been a good one, that it had been on target. That was one of the moments in which I felt that this was exactly what I wanted to do. Because at the beginning you always wonder, will it turn out, will it be the way I want it to be. Will she do what she said, or in the end will she make it only what she wants, that's what you always ask yourself, there are so many questions. And also that time we were here and after a while Juan arrived and got into the conversation, ah? Although he was acting slippery, he didn't want to get involved in it and talk too much. That time, too, I thought to myself, this is what I want. I don't know if you, too, felt that sense of easy flow.

F: *I remember two moments here in your house when I did feel that, for different reasons. One was the conversation with you when Juan got involved, and if I remember correctly we were talking about the Mapuche movement and the changes that occurred during the 1980s. And the other moment was when we were talking with Elvira about the different people in your family, and about Mapuche courtship. Remember?*

That can't appear in the book! (Laughter.)

RAMÓN: *Yes, it can. All of that has to appear in the book.*

Yes, it will.

RAMÓN: *Is it true, Mom, that all of this will come out in the book?*
F: *Yes, but Isolde is the one who decides. We can twist her arm, but in the end she decides.*
RAMÓN: *That's right.*

But he's the referee (laughter). You're the referee here, you need to make sure it all comes out all right.

F: *But those two conversations, for different reasons, gave me confidence. I don't know if you agree, but the one about the Mapuche movement was the first.*

Yes. I was especially impressed by the reflections Juan and I shared, something we hadn't been able to do for quite a while. We talked at a very general level about the movement: what we had been trying to do, what we had been hoping to find. In general we tend to reflect on more immediate things, rather than connecting our present moment to the past, all the way to the beginning, the way we did that day. It's harder to get outside our present-day box and think back to what happened before, what worked and what didn't work, ah? I really needed to get some historical perspective, so that I could get a better feel for where we're standing now.

F: *Yes. You know, the part that I remember about that conversation, that impressed me and made me feel optimistic, was that I came prepared with two or three different versions of what had happened in the Mapuche movement, and each time I offered one up, you'd just sit there looking at it.*

Did we pull it apart, or what?

F: *Yes. You'd look over the explanation I was offering, Juan also would look at it, and then you'd say, well, this part works, but not that part. We'll keep this thread, but the rest goes in the trash. Then I'd take out another explanation and you'd both look it over and say OK, we'll add these two pieces to the little thread that we took out before, but the rest is useless. And I really liked that. Precisely for the reason you mentioned earlier, when you said you thought I didn't have my hypotheses all made up ahead of time. I loved the fact that we were coming up with something new, analyzing deeply instead of just accepting a prepackaged explanation. I liked that a lot.*

RAMÓN: *Such a great historian you are, Mom. You like it when people tell you your explanations are useless.*

F: *But I think Isolde liked me because I'm strange (laughter).*

An atypical historian.

RAMÓN: *Atypical, and that's why she was attracted to an atypical community (laughter).*

And that's also why she has such an atypical son (laughter).

F: *Well. In the midst of all these atypical things, it seems we more or less got the project to work out. Isolde, if you could talk to the reader who's going to pick up this book and say, "Look, if you get nothing else out of this book, what I want you to know is this"—what would it be? What are the things the reader really has to understand in order to appreciate your story?*

Let's see. I think there are several points. On the one hand there's the testimony of an indigenous woman who has ventured beyond the boundaries of her community. On the other hand there's the Mapuche leader who has had to prove she's as good as the men in terms of potential, action, content, and response to crisis. But perhaps most important is the story of persistence in pursuit of your goal, in this case making sure that the Mapuche people maintain their own culture. And in relation to this last point I think it's important to emphasize the right of all peoples to autonomy. This is what I'd like readers to see in my book, but if I want to boil it down even further, I'd say that I hope they see how difficult it is to be a social and political leader in the kind of world we're living in at the turn of the century.

F: *With this last comment you also cross other boundaries, because even if the Mapuche people and their leaders face difficulties with political organization in today's world, so do the rest of us.*

I think that's right. I think all leaders who go public and step outside their house and their family face the scrutiny of the larger society, the positive and negative comments about what they did and didn't do. You lose your privacy and that of your family, and what you say is no longer simply your opinion but represents others. Other people start seeing you as a role model. Maybe this is something we didn't touch on at length in the book, but in many of the fifteen-hundred communities I visited when I was Secretary General of the Centros Culturales and of Ad-Mapu, today there are little girls between the ages of seven and twelve whose name is Isolde. These are things that maybe you don't entirely appreciate at the time. Or maybe at that moment there are a lot of men who are saying, look, why don't you come to my community, I'll organize a meeting for you; and as a woman you always wonder and you hide behind your armor, because you're speculating if a man is inviting you as a leader or as a woman. I'm sure that in some cases there was a double motive, and that some men organized a meeting in their communities with the idea that they could be near me and make a different kind of proposition. In some cases they made a subtle attempt at it; in other cases they didn't dare try. But the end result was that their daughters today carry my name, and some couples have actually told me, look, my child carries that name in your honor. These are things that affect you, that increase your self-esteem. The movement was a watershed in the history of many communities, and even if it may seem lost, it's not.

Those are the moments when you see yourself as a role model for others, and you realize how difficult it is to be a role model. Now I don't mean a model in the physical sense, but in the sense of taking action, being a leader, behaving in a certain way that conforms to Mapuche standards of morality. So I don't have the right to make a mistake, which becomes an enormous responsibility. Sometimes, when in a community I see the results of my actions, I get a little scared because I wonder if I really know what I'm doing. Sometimes I have a hard time expressing an opinion, precisely because I know a lot of people are waiting to see what I'm going to say. And this is hard, also because both Mapuches and non-Mapuches tell me they're waiting to hear what I have to say.

When you say that all social and political leaders, not only indigenous but nonindigenous as well, face these challenges, I say you're right, even if our perspectives, characteristics, and objectives might be different. All the leaders in the world, all the way from the smallest group at the community level to the very top, lose the personal dimension of their lives. They're distanced from their families. They get closer to their people, but at the same time they're distanced from their people, because everyone is waiting to see what the leader's reaction is going to be. They're waiting for the leader's opinion in order to say, look, this is the road we need to take. I've heard people say, well, Isolde needs to give her opinion. And then if I come forward, they're waiting in order to respond or find a compromise solution. Even these days, when the Mapuche movement isn't as strong, there are many people who say: look what's happening, Isolde: what do you think?

F: *And this is both a privilege and a burden, no?*

It's a privilege that carries a tremendous responsibility, as well as many worries and frustrations. As a woman I need to be honest with the people who are going to read my book and say that this scares me. Many times I'm scared by the responsibility, by the effect my words can have on others. On another level it's also a huge challenge, because you have to be learning every day, reading, listening to the news, analyzing things, talking with other leaders, communicating with people. And in addition to talking to people, you're also responsible for what's on paper. Because what I feel when I have a problem may not be what the law tells me I should feel, and the solution that first comes to me as the one affected by the problem may not be permissible under the law. So as a leader I'm responsible for knowing the difference between what is permitted by law, and the reality of what people suffer. These are the things a leader needs to know and worry about. Leaders who don't read, who don't worry, who aren't up to date, sooner or later reach their limit. They'll reach the end of their time in office and won't be able to go further as guides or teachers of their people.

F: *So you need to be reborn every day.*

Every day. If you wish it, you can be reborn and renewed every day.

 GLOSSARY

achiñurrada Putting on airs, stuck-up; looking down on one's Mapuche heritage and origins.

ANECAP National Association of Domestic Workers (*Asociación Nacional de Empleadas de Casa Particular*).

awarkuzen A game played with broad beans (*habas*).

boldo A large, oaklike native tree whose leaves can be used for a variety of medicinal purposes, especially to aid digestion when steeped in hot water and served as tea.

cacique Originally a Carib word for "leader" or "headman," during the colonial period it was generalized to mean any indigenous leader. In the case of the Mapuche it is often used as a synonym for logko.

cabestro halter for a horse.

Caleuche A ghostly ship or galleon that moves eternally through the foggy waters of Chile's southern coast, with a bevy of ghosts partying merrily aboard, occasionally taking on additional passengers. This story is especially common among Huilliche inhabitants in Chiloé.

CAPIDE Center for Training, Research, and Development (*Capacitación, Investigación y Desarrollo*) for the Mapuche People. A nongovernmental organization begun by a group of anthropologists at the university in Temuco, which then expanded dramatically during the period of international funding in the 1980s. The head of the group was anthropologist Mireya Zambrano.

CEDEM Center for Women's Development, or *Centro de Desarrollo de la Mujer*. A Santiago-based NGO involved in grassroots women's organizing from a leftist-feminist perspective.

CEPI *Comisión Especial de Pueblos Indígenas*, or Special Commission of Indigenous Peoples. The first institution created by the *Concertación* government as a response to the demands of indigenous peoples, it was created by Presidential Decree on May 17, 1990, at the beginning of the Aylwin government.

chamal The sleeveless, black, shiftlike dress that forms the core of a Mapuche woman's traditional dress.

chem Thing.

CODEJU *Comisión de Derechos Juveniles*, or Commission for the Rights of Youth.

CONADI *Corporación Nacional de Desarrollo Indígena*, or Indigenous Development Corporation. An agency created by the 1993 Indigenous Law to oversee the programs and moneys intended for indigenous development programs, as well as to mediate for and protect the integrity of indigenous communities.

CORFO *Corporación de Fomento a la Producción*, a government development corporation founded under the first Popular Front Government (1938–1942) to help facilitate investment in production and industry by encouraging partnerships between the state and private capital.

CRAV *Compañía Refinadora del Azúcar de Viña del Mar*, or Sugar Refining Company of Viña del Mar. When this company went belly-up in 1981 it helped generate the deepest economic and bank crisis faced by the Pinochet regime.

epeu Storytelling competition.

fogón The central hearth or fireplace around which a traditional Mapuche home, or ruka, is constructed.

FOSIS A fund for social projects created at the beginning of the Aylwin administration. Funds are disbursed through a competition among formal proposals.

gillatufe Religious specialists who help with the prayers in Mapuche religious ceremonies.

gillatun One of the most important Mapuche religious and communal ceremonies, in which neighboring communities reestablish reciprocal ties through a ceremony of prayer and reflection that lasts several days. While it can be organized at specific moments to plead with God to resolve specific problems, in general it occurs in a community once every four years and is carried out on a special field which that year is consecrated exclusively for that purpose.

Günechen God or Supreme Being.

hualle Variety of tree native to the Chilean south, occurring abundantly in the original forests of the Mapuche region.

IANSA One of the industrial firms that, during the dictatorship, cooperated with CORFO in providing seeds, fertilizers, or other in-kind credits to small producers interested in raising crops for industrial transformation, such as sugar beets.

ilkantun Improvisational song competition, in which individuals compete by composing verses on the spot.

INDAP Institute for Agrarian and Livestock Development, or *Instituto de Desarrollo Agropecuario*. Along with the Corporation for Agrarian Reform (*Corporación de la Reforma Agraria*, or CORA), INDAP was an institution created in the 1960s to facilitate the process of agrarian reform and development carried out between 1964 and 1973. In contrast to CORA, which was abolished by the military government after the completion of the agrarian counterreform in 1978, INDAP today still provides loans to small agricultural producers, though now very much under market criteria. In 1979, the previously existing Indigenous Development Institute (*Instituto de*

Desarrollo Indígena, or IDI) was abolished and its functions integrated into INDAP.

kamarikun Central ceremony of the gillatun. Also the field designated for the ceremony.

kamikan A Mapuche parlor game.

kelluwun Mutual aid, or labor cooperation in community projects.

kona A Mapuche commoner, of humble origin or lineage.

kulkul Traditional Mapuche wind instrument.

kulxun Sacred ceremonial drum beaten at most Mapuche rituals and ceremonies; a machi also uses a kulxun in most of her or his ceremonial and healing practices.

lamñen Sister, relative.

logko In the Mapuche language, mapunzugun, the word means "head." Designates the recognized leader of a Mapuche community, who organizes ritual, mediates in a crisis, and handles the relationship of the community to the outside world.

machi A shaman or ritual specialist in Mapuche culture. She or he officiates at various forms of religious ritual and stores and transmits knowledge concerning healing, spirituality, and past events. A machi is both greatly respected and greatly feared in the community.

machitun Healing ceremony performed by a machi.

Manquián A spirit or apparition taking the shape of a girl with golden hair, who appears to people in a variety of places and environments.

mapunzugun The language of the Mapuche people.

mate A caffeinated, tealike beverage traditionally drunk on the plains of Argentina and surrounding regions. While in Argentina it is today a widespread practice to drink mate, in some parts of Chile to do so is marked as a Mapuche custom.

merken A powder made of combined chili peppers and salt, used as condiments in Chilean food, but especially in Mapuche households.

MIDEPLAN Ministry of Planning (*Ministerio de Planificación*), under whose jursidiction CONADI was placed.

mote A stew made of boiled grains, usually corn or wheat.

muday A traditional drink made from grain, usually wheat, that is used at most Mapuche religious ceremonies. It can be fermented or not fermented.

newen The personal spirit helping each individual in Mapuche culture; but especially the special helper-spirit who aids the machi in her work.

Newen Lelfn Roughly translated, it means "spirit of youth" or "youthful spirit." The Mapuche youth organization in Chanco.

norporrufe A sergeant at the gillatun ceremony who clears the area and makes sure the boundaries of the field are well defined and maintained.

Nütram A magazine put out by the Centro Ecuménico Diego de Medellín in Santiago, edited by Rolf Foerster and R. Rupailaf. Beginning in 1985, its goal was to support an understanding of Mapuche culture and of the Mapuche's struggle for liberation.

ñeikurewen Dance of the machi through which she or he renews a commitment to the community, to her or his newen, and to the practices and identity associated with being a machi.

ñukekurre Traditional custom in which a Mapuche man has first right to marry his brother's widow.

pakarwa Toad.

palin A sport similar to field hockey, played with sticks and a wooden ball. The competition is usually between communities, each of which arrives at the field with large representations headed by machis. The sport used to be played as part of their training by Mapuche warriors.

peñi Brother.

pewen Mapuche name for the Araucaria pine native to the Chilean southern temperate rainforest.

pidén A bird native to the Chilean south and known for its distinctive call.

pixtu Allergic rash.

PRODEMU A regionally grounded but nationally organized women's training organization under the control of the First Lady of the Republic.

ramada A temporary shelter made of tree branches. In addition to being used to shelter participants in a gillatun, it is a common form of shelter for fairs and other forms of mobile gatherings throughout rural Chile.

rewe A carved post resembling a totem that designates a machi's house; also, the carved post representing the community or lineage that is exhibited at a gillatun.

ruka Traditional Mapuche dwelling, with a thatched roof and a large hearth at its center around which the rest of the house is built.

SEREMI *Secretaría Regional Ministerial*, or regional office of a particular Ministry. During the administrative decentralization carried out under the military government, each region was to establish an office to carry out policy for each of the national-level ministries. Since 1990, these offices have moved into a position to actually help revise and formulate locally specific policy in some cases. The SEREMIS form part of the regional intendancy system and the positions are filled through political appointment.

SERNAM *Servicio Nacional de la Mujer*, or National Women's Service (with ministerial status).

SERPAJ *Servicio de Paz y Justicia*, or Service for Peace and Justice. An international human rights organization formed in the early 1980s, with the participation of Nobel Prize winner Adolfo Pérez Esquivel.

sopaipillas A form of fried bread which is cooked in animal fat and has become very traditional throughout rural Chile in particular. When made for a gillatun, they are especially large.

Trauco A tiny, mythical figure most common in Huilliche stories from Chiloé, who walks through the forest on stump feet, carrying an ax. He is sometimes associated with the seduction of young women.

ülmen Like a logko, one of the important leaders of Mapuche society.

weñufolle Special flag carried during a palin competition representing the *ramada* of a specific lineage or community. People say it has magical properties that allows its carriers to emerge victorious in the competition.

wigka The word used today in mapunzugun to designate non-Mapuches, it originally meant "thief who operates quickly and violently."

xapi ají or chili peppers.

xarilogko A woman's headress, composed of ribbons and decorative flowers

xariwe A woman's sash or belt made of woven wool. Traditionally the design would have designated a woman's marital status.

xuxuka Traditional Mapuche wind instrument.

zugumachife A special ritual mediator or translator who makes sense of a machi's utterings while she or he is in a trance.

NOTES

Editor's Introduction

1   On the early twentieth-century Mapuche organizations, see Rolf Foerster and Sonia Montecino, *Organizaciones, líderes y contiendas mapuches (1900–1910)* (Santiago: Centro de Estudios de la Mujer, 1988).
2   The figures from the 1992 census are best analyzed in *XVI Censo Nacional de Población 1992: Población Mapuche: Tabulaciones Especiales*, a joint publication of the Instituto de Estudios Indígenas/Universidad de la Frontera, Instituto Nacional de Estadísticas, Corporación Nacional de Desarrollo Indígena, Comisión Económica para América Latina y el Caribe, and the Centro Latinoamericano de Demografía (Temuco: Instituto de Estudios Indígenas/UFRO, 1998). Some of the ethnographies of the Mapuche are: Ximena Bunster, "Adaptation in Mapuche Life: Natural and Directed," Ph.D. diss., Columbia University, 1968; Tom D. Dillehay, *Araucanía, presente y pasado* (Santiago: Editorial Andrés Bello, 1990); Louis C. Faron, *Hawks of the Sun: Mapuche Morality and its Ritual Attributes* (Pittsburgh: University of Pittsburgh Press, 1964), and *The Mapuche Indians of Chile* (New York: Holt, Rinehart and Winston, 1968); Rolf Foerster, *Introducción a la religiosidad mapuche* (Santiago: Editorial Universitaria, 1993), and *Vida religiosa de los huilliches de San Juan de la Costa* (Santiago: Ediciones Rehue, 1985); Julian H. Steward and Louis C. Faron, *Native Peoples of South America* (New York: McGraw-Hill, 1959); Milan Stuchlik, *Life on a Half Share: Mechanisms of Social Recruitment among the Mapuche of Southern Chile* (London: C. Hurst, 1976).
3   Sources on the relationship between international human rights and indigenous movements include: Guillermo Bonfil Batalla, ed., *Utopía y revolución: El pensamiento político contemporáneo de los indios en América Latina* (Mexico, D.F.: Editorial Nueva Imagen, 1981); Héctor Díaz Polanco, *Indigenous Peoples in Latin America: The Quest for Self-Determination*, trans. Lucía Rayas (Boulder: Westview Press, 1997); Documentos de la Segunda Reunión de Barbados, *Indianidad y descolonización en América Latina* (Mexico, D.F.: Editorial Nueva Imagen, 1979); Alexander Ewen, ed., *Voice of Indigenous Peoples: Native People Address the United Nations* (Santa Fe: Clear Light Publishers, 1994); Rigoberta Menchú, with Dante Liano

and Gianni Mina, *Rigoberta: La nieta de los mayas* (Mexico, D.F.: Aguilar, Altea, Taurus, Alfaguara, S.A. de C.V., 1998); Rodolfo Stavenhagen, *Ethnic Conflicts and the Nation-State*, United Nations Research Institute for Social Development (New York: St. Martin's Press, 1996), and "Indian Ethnic Movements and State Policies in Latin America," *IFDA Dossier* no. 36 (July/August, 1983): 3–16; and *Derecho Indígena y derechos humanos en América Latina* (Mexico, D.F.: El Colegio de México, 1988); Rodolfo Stavenhagen and Diego Iturralde, eds., *Entre la ley y la costumbre: El derecho consuetudinario indígena en América Latina* (Mexico, D.F.: Instituto Indigenista Interamericano e Instituto Interamericano de Derechos Humanos de San José, Costa Rica, 1990); and Donna Lee Van Cott, ed., *Indigenous Peoples and Democracy in Latin America* (New York: St. Martin's Press and The Inter-American Dialogue, 1994). A particularly creative use of international human rights discourse to confront the situation of the Maya people in Guatemala can be found in the work of Demetrio Cojtí Cuxil. See, for example, Demetrio Cojtí Cuxil, "The Politics of Maya Revindication," in Edward F. Fischer and R. McKenna Brown, eds., *Maya Cultural Activism in Guatemala* (Austin: University of Texas Press, 1996), pp. 19–50. For an overview of the discourse of the Maya movement, see Kay B. Warren, *Indigenous Movements and their Critics: Pan-Maya Activism in Guatemala* (Princeton: Princeton University Press, 1998).

4   Lynn Stephen, ed., *Hear My Testimony: María Teresa Tula, Human Rights Activist of El Salvador* (Boston: South End Press, 1994).

5   Pewenche and Lafkenche people are both ecologically specific subgroups within the more general category of Mapuche. *Pewenche* means "people of the pewen," Mapuche name for the araucaria pine native to the southern temperate rainforest. Pewenche people have developed a seasonally migrant adaptation to the extreme winters of the Andes Mountains, in which during the summer months they live in the top area of the Andes Mountains in what they call *veranadas*, grazing their herds and gathering the araucaria pine nuts that then form an important part of their protein supply throughout the year. In the winter months they move closer to the river valley floors to regions they call *invernadas*, where they grow crops. *Lafkenche* means "people of the water" and denotes those communities that have historically lived near rivers, lakes, or the ocean. They complement their agricultural and livestock activities with fishing and gathering of aquatic products.

6   For a more detailed description of this process, see José Bengoa, *Historia del pueblo Mapuche, siglos XVII a XX* (Santiago: Ediciones Sur, 1985), 345–64. For the original *título de merced* of Isolde's community, see Archivo de Asuntos Indígenas, T.M. 1921: Comunidad de Rosario Coñoen v. de Lefihual, Chanco, Pitrufquén, provincia de Valdivia, otorgado 16 de junio de

1910. Evidence concerning the land conflicts and delays with the titling process in the Pitrufquén area can be found in Archivo Siglo XX, Ministerio de Relaciones Exteriores, Vol. 1116, 1904: "Oficio de los indígenas de la Subdelegación No. 14 de Pitrufquén, provincia de Valdivia, al Ministerio de RR.EE., pidiendo que los ingenieros de colonización los radiquen en el terreno que ocupan," Pitrufquén, April 1904. Evidence about don Ernesto Reuque's purchase of lands in Coñoen de Lefihual comes, in addition to the conversations with Isolde and her family, from Carpeta Administrativa, T.M. 1921: "Autorización para enajenar: Comunidad Rosario Coñoen; Vendedor: Marcelina Millaleo; Comprador: Ernesto Reuque," Causa No. 5455, Leg. 6–2, Juzgado de Pitrufquén, 1947.

7   How to define Mapuche culture and identity—in essence, how to decide who is "in" and who is "out"—is a complex question indeed. The 1993 Ley Indígena provides an answer based on a combination of self-definition, membership in a legally constituted indigenous community, and familial heritage. Before the Pinochet Land Division Law of 1979, people could "prove" they were Mapuche by demonstrating that they were descended from one of the family lines contained in the *títulos de merced*, or original land-grant documents. Since each community received the name of the man considered, at the moment of settlement, to be the logko or cacique, Mapuche last names also took on great importance in this process of definition. At the same time, however, increasing rural to urban migration across the twentieth century, combined with differential commitment in the communities to preserving the language, religious rituals, customs, and dress considered distinctive to the Mapuche, made defining Mapuche identity increasingly problematic. Beginning in the 1970s, the commitment to ethnic revival—including the revindication of the Mapuche language; of rituals such as the gillatun; of traditional dress, especially among women; of literature, other forms of narrative, and music; and of sports traditions such as palin—has spread through previously more assimilated communities and into the urban areas (where, after all, the majority of Mapuche today live).

8   For the adaptation of the community of Juan Catrilaf, I have relied on an interview with Aurelio Catrilaf Parra and Norma Catrilaf, Ñinquilco, 18 June 1997. I treat the adaptation of the community of Nicolás Ailío in "Courage Tastes of Blood: The Mapuche Community of Nicolás Ailío and the Chilean State, 1906–2001," ms. On the story itself, comparative examples of devil contract stories for other parts of Latin America are presented by Michael T. Taussig, *The Devil and Commodity Fetishism in South America* (Chapel Hill: University of North Carolina Press, 1980). I am also grateful to Juan Sánchez Curihuentro, Isolde's husband, for his explanation of how political crises can generate transferences of power from one

lineage to another in Mapuche communities. Finally, however, it is important to note that not all Mapuche agree that the figure of the devil exists in Mapuche culture. According to machi don Víctor Caniullan, for example, the concept of evil is very different among the Mapuche and has been misinterpreted by scholars analyzing Mapuche belief systems as referring to the devil.

9 Organizing experience around particular patterns of meaning is, of course, a more general strategy people use in narrating a life. Daniel James calls it a "key pattern" (*Doña María's Story: Life History, Memory, and Political Identity* [Durham: Duke University Press, 2000], 161). Alessandro Portelli refers to a similar idea in *The Death of Luigi Trastulli and Other Stories: Form and Meaning in Oral History* (Albany: SUNY Press, 1991), which he calls a "central core of meaning" (65).

10 The gillatun is one of the most important Mapuche religious and communal ceremonies, in which neighboring communities reestablish reciprocal ties through a ceremony of prayer and reflection that lasts several days. While it can be organized at specific moments to plead with God to resolve specific problems, in general it occurs in a community once every four years and is carried out on a special field which that year is consecrated exclusively for that purpose. In the years between about 1960 and 1978, many communities began to abandon the gillatun as the older generation—and especially the first reducción generation of logkos and machis, the leaders needed to reproduce the ritual—began to die out.

11 For an interesting comparative perspective on ethnic revitalization or revival, see Joane Nagel, *American Indian Ethnic Renewal: Red Power and the Resurgence of Identity and Culture* (New York: Oxford University Press, 1996). On this process in other parts of Latin America, see, among other works, Joanne Rappaport, *The Politics of Memory: Native Historical Interpretation in the Colombian Andes* (Cambridge: Cambridge University Press, 1990), and *Cumbe Reborn: An Andean Ethnography of History* (Chicago: University of Chicago Press, 1994); Diane M. Nelson, *A Finger in the Wound: Body Politics in Quincentennial Guatemala* (Berkeley: University of California Press, 1999); Kay B. Warren, *Indigenous Movements and their Critics: Pan-Maya Activism in Guatemala* (Princeton: Princeton University Press, 1998); Melina Selverson-Scher, *Ethnopolitics in Ecuador: Indigenous Rights and the Strengthening of Democracy* (Coral Gables: North-South Center Press, 2001); Alcida Rita Ramos, *Indigenism: Ethnic Politics in Brazil* (Madison: University of Wisconsin Press, 1998); Seth Garfield, *Indigenous Struggle at the Heart of Brazil: State Policy, Frontier Expansion, and the Xavante Indians, 1937–1988* (Durham: Duke University Press, 2001); Jonathan Warren, *Racial Revolutions: Antiracism and Indian Resurgence in Brazil* (Durham: Duke University Press, 2001); Lynn Stephen and George A.

Collier, eds., *Reconfiguring Ethnicity, Identity, and Citizenship in the Wake of the Zapatista Rebellion*, special issue of the *Journal of Latin American Anthropology* 3, no. 1 (1997); and Charles R. Hale, *Resistance and Contradiction: Miskitu Indians and the Nicaraguan State, 1894–1987* (Stanford: Stanford University Press, 1994).

12 Sidney W. Mintz, *Worker in the Cane: A Puerto Rican Life History* (New York: Norton, 1974; orig. ed., Yale University Press, 1960).

13 For some illuminating discussions of the problems with transcription, see Victoriano Camas Baena and Ignacio García Borrego, "La transcripción en historial oral: Para un modelo 'vivo' del paso de lo oral a lo escrito," *Historia, Antropología y fuentes orales* 2, no. 18 (1997); Kate Moore, "Perversión de la palabra: La función de las transcripciones en la historial oral," *Historia, Antropología y fuentes orales* 2, no. 18 (1997): 13–24; followed in the same issue by the comments of Rosemary Block (25–28) and Michael Frisch (29–33) and rejoinder by Moore (35–39); and Alessandro Portelli, "What Makes Oral History Different," in *The Death of Luigi Trastulli*, 45–58.

14 Daniel James, in *Doña María's Story*, struggled with some of these same issues, though in his case it is only one performer who inhabits the stage. He referred to this question by coining the concept of "performed stories" (183).

15 I have begun to suspect, for example, that by organizing Rigoberta Menchú's testimony into recognizable anthropological categories, Elisabeth Burgos Debray (and, apparently, Arturo Taracena) may have emphasized the "indigenous" part of the text to a much larger degree than the original conversations had suggested. For more on the case of Rigoberta Menchú, see below.

16 In this sense I have opted for a more interventionist role in the conversation than recommended by some oral historians (Paul Richard Thompson, *The Voice of the Past: Oral History* [New York: Oxford University Press, 1978]; Eugenia Meyer, "América Latina, ¿Una realidad virtual? A propósito del artículo de Dora Schwartzstein," *Historia, Antropología y Fuentes Orales* 1, no. 16 (1996): 141–49, and "Deconstrucción de la memoria, construcción de la historia," *Historia, Antropología y Fuentes Orales* 1, no. 19 (1998). On the other side of this debate, however, are people like Alessandro Portelli, who emphasizes cooperation between interviewer and interviewee in the fashioning of a narrative. See *The Death of Luigi Trastulli* and *The Battle of Valle Giulia: Oral History and the Art of Dialogue* (Madison: University of Wisconsin Press, 1997). An early and complex intervention in these debates was Sherna Berger Gluck and Daphne Patai, eds., *Women's Words: The Feminist Practice of Oral History* (New York: Routledge, 1991).

17   Perhaps an extreme example of pretended horizontality or equality occurs in Ruth Behar, *Translated Woman: Crossing the Border with Esperanza's Story* (Boston: Beacon Press, 1993), a life history of a Mexican peasant woman, when Behar compares her conflictual experiences as the middle-class daughter of a strict, authoritarian Cuban father who tore the letters she had sent him and threw the pieces in her face, and later as a North American academic who did not receive the recognition she felt she deserved, with the life of a peasant woman who knew bitter poverty and dangerous and repeated physical abuse from her father, her husband, and her mother-in-law.

18   Already when we recorded the introduction and conclusion to this book in August 1998, a revitalized Mapuche movement had begun to confront the Chilean state and the large lumber companies over the ownership and exploitation of forest resources in Lumaco and other parts of the IX Region. Since then, similar conflicts have erupted further north, in the region of Arauco. Though the Mapuche movement is no longer in retreat in the same way, however, the urgency of incorporating lessons learned in the earlier cycle of mobilization has not diminished. If anything, it may have increased.

19   Doris Sommer wrote an early article about the concept of "secrets" in Rigoberta Menchú's first testimonio: "Rigoberta's Secrets," *Latin American Perspectives*, issue 70, vol. 18, no. 3 (summer 1991): 32–50.

20   The original Spanish edition of Menchú's first testimony was published in Spain: Elisabeth Burgos Debray, ed., *Me llamo Rigoberta Menchú y así me nació la conciencia* (Barcelona: Editorial Argos Vergara, 1983). By 1997 the Spanish text had gone through fourteen editions and had been translated into many languages, including, of course, English.

21   Rigoberta Menchú, with Dante Liano and Dianni Mina, *Rigoberta: La nieta de los mayas* (Mexico, D.F.: Aguilar, Altea, Taurus, Alfaguara, 1998). See especially 252–56 for a description of the process of the first testimony.

22   David Stoll, *Rigoberta Menchú and the Story of All Poor Guatemalans* (Boulder: Westview Press, 1999). The phrase about "revolutionary thinking" appears on 194. Reproducing a list of Stoll's specific allegations is not relevant to our subject here and in any case has been done in other texts that are direct interventions in the debate about Menchú's first testimonio. See Arturo Arias, ed., *The Rigoberta Menchú Controversy* (Minneapolis: University of Minnesota Press, 2001), and *If Truth Be Told: A Forum on David Stoll's* Rigoberta Menchú and the Story of All Poor Guatemalans, *Latin American Perspectives*, issue 109 (coordinated by Jan Rus), November 1999.

23   John Beverley, "The Real Thing," in Georg M. Gugelberger, ed., *The Real Thing: Testimonial Discourse and Latin America* (Durham: Duke University Press, 1996), 266–86; direct quotation on 281.

24 Sidney W. Mintz, *Taso: Trabajador de la caña*, con estudio preliminar, bibliografía y cronología de Francisco A. Scarano (Río Piedras, P.R.: Ediciones Huracán, 1988), 65; translation mine. The results of the seminar mentioned earlier in the paragraph were published as James Clifford and George E. Marcus, eds., *Writing Culture: The Poetics and Politics of Ethnography* (Berkeley: University of California Press, 1986).

25 For some complex reflections on these issues, see (among many others) James Clifford, *The Predicament of Culture: Twentieth-Century Ethnography, Literature, and Art* (Cambridge: Harvard University Press, 1988); *Hispanic American Historical Review*, "Special Issue: Mexico's New Cultural History: ¿Una lucha libre?," 79, no. 2 (May 1999); Renato Rosaldo, *Culture and Truth: The Remaking of Social Analysis*, 2d ed. (Boston: Beacon Press, 1993); Barbara Tedlock, "From Participant Observation to the Observation of Participation: The Emergence of Narrative Ethnography," *Journal of Anthropological Research* 47 (1991): 69–97; and Lila Abu Lughod, *Writing Women's Worlds: Bedouin Stories* (Berkeley: University of California Press, 1993), especially 6–42.

26 John Beverley, "The Margin at the Center: On Testimonio (Testimonial Narrative)," originally published in 1989 and reproduced in Gugelberger, ed., *The Real Thing*, 23–41; direct quotations on 31 and 33.

27 All the authors in *The Real Thing* agree that testimonio, as a genre, has been increasingly integrated into academic discourse, thus losing its capacity to transgress. For the deepest analysis, using the Bolivian case, of the changes brought on by globalization, see Javier Sanjinés, "Beyond Testimonial Discourse: New Popular Trends in Bolivia," in the same volume, 254–65. Beverley's critique appears in "The Real Thing," 266–68; direct quotations are on 281–82.

28 Margaret Randall, *Christians in the Nicaraguan Revolution* (Vancouver: New Star Books, 1983), *Todas estamos despiertas: Testimonios de la mujer nicaragüense de hoy* (Mexico, D.F.: Siglo XXI Editores, 1980), *Sandino's Daughters Revisited: Feminism in Nicaragua* (New Brunswick: Rutgers University Press, 1994); Domitila Barrios de Chungara, with Moema Viezzer, *"Si me permiten hablar—": Testimonio de Domitila, una mujer de las minas de Bolivia* (Mexico, D.F.: Siglo XXI Editores, 1977); Oscar Lewis, *The Children of Sánchez: Autobiography of a Mexican Family* (New York: Random House, 1961), *A Death in the Sánchez Family* (New York: Random House, 1969), *Five Families: Mexican Case Studies in the Culture of Poverty* (New York: Basic Books, 1959), *Living the Revolution: An Oral History of Contemporary Cuba* (Urbana: University of Illinois Press, 1977), *Four Women: Living the Revolution* (Urbana: University of Illinois Press, 1977), *Pedro Martínez: A Mexican Peasant and his Family* (New York: Random House, 1964), *La Vida: A Puerto Rican Family in the Culture of Poverty* (New York: Random House, 1966); Elena Poniatowska, *Fuerte es el silencio*

(Mexico, D.F.: Ediciones Era, 1982), *Hasta no verte, Jesús mío* (Mexico, D.F.: Ediciones Era, 1969), *Nada, nadie: Las voces del temblor* (Mexico, D.F.: Ediciones Era, 1988), *La noche de Tlatelolco: Testimonios de historia oral* (Mexico, D.F.: Ediciones Era, 1971); Miguel Barnet, *Canción de Rachel* (Buenos Aires: Editorial Galerna, 1969), *Biografía de un cimarrón* (Buenos Aires: Editorial Galerna, 1968). Elena Poniatowska's role as research assistant to Oscar Lewis is mentioned in Susan M. Rigdon, *The Culture Facade: Art, Science, and Politics in the Work of Oscar Lewis* (Urbana: University of Illinois Press, 1988). See also June Nash, *We Eat the Mines and the Mines Eat Us: Dependency and Exploitation in Bolivian Tin Mines* (New York: Columbia University Press, 1979), and *I Spent My Life in the Mines* (New York: Columbia University Press, 1992).

Testimonial and life history texts in Chilean literature, especially those relating to Mapuche culture, include: Pascual Coña, *Testimonio de un cacique mapuche*, dictated to Father Ernesto Wilhelm de Moesbach, 3rd ed. (Santiago: Pehuén, 1984); Sonia Montecino Aguirre, *Grupo de mujeres de la ciudad: Una experiencia múltiple* (Santiago: Programa de Estudios y Capacitación de la Mujer Campesina e Indígena, Círculo de Estudios de la Mujer, Academia de Humanismo Cristiano, 1983); Montecino, *Mujeres de la tierra* (Santiago: CEM-PEMCI, 1984); Montecino, *Los sueños de Lucinda Nahuelhual* (Santiago: Programa de Estudios y Capacitación de la Mujer Campesina e Indígena, PEMCI, Círculo de Estudios de la Mujer, Academia de Humanismo Cristiano, 1984); and Martín Painemal Huenchual, with Rolf Foerster, *Vida de un dirigente mapuche* (Santiago: Grupo de Investigaciones Agrarias, Academia de Humanismo Cristiano, 1984).

29   Stoll, *Rigoberta Menchú*, 185. At the same time we should not lose sight of the fact that, by the time Stoll interviewed Burgos Debray their interests were converging, according to Menchú's long-time mentor and Guatemalan historian Arturo Taracena, because Burgos Debray was in the process of distancing herself from the Latin American left. Taracena's version of how Menchú's first testimony was produced appears in Peter Canby's review of Stoll and Menchú, *New York Review of Books* 46, no. 6 (8 April 1999): 28–33. In addition to a detailed narrative about his role in the production of the first testimonial, a role Burgos Debray seems to have buried for quite a while, Taracena apparently confirms (32) that Burgos Debray's original intention was to write a magazine article. Further comments by Taracena can be found in Luis Aceituno, "Entrevista a Arturo Taracena sobre Rigoberta Menchú: Arturo Taracena rompe el silencio," in *The Rigoberta Menchu Controversy*, ed. Arturo Arias (Minneapolis: University of Minnesota Press, 2001), where he suggests that their original model for the testimonio was Domitila Barrios de Chungara.

30   Aceituno, "Entrevista a Arturo Taracena"; Kay B. Warren, "Telling Truths:

Taking David Stoll and the Rigoberta Menchú Exposé Seriously," in Arias, ed., *The Rigoberta Menchú Controversy*, 198–218. An English translation of Arturo Aracena's interview appears in the same book, 82–94.

31 Another of the unfortunate tendencies in the Stoll book is to lose sight of the amazing disparity between the firepower and cruelty of the army and of the guerrillas, a disparity clearly reflected in the commission's figures. For the report see the *New York Times*, 27 February 1999, A4, and 1 March 1999, A10. See also the summary available on the Web at http://hrdata .aaas.org/ceh/report/english/toc.html.

32 This issue came up again at a panel at the 2001 Latin American Studies Association meetings in Washington, D.C., when commentator Doris Sommer congratulated the panelists who were debating David Stoll for beginning to take facts seriously.

33 An important contrast can be seen, in this context, between the treatment received by Menchú's text and other memoirs of repression or *denuncia* that, because they are not by indigenous authors, are not transformed into ethnography. For the Guatemalan case we have the testimony of guerrilla fighter Mario Payeras, published originally in Spanish as *Días de la selva* (Havana: Casa de las Américas, 1980). In an essay comparing the two testimonios Marc Zimmerman refers to Payeras by his last name, and to Menchú as "Rigoberta" ("Testimonio in Guatemala: Payeras, Rigoberta, and Beyond," in Gugelberger, ed., 101–29), thus constructing ethnographic intimacy only in the case of of a denuncia text produced by an indigenous woman. The essays by Duncan Earle, "Menchú Tales and Maya Social Landscapes: The Silencing of Words and Worlds," and Victor D. Montejo, "Truth, Human Rights, and Representation: The Case of Rigoberta Menchú," both appear in the Arias anthology, 288–308 and 372–91, respectively. Both authors suggest that the left and the solidarity movement also helped canonize Menchú and thus partially marginalized other Maya voices and texts of denuncia, such as Montejo's own *Testimony: Death of a Guatemalan Village* (Willimantic, Conn.: Curbstone Press, 1987).

Among the many texts of denuncia produced for the Chilean case, see Luz Arce, *El infierno* (Santiago: Planeta, 1993); Sergio Bitar, *Isla 10* (Santiago: Pehuén, 1987); CODEPU, *Chile: Recuerdos de la guerra: Valdivia-Neltume- Chihuio- Liquiñe* (Santiago: CODEPU-Emisión, n.d.); Hernán Valdés, *Tejas Verdes (Diario de un campo de concentración en Chile* (Barcelona: Editorial Laia, 1978). Interestingly, in the Chilean case the Mapuche experience of repression has not received much attention in its own right, with the exception of Roberta Bacic et al., *Memorias recientes de mi pueblo, 1973–1990, Araucanía: Muerte y desaparición forzada en la Araucanía: Una aproximación etnica* (Temuco: Centro de Estudios Socio Culturales, Universidad Católica de Temuco, 1997).

34   Coña, *Testimonio de un cacique mapuche*; Painemal Huenchual, *Vida de un dirigente mapuche*; and Sonia Sotomayor Cantero, "Comprensión del proceso de formación y gestión de un lider mapuche evolue. Análisis de la historia de vida de José Santos Millao Palacios," M.A. thesis, Universidad de la Frontera, Temuco, 1995.

35   The article about the Mapuche woman leader is by Ximena Bunster, "The Emergence of a Mapuche Leader: Chile," in June Nash and Helen Icken Safa, eds., *Sex and Class in Latin America* (New York: Praeger, 1976), 302–19. It is a shame that the promised book-length autobiography of this leader, given the name of Llanquitray, to my knowledge never materialized. Other sources on Mapuche women include Montecino, *Grupo de mujeres de la ciudad*; *Mujeres de la tierra*; and *Los sueños de Lucinda Nahuelhual*. Sonia Montecino Aguirre's acclaimed novelized biography of a machi is *Sueño con menguante: Biografía de una machi* (Santiago: Editorial Sudamericana, 1999).

36   To all of this has been added Isolde's most recent participation in CONADI, first in an unsuccessful campaign for an elected seat on its national council, then as President Ricardo Lagos's designated council member. This new position has resulted in her being labeled, once again, an *oficialista*, someone who goes along with government policy, by implication an enemy of the more militant Mapuche movement. There is an element of deja vu here, of course; the same thing happened to her, as a Catholic activist, in the early 1980s.

37   See chapter 4.

38   It was only recently, after the manuscript was in the final process of revision, that I came across a very similar phrase in the conclusion to another life history: "Life is reborn with every dawn and so am I." María de los Reyes Castillo Bueno, *Reyita: The Life of a Black Cuban Woman in the Twentieth Century* (Durham: Duke University Press, 2000), 170. Despite the many differences between the two lives and the two texts, I was struck by the parallel and stubborn optimism that stands at the center of how both women narrate their stories.

1   Chanco: Family, Land, and Culture

1   Across the twentieth century, Mapuche land-grant communities have been affected by a series of different laws that have established the rules of the game, so to speak, for maintaining or dividing up indigenous property. Since 1928, when the first Land Division Law was passed, the main variation has been around what conditions, and with what percentage of the community's approval, a process of subdivision could occur. Law 17129 was passed under the Popular Unity government, and its big difference was that a majority of the community's population needed to approve a peti-

tion for subdivision and privatization. The so-called Pinochet Law 2568 was allegedly only a modification of Law 17129 rather than an entirely new law, but it envisioned a complete change in the principle of subdivision in the sense that it was a land to the occupant law, rather than a law subdividing the land among legally recognized members of the community, some of whom were in the city at the time of the process. See chapter 2 for a more extensive discussion of the issues surrounding the Pinochet Law.

2   Throughout our conversation, doña Martina is negotiating with her daughters as to how much she'll actually say, and when her husband comes in, she begins crying and the tone of her recollections becomes tragic. Her daughter Elvira, who had just received a degree in journalism from the University of Temuco, is also trying to provide historical context for the importance of the Paillalef family, one of the most prosperous Mapuche lineages, in part because of their history of livestock herding and trade between Chile and Argentina.

3   *Unidad Popular* or Popular Unity, the name popularly given to Salvador Allende's government (1970–1973) because the electoral coalition that brought him to power, composed mainly of the Communist, Socialist, and Radical parties, went by that name.

4   "Gute" refers to Gutenberg Martínez, in 1997 one of the more important "new wave" leaders of the Christian Democratic Party.

5   The Rettig Commission was created by President Patricio Aylwin upon taking office in 1990. Its three-volume official report, issued in February 1991, found enough evidence to confirm the disappearance of only 3,000. Pedro Curihual Paillán was one of them. *Informe de la Comisión Nacional de Verdad y Reconciliación* (Santiago: Secretaría de Comunicación y Cultura, Ministerio Secretaría General de Gobierno, 1991), vol. 2, 119.

6   To some extent, people's fears toward the machi, as well as her ambivalence about her own role, are quite recognizable in Mapuche culture. Taking on such a huge responsibility almost always entails ambivalence, and others in the community fear and sometimes envy the machi. See, for example, Sonia Montecino, *Sueño con menguante: Biografía de una machi* (Santiago: Editorial Sudamericana, 1999). Another perspective on the ambivalences associated with becoming a machi was given in a lecture by machi Víctor Caniullan, Universidad Católica de Temuco, August 1998.

7   Today the most radical and fundamentalist Mapuche organization, the *Consejo de Todas las Tierras* takes a strong position on cultural and territorial autonomy and has, since 1992, helped organize two waves of land invasions whose purpose was to recuperate the lands usurped from Mapuche communities after the so-called Pacification of the 1880s. Since the resurgence of the Mapuche movement in 1997, its increasing militancy has also helped increase the visibility and influence of the *Consejo* once again.

8   Lionel's story, prompted by my mention of earlier Mapuche intellectuals about

whom I've read, is especially riveting because of its periodization, which begins with a young man defeating the Spanish conquerors, an event usually associated in Chilean history with the second half of the seventeenth century, and then living to negotiate an arrangement with the Chilean state at the end of the nineteenth century. The fable-like, almost timeless quality of the story suggests that often, in Mapuche narrative, the distinction between the Spanish and the Chilean adversaries can become muddied.

9 Here Lionel is referring to Aucán Huilcaman, the leader in charge of the *Consejo de Todas las Tierras*, who at one point attempted to begin organizing the Mapuche communities near Pitrufquén.

10 Here I'm falling into a romanticization of the communal and collective nature of Mapuche religiosity and culture, which is part of ongoing debates about the nature of Mapuche society. Starting with the revitalization movement of the late 1970s, there emerged a tendency to see the Mapuche as a collectively and communally organized people, which in a strict historical sense was never the case. Lionel will soon bring up his doubts about my formulation when he discusses the existence of hierarchy in Mapuche religion.

2 The Mapuche Movement under Dictatorship, 1973–1989

1 Pedro de Valdivia, formally known as the conqueror of Chile, led the first expedition of explorers south from Peru, founding the city of Santiago in 1541. He was killed in Tucapel, during an expedition against the Mapuche, on 1 January 1554.

2 This is a reference to Aucán Huilcaman, who at the end of the 1980s would become the leader in charge of the radical Mapuche organization the *Consejo de Todas las Tierras*. See below, this chapter, and chapter 3 for a more extensive discussion of this organization.

3 Calling policemen "toads" has a double meaning in Chile, because the dark olive green of their uniforms was toad-like.

4 General César Mendoza Duran was the representative of the *Carabineros*, or militarized police, on the Military Junta. Among his assigned duties was supervising policy for the agrarian sector.

5 Author of *Historia del Pueblo Mapuche: Siglos XIX y XX*, José Bengoa is today considered one of the most prestigious historians of the Mapuche people as well as of rural Chile. He also served as first director of the *Consejo Especial de Pueblos Indígenas* (cepi), the transition indigenous organization created under President Patricio Aylwin (see chapters 3 and 4). José Mariman is a prominent Mapuche historian and intellectual, presently residing in the United States, who was a part of Ad-Mapu in the second half of the 1980s and has written several important and influential

essays on Mapuche politics, including "La Organización mapuche Aukiñ Wallmapu Ngulam," 1995, http://www.xs4all.nl/~rehue/art/jmar2.html; "Transición democrática en Chile: ¿Nuevo ciclo reivindicativo mapuche?" 1994, http://www.xs4all.nl/~rehue/art/jmar5a.html; and "Lumaco y el Movimiento Mapuche," 1998, http://www.xs4all.nl/~rehue/art/jmar6. html. In contrast to Isolde, both of these intellectuals have always been firmly in the socialist political camp.

6 José Santos Millao became active in Ad-Mapu upon his return from exile in the Soviet Union and became a public leader after the split in late 1982– early 1983. A member of the Communist Party, Millao from the beginning was interested in turning the organization in a more classic political direction. The memoir cited is Sonia Sotomayor Cantero, "Comprensión del proceso de formación y gestión de un líder Mapuche evolue: Análisis de la historia de vida de José Santos Millao Palacios," M.A. thesis, Universidad de la Frontera, Temuco, August 1995.

7 *Mapuchista* is best translated as Mapuche-ist, or someone supporting the Mapuche cause. *Indianista* would be indigenous-ist, someone supporting the indigenous cause. *Gremialista*, while meaning syndicalist, also had a special meaning during the dictatorship, because it signified those people in trade associations who had supported the overthrow of Allende. While the dictatorship had turned away from responding to gremialista demands by the early to mid-1980s and many gremialistas had gone into opposition, for people on the left the term still had very negative connotations.

8 The *Asamblea de la Civilidad* was a broad-based grassroots coalition formed in 1986 in opposition to the dictatorship; its main purpose was to attempt to unify all opposition forces above and beyond political party lines and divisions.

9 Isolde made these comments near the beginning of our conversations, at the beginning of 1997, before the resurgence of a militant Mapuche movement. While here she clearly reflects the mood at that particular time, it's also true that the deeper frustration about the inability fully to institutionalize Mapuche gains, about the ongoing confrontations with the state simply to maintain access to basic resources and rights, remains an enduring problem today.

10 In the original Spanish text, Isolde says "*Terminamos bien taconeados, decía yo en broma, pero fué muy rico.*" *Taconeado* is a wordplay on *taco*, but since in Spanish *taco* also means the heel of a shoe, *taconeado* can also mean "trampled" or "battered." This is a reference to the wear and tear that such a long trip can inflict on the travelers, even as they are being hosted and feted.

11 There has been quite a heated debate in the U.S.-based historiography on Latin American labor about the American Institute for Free Labor Development, which some scholars have seen as a CIA front. Certainly at

about this time, between 1985 and 1986, the United States was involved in attempting to influence the shape of the Chilean transition to democracy and was facilitating, through a series of programs—most notably the United States Information Agency—a string of cultural exchanges in both directions to foster the formation of younger Christian Democratic leaders. I personally remember meeting in Madison, Wisconsin, with Delia Del Gatto, whom Isolde mentions in her next paragraph, who was on a U.S.-government-sponsored tour of universities at that point.

12 Teodoro Schmidt was an Austrian immigrant engineer who was made responsible for the mapping of all territory controlled by the Mapuche prior to the so-called Pacification in the early 1880s. He was also rumored to have used his position to accumulate a large personal fortune, especially through the accumulation of choice pieces of land his family later used for commercial agriculture and lumber. Since Lautaro was one of the most famous and militant Mapuche warriors, renaming the plaza clearly had a deep political and symbolic significance.

3 The Transition to Democracy

1 All of the places mentioned in this paragraph—Curarrehue, Lonquimay, Villarrica, Panguipulli, and Neltume—are located in the farther reaches of the Andes foothills. Panguipulli, Neltume, Villarrica, and Curarrehue had reputations of being open to MIR influence during the Popular Unity government.

2 The Group of 24 was a group of jurists, mainly from the centrist opposition to the Pinochet dictatorship, that began meeting in 1978 in an attempt to find a more democratic alternative to the process of institutionalization that ultimately culminated in the 1980 Constitution. Though the group no longer had any formal role by the second half of the 1980s, as Isolde points out here its members were prestigious political leaders who were intimately involved in the process of negotiating a transition toward democratic rule.

3 Published in Santiago in the 1980s, under the leadership of anthropologist Rolf Foerster, *Nütram* was a periodical with "restricted circulation," which allowed it to address certain political issues not allowed in more mainstream media at the time. It provided a forum for the discussion of political and cultural issues concerning the Mapuche movement.

4 José A. Mariman, "La Organización mapuche Aukiñ Wallmapu Ngulam," 1995; http://www.xs4all.nl/~rehue/art/jmar2.html. An earlier manuscript version, which was the only version I had seen when Isolde and I had this conversation, was also available in the documents collection at the Sociedad Liwen in Temuco.

5   The Pact of Quilín was the first peace accord reached between the Mapuche and the Spanish forces, in January 1641. Mediated by Jesuit clerics, it set the standard for all future negotiations by accepting Mapuche independence and autonomy between the Bío-Bío and Toltén rivers. For INDAP-DASIN, see note 6 below.

6   Galvarino, a famous Mapuche leader, was gruesomely tortured in the 1550s by Spanish soldiers during one of the many campaigns of conquest the Spanish attempted against the Mapuche. His story is dramatically told in Alonso de Ercilla's famous epic poem, *La Araucana*.

7   There was an irony to the continuity, both in office space and personnel, between INDAP-DASIN and CONADI. INDAP-DASIN had been the Pinochet dictatorship's institutional arm in the countryside, not only in the undoing of the Agrarian Reform, but also in the subdivision and privatization of Mapuche land. When CORA, the Agrarian Reform Corporation, was abolished by the military government after the completion of the agrarian counterreform in 1978, INDAP became the main government arm in the countryside. In 1979, the previously existing Indigenous Development Institute (*Instituto de Desarrollo Indígena*, or IDI) was abolished and its functions integrated into INDAP. The social welfare functions earlier a part of IDI were distributed to the various relevant ministries. After the 1981–85 economic crisis, when the military government created a Secretariat of Development and Social Welfare (*Desarrollo y Asistencia Social*), the forms of social welfare targeted through DAS for indigenous people were administered locally through DASIN.

8   The battle for constitutional recognition, and for the approval of ILO convention 169, continues as of this writing (2001). There is good reason to believe that the cutting and chopping away at the Indigenous Law that occurred in Congress sent a broader message to the society as a whole, that indigenous rights were not to be taken as seriously as had initially been believed.

9   The projected Ralco hydroelectric plant is the second in a series of plants planned by ENDESA, one of two state-owned electric companies privatized in the 1980s and today with substantial Spanish investment, along the Bío-Bío river. The first one, named Pangue, was inaugurated in the mid-1990s after a great deal of controversy. Ralco has inspired major confrontations between ENDESA, generally supported by the government under the presidency of Eduardo Frei-Ruiz Tagle (1994–2000), and a coalition of environmentalists, human rights activists, Mapuche organizations, and a faction of the leaders from the Pewenche communities that would be flooded by the new dam. See below, chapter 4, for a more detailed discussion of this issue and its ramifications.

10 *La Cuarta* is an afternoon daily distributed nationally, known for its sensa-

tionalist headlines and for featuring a picture of a scantily clad young woman on the front page every day.

11   *Renovación Nacional* is considered the more moderate or "reasonable" of the political parties on the Chilean right and is numerically a comparative small party.

12   Here Isolde is making a play on words between the internal party nicknames as descriptions of a physical characteristic, and their meaning that designates a factional allegiance, while at the same time poking fun at herself as güatona (pudgy or pot-bellied). The internal elections she mentions, held in 1997, were extremely acrimonious within the Christian Democratic Party and pitted the "old guard" led by Enrique Krauss, Christian Democratic congressman during the UP government and Minister of the Interior in the Aylwin government, against younger and more "modern" leader Gutenberg Martínez.

13   Francisco Huenchumilla, during the dictatorship a lawyer who defended political prisoners in the Temuco courts, became a congressman with the transition to democratic rule. He spoke out on human rights issues, especially around the time of the Commission on Truth and Reconciliation. Since 1997, which was when Isolde made these comments, he has assumed a more public position on the need for Mapuche representation in the political system, and my impression is that Isolde herself has been one of the people influencing him in that direction. In addition, after losing in a senatorial primary in 2000, Huenchumilla has come out more and more publicly in favor of the new Mapuche movement.

14   When Isolde says "today," she means the first half of 1997, when the Mapuche movement was at one of its lowest ebbs. Since then, as she discusses in the concluding chapter, the antilogging and land recuperation campaigns have galvanized political activism in many communities and in the cities. Isolde points out below that this new wave of activism has facilitated the rise of a new, younger leadership who did not have direct experience with the struggles of the 1970s and 1980s.

4   The Mapuche Movement under Democracy, 1990–1998

1   At the time we were talking, in the first half of 1997, there were approximately four hundred pesos to the dollar.

2   This conversation took place in 1997.

3   *Ñimen Rayen* means, roughly translated, "weaving or embroidering flowers" (*ñimen*, pattern or design in a weaving or embroidery; *rayen*, flower).

4   This conversation took place in 1997, shortly before a community-based movement of resistance against the large lumber companies helped ignite a new round of militance in the Mapuche movement that has, up until this

writing (November 2000), lessened the effectiveness of CONADI as representative of the Mapuche people.

5 Between 1997 and 1999, protest coalesced around a series of development projects in the center-south that threatened Mapuche control over their own resources. Aside from the Ralco project, the government began building a coastal superhighway that was to open up the southern regions more easily to tourism. A number of communities were affected by this project all along the coast, from Concepción to Valdivia. A projected by-pass for the Panamerican highway, which was to circumvent downtown Temuco and go through the territory of a group of Mapuche communities along the southern bank of the Cautín river, was also hotly protested in this period. A paper factory to be built in the X Region, Valdivia province, was also contested on grounds of pollution, which given what has happened further north, between Temuco and Concepción, was not a wild-eyed claim in the least.

6 When Mauricio Huenchulaf was replaced as National Director of CONADI in the first half of 1997, Isolde's perspective on the relationship between his ouster and the Ralco conflict was quite appropriate and clear-headed, though many people did not agree with her. A little over a year later, as becomes clear in the Conclusion section of this book, which we recorded in August 1998, the situation was very different, because Huenchulaf's replacement, Domingo Namuncura, was fired precisely because he opposed the construction of Ralco.

7 Though Isolde's vision of how CONADI's autonomy could be improved was a good one, events in 1998 and 1999 would move in the opposite direction. After Namuncura was fired, the first non-Mapuche head of CONADI was named by President Frei. After Ricardo Lagos was elected in January 2000, the position became vacant, reflecting the deepening crisis of the institution, precisely because it had no autonomy and little legitimacy left vis-à-vis the Mapuche movement more broadly. The current Director (2001) is a Mapuche technocrat who, according to most reports, has little broad leadership ability.

8 This statement actually proved quite prescient. When Namuncura was removed in late July 1998, it was precisely because his commitment to human rights principles prevented him from supporting Ralco. See Domingo Namuncura, *Ralco: ¿Represa o pobreza?* (Santiago: LOM Editores, 1999).

9 Edith Meyer Durán is a career archivist who has been in charge of the *Archivo de Asuntos Indígenas*, which holds all the administrative and judicial files and documents pertaining to indigenous communities with *títulos de merced*, for many years. Here Isolde is referring to the fact that Mrs. Meyer was the archivist throughout the Pinochet dictatorship and is

one of the leaders among the functionaries in CONADI who have remained from the previous regime. When I worked in her archive, she insisted that I get a signed letter of permission from the National Director, at that point Mauricio Huenchulaf, before she would allow me to see any papers.

10   A reference to Gutenberg Martínez, leader of the younger, more reformist faction of the Christian Democratic Party who lost the election for head of the party in 1997 to the older, more traditional Enrique Krauss.

11   Between the time we were discussing this situation and mid-1999, Isolde did hold a paid position in PRODEMU, a woman's grassroots organization under the control of the First Lady of the Republic. Despite not having the requisite degrees she did excellent work until she was fired, as she saw it, for having spoken up on the Ralco controversy. After having been very active in the Lagos campaign in Temuco, she received the presidential appointment as Councilmember on CONADI's National Council, which is an ad honorem position. She is therefore still technically unemployed, even as she has become extremely active in CONADI during the Lagos administration.

12   The specific reason for this, though Isolde does not say it outright, is that Llao and Avendaño are both active in the socialist and communist left.

13   The Institute of Indigenous Studies (*Instituto de Estudios Indígenas*) was an initiative of the Universidad de la Frontera in Temuco, with funding from the Ford Foundation, to help foster discussion, research, teaching, and outreach on indigenous issues. Its first director was José Aylwin, an important human rights lawyer active in indigenous issues during the transition. Its second director was Julio Tereucan, a Mapuche social scientist.

14   Here it's important to remember that Isolde has waged an intense ideological battle, as a Mapuche feminist, against polygamy and what she sees as the sexual abuse of women in her own culture. Thus, for her, debates on polygamy are not merely theoretical.

15   This is a reference to the fact that, in Spanish, all nouns have a gender, and this is one of the basic elements of the language that is learned in elementary school. By saying this, of course, Isolde is making fun of the intellectual level of the discussion in which the women of the right were engaged.

Conclusion

1   This discussion obviously occurred before Pinochet was arrested in London, finally sent back to Chile, and had his senatorial immunity judicially removed. The balance of power between the government and the military has begun to change, and people are no longer silent on issues of human rights abuse and impunity. Where all this will lead, however, is still unclear. It is also important to remember that, as late as the second half of 1997, the

feelings of frustration about the transition Isolde expresses here were current for a good part of the Chilean population. Also, the issues she raises about the law and indigenous peoples, and about the relationship of the state to global capitalism, remain current today.

Afterword

1 Literally, *pelar* means to peel; but in Chilean slang it also means to gossip about people. When you drink mate for a long time, adding water repeatedly until the leaves no longer have much taste, you say you are "peeling" (*pelando*) the mate. Such an activity is also a good opportunity to converse and/or gossip at an easy pace, among friends. Thus *pelando el mate* means a long, leisurely conversation during which much gossip has the opportunity to surface.

INDEX

ROSA ISOLDE REUQUE PAILLALEF is a leading Mapuche feminist in Chile. A founder of the first Mapuche ethnic organization in 1978, and of the first Mapuche feminist organization in 1991, she was also active in the Chilean human rights movement. She participated in the 1996 International Women's Conference in Beijing and continues to speak out for indigenous rights, for stronger, more significant representation for the Mapuche in the Chilean government, for progress on women's issues, and for the value of Mapuche religiosity as a spiritual inspiration and resource in today's increasingly homogeneous world.

FLORENCIA E. MALLON is Professor of Modern Latin American History at the University of Wisconsin. She is the author of *Peasant and Nation: The Making of Postcolonial Mexico and Peru* (1995) and *The Defense of Community in Peru's Central Highlands: Peasant Struggle and Capitalist Transition, 1860–1940* (1983), and has been doing research on the Mapuche since 1996.

Library of Congress Cataloging-in-Publication Data

Reuque Paillalef, Rosa Isolde.
   When a flower is reborn : the life and times of a Mapuche feminist / Rosa Isolde Reuque Paillalef ; edited and translated by Florencia E. Mallon.
      p. cm.
Includes index.
ISBN 0-8223-2934-4 (cloth : alk. paper) — ISBN 0-8223-2962-X (pbk. : alk. paper)
1. Reuque Paillalef, Rosa Isolde 2. Mapuche women—Biography. 3. Feminists—Chile—Biography. 4. Women social reformers—Chile—Biography. 5. Mapuche women—Social conditions. 6. Mapuche Indians—Land tenure. 7. Mapuche Indians—Politics and government. 8. Chile—History—Coup d'âetat, 1973. 9. Chile—Politics and government—1973–1988. I. Mallon, Florencia E. II. Title.
F3126.R49 A3 2002
983.06'5'092—dc21   2002001762